Stepping in the Madang

Donna Lee Kwon

STEPPING
IN THE MADANG

Sustaining Expressive Ecologies of

Korean Drumming and Dance

Wesleyan University Press   Middletown, Connecticut

Wesleyan University Press
Middletown CT 06459
www.wesleyan.edu/wespress
© 2024 Donna Lee Kwon
All rights reserved
Manufactured in the United States of America
Designed by Mindy Basinger Hill / Typeset in Minion Pro

The Publisher gratefully acknowledges the AMS 75 PAYS Fund of the American Musicological Society, supported in part by the National Endowment for the Humanities and the Andrew W. Mellon Foundation.

Acknowledgments for previously published materials used with permission:

"'Becoming One': Embodying Korean P'ungmul Percussion Band Music and Dance through Site-Specific Intermodal Transmission." *Ethnomusicology* 59, no. 1 (2015): 31–60.

Library of Congress Cataloging-in-Publication Data available upon request

cloth ISBN 978-08195-0140-0
paper ISBN 978-08195-0141-7
ebook ISBN 978-08195-0142-4

5 4 3 2 1

CONTENTS

Acknowledgments vii

Note on the Companion Site xiii

Note on Language xvii

INTRODUCTION Stepping in the Madang 1

PART I LOCAL TRANSMISSION AND RITUAL PERFORMANCE

ONE Pathways to Pilbong 23

TWO "Becoming One" through Site-Specific Intermodal Transmission 57

THREE Cultivating the Village, Preparing for Ritual 89

FOUR "Abundant Kut, Abundant Life": The Place of Ritual P'ungmul 108

PART II ARTICULATING REGIONAL, NATIONAL, AND TRANSNATIONAL CONNECTIONS

FIVE The Madang on the Move 149

SIX Creative Korean Performing Arts in National Urban Spaces 174

SEVEN The Politics of Sounding Space in the Korean American Community 197

Conclusion 232

Notes 239

Bibliography 253

Index-Glossary 265

ACKNOWLEDGMENTS

This book is the result of a long engagement with *madang*-based Korean performing arts traditions that has spanned several decades. This journey has elicited the full range of emotions, one of which is gratitude to the many wondrous individuals with whom I have shared in this journey. I must first thank Bonnie C. Wade, for believing in me and for being such an encouraging and effective professor, advisor, reader, and mentor. My work benefits from her unerring guidance, but beyond this, I have learned so much from her about how to survive and persevere in academia. As a role model, Bonnie occupies rarefied air in giving back to students and for her commitment to the discipline of ethnomusicology. I also want to thank Thomas Turino for generously reading my full manuscript and providing such honest, constructive, eloquent, and incisive feedback. I am humbled by his thoughtfulness in reading my work, and his scholarship on participatory music and applying Peircean semiotic theories to music has greatly informed my work and teaching.

I also want to thank Suzanna Tamminen, the editor of Wesleyan University Press, and the rest of her team. Sincere thanks goes to Ally Findley for her excellent copyediting and to Jess Herdman for providing much-needed expertise in preparing the Index-Glossary. I am especially grateful to the anonymous reviewers of this manuscript and was fortunate to have received such detailed and engaged comments that were immensely helpful in the revision process. Thanks also to the Music/Culture series editors, Deborah Wong, Sherrie Tucker, and Jeremy Wallach, for supporting the review of this manuscript. Lastly, I am indebted to Stephen Stuempfle for graciously granting permission to publish a revised version of my *Ethnomusicology* journal article entitled "'Becoming One': Embodying Korean *P'ungmul* Percussion Band Music and Dance Through Site-Specific Intermodal Transmission" (2015) as the basis for chapter 2 in this manuscript.

Like many scholars, my time in the field, mainly in South Korea, has been the highlight of my life as an ethnomusicologist. Over the years, I am thankful to all the generous funding organizations who have supported field research for this project. These include a Fulbright IIE Fellowship from the Fulbright Institute for International Education/Korean American Educational Commission from 2001 to 2002, the Korea Foundation Instructional Materials Development Grant from 2006 to 2007, and the American Council of Learned Societies Fellowship from 2015 to 2016. In addition to these more longer-term grants, I also want to thank the Friends of Music and the College of Fine Arts travel grant from the University of Kentucky for helping to fund travel for shorter trips in 2009 and 2012.

On the ground in South Korea, I want to thank the National Gugak Center (*Kungnip Kugakwon*) for allowing me to use their library and facilities and for always being a touchstone for high-quality Korean music and dance. From the depths of my gratitude, I also want to thank the Imshil Pilbong Nongak Preservation Association (Imshil Pilbong Nongak Pojonhoe), the group with which I based much of my ethnographic research and analysis on *p'ungmul* (percussion band music and dance). I want to begin by personally thanking the entire Yang family for welcoming me into their lives. In particular, I want to thank Yang Chinsŏng, their leader and *sangsoe*, for taking the time out to allow me to interview him and for granting permission to reproduce a map and include a nicely recorded audio sample that they produced. I also appreciate the many stories that he shared as well as his unique perspective, wisdom, and energy. If I improved at all as a player while in Korea, it would be due to his close attention, care, and candor. I also want to thank Yang Chinhwan and Oh Mi-ae for their insightful comments during interviews. Given that there were not as many women in the group at the time, I am grateful to Oh Mi-ae for opening her home to me in Gwangju and for being such an inspiration as a *p'ungmul* practitioner, mother, and friend. I also want to thank Yang Oklan for her friendship, warmth, and willingness to teach me Korean folksongs and *p'ansori*. I am also thankful to Yang Chongyun (Yang Chinsŏng's son) and it was lovely to experience life coming full circle when I was able to invite him to my home while he was in residence at the Korean Performing Arts Institute of Chicago to give a wonderful performance at the University of Kentucky. Lastly, I owe much gratitude to teachers Ch'oe Ho-in and Han Chaehun (who gave me a handmade *kkwaenggwari* mallet that I still use religiously).

While living in Seoul, I attended the Seoul Pilbong transmission center. Here,

I met many wonderful people who were overflowing with *shinmyŏng* (spirit). I am particularly indebted to Cho Ch'unyŏng who took great interest in my project and shared many invaluable insights with me during my fieldwork year. In addition, I want to thank Amber Heaton, who I met through the Korean Youth Cultural Center and who was also a fellow Fulbright grantee in Korea while I was there between 2001 and 2002. Because she also cultivated a strong relationship with the Pilbong *p'ungmul* group, I am grateful for her sensitive companionship and willing ear, as we bounced thoughts back and forth on our overlapping experiences in Korea.

I also spent considerable time with the Goseong Ogwangdae Preservation Association, documenting their performances and attending their transmission sessions. Although I do not dedicate much textual space to them in this book, I cannot overstate how much my work is informed by their tasteful expression (*mat*), spirit (*shinmyŏng*), and sense of abundant community. In particular, I want to thank Yi Yunsŏk, Chŏn Kwangyŏl, and Hwang Chonguk for welcoming me into their world. I also want to thank Yun Hyŏnho for his friendship and for patiently teaching me how to play the conical double-reed (*t'aep'yŏngso*). In the arena of creative traditional performing arts (*ch'angjak yŏnhŭi*), I am thankful to Hŏ Ch'angyŏl, Pak Insu, and Kim So Ra, for allowing me to interview them and follow them around to various performances.

I also want to thank Korean scholars and thinkers Yi Chongjin and Pak Hŭngchu for their insights on Pilbong *p'ungmul* and *kut* (shamanist ritual) as well as Yi Yŏng-mi for meeting with me and providing her invaluable help in navigating the confusing terrain of the *madang* and *p'an*. I am also grateful to Chan E. Park, whose rigorous and performance-oriented approach to *p'ansori* continues to inspire. I also give thanks to other members of a tightknit community of Korean music and sound studies scholars, including Hyun Kyong Chang, Hyun Kyung Chae, Jocelyn Clark, Hilary Finchum-Sung, Nathan Hesselink, Hee-sun Kim, Sun Hee Koo, Roald Maliangkay, Ruth Mueller, Mi-Kyung Park, Shingil Park, Joshua Pilzer, CedarBough Saeji, Anderson Sutton, Haekyung Um, and Heather Willoughby. In particular, I want to thank CedarBough Saeji and Heather Willoughby for being tremendous hosts while I was staying in Korea; I always appreciate their unique perspectives, aspirational work ethic, and warm collegiality. As friends from graduate school, I have many things to thank Michael Hurt for, including hosting me in Korea and granting permission to include some of his amazing photography and videos on the companion website. Finally, I am incredibly grateful to have Katherine Lee in my circle of colleagues. From early on, our spheres of interest overlapped, and my work has been significantly enhanced by her generous spirit, deep thinking, and careful scholarship.

In the Korean American diaspora *p'ungmul* community, I want to thank members of the Korean Youth Cultural Center including Ko Misuk and the late Ko Chaeho, Jang Woo Nam, Hojung Choi, Jongsuk Lee, Jenny Cho, Minjoon Kouh, Ann Kwon, Patrick Chew, Keeyoung Kim, Dohee Lee, Helen Min, Chaehong Chin (whose master's thesis I also cite in this book), Kyung Jin Lee, Eunyoung Kwon, the late Peter Kim, John Kim, and Elisa Gahng. In particular, I am grateful to Ann Kwon and Patrick Chew for perpetually nurturing the healing power of laughter, storytelling, and food. I also want to thank members of other *p'ungmul* groups who were helpful in this research, including Helen S. Kim, Miriam Ching Louie, Ju Bum Cha, Liz Chong Eun Rhee, Juliet Hyun Jung Hwang, Byoung Sug Kim, Gina Choi, Suwan Choi, Yong Sok Chung, and Kim Hyonchong, as well as members of Ieumsae.

In the larger world of ethnomusicology, I have had the great fortune of gaining input and inspiration from many scholars. In particular, I would like to thank my graduate professors, including Mark Slobin, Su Zheng, Sumarsam, Ben Brinner, and Jocelyne Guilbault. Additionally, I am grateful to Deborah Wong and Tomie Hahn, whose scholarship and presence in the field have been so meaningful to me. I also want to thank supportive peers, such as Partow Hooshmandrad for inviting me to present my scholarship at Fresno State University, as well as Henry Spiller, Marié Abe, Shalini Ayyagari, Christina Sunardi, Carla Brunet, Mari Arko Klemenc, Susie Lim Koh, Francesca Rivera, and Rebecca Bodenheimer. I am also thankful to Maria Mendonça, Robert Lancefield, Junko Oba, Tim Eriksen, Michael Veal, and the late Mirjana Laušević, who was unparalleled in her ability to bring people together. I also want to thank Meredith Schweig and Lei X. Ouyang for providing valuable insights into Asian music studies and the publishing process.

Having taught for over a decade at the University of Kentucky, I am so blessed to be surrounded by such a supportive, eclectic, and special group of music scholars. To Ron Pen, I thank you for always being a consummate host, teacher, and scholar, who never fails to radiate warmth, intelligence, and humanity, even during my first frigid visit to Lexington during an ice storm. In addition, I want to thank my other senior colleagues—Jon Glixon, Beth Glixon, Diana Hallman, Benjamin Arnold, and Lance Brunner—for their effective mentoring, inspirational scholarship, and commitment to hosting extraordinary potlucks. I am also thankful to Erin Walker Bliss and Revell Carr, my accomplished and always delightful colleagues in world music and ethnomusicology. In addition, I want to thank the Director of the School of Music Stanley Pelkey and College of Fine Arts Dean Mark Shanda for their commitment to supporting faculty research. Thanks also to my larger community of colleagues, including Jennifer Campbell, Martina Vasil, Liang Luo, Keiko Tanaka, Akiko Takenaka, Wei Jiang, Ali Meyer Rossi, Jairus Rossi, Srimati Basu, Sharon Yam, Goeun Lee, Jonghee Caldararo, Rae Goodwin, Melissa Vandenberg, Sujin Kim, Deborah Chung, Eun Young Lee, Dong Han, and Yuha Jung, for their support. I also want to express my thanks to all the graduate students who have played *p'ungmul* with me over the years, including Tanner Jones, Megan Murph, Justin Balcor, Isaac Maupin, Elizabeth Varnado, David Boyd, Joshua Cohen, Samantha Vivian, Reyers Brusoe, and Hada Jang. Finally, I owe a great deal of my peace of mind to being able to take part in the "*madangs*" of several participatory musical communities in Lexington, including the hollow square of the Appalachian Association of Sacred Harp Singers, the central circle of the old-time jam, and the metaphorical *banjar* of the Balinese Gamelan Angklung Langen Kerti at the University of Kentucky.

In conclusion, I want to thank my mother and father, Kyumeen and O Kuk Kwon, and my sister Gina and her family (Craig, Pat, Ben, Christy, Luke, and Lily), for their gentle encouragement and endless reservoir of love, prayers, and support. I have also been blessed with many cousins who have been the source of much joy and companionship over the years. I am especially thankful to James Bai for producing a Korean popular culture YouTube channel with me (@hallyulikethat). Finally, I dedicate this book to my amazing husband Robert and my quick-witted daughter Sophie. They are the grounding forces of my life, and their humor, warmth, and love make life infinitely more meaningful.

NOTE ON THE COMPANION SITE

Supplementary audio, visual, and audiovisual materials are available on the accompanying Reader's Companion: https://www.weslpress.org/readers-companions/. Access using the password: SITM01417. Videos with subtitles are provided to both help introduce readers to the genres discussed as well as heighten understanding of the more in-depth analytical sections. In addition, color photos are available and will be marked with the symbol ⊙ before the figure number; these should not be confused with figures that are included in the text. References to audio materials are marked 🔊, and references to audiovisual materials are marked 📢. Readers are highly encouraged to consult the website as they read through this book.

MULTIMEDIA AVAILABLE ON THE COMPANION SITE

Chapter 2

AUDIO 2.1 *Hoho-kut* and *P'ungnyu-kut* performed and recorded by members of the Imshil Pilbong Nongak Preservation Association, with the *pan-p'ungnyu* rhythm beginning at 9:11 in the track (2017). 80

VIDEO 2.1 *Madangbalbi* performed by the Imshil Pilbong Nongak Preservation Association with participants dancing the shoulder dance, Pilbong village (2002). 57

Chapter 3

FIGURE 3.1 Example of a log cabin–style home in the village of Pilbong (2016). 99

FIGURE 3.2 A sign that reads: "Original location of Pilbong-kut that is recognized by UNESCO as Important Intangible Cultural Property 11-5 by the South Korean government," Pilbong village (2016). 100

FIGURE 3.3 Pilbong Lunar New Year Ritual Cloth Map displaying the "mini village within a village," Pilbong village (2016). 100

Chapter 4

VIDEO 4.1 *Tangsanje* performed by the Imshil Pilbong Nongak Preservation Association, Pilbong village (2002). 113

VIDEO 4.2 *Saem-kut* performed by the Imshil Pilbong Nongak Preservation Association, Pilbong village (2002). 115

VIDEO 4.3 *Taep'osu Solo* performed by the Imshil Pilbong Nongak Preservation Association during *madangbalbi*, Pilbong village (2002). 125

VIDEO 4.4 *Ap-kut* or the front half of the *p'an-kut* performed by the Imshil Pilbong Nongak Preservation Association, Pilbong village (2002). 133

VIDEO 4.5 *Twi-kut* or the back half of the *p'an-kut* performed by the Imshil Pilbong Nongak Preservation Association, Pilbong village (2002). 135

FIGURE 4.1 Performers of the Imshil Pilbong Nongak Preservation Association playing *Ki-kut* in the village common area (*tongch'ŏng madang*), Pilbong village (2016). 112

FIGURE 4.2 Pilbong Lunar New Year Ritual participants crowded around the guardian spirit tree in the Tangsan ceremony, Pilbong village (2016). 136

FIGURE 4.3 Dancing in the newly constructed *kut-madang*, Pilbong village (2016). 140

FIGURE 4.4 Yang Chinsŏng and Koh Yonse, Pilbong village (2016). 140

Chapter 5

VIDEO 5.1 Goseong Ogwangdae selected scenes performed by the Goseong Ogwangdae Preservation Association during their annual performance (2002). 165

FIGURE 5.1 Tongyeong Ogwangdae mask dance transmission center *madang* by the river in Tongyeong (2002). 151

FIGURE 5.2 National Gugak Center Yŏnhŭi Madang, Seoul (2015). 154

Chapter 6

VIDEO 6.1 *Norikkot P'ida* interactive scenes, performed by Norikkot, Seoul (2015). 184

VIDEO 6.2 *Miyal Halmi* performed by The Greatest Masque, Incheon (2015). 187

VIDEO 6.3 *Mundungi* performed by The Greatest Masque, Incheon (2015). 187

VIDEO 6.4 *Imae* performed by The Greatest Masque, Incheon (2015). 189

FIGURE 6.1 Yŏnhŭi Chipdan the Kwangdae performing in the Naminsa Madang in Insadong, Seoul (2015). 181

FIGURE 6.2 Norikkot performing in Namsan Hanok Village, Seoul (2015). 184

FIGURE 6.3 Kim Jungwoon of Norikkot performing the spinning disk *pŏna* segment in Namsan Hanok Village, Seoul (2015). 185

FIGURE 6.4 Kim Jungwoon of Norikkot with her final "suitor" at the conclusion of her spinning disk *pŏna* segment, Namsan Hanok Village, Seoul (2015). 185

Chapter 7

VIDEO 7.1 *Performing Korea*, draft documentary on the Korean Youth Cultural Center, Oakland, CA (2001). Recorded and edited by Michael Hurt. 223

FIGURE 7.1 Yun Hanbong, founder of the Minjok Future Research Institute, Gwangju (1995). 199

FIGURE 7.2 *Chishinpalpki* performed and organized by Pinari of the MinKwon Center, New York (date unknown). 205

FIGURE 7.3 Report by the *Korea Times* (San Francisco branch) on the Korean Youth Cultural Center's Annual Performance in Golden Gate Park's Marx Meadow in San Francisco (Monday, September 24, 2001). 221

FIGURE 7.4 Members of Pinari from the MinKwon Center and NYURI from New York University at Battery Park memorializing the victims of 9/11, New York (2002). 223

FIGURE 7.5 Author with small gong in the center with members of Hanulchida at the Lexington Women's March, Lexington, Kentucky (2017). 227

Note on the Companion Site **xv**

NOTE ON LANGUAGE

Most Korean words have been romanized according to the McCune-Reischauer system, with some notable exceptions. For example, I have elected to specify the "ㅅ" character as "sh" (instead of "s") to specify when it is pronounced in this fashion, as in the words *shinmyŏng* (신명) or the county of Imshil (임실). Other exceptions include the alternatively romanized names of Korean authors who have published in English and well-known figures such as former President Park Chung Hee [Pak Chŏnghŭi/박정희]. Here, I will generally provide the McCune-Reischauer romanization in brackets upon first appearance in the text. In addition, Korean family names that would be romanized as a single letter will be alternatively romanized according to common practice. For example, the common last name of "이" will be romanized to "Yi" instead of "I," and "오" will be romanized as "Oh" instead of "O." To benefit those familiar with South Korea or for those wishing to engage with contemporary maps or even visit some of the places mentioned in the text, I have chosen to romanize all Korean locations according to the Revised Romanization of Korean as devised by the South Korean Ministry of Culture and Tourism. Examples include the South Korean metropolis of Seoul (서울), smaller villages such as Pilbong (필봉), provincial names such as Jeolla province (전라도), as well as all geographical landmarks, islands, mountains, seas, etc.

Korean names of figures and authors (who publish mainly in Korean) are generally written according to standard usage in Korea, with family names preceding given names. When discussing authors with Korean names who publish predominantly in English, I follow standard English practice. Korean terms will be italicized throughout (including titles of artistic works, rhythms, and song titles), with the exception of proper nouns such as group or organizational names, geographical place names, landmarks, and cities. My intention is that the continued italicization of foreign terms will help remind readers to consult the glossary that is integrated with the index. Unless otherwise noted, all translations from Korean to English are mine.

Stepping in the Madang

INTRODUCTION

Stepping in the Madang

"Are you a *madang* (village courtyard) type or a *mudae* (stage) type?" I was asked this question by a visiting Korean music teacher named Mr. Ko in the mid-1990s, prodding me to re-think what kind of performance space I should align myself with as a community-based performer and scholar. For him, the *madang* was the only right answer. Intrigued, I decided to follow this thread and discovered that the *madang* operates as a multidimensional cultural trope, conveying a core of spatial, temporal, and social meanings as a courtyard, common, or field, an expressive occasion in time, and a cultural space of embodied participation. I vividly remember the first time I stepped into the *madang* of a Korean village home to experience *p'ungmul* (percussion band music and dance) for a Lunar New Year ritual, the reddish-tinged earth giving ever so slightly under my feet.[1] I often think back on this feeling of the ground "giving back" as a gentle reminder of the spiritual function of Korean drummers playing and stamping out the mischievous spirits from the courtyard of a village home during a seasonal ritual.

Since then, the importance of "stepping in the *madang*" has emerged in varied ways as a guiding concept in my research. For example, Kim Inu is well known for highlighting the saying that "*p'ungmul* must be played with one's heel!" (Kim 1987, 113), emphasizing the importance of bodily engagement and movement in the *madang*. In classes that I attended, the act of bending one's knees and stepping in the *madang* was taken down to an excruciatingly slow tempo, bringing out what Thomas Csordas calls "somatic modes of attention" (1993, 139) and instilling an embodied understanding of *p'ungmul*'s connections to agricultural labor. Similarly, I have also experienced intense moments in the *madang* that would fall under what Tomie Hahn has called the realm of the "sensually extreme" that "bring to the surface extraordinary cultural insights, as well as personally transforming orientations" (Hahn 2006, 89). Lastly, one of my main interlocutors, Yang Chinsŏng, reminds us that the pathways that take us from one *madang* to the next are what ultimately connects people in the rituals of daily life.

In today's hyper-globalized South Korea, the reality is that most Koreans experience "traditional" culture in ways that are increasingly mediated and "schizophonic"—that is, detached from earlier socio-cultural contexts and local environments. As the practice of Korean folk expressive culture continues to flow from local, rural environments to urban, national, and even transnational contexts, this book examines how some practitioners have responded by intentionally stepping in the *madang*—both literally and metaphorically—as a means of bringing one's feet and body into purposeful contact with the site, time, and place of performance. In theoretical terms, I posit that this continued engagement with the *madang* works against what Marilyn Ivy views as the "phantasmatic" nature of tradition, whereby forms that are constructed as "folk" are rendered ephemeral through their perpetual association to an ever-receding, pre-colonial past (1995). Building upon the idea of "stepping in the *madang*," I contend that the participatory and communal ways of being that are cultivated in the *madang* can counteract this phantasmatic tendency by placing more focus on bringing these folk practices more fully into the embodied present, even if in an idealized fashion.

Anthropologist Arjun Appadurai argues that the term "folk" homogenizes or masks differences in areas such as class, gender, region, and skill (1991). It can also relegate a genre to an idealized past and perpetuate a more singular and canonic notion of what constitutes a given tradition. However, following the lead of ethnomusicologist Stefan Fiol (2017), I choose to continue to use this term with the awareness that what is considered "folk" is a fluid discursive process, subject to the forces of the present as much as the past. In this way, I intend to remain consistent with Korean ways of categorizing certain genres in the folk or *minsok* category, in part to acknowledge how Korean folk genres were heavily politicized and embraced by the progressive left during the democratization movement in South Korea (from the 1960s to 1980s). Around the same time, the government also supported folk genres as part of a policy of cultural asset designation and preservation. While these trends produced conflicting folk discourses, they both had the effect of privileging tradition-bearers who were older, more working class, and locally based in representative regions. In general, practitioners emphasized the role of transmission and promoted the notion that anyone could learn and derive meaning through intensive, participatory engagement. In the new millennium, the association of folk with the progressive left has diminished, and with this, differentiations between folk genres and other categories have become less fraught. I tend to use the term "expressive folk culture" over "folk music" (*minsok-ak*) or "folk dance" (*minsok-ch'um*) to emphasize the highly integrated nature of Korean music and dance.

Although I cannot cover all of the relevant Korean expressive folk genres in this book, my central aim is to convey the power and limits of the *madang* to engender site-specific expressive ecologies—defined loosely as sited practices of performance and transmission—that evoke cultural continuity with the past while also encouraging its embodied participation in the present. Part 1 serves as a case study that shows how Korean *p'ungmul* practitioners must work constantly to sustain a site-specific, village-based expressive ecology. Here, I carefully document how this expressive ecology is supported through historical trends, transmission practices, communal labor, and performative ritual. In part 2, I examine how these practices resonate beyond the village in regional, national, and transnational contexts. My aim is to demonstrate how site-specific and site-oriented expressive ecologies create opportunities for multiple generations of people to express themselves in a broad array of contexts to participate wholeheartedly in the *madang*, thereby deepening their connections to each other, to place, and potentially to the environment.

YANGCHON VILLAGE (NEAR ANSEONG CITY), GYEONGGI PROVINCE

Although part 1 is focused primarily on the village of Pilbong, I begin with a slight detour. One Sunday in March, 2002—deep into my fieldwork year—I found myself stepping in the *madangs* of Yangchon village. At the time, I had been taking *p'ungmul* classes at a satellite transmission center in Seoul associated with the Imshil Pilbong *p'ungmul* style. The Seoul transmission center had received a special invitation from Yangchon and had asked several other Seoul-based community and college organizations to play with them to wish the village residents good fortune during the Lunar New Year season. Altogether, there were about thirty-eight people playing percussion-based instruments, two *t'aep'yŏngso* (conical double-reed) players, and four *chapsaek* or character actors/dancers. In addition, there were perhaps twenty village residents and fifty to seventy spectators. Affectionately called *kugyŏngkkun* in Korean, these spectators were exceptionally well informed and participated enthusiastically with an array of embodied movements and vocal interactions. Going against my usual mode of fieldwork, I decided to leave my video camera at home and just participate as a performing member by playing the *changgo* (Korean hourglass drum). Although some of the performing members overlapped with the official Imshil Pilbong Nongak Preservation Association, this was not an "official" Imshil Pilbong event. This, no doubt, informed my decision to focus on playing and experiencing the flow of the event. Even though I have little documentation besides my fieldnotes, I am glad I did fully participate, because it taught me something about the *madang* that very few other events did over the course of my research.

The day began much like other village-based *p'ungmul* rituals do during the Lunar New Year period. We started playing in front of the village center building, or *maŭl hoegwan*, where there was a shrine set up with sacrificial foods for the village spirits. From there, the group travelled to a village water tank. Even though it was surrounded by a metal wire fence, they did try to bend down over the fence to sample and bless the water. In the pre-industrial period, *p'ungmul* troupes would visit the village spring or well. While some villages like Pilbong choose to focus on older sites (even if they are currently defunct), the village of Yangchon decided to stay true to the function of the ritual and direct the troupe toward the modern-day sources of water for the village, even if they were not perhaps as picturesque. From here, we proceeded into the *madangbalbi* portion of the ritual, where the group visits individual village residents who want the performers to perform a personalized ritual in their home to chase away bad spirits and energy and usher in blessings for the year.

We visited around ten homes over the course of the day. Some were older, more traditional homes with intimate, enclosed *madang* courtyards; others were made of modern brick construction, many with open *madangs* that exposed the performers to the cold wind. My favorite *madang* was enclosed and laid with stone. We played there for a long time; the owner sang many songs and served us homemade pine-needle *makkŏlli* rice alcohol. At another home, we encountered an older *halmŏni* (grandmother) who had just lost her husband. As the leader tried to help her reckon with her emotions and perform rituals that would usher in better fortune in the coming year, she cried so uncontrollably that many of us could not help but be moved during our visit with her.

Another unmistakable character was an older *harabŏji* (grandfather) dressed in an orange and navy *hanbok*, or Korean-style dress. He followed us around and became increasingly agitated as the day wore on. At one point, he even managed to pull a flower hat (*kokkal moja*) off of one of our female *changgo* players, ripping it to shreds; given that it was tightly fastened around her neck, this action caused a measure of shock and discomfort (but no lasting injuries, thankfully). On this and several other occasions, he had to be restrained by members of the village. Although this does not excuse the way he lashed out at our members, it turned out that he was the president of the elder village center organization (*noin maŭl hoegwan hwejang*) and was upset that we had not visited his home first. I heard later that the leader of the group intended to visit his home last. Whether his behavior was due to a miscommunication or something else, it did inject some unexpected real-life tension, drama, and chaos (*nanjang*) that further heightened the social aspect of the ritual. When we finally arrived at his abode, the performing troupe was very generous in spending a lot of time playing at his house, performing rituals both indoors and outdoors. One of our leading performing members even gave him a huge, cathartic embrace, as if to cement the resolution of this conflict in one heartfelt, embodied gesture.

In the end, this offered a rare glimpse of what much of the literature and my interviews confirm about the *madang*—namely, that it is about much more than an adherence to a particular spatial or temporal format. In the best of circumstances, *madang* events should be fully invested participatory occasions where real-life social conflicts, histories, or moments of chaos may arise, begging for resolution.

FROM SITE-SPECIFIC PERFORMANCE TO THE EXPRESSIVE ECOLOGY OF KOREAN FOLK CULTURE

This scene from my fieldwork illustrates how various community and college *p'ungmul* groups came together to perform and engage wholeheartedly with the particularities of *site*: its people, stories, *madangs*, resources, and so on. While *madang* discourses and practices evident in this event tend to emphasize communal ideals and "participatory performance" as theorized by Thomas Turino (2008), this process is fluid, complex, and capricious, and therefore subject to continual cultivation and production. Case in point, visiting Yangchon village during Lunar New Year and playing *p'ungmul* did not regularly recur much beyond 2002. In site-specific expressive ecologies more generally, I argue that the cultivation of participatory expressive culture is guided through *madang*-related discourses and practices whereby: (1) the phenomenological experience of the body is privileged, (2) attention is drawn toward engaging with the features and fluid conditions of a given site, and (3) the spirit of openness in performances is encouraged in order to enable a more dynamic range of social relations and interactions.

My work intersects with and differs from how site-specific performance or art has been theorized in the fields of performance studies, theater, dance, and art. While its definition has been evolving since its emergence in the late 1960s, many scholars cite art historian Miwon Kwon's definition of early site-specific art as necessitating "an inextricable, indivisible relationship between the work and its site" (2002, 12) where artists strive to engage with "the site itself as another *medium*, as an 'other language'" (2002, 75). Nick Kaye similarly defines site-specific art as "articulate exchanges between the work of art and the places in which its meanings are defined" (2000, 1). In both cases—and in much site-specific art scholarship—there is a privileging of *new* works of site-specific art over older forms of expressive culture that emerge more organically from a particular location, and my motivation is to explore the potential of these types of practices within ethnomusicological contexts.[2]

One area of site-specific performance theory that resonates with ethnomusicological approaches is the "phenomenological or experiential understanding of site, defined primarily as an agglomeration of the actual physical attributes of a particular location" (Kwon 2002, 3). This approach to site demands "the physical presence of the viewer" (2002, 12) where site-specific analysis encourages a heightened consideration of the relationships between the site, the body of the performer, and the performance itself; these relationships are not taken as given but are variously read for their potential to reveal new meanings, tensions, questions, or resolutions. In her survey of site-specific performance in Britain, theatre scholar Fiona Wilkie writes that while there is a notion that the "performance 'fit' the site and vice versa," she observes that the "fit" may not be a comfortable merging with the resonance of the site but might be a reaction against it (2002, 149). In the Yangchon example above, the lack of "fit" between the performers and the villagers was a source of tension, but ended up contributing to the developing drama of the day's events.

Wilkie also encourages a multi-layered approach by defining site-specific performance as "specifically generated from/for one selected site" where "layers of the site are revealed through reference to: historical documentation; site usage (past and present); found text, objects, actions, sounds, etc.; anecdotal guidance; personal association; half-truths and lies, site morphology (physical and vocal explorations of site)" (2002, 150). While site-specific performance theory and practice might not have been conceived in relation to older, more continuous forms of expressive culture, Wilkie's multi-layered approach provides alternative ways of thinking about the mutually constitutive relationship between expressive content and the actuality of site. Although some scholars are keen on differentiating the boundaries between site-specific art and what has variously been called site-oriented, site-sympathetic, or site-responsive art (to name a few), I approach these categories as more of an overlapping, fluid continuum. In this way, the approach of this book is site-specific in part 1 and more site-oriented, or even *madang*-oriented, in part 2.

Stemming from my concern with the intersection of expressive culture and place, I am also interested in exploring the relationship between site-specific performance and the promotion of cultural heritage. In the context of South Korean cultural heritage promotion, site-specific events are performative: when done regularly, they signify and cement the bonds between a given expressive folk culture tradition, the place of performance, and the participating community. Cultural heritage events perform place in ways that can potentially go further than many other types of site-specific performances because they tend to occur for a longer period, whereas the latter often have a limited run. When regularly recurring cultural heritage performances are conducted in ways that balance repetition with dynamic change and creativity in response to individual and community needs, they can help cultivate deep connections between individuals and the community, as well as to place and the environment. All too often, however, cultural heritage events can become static, routine, and monetized according to the logic of individual gain, government-sponsored nationalism, or neoliberalism. I remain optimistic that the cultural heritage world will remain diverse, however, and assert that more case studies—such as the one presented in this book—should be documented in close detail.

In this way, one of the primary lines of inquiry in this book is to investigate how cultural heritage practitioners go about sustaining what I would define as the *expressive ecology* of a site-based tradition. While indebted to pioneering scholars in the emerging field of ecomusicology such as Nancy Guy (2009), Aaron Allen (2011, 2014), and Jeff Todd Titon (2013, later "sound ecology" in 2020), I have opted to proceed with the alternative of "expressive ecology" in order to go beyond the realm of music and sound to better speak to comprehensive expressive cultural forms, such as *p'ungmul*, where movement, ritual, dialogue, drama, labor and other elements (many of which are participatory) are equally important. I further define expressive ecology as a term that takes into consideration all that goes into sustaining or giving life to a sited expressive cultural form; this may include how participants engage with, relate to, or conceptualize the surrounding environment and living things, all within the context of various forces, movements, or trends. In this way, I am inspired by the field of political ecology, which seeks to critically analyze the complex interaction of various forces—economic, political, social, technological—and their impacts on the environment. Furthermore, my definition of the study of an expressive ecology encompasses how expressive practices contribute to the phenomenological experience of site or place as well as its material and discursive construction.

Another relevant area that informs my thinking on expressive ecology is the field of acoustemology proposed by Steven Feld (1996). Feld's epistemological theorization of "sound as a way of knowing" remains inspirational despite my desire to move beyond sound as a central analytic (Feld 2015, 12). Perhaps even more crucial than sonic awareness in the *madang* are other forms of sensory knowledge, especially embodied modes of knowledge or learning, theorized by Thomas Csordas (1990) as "embodiment," and conceived variously by ethnomusicologists such as Tomie Hahn (1996) as "kinesthetic transmission" and Kyra Gaunt as "kinetic orality" (2006). Embodied knowledge is essential in the transmission of *p'ungmul* but is also critical in guiding how one interacts expressively with others in the *madang* or site.

In examining why a group or an individual might be motivated to participate in a site-specific expressive ecology, I turn to Thomas Turino's reading of Gregory Bateson's far-reaching text, *An Ecology of Mind*. According to Turino, Bateson "suggests that artists communicate through the presentation of *forms and patterns that serve as integrated maps of sensations, imagination and experience* and that it is through these patterns that we are most deeply connected to and part of the natural world" (Turino 2008, 3, my emphasis). Turino further explains that:

> Bateson's hypothesis is that artistic patterns and forms are both the result of and articulate this integration of different parts of the self and thus facilitate wholeness. He concludes that the integrative wholeness of individuals developed through artistic experience—the balancing of connective inner life with reason, sensitivity, and sense—is crucial to experiencing deep connections with others and with the environment, which is crucial for social and ecological survival. (Turino 2008, 3–4)

Bateson adds that he is "concerned with what important psychic information is in the art object quite apart from what it may 'represent'" and that he values what may be implicit in the "style, composition, rhythm, skill, and so on" (Bateson 2000, 130). With this said, individual experiences vary and this analytic should be carefully applied by integrating it with cultural, social, and historical analysis. Some scholars, such as anthropologist Adrian Vickers (1989), have been critical of Gregory Bateson and his research partner and wife Margaret Mead for not doing this enough in their work in Bali (Downing 2019, 17). In South Korea, *p'ungmul* is often touted as a genre that fosters community or "deep connections with others" and several authors have gone further to analyze how its rhythms, stylized chants, and movements embody and cultivate this sense of community and dynamism according to the norms of specific groups (Kim Inu 1987, Hesselink 2011, Lee 2018). Continuing along these lines, I aim to further articulate Bateson and Turino's assertion that participating in the arts can facilitate deeper connections to the natural world and/or the surrounding environment. Specifically, I posit that site-specific expressive cultures can enable deeper connections to the environment by providing a range of "artistic patterns and forms that serve as integrated maps of sensations, imagination and experience" (Turino 2008, 3) that participants can performatively enact within a given space, place, and time.

As much as this book takes "sitedness" seriously, terms such as "site" or "place" fail to do justice to the *madang* and its full scope of meanings. Because of this, I contend that the notion of the *madang* is central to the patterning of the genres explored in this text. As a multi-dimensional cultural trope with a rich body of closely associated discourses, the *madang* serves as an "integrated map of sensations, imagination and experience" (Turino 2008, 3) that helps guide and inform Korean folk expressive culture activities. To take this further, the *madang* is an example of a trope or metaphor that can infuse multiple domains, frames, or layers of meaning, much like the "blues" and "ring shout" tropes in African American musical traditions (figure 0.1). According to metaphor theorists Mark Johnson, George Lakoff, and Naomi Quinn, a "metaphor is a mapping from some *source domain* to some *target domain*" (Quinn 1991, 57, my emphasis) where source domains are often familiar, basic, and "most often of the physical world" (building on the work of Lakoff and Johnson) and target domains are "best thought of as 'abstract' conceptual domains, often of the internal mental or emotional world, sometimes of the social world" (Quinn 1991, 57). In this scheme, the meaning of the *madang* as a courtyard, common, or field is the source domain that is then mapped onto other target domains such as the temporal and social target domains.

These spatial/material, temporal, and social dimensions can also be produc-

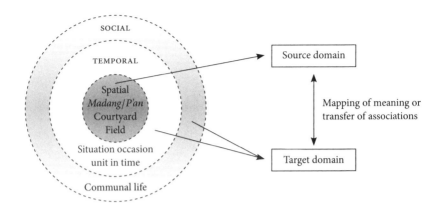

FIGURE 0.1 The *Madang* trope.

tively conceived of as *frames*, as permeable layers that are all potentially integral to the *madang*. Expanding upon the *madang* trope in figure 0.1, an expressive folk culture event could include additional frames or concentric circles such as: (1) process and preparation; (2) form, content, and expression; and (3) ritual. The *process and preparation* frame could include pedagogical methods, transmission, and all the planning sessions, cooking, cleaning, and other aspects of preparation that go into an event. This is an extremely important area in which many participants (performers, villagers, students, for example) can contribute and become involved. The *form, content, and expression* frame refers to all the music, dance, movement, or text-related elements that can be discerned in each event or performance and includes group and individual styles or expressions. This frame also includes structural aspects, such as the order of dances, songs, or scenes. The *ritual* frame includes specific ceremonies and is extremely crucial, because it is through this frame that the *madang* is seen as a transformative spiritual space where participants experience "oneness" or group *shinmyŏng* (ecstatic joy). Here I draw on the work of Travis Jackson, who theorizes frames around a jazz event (such as form, head, tune, temporal, spatial, ritual, scene, and blues aesthetic). While Jackson's jazz frames are not the same, they operate similarly in that they serve as "different areas in which participants in musical events can creatively manipulate and respond to the materials they have" (2000, 66).[3]

Based on this expanded view of a *madang* event, the *madang* source metaphor is mapped onto each successive target domain, becoming a central guide or iconic feeling that affects how different areas of an event are shaped and experienced. The way the *madang* metaphor becomes a connective force between expressive culture domains is akin to what Judith and Alton Becker call "iconicity" or what Feld similarly calls the "iconicity of style" (Becker and Becker 1981, 203; Feld 1994, 131). According to Feld, metaphors become "iconic" when they are "felt to be naturally real, obvious, complete, and thorough . . . and are experienced as feelingfully synonymous from one domain or level of image and experience to another" (Feld 1994, 132).

By examining the Korean literature on the *madang*, I have found that participants have developed new indexical meanings for the *madang* by associating it with a range of other concepts. The resulting web of discourses associated with the *madang* can be loosely sorted into the following categories: (1) the spatial-temporal, (2) social-relational, (3) transformative or dynamic, and (4) experiential (Kwon 2005, 117–24) (table 0.1).[4]

To better explain these *madang* discourses, I will first introduce the main genres explored in this book, namely *p'ungmul* and *kamyŏn'gŭk*. *P'ungmul* (literally "wind objects," also called *nongak*) is a Korean form of percussion band music and dance, normally played outdoors in *madang* spaces with the instru-

TABLE 0.1 Discourses of the *Madang*

CATEGORY	THEMATIC MEANINGS
1. Spatial/temporal	*Madang* as an integrated spatio-temporal field
	Madang as a space of "openness" or "open emptiness"
	Madang as a space that encourages an inclusive audience/performer relationship of "becoming one"
2. Social/relational	*Madang* as a space of "community" (*kongdongch'e*)
	Madang as a space of "cooperative labor" (*ture*)
3. Transformative/dynamic	*Madang* as space of "ritual" (*kut*)
	Madang as space of "spiritual catharsis" (*shinmyŏng*)
	Madang as a space of "chaos" and "topsy-turvy" (*nanjang*)
	Madang as a cosmological space of nature
4. Experiential	*Madang* as a space of "play" (*nori*)
	Madang as a space of "being in the moment" (*hyŏnjang*)

Introduction: Stepping in the Madang 11

mentalists playing the small gong (*soe*), large gong (*ching*), hourglass drum (*changgo*), barrel drum (*puk*), and handheld drum (*sogo*). This is combined with other performance elements such as stylized speech, movement, choreography, singing, character actors, and melodic improvisation played on the *t'aep'yŏngso* (conical double-reed). *Kamyŏn'gŭk* (literally "mask theater," also called *t'alch'um* or "mask dance") is the umbrella term for mask dance drama and is also performed in a circular *madang* formation. It is a boisterous genre that is organized into a series of acts that feature archetypal characters, often with musical accompaniment that includes many of the same instruments found in *p'ungmul*. The embodied energy, sound, and visual appeal of these genres continues to engage contemporary participants—both domestically as well as with diasporic and international communities (see companion website for video examples).

Behind the scenes, however, I posit that the *madang*-related discourses in table 0.1 have been instrumental in helping practitioners articulate and understand how to better elicit and shape the aesthetics of participation. For example, the spatial/temporal discourses help groups prepare or select appropriate performance sites or spaces that foster openness and an inclusive audience/performer environment that promotes the feeling of "becoming one." The social/relational discourses of *kondongch'e* (community) and the model of *ture* (a cooperative agricultural labor organization) serve to encourage practitioners to not just focus on improving performance skills, but to develop a communal mindset toward doing the work necessary for a successful *madang* event. In pre-industrial times, some *ture* organizations incorporated *p'ungmul* to facilitate a balance of work and play or tension and release that served to enhance productivity.

Of the transformative discourses, the concepts of *kut* (shamanist ritual) and *shinmyŏng* are the most frequently mentioned. The framing of *p'ungmul* as *kut* is central to the style of *p'ungmul* that I focus on in this book and will be discussed in more depth in chapters 3 and 4. Another shamanism-related term, *shinmyŏng*, literally means "shining with the spirit" and refers to that elusive state of "spiritual catharsis" during which participants let go of inhibitions and express their emotions. Although *shinmyŏng* is discussed in mask dance drama circles, it is considered a core aesthetic in *p'ungmul* (Yi Chongjin 1996, 1; Kim Inu 1987, 141). Korean scholar Song Soonam [Song Sunam] suggests that *shinmyŏng* is especially important in encouraging embodied participation in the *madang* and writes that it is best "realized in Korean group dance performance," uniting the "dancer [or performer] with the audience, making them one" (1990, 34–35). *Nanjang* or "chaos" can carry negative connotations of disorder, but it is one of the more intriguing *madang*-related concepts. In *p'ungmul*, *nanjang* can be seen as an "anything goes" mode of spontaneity and freedom from order that can change the course of an event. Some scholars relegate *nanjang* to the freeform play or dance that occurs at the end of an event (Chu Kanghyŏn 1992, 220; Kwŏn Tuhyŏn 1992, 49), but it can occur at other times. Reminiscent of Victor Turner's "communitas" (1974), *nanjang* can be defined as a state of "temporary suspension of the usual order of things, where the boundaries between men and women, old and young, rich and poor are dropped" (Park 2000, 160). *Nanjang* can also been seen as a negation of the self and the expansion of one's awareness of the community (Kim Iktu 1995, 116–17).

The last theme within the transformative category is the emphasis on cosmological views of space and patterns of nature that are reproduced temporally, experientially, and spatially in the *madang*. According to Asian cosmological beliefs, space is mapped according to *ohaeng* or "five directions": east, west, north, south, and center. Each direction correlates symbolically to a complex of elements and forces (colors, seasons, natural elements, etc.). When *p'ungmul* is choreographed according to these directions, it is believed to balance these forces and instill harmony. Patterns of nature pertinent to *p'ungmul* include the regular sounds of breathing, heartbeats, rain, or wind, and even fractals that are reproduced in nature. Many patterns in *p'ungmul* possess a fractal-like quality in the way that they can be found to be repeated or reproduced on various scales, from the articulation of a single rhythmic pattern to the way rhythms and tempos are ordered and bound together, to the way the energy is shaped over the course of the whole day's events.[5] Though this concept applies mostly to the way a *madang* is experienced temporally, one can also see the fractal-like shape emerge from the circular motion of the *p'ungmul* troupe as it travels from one village *madang* to another.

In the final experiential category, the concepts of *nori* (play) and the *hyŏnjang* (being in the contemporary moment or place) are extremely important in guiding participation. The most common space for play in a *p'ungmul* or mask dance drama performance usually occurs at the end of a performance, when *all* the participants are invited to enter the *madang*. When this takes the form of simple games or organized movements, this is often called *taedongnori* (literally "large group play"). Otherwise, when teachers tell students that they have to "*play more,*" it usually means that they need to focus on smiling and interacting with others, or contribute to the liveliness of the *madang* by improvising movements, rhythms, or vocalizations. The *hyŏnjang* refers to being in the "actual spot, moment or scene." It is what Im Chint'aek and Ch'ae Hŭiwan call *hyŏnjangjŏkin undongsŏng*, or "the philosophy of being attuned to the dynamics of the moment/scene" (Im 1990, 85; Ch'ae 1992, 64–68). In effect, to be in the *madang* is to always be ready to respond to whatever may happen in a given moment.

With this arsenal of meanings coupled with its "iconicity of style" that infuses multiple domains, it should be evident that the *madang* is integral to the patterning of *p'ungmul* and other related arts. According to Turino, these "patterns" or "integrative maps" provide avenues for participants to achieve a sense of wholeness or "becoming one" (in the language of *p'ungmul* practitioners), while also becoming more connected to the environment.

CHAPTER OVERVIEW AND METHODOLOGY

This book's overall structure flows from a thorough grounding in the local and proceeds outward to delve into the workings of the *madang* in facilitating integrative practices in regional, national, and transnational settings. Following the introduction, part 1 is a case-study of a site-specific expressive ecology of *p'ungmul* based in the village of Pilbong. *P'ungmul* or *nongak* was designated as Important Intangible Cultural Property no. 11 in 1985 by the South Korean government (with the Pilbong style being recognized in 1988), and as an Intangible Cultural Heritage for Humanity by UNESCO in 2014. Part 2 expands centrifugally to explore site-oriented or *madang*-oriented expressive ecologies that resonate beyond the village in a broad array of contexts. To provide an overview of part 1, the chapters explore the expressive ecology of Pilbong as it has been cultivated through certain historic conditions and paths (chapter 1), site-specific transmission (chapter 2), village preparation and labor (chapter 3), and performative ritual (chapter 4).

In chapter 1, I provide the larger context of site-specific transmission and performance through the lens of Pilbong's history as a destination of site-specific heritage and culture from the 1970s until the early 2020s. Here, I operate from a theoretical position of place as constructed. While aspects of place may possess and be limited by physical or material realities, I am sympathetic with Doreen Massey's theorization of place and space as inherently relational and integral with time. Specifically, Massey defines place as a node in an interlocking web of social relations that is subject to the heterogeneous effects of globalization and unequal power geometries (Massey 1994). In terms of the place of Pilbong, I apply these ideas by challenging the assumed isomorphic relationship between a regional style (such as Pilbong *p'ungmul*) and the place it is attributed to (the village of Pilbong) by telling the complex and unpredictably mobile history of its key actors in relation to its major sites of transmission from the 1970s until the end of the first decade of the twenty-first century. Chapter 1 also delves into adjacent practices that enabled the development of Pilbong as a cultural destination, including the practice of *nonghwal*, a form of rural activism that targeted farmers living in villages, and a domestic cultural tourism trend called *tapsa*.

Chapter 2 looks at how transmission practices structure the experience of a Korean expressive folk culture form by emphasizing site-specific instruction and intermodal pedagogical techniques that train the body to engage with space and place in certain patterned ways. Here, I highlight the role of *madang* discourses as they inform the site-specific practice of going to transmission camps called *chŏnsu*—popular among expressive folk culture practitioners—to attend intensive sessions of instruction in or near the place where a given tradition or style is believed to have originated. I contextualize these transmission centers or *chŏnsugwan* as important alternative institutions for the transmission of Korean music and dance. In the rest of the chapter, I take the reader inside a week at the Pilbong transmission center and provide rich ethnographic description of the major, site-specific activities of a typical training session. I conclude by providing a microanalysis of how Pilbong teachers transmit the distinctive regional groove of the Pilbong rhythmic style by examining intermodal pedagogical strategies that target the body.

Chapter 3 acquaints the reader with Pilbong village and shares how its residents and associated *p'ungmul* practitioners strive to maintain the expressive ecology of the village and its environs, especially during a time when so many factors threaten the integrity of rural village life in South Korea. Here, I share an intimate view of this effort by sharing a self-reflexive account of how the group prepares to host the Lunar New Year Ritual in Pilbong. I was fortunate to be there during the pivotal years of 2001–2002 and 2016 to observe and personally help with various preparations including cooking, cleaning, and decorating the various village *madangs*. I also draw from other visits in 2007, 2009, 2012, and 2015. Lastly, I chronicle the tremendous efforts that have occurred over the years to maintain and re-make Pilbong's landscape, pathways, and architecture in its steady journey to become more of a cultural heritage destination.

Chapter 4 is the culmination of part 1 and details the performance and ritual elements of the Lunar New Year Ritual in 2002 and 2016. Here, I argue that site-specific performance and ritual can enable stronger connections to the environment by providing a range of aesthetic patterns, sensations, and experiences that participants can then engage and play with in both time and space. In this way, I argue that these rituals create a space to perform dialogues about relationships with each other and with the animistic spirit realm—all in response to the forces of modernity—as they play out in performative rites, improvisational gender play, and even Turnerian social drama. I posit that these modes create moments of open-ended social engagement that articulate and reiterate our connections to each other and to the environment (or lack thereof) and are crucial to the continued relevance of the form. Finally, I reflect on the ongoing influence of cultural heritage preservation and tourism that has been there from the outset but has become more influential over time.

The overarching inquiry of part 2 is to investigate whether Korean folk expressive culture can still forge meaningful connections between people, place, and the environment when the "site" moves to other locations and contexts beyond the village-based ritual. Here, I examine how *madang*-oriented or site-oriented performances of Korean folk expressive culture operate on larger scales, such as the regional in chapter 5, the urban/national in chapter 6, and the transnational in chapter 7.

In chapter 5, the main line of inquiry is to investigate whether *madang*-type performances can still forge "resonant" connections between people, place, and the environment when a regionally based group goes on tour or performs at another regional location not exclusively associated with their tradition. Here, I draw productively from Marié Abe's insightful work on *chindon-ya* practitioners whose philosophy of "resonance" (*hibiki* in Japanese) she defines as "a simultaneously acoustic and affective work of sounding that articulates latent socialities, the acoustic environment, and sedimented histories" (Abe 2018, 29). In this way, I look at how region, history, and memory are woven together by examining two festivals. The first was a festival that commemorated the revolt of peasants in the *Tonghak* Uprising (1894), where all the participants were asked to physically gather and march in key historic locations of this movement, thereby embodying history in space and place. The second festival was organized by the Goseong Ogwangdae mask dance drama group and was meant to commemorate the victory of the famous Korean naval commander Yi Sunshin (1545–1598) over the Japanese in the battle of Danghangpo harbor in 1592. As in the previous example, this festival highlighted historic events that can be framed both in terms of their regional specificity as well as for their national historic import.

In chapter 6, I explore how the younger generation of creative folk expressive culture practitioners perform in urban, national settings in Seoul, the capital of South Korea. Here, I focus on creative folk expressive culture groups working in a genre called *ch'angjak yŏnhŭi*, such as Yŏnhŭi Chipdan The Kwangdae, The Greatest Masque, Norikkundŭl Todam Todam, and the all-female Norikkot. I examine how these teams continue to draw upon *madang* discourses to reach increasingly diverse audiences in a range of urban spaces—from public urban *madangs* to intimate senior centers, elegant palatial parks to bustling city streets. Using an arsenal of different expressive modes, I argue that these performers are on the frontlines of creating *madang*-oriented expressive ecologies in urban spaces by eliciting bodily and social participation from various groups of people who reside in or visit South Korea.

In chapter 7, I extend this inquiry further by looking at how the *madang* has been used as a powerful format in site-oriented performances by Korean Americans living in the United States, especially during challenging times such as in the immediate aftermath of 9/11. Here, I focus on groups practicing in the San Francisco and New York metropolitan areas and examine how the politics of gathering and performing in public spaces in the United States can have diverse consequences, especially for marginalized groups. I also come back to the use of ritual, but here as adapted to forge political solidarity and community healing. Lastly, I assess the power and limits of these site-specific performances to create an effective means of achieving a sense of integrative wholeness and stronger connections to place and to each other when a group's claim to a given public space is tenuous at best. The conclusion offers a reflection of the lessons that can be learned from *madang*-based, site-specific practices, and articulates some of the implications of this research.

This project is the result of a fieldwork-based, longitudinal study that has spanned over two decades, aligning with what Kay Kaufman Shelemay defines as a "medium-term," "multitemporal" study (Shelemay 2022, chap. 1). This has enabled me to step in myriad *madangs* during my research, mostly in South Korea but also in the United States. Prior to embarking on dissertation fieldwork, I had spent several summers (1994, 1999, 2000) and a half-year exchange (1992) in South Korea engaged in learning about Korean music and dance. During my long-term dissertation fieldwork year in South Korea in 2001–2002, I visited so many *madangs* that I quickly earned the label of *madangbal* (literally "*madang*-foot" or "wide foot"), a somewhat affectionate moniker for someone who covers a lot of ground and circulates among various social circles. This literal and metaphorical attention to the expressive interface between feet and ground, body and site, has necessitated an embodied, experiential, and, ultimately, self-reflexive approach to fieldwork and ethnography. After my dissertation was completed, I continued to follow up with research visits to South Korea in 2007, 2009, 2012, 2015, and 2016. My US-based activities with Korean American groups were most intensive from 1999 to 2001 and 2002 to 2005, while I was active with the Korean Youth Cultural Center in Oakland, California. After this, I continued to be in contact with US-based groups across the country through the early 2020s.

Like many authors, the subject of my research reflects who I am as a person. While my initial attraction to Korean music and culture stemmed from a desire to learn more about my heritage, growing up as a code-switching, second-generation Korean American also prompted a deep-seated awareness of my "space" and "place" in the world. This explains why I was initially so drawn to the possibilities of the *madang* as a distinctly participatory cultural space. In the field and beyond, I have had to negotiate my complex position as a second-generation Korean American woman, scholar, and practitioner. On the one hand, my identity gives me a certain degree of insider status and sense of belonging and has provided a productive diasporic link to the Korean genres I have studied. On the other, I have found that my outsider status as a second-generation American, as well as my position as a scholar, has profoundly complicated this link, especially when combined with my reception as a woman in a more patriarchal society such as South Korea. Over the years, I have learned not to try to reconcile these binary insider/outsider positions but have negotiated and built upon them. By engaging in the *madang* in multiple ways—as audience member, performer, videographer, ethnographer, scholar, activist, and teacher—I aim to provide a more multifaceted account.

Following the well-trodden path of Mantle Hood (1960) and countless other ethnomusicologists, my approach has been a journey in learning to become more "bi-musical" or, perhaps more accurately, "multi-musical."[6] Further, since I was active in the Korean American and Asian American community-based performing arts scenes in the San Francisco Bay Area, I found myself applying what I learned from the field directly to these activities. I realize now that I was engaging in the concurrent learning, performance, and writing of culture. For additional context, the dissertation fieldwork and writing period from which much of this book derives coincided with the September 11 attacks and the subsequent War on Terror and the invasion of Iraq in 2003. As a result, I was called upon many times to respond to these events by participating in peace protests involving Korean drumming or *p'ungmul* and other performances that included various Korean music and dance. I realize now that I was practicing a kind of politically engaged performative ethnography (Wong 2008), even though at the time I was trying to keep my academic and performance/political worlds separate. As a result, a more auto-ethnographic attention to the politics of performance did not always make it into my ethnographic writing, although it certainly informed it. In many ways, this book represents a more personal attempt to rectify this gap, spurring me to integrate and reflect upon what the politics of site-specific performance has meant for me and my interlocutors in this study.

PART I
Local Transmission and Ritual Performance

ONE

Pathways to Pilbong

> For me, the village just means the space where people live. It's a matter of space or the *madang*. When we think about the village, I don't just think about the people, I think about all the creatures, all of nature, all of the life that is exuded in this space. It is not just a space-of-play, it is a work-space. There are a lot of paths throughout the village, the path where you go to play, the path where you go to collect wood. When someone dies, there's a path you have to go for that. All of these things.
>
> Yang Chinsŏng interview, October 5, 2003

As the leader of the Imshil Pilbong *p'ungmul* group, Yang Chinsŏng spoke often about the village of Pilbong and the importance of its *madang* spaces and paths. He reminds us that while the paths may be interconnected, each one is cleared with a distinct destination and purpose in mind. It is our job then to map their interconnections and try to determine their specific trajectories. In this chapter, I will explore some of the pathways and material conditions that have enabled such robust site-specific expressive activity in South Korea and note some of the changes that have occurred over time in my primary case study. Then, I will examine two important practices or paths that are closely intertwined with site-specific performance and transmission, namely *tapsa* (field visits) and *nonghwal* (literally "farming activity").[1] Going on *tapsa*, or the act of visiting cultural field sites throughout South Korea, has been popular since the 1990s (Oppenheim 2010, 105). *Nonghwal* is a service activity where students or young activists volunteer on a farm for a week or longer to experience the "life" of a farmer in order to better advocate for them. Because of *p'ungmul*'s historical connections to agricultural labor, many *p'ungmul* enthusiasts have had some experience with *nonghwal*. In looking at site-specific performance and transmission, my primary case study for part 1 of this book is Imshil Pilbong Nongak (Important Intangible Cultural Property No. 11-5) and its activities in the village of Pilbong in North Jeolla province. This chapter serves the dual purpose of giving some background history as an introduction to Imshil Pilbong Nongak while also demonstrating the fluidity of the relationship between a regional style of *nongak* (also called *p'ungmul*) and the place with which it is identified. I do this by telling the unpredictably mobile history of its transmission center from the 1970s until the end of the first decade of the twenty-first century. Central to my thesis is the idea that musical or cultural attachments to place are not necessarily "natural" or eternal but must be continuously cultivated.

SETTING THE SCENE: A PICTURE OF PILBONG

Despite its small size, South Korea has cultivated a strong national identity while also maintaining distinct regional identities, often playfully articulated in the media in terms of dialects, regional cuisines, and even gendered personality types. To give some perspective, the entire Korean peninsula is about the size of the United Kingdom, with South Korea being just a little larger than Portugal, but home to over fifty million residents. Korea is rugged territory and its mountain ranges have long served as natural borders between regions. For example, the Sobaek range that bisects the southern portion of the peninsula is a significant material feature that has divided the cultural and historical Honam and Yeongnam regions. South Korea's outer borders have also been defined by geography and politics; oceans line the eastern, western, and southern borders of the country while the Korean Demilitarized Zone (DMZ) that lies at the thirty-eighth parallel serves as its de facto northern border with North Korea. While human politics and historical struggles have certainly had an impact on the development of Korea's distinctive combination of national and regional identities, its material geographic conditions have also played a major role.

In terms of site-specific performance and transmission, then, South Korea's combination of relatively manageable size, dense population, comprehensive transportation infrastructure, and history of regional development or *chibanghwa* have all contributed to fertile conditions of possibility for robust regional practices to thrive. In addition, affordable transportation coupled with a rising middle-class nostalgia for the "country" on the one hand and a desire for alternative modes of travel and leisure on the other are important driving factors. Geography and the concentration of power in certain cities play a role in contouring the routes and nodes of travel. For example, it is easier to move vertically north and south versus east and west because of the mountain ranges that bisect the peninsula. Given that Seoul is the capital of South Korea and its major metropolitan center, it is generally simpler and faster to get anywhere from Seoul than to travel in the east-west direction. This geographic mapping of routes and nodes has impacted the flow of people who might engage in a given expressive genre. While there are many exceptions, divisions between regions tend to persist as a result, while at the same time facilitating certain kinds of interactions between the residents of: (1) the Seoul metropolitan area and almost any other location easily accessible by bus or train, (2) cities or towns that may be geographically distant but are still within the same region (Honam or Yeongnam) or province, and (3) cities or towns that are in close proximity.

My field research drew me to many locations south of Seoul, but the place I visited most regularly was the village of Pilbong, located in Imshil County in North Jeolla province. This is the home of the Korean rural percussion band tradition of Imshil Pilbong Nongak (Intangible Cultural Property 11-5).[2] Following the lead of practitioners, I will often refer to the style as "Pilbong *p'ungmul*," "Pilbong *p'ungmul-kut*," or "Pilbong *nongak*" somewhat interchangeably, but when referring to the organization, I will use their official name of Imshil Pilbong Nongak Pojonhoe (Imshil Pilbong Nongak Preservation Association). When I first started visiting in 1999 and 2000, I had to travel by bus first to the city of Jeonju and then transfer to the neighboring town of Gangjin, which took roughly six hours. Approximately fifteen years later, there is now a direct bus from Seoul to Gangjin that cuts this time by an hour or two. Once in the town of Gangjin, it is an easy walk to the Imshil Pilbong Nongak transmission center. From there, all one needs to do is glance across the highway to make out the rounded calligraphy brush–like symmetry of Pilbong mountain that is often emphasized as a prominent marker of place and locality among residents (figure 1.1). This geographical mountain feature of Pilbong has come to inscribe not only the name of the village, but also the name of the style of *nongak* or *p'ungmul* that is associated with this village. My former teacher, Han Chaehun explains:

> The village of Pilbong is named after the Pilbong mountain. The mountain is called Pilbong because it resembles the tip of a large calligraphy brush [literal meaning of "Pilbong"] . . . There are fewer people living in Pilbong than there

FIGURE 1.1 View of Pilbong mountain from the Pilbong transmission center (2016). Photo by the author.

are performing members. There are no young people—it's a very small place, a very, very small place—well maybe if you include all the small children it equals out. There are no young adults—all of the countryside is like that. Everyone has left. They all dispersed to the cities. Well, there are some students who are thinking about coming in. (Han Chaehun recording, January 15, 2002)

In the 1970s, there were approximately fifty households with 148 residents. By 1987, the number of households decreased to thirty-eight. A survey taken in 1994 states that there were thirty-four households with about 100 residents (Kim Iktu et al. 1994, 135). By 1996, there were twenty-four households with seventy-four residents (Yi Chongjin 1996, 14). In 2008, there were twenty-two households with sixty residents remaining in the village (Yang Chinsŏng 2008, 14). Regardless of these changes, entry to the village is still more or less the same. After turning off a busy two-lane highway and crossing over a medium-size stream, it is a quick walk up a narrow road before reaching the village center. In the distance, burial mounds can be seen on the higher plateaus. As you approach the village, there is a large *tangsan namu*, or grandfather tutelary (guardian) spirit tree, on the right, located just before a bend in the road that leads into the village center.

THE SIGHTS AND SOUNDS OF PILBONG *P'UNGMUL*

P'ungmul is an unabashedly loud and colorful music and dance form that is perhaps best appreciated outdoors, preferably against the backdrop of dirt, trees, mountains, rocks, and streams. In order to make enough of a sonic and visual impact in this setting, a *p'ungmul* ensemble is typically rather large. The Imshil Pilbong Nongak Preservation Association (hereafter abbreviated as IPNPA) consists of fifty to seventy-five members called *ch'ibae*, who all stand and/or move as they perform. This ensemble consists of percussionists, character actors, supplemental wind instrumentalists, and large flagholders (table 1.1). The *sangsoe*, or lead small gong, determines the overall membership and designates who performs which role. The percussionists consist of the *soe* (small gong), *ching* (large gong), *changgo* (hourglass drum), *puk* (barrel drum), *kokkal sogo* and *ch'aesang sogo* (different types of handheld drum) players, who generally play in this order. The character actors, or *chapsaek*, usually take their position behind the *sogo* players, although they are also free to roam around, as long as it is not a pivotal section of choreography. These character actors represent classic village archetypes in Korean society. Some, like the *taep'osu* (hunter), the *kakshi* (young woman or bride), and *halmi* (grandmother), are more important than others. Supplemental instrumentalists include players of the conical double-reed instrument called the *t'aep'yŏngso* and the valveless long-neck bugle or *nabal*. Supplemental players usually stand to the side and do not perform the choreographed movements. Flagholders also spend most of the time standing to the side, but they can be positioned in the center of the circle (as in the flag ceremony) or walk as part of the troupe either in the front or rear position (usually when traveling from one location to the next). These flagholders carry four flags: two of the flags, called *yŏng-gi*, are rectangular and mounted horizontally on six-foot poles, while the other two are twelve- to fifteen-foot banners (*nong-gi*) that hang down vertically. Sometimes, they also carry or mount a large flag with a dragon on it, called a *yong-gi*.[3]

When the whole ensemble is playing the overall sound is full but with a bal-

TABLE 1.1 Pilbong *P'ungmul* Ensemble Roles

INSTRUMENT/TITLE	NUMBER	ROLE
Sangsoe (lead small gong player)	1	Lead small gong player, played with wooden mallet. Commands the whole ensemble, cues changes, and improvises within the rhythmic cycle.
Soe or *kkwaenggwari* (small gong)	4–7	Additional small gongs, played with wooden mallet. Sometimes plays hocketing patterns with the *sangsoe*. All *soe* players wear white *minbok*, black satin vests with rainbow-striped sleeves, colorful sashes, and a *pup'o sangmo* hat with a spinning tassel that is decorated with a cluster of white feathers.
Ching (large gong)	3–5	Large gong, played with soft mallet. Emphasizes the first beat of the rhythmic cycle. Wears a white *minbok*, blue vest, and sashes.
Changgo (hourglass drum)	8–12	Two-headed hourglass drums, played with wooden mallet and thin bamboo stick. Lays out drum stroke patterns that closely follow the rhythmic cycle. Wears a white *minbok*, blue vest, and colorful sashes.
Puk (barrel drum)	4–7	Two-headed barrel drums, played with a thick wooden stick. Accents the strong beats. Wears a white *minbok*, blue vest, and colorful sashes.
Kokkal sogo (flower hat handheld drum)	7–17	Small drum dancers with flower (*kokkal*) hats in white, yellow, and red. Though the handheld drum is played with a stick, the main role is to provide dance and movement. Wears a white *minbok*, blue vest, and colorful sashes.
Ch'aesang sogo (twirling ribbon hat handheld drum)	5–13	Small drum dancers with twirling ribbon hats (*ch'aesang sangmo*). Though the handheld drum is played with a stick, the main role is to dance and create vertical/circular interest. Wears a white *minbok*, blue vest, and colorful sashes.

anced and robust percussive texture. Each instrument group adds their own necessary color to the overall sound. The small gongs (*soe*) clang with a high, shimmery sonority, while the larger gongs (*ching*) ring with a low, continuous "wah"-like sound that really fills out the lower frequency spectrum and, according to Yang Chinsŏng, is "what makes some villagers go crazy for the sound of *p'ungmul*." The *puk* provides a very discernible bass, accenting the strong beats of the rhythms while the *changgo* fills the space in between. The distinctive high and bright timbre of the *t'aep'yŏngso* (conical double-reed) adds a great deal of improvisatory melodic interest with its unique style of ornamentation, heavy vibrato, and bending inflections. The *t'aep'yŏngso* player performs continuously

INSTRUMENT/TITLE	NUMBER	ROLE
T'aep'yŏngso (conical double-reed)	1	Conical double-reed, provides soaring, improvisational melodies that shift according to the rhythmic cycle and energy level, usually stands to the side. Wears a long robe.
Nabal (valveless long-neck bugle)	1	Valveless long-neck bugle. Sounds three times to alert the village and the performers that the event will be beginning.
Kisu (flagholder)	4–5	Flagholders.
Taep'osu	1	Hunter, male, wears a white *minbok*, red satin vest, black beard, wooden rifle prop, woven knapsack, and a brass crown.
Yangban	1	Aristocrat, male. Wears a long white robe, white beard, and black headpiece, and holds a fan and a long pipe.
Ch'angbu	1	Village character, usually male. Wears a long blue robe, a straw hat with feathers, and a long sash.
Hwadong	1	Village character, usually male. Wears a long robe and a long sash.
Chorijung	1	Monk, male, wears a gray robe, conical straw hat, and holds a wooden temple block.
Kakshi	1	Literally "bride" or "doll," but also refers to a young woman or maiden, usually played by women but can also be played by men. Wears a *hanbok* with a red skirt and yellow top, and a white scarf on her head.
Halmi	1	Grandmother, female. Wears a white hanbok and a white scarf on her head and holds a long pipe and a wooden cane.

but has the freedom to come in and out where appropriate. In contrast, the *nabal* is traditionally sounded three times in the beginning, with significant pauses in between each blow, to alert the village that the start of the ritual is imminent. Aside from the *nabal*, all the instruments are usually played at the same time, although there are moments when the *soes* might drop out temporarily. Other times, the whole ensemble might quiet down or drop out completely for instrumental solos or the singing of songs. Amplification is generally not used, but the *t'aep'yŏngso* is sometimes given a stationary microphone in certain key locations. When the voice is highlighted, in songs for example, the singer may also be provided with a clip-on microphone.

Today, very few of the forty-five to fifty-five members of the IPNPA actually reside in Pilbong full-time. The current leader Yang Chinsŏng and his brother Yang Chinhwan have strong ties to the village and stay there often, but maintain other residences with their own families. Although they may not live in Pilbong, most of the elder players that were active in the early 2000s live nearby in neighboring villages and towns. Many of them are now deceased or are too old to maintain the rigors of performing with the group regularly. Among the younger generation of players who now comprise most of the performers, some reside at the Pilbong transmission center nearby, while most live in cities such as Jeonju, Gwangju, and Seoul (Yang Chinsŏng 2000, 267–68). In terms of gender, the troupe tends to be male dominated. However, in the last decade or so, especially among the younger generation, more and more women have joined the IPNPA.[4]

The transmission center complex or *chŏnsugwan* (also called *chŏnsuhoegwan*) is located just across from the village, on the other side of a small highway. Less than a fifteen-minute walk away, it sits on an expansive property carved out of the hills. It is here where all the administrative, transmission-related, overnight accommodation, and educational activities of the IPNPA take place. Since the late 1990s I have witnessed this transmission center grow from a single "original" transmission building into a complex of over twenty buildings and other structures that include traditional architectural residential spaces, indoor and outdoor rehearsal and performance venues, classrooms, a cafeteria, a residence hall, a museum, gardens, and walking paths (figure 1.2). Despite the almost unrivaled expansion and success of this transmission center, the paths that led to this point were plural, contentious at times, and non-linear. Given this, the assumed isomorphic relationship between the transmission of this genre and its place of origin in the village of Pilbong was not automatic and was complicated by several factors that will be better explained in the sections that follow.

TAPSA AND SITE-SPECIFIC PERFORMANCE

Ch'ae Hŭiwan describes being in the *madang* as an engagement with the "actual everyday cultural space of life" (1992, 64).[5] In the context of Korean performance, this means seeking out expressive culture as it occurs naturally in daily life. For folk genres such as *p'ungmul*, this would have naturally occurred in pre-industrial village life settings—either out in the fields in conjunction with agricultural labor or in various *madangs* throughout the village during periods of recreation or ritual. In some cases, one might have encountered *p'ungmul* in more itinerant

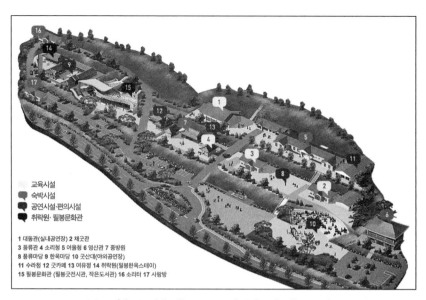

FIGURE 1.2 Map of the Imshil Pilbong *Nongak* Cultural Village and Transmission Center (2023). Used with permission of Yang Chinsŏng.

settings, where performers traveled from town to town, often aiming for market days when people from multiple villages would gather. Today, one might see people playing in urban plazas, parks, or even on the streets, especially during holidays like Lunar New Year. Even so, there continues to be a widespread belief that in order to truly understand genres like *p'ungmul*, one must travel to the villages where music and dance is believed to be better integrated with the rhythms and rituals of everyday life in certain sites (Kwon 2015; Saeji 2013, 74).

These ideas are very much in line with the cultural field-visiting practice known as *tapsa*. Anthropologist Robert Oppenheim has defined *tapsa* as a "practical genre of interacting with historic things" and credits its popularity to Professor Yu Hongjun, who became famous for his two-volume work entitled *Na ŭi Munhwa Yusan Tapsagi* (The Chronicle of My Field Investigation of Cultural Remains) (Oppenheim 2008, 83–84). And while the writings of Oppenheim and Yu are inclusive of cultural heritage performances and practices, both are somewhat more focused on the objects or "things" (in Oppenheim's theorization) of material culture. This approach generally mirrors the divide in the heritage world between "tangible" and "intangible" culture. And while both tangible and intangible culture are considered valuable on multiple scales (local, national,

Pathways to Pilbong 31

international), they are often quantified and managed in very different ways. Depending upon the degree to which one's orientation toward *tapsa* is based upon tangible or intangible culture (or both), one might categorize the practice of site-specific cultural performance as either parallel to *tapsa* or more inclusively as a performance-oriented branch within *tapsa*. Either way, both practices have come to circumscribe a range of activity that spans from touristic, free-flowing, and individualistic travel to serious group study. For example, *tapsa* travels have often been described online or in "culture" or "weekend" sections of a newspaper for the benefit of individuals, families, or groups. I have also seen the term co-opted by commercial tourist agencies that advertise multi-site tours of various cultural destinations within a city. Robert Oppenheim writes that it "would not be wrong to describe *tapsa* as a sort of domestic heritage tourism, but that description would risk obscuring its weight as a practice of encounter often taken quite seriously amid shifting terrains of history, historical experience and democracy alike" (2008, 83–84). In my research, I have observed that while some city people who travel to see site-specific performances can be described as casual tourists, many who come are part of college- or community-based "folk culture research organizations" (*minsok munhwa yŏnguhoe*) who meet regularly to read, discuss, and even learn the music or dance that is being performed.

Oppenheim writes that *tapsa* is about "interacting with historic things" (2008, 83) while Yu defines it as "leaving the road to find places with a history" (Yu Hongjun 1993, 95). Site-specific performance, then, can be further defined in this context as participating in performances, rituals, or other expressive practices that have a relatively long and continuous history of being conducted in a particular site or regional location. Lunar New Year village-based rituals performed by *p'ungmul* practitioners and the UNESCO-recognized Gangneung *Tano* festival that falls on the fifth day of the fifth month of the Korean lunar calendar are both good examples. In the case where an event may have been practiced for a long time but was interrupted in some way or subsided from practice (but not memory), careful revival is possible and can also be considered site-specific performance. With South Korea's modern history of colonial occupation, war, and relatively rapid industrialization, the interruption of practice is much more the norm. As we will see later in this chapter, some practices may have been continued, but not necessarily always in the same place.[6]

Oppenheim situates Yu's framing of *tapsa* as a project of citizenship as well as history. In terms of citizenship, Yu's work has taken *tapsa* from its more limited academic environs and opened it up to all citizens. This encourages them to engage with historical objects to make their own sense of history, purportedly free from the authority of textbook-based national narratives. Theoretically, this is supposed to democratize the engagement with historical artifacts, but also authority itself, especially as regular citizens gain practical knowledge and are able to lead *tapsa* on their own. According to his critics, Yu failed in these intentions and inadvertently created his own overly prescriptive "dominant discourse" as his readers strived to experience objects as described in his texts (Oppenheim 2008, 92).

Because there are fewer authoritative *tapsa* accounts about site-specific performance or ritual events written for general audiences, I do not get a sense that there is a highly detailed dominant discourse about how to experience them. With this said, I have repeatedly experienced a push toward participating collectively and wholeheartedly in an event. For Korean expressive folk culture such as *p'ungmul* and mask dance drama, there is a somewhat learned or prescriptive quality to this that I will detail in the next chapter but, in short, this usually translates into interjecting *ch'uimsae* (shouts of encouragement) or dancing, usually by bouncing up and down or moving one's arms from side to side from the sidelines. At other times, this may even entail coming into the center of the performance space during participatory "group-play" sections called *taedongnori* when the performers encourage audience members to come into the *madang*.

The act of seeking out older site-specific performances can also be seen as an engagement with history at large. Oppenheim interprets Yu's *tapsa* practice as a corrective balm or reckoning with Korea's "twisted" history (2008, 93–99). Similarly, the student-led revival of folk genres that was associated with the *minjung* movement (literally "people's movement," also called the democratization movement) in the 1970s and 1980s can be seen as a desire to respond to what Namhee Lee calls the narrative of "negative modernity" that has come to characterize Korea's colonial and post-colonial history (2007, 3). At a basic level, this works simply by enabling more people to participate in expressive culture practices that are considered more continuous with pre-division Korean culture and history, thereby recovering an embodied knowledge largely lost to several generations of Koreans who have grown up predominantly with Western and Japanese-influenced cultural forms. In addition, Namhee Lee argues that *minjung* movement activists were striving for ways to create a "counterpublic sphere" through *madang*-related practices (especially *madang* theater or *madangguk*) that could provide a grassroots alternative to the ways in which the Park Chung Hee regime was using folk genres to bolster the legitimacy of the state through the staging of national folk arts contests (Lee 2007, 190). In my fieldwork, I encountered many elder *p'ungmul* practitioners denigrating these folk arts contests as de-personalized and shallow "mass game" culture. While the government did help provide resources through the Intangible Cultural Property system to create local transmission centers and support designated local artists, some *minjung* movement–influenced scholars and practitioners helped to re-situate folk genres in ways that were more historically and regionally consistent with earlier practices. Interestingly, as the *minjung* movement perspective became more accepted throughout the mid-1980s and '90s, some of these ideas circled back to influence the governmental designation process of Intangible Cultural Properties. While participating in site-specific performance may not be as detailed an engagement with history as *tapsa* can be (with its close attention to architecture and artifacts from various periods in Korea's history), it nevertheless shares some similar motivations and, perhaps more importantly, speaks to the same thorny tensions involved in citizenship, activism, and the embodied engagement with history in South Korea.

Perhaps the most relevant correlation between *tapsa* and site-specific performance is the philosophy behind the famous phrase "museum without walls," first articulated in an essay by André Malraux (1967) but often used in Korea to describe the city of Gyeongju. Inherent in this phrase is the assertion that if art includes what Yu considers as valuable artifacts of cultural heritage, such as sculpture, pagodas, and architecture, then it follows that these artifacts must be appreciated *in situ*. This necessitates an encounter that is embodied and personal—often involving walking, hiking, and multi-sensory observation—ideally with consideration to how these objects engage with nature and the surrounding geographical environment. According to Yu, this may include appreciating or critiquing the way certain objects enhance or perhaps obscure the natural beauty of the surrounding landscape or architecture, or even looking at the way light falls on an object at different times of day. Oppenheim notes that Yu is an advocate for moving artifacts that were once displayed in museums and re-situating them back in context, for "only when it is in its own location can the light of a relic really shine forth" (Yu Hongjun 1993, 5, cited in Oppenheim 2008, 88). Translating this sentiment into the realm of sound and expressive intangible culture, this correlates directly with the move toward presenting Korean expressive folk genres in outdoor *madangs* or in the actual spatio-temporal context or *hyŏnjang*, versus indoor concert halls. As a researcher, this philosophy may include attuning oneself to how the overall sound resonates in a given environment and analyzing how performers adjust and respond to a given socio-acoustic setting. Another unexpected consideration that came up in my research was the impact of natural versus artificial lighting, so eloquently articulated here by the current leader of the IPNPA, Yang Chinsŏng:

> When I was young, I was exposed to [*p'ungmul* under] the natural lighting of the moon. Under this moon just floating by itself, eternal, what I saw was the *madang*. Lately, I have also been exposed to the bright and colorful culture of artificial lighting. And though the culture of moonlight is not as bright, the kinds of things that happen . . . by the light of the moon is what I have come to see as truly beautiful. (Yang Chinsŏng interview, October 9, 2002)

These are the kinds of intersections I hope to highlight in this study by taking into account both human and non-human actors in a way that bridges the divide between "human" and "nature," and between the anthropocentric "art object" and its social, spatial, and environmental context. In this endeavor, my goal is to present a study of the expressive ecology that embraces the implications of site-specific transmission and performance in terms of both the politics of decolonization on the one hand, and cultural and environmental sustainability on the other.

NONGHWAL AND SITE-SPECIFIC TRANSMISSION

If the practice of observing site-specific performances is most analogous to the *tapsa* phenomenon, then site-specific transmission, or *chŏnsu*, correlates most closely to the practice of *nonghwal*. The term *nonghwal* is technically an abbreviation of *nongch'on hwaldong*, which literally means "farming village activism." In its abbreviated form, the term is reminiscent of the common word for "living," or *saenghwal*, and as such, conveys the notion that it is akin to experiencing the life of a farmer. While *tapsa*, *nonghwal*, and *chŏnsu* all have close ties to Korean academia, *chŏnsu* and *nonghwal* are more intimately related in that they usually involve groups of university students going on intensive (usually week-long) trips during school breaks to a countryside location to embark on an immersive experience that may include some combination of instruction, work, activism, group reflection and discussion, the sharing of food and drink, and most importantly, the building of relationships. Participants of site-specific transmission or *chŏnsu* typically travel to a *chŏnsugwan* or transmission center to learn a given performance tradition, at or near the place where it is said to have originated.[7]

Similarly in *nonghwal*, students travel to a participating village and then divide into smaller groups (usually by gender), often staying with families in the village. Later, these activities also came to include community members and activists.

Although there is evidence of service-minded students visiting the countryside in the 1920s and 1930s, the roots of *nonghwal* as we know it today began in the 1960s (Abelmann 1996, 155). It became more established in the late 1970s, only to become yet more widely practiced in the 1980s and early 1990s. Early *nonghwal* was more service-minded and was sometimes appropriately called "farming village service activity," or *nongch'on bongsa hwaldong*. As South Korea's climate grew increasingly more repressive during the Yushin Constitution era (1972–1979), however, the focus of *nonghwal* became more explicitly political. Essentially, the Yushin Constitution was a blatant attempt to extend the third-term presidency of Park Chung Hee into a long-term dictatorship; this was accompanied by higher levels of government censorship and control. In response to these and other developments, *nonghwal* participants gradually shifted focus in the 1970s and began to move beyond just engaging in service activities with the farmers and instead aimed further to organize, "enlighten," or change the political consciousness of farmers. This change was marked by a gradual shift in terminology to *nongch'on hwaldong*, or "farming village activism." By the 1980s, student *nonghwal* activists began to work more directly with farmer coalition groups and "the distance from farmers' movements . . . was consciously reversed in the second half of the 1980s" (Abelmann 1996, 156).

The site-specific transmission of expressive folk genres such as *p'ungmul* (rural percussion band music and dance) and *t'alch'um* (mask dance) are historically intertwined with *nonghwal* in ways that have not really been fully explored in the literature. While it is widely known that democratization activists found some measure of refuge in *p'ungmul* and *t'alch'um* groups on campuses during the Yushin era, I have not found a lot of documentation that focuses on *nonghwal* activists in particular. Unlike more explicitly political groups, *p'ungmul* and *t'alch'um* organizations were allowed to continue under the gloss of researching or learning Korean folk culture. However, I have heard much anecdotal evidence from my interlocutors active at this time that this "refuge" was limited because practice spaces were believed to be wiretapped and monitored by the government. Even so, Pak Ch'ansuk writes in her "30 Year Report on the Origins of the Back-to-the-Earth Farmer Movement" that the *t'alch'um* group at her alma mater, Ewha University, "devoted much of its time to *nonghwal* and went four times between the winter of 1978 and the summer of 1979" (Pak 2013, 42).

While this account mentions *t'alch'um* groups, there is strong reason to believe that *nonghwal* activists overlapped significantly with *p'ungmul* groups as well. For one, *nonghwal* activities often included the playing of *p'ungmul* as part of a weekly program, usually as a mode of cathartic release during social events that combined *p'ungmul*, singing, dancing, and drinking around a bonfire. I have even read an account that documents the use of *p'ungmul* in 2001 by a student *nonghwal* group from Sungkyunkwan University in a culminating politicized ritual to "exorcise" the "demons" of neoliberal oppression such as the WTO and the IMF, the recent policies of which have negatively impacted the livelihood of Korean farmers (Pak Chinhŭi 2001, 30). During my primary fieldwork years around the time that this article was published, I learned from my conversations and interviews with *p'ungmul chŏnsu* participants that many groups made a conscious effort to participate in *nonghwal* as well, sometimes consolidating the two experiences by doing one first and going straight to the other during a two-week period.

My research also suggests that early *p'ungmul* transmission or *chŏnsu* programs often brought participants in close contact with working farmers in village settings, which would have been appealing to *nonghwal* activists. In fact, nascent *p'ungmul chŏnsu* programs, with their more informal village home-stay settings (as opposed to the more institutional local transmission centers that became more common later), offered a very similar environment to that of *nonghwal* during the 1970s and '80s. While *nonghwal* was certainly more intense in terms of work and political activism, both required a high service and work ethic as well as a commitment to roughing it in rural, camp-like conditions, where sleep, hot showers, and privacy were rare and work, socializing, alcohol, and mosquitoes were plentiful. While *p'ungmul chŏnsu* did have more of a focus on learning the rhythms and movements of *p'ungmul*, there was also a tacit expectation that everyone would have to work collectively to keep the *chŏnsu* running. While this did not normally include agricultural labor, it certainly meant that everyone had to help clean and prepare their own food. These conditions created a rarefied environment that immersed both the body and the mind, often producing eye-opening and even life-changing experiences for its participants. Nancy Abelmann documents in fine ethnographic detail the transformative experience of *nonghwal* in her landmark study, *Echoes of the Past, Epics of Dissent*, that chronicles a period that brought together farmers, student activists, and organizers to protest the corporate ownership of tenant plots. For one of the students she interviewed, "*nonghwal* was the climax of her spring and summer initiation into the student movement" (1996, 150). Just as there were overlapping concerns among those participating in *p'ungmul chŏnsu* and *nonghwal*, there was also significant fluidity between these realms and the larger democratization movement (also called *minjung undong*) that was so volatile at the time.

The volatility of this movement was due to government pushback that tried to influence mainstream opinion by painting students involved in these types of activity as communists or "reds," the labeling of which was especially effective for older-generation South Koreans who had lived through the Korean War. Due to the widely assumed association between *p'ungmul* participation and political protest during the 1980s and beyond, both *p'ungmul chŏnsu* students and *nonghwal* activists were subject to surveillance and even barred from entering villages by the local police (Abelmann 1996, 61–62; Lee 2012, 180). These tensions peaked in the mid-1980s, but eased considerably after 1989, after which student participation in *nonghwal* and *p'ungmul* began to soar. This politically charged atmosphere was a major factor precipitating the peripatetic and divided existence of Pilbong *nongak* from 1984 to 2000, which will be detailed in more depth in the following section. From the late 1980s, *nonghwal* became more aligned with the growing power of the democratization movement, which was gaining momentum and broader acceptance during this period. Increased solidarity among student and farmer activists led to the increased visibility of organizations such as the National Farmers Coalition, and of the farmers' movement in general. By the 1990s, *nonghwal* continued to be one of the most popular volunteer service activities on campuses. As gains were made in South Korea's democratic process, *nonghwal* became less explicitly political and more diverse in the late 1990s and 2000s to include other concerns such as organic farming, environmentally sustainable agriculture, and back-to-earth village community building. In my more recent conversations with college-age *p'ungmul* enthusiasts in 2015, I was surprised to hear that *nonghwal* participation was still common. However, because of the increased professionalization of *p'ungmul* on one hand and the diversification of *nonghwal* on the other, the link between *nonghwal* and *p'ungmul* can no longer be assumed. Although college students who engage in *p'ungmul* may also tend to participate in *nonghwal*, they do so with separate student organizations.

Despite these historical links, there are important differences in philosophy between *nonghwal* and *p'ungmul chŏnsu* that are worth noting here. For one, unlike *nonghwal*, *p'ungmul* practitioners did not generally seek to transform the political consciousness of farmers with whom they had contact. Another important difference is that *p'ungmul* practitioners sought out farmers who were especially skilled in *p'ungmul* and interested in preserving it along with other traditional forms. As Nancy Abelmann suggests, the smaller subset of farmers interested in *p'ungmul* did not represent the vast majority who were turning away from older ways of life and more interested in improving their lives through modern modes of work and leisure. Because student activists largely turned to traditional culture to express opposition, this contributed to a paradoxical situation whereby "the 'subjects' (farmers) turned their heads away from 'traditional culture' whereas students maintained it" (Abelmann 1996, 160). Abelmann continues to write that these students did this because they "wanted these subjects to recapture their own 'healthy' culture" (1996, 160). However, in order to re-introduce traditional forms—like *p'ungmul*—to farmers who had become unfamiliar with them, the students had to become proficient themselves. Although many activists learned *p'ungmul* from other students in their student circles, or *dongari*, or from other teachers in neighborhood community organizations, those who were serious about learning *p'ungmul* went to *chŏnsu*. Unlike *nonghwal*, however, students were primarily there to learn from elder master teachers (who were farmers or grew up in farming villages), so the resulting political dynamic was very different from *nonghwal*.

In my experiences attending various types of *chŏnsu*, students often went out of their way to treat their instructors with the utmost respect as elders or "master teachers." This often meant bringing gifts at the start of *chŏnsu* and perhaps even cooking, cleaning, or doing other types of chores for the teachers. I also observed students listening to their teachers almost unconditionally, rarely speaking up if the teachers were late for instruction or challenging them publicly if they disagreed with them or disapproved of their methods. This attitude differed significantly from what has come to be known as "farmer-as-object" *nonghwal* and "farmer-as-subject" *nonghwal*. Nancy Abelmann characterizes the "farmer-as-object" stance as an earlier stage of *nonghwal* where students objectified the farmers as the recipients of student service (Abelmann 1996, 157); this one-sided relationship meant that farmers had less of a voice to determine what they wanted out of *nonghwal*.

Students later wanted to overcome this tendency by shifting to "farmer-as-subject" *nonghwal*, in which the goal was for farmers to realize their own subjectivity and political agency. In my view, this stance still failed to put the students and farmers on equal footing, but at least it did open more space for mutual dialogue and reflection. In site-specific transmission, or *chŏnsu*, the power dynamics are very different, if not the reverse of that of *nonghwal*. While both can be seen as student driven, transmission camps tend to be run more on the teacher's terms. I would argue that most of the students I observed or interviewed treated farmer/teachers with the assumption that they were already realizing their own subjectivity and agency as performers and teachers. The students' main agenda was to learn from the teachers (and not the other way around), and they generally did not try to organize or transform the consciousness of the teachers or fellow farmers during *chŏnsu*. If anything, *p'ungmul chŏnsu* students strove to learn and ultimately embody the consciousness and collectivity (*kongdongch'e*) of the farmers through their playing or dancing.

Despite their differences, the practice of *nonghwal* and the site-specific transmission of certain expressive folk cultural traditions such as *p'ungmul* and *kamyŏn'gŭk* (mask dance drama) were historically intertwined. *Nonghwal* set a precedent for bringing college students from primarily urban areas into close, immersive contact with people and place in rural farming villages. When *nonghwal* was more explicitly banned by the government or local police, this activity continued temporarily under the guise of *chŏnsu*. Many students participated in both activities, and if they did not, they were at least highly sympathetic to the other, until the late 1990s. While history certainly proved that the political drive behind *nonghwal* overlapped with *chŏnsu*, there are other political intersections that are worth exploring. For example, if *nonghwal* was ultimately concerned with the rights of farmers and the sustainability of farming and village life, then *chŏnsu* was concerned with the sustainability of a cultural form that sprang from this way of life. The fact that the two are mutually interdependent was not lost on the participants of both *nonghwal* and *chŏnsu*. The issue of environmental sustainability is also relevant and has become more of a concern in the twenty-first century. Both *nonghwal* and *chŏnsu* served to bring more meaning and political weight to marginalized areas by opening more pathways to them, thereby increasing the connections between people and place. In this way, *nonghwal*'s connection to *chŏnsu* is a critical reminder that an expressive ecology of a traditional cultural form must consider multiple interdependent dimensions of sustainability.

"ABUNDANT *KUT*, ABUNDANT LIFE": THE HISTORICAL TRAJECTORY OF PILBONG *P'UNGMUL* TRANSMISSION

While public performances of *p'ungmul* have certainly brought people to Pilbong, it is the site-specific practice of transmission, or *chŏnsu*, that has really drawn people into the real and imagined community of Pilbong, in both quantitative and qualitative ways. By tracing the transmission of this regional genre, I aim to provide a better understanding of how an expressive genre functions as a motivating force in the cultivation of a site-specific expressive ecology. The regional style of Pilbong *p'ungmul* is an especially revealing case study because its center of transmission moved several times before coming back to Pilbong. In detailing this history, I will demonstrate the various ways in which meaningful attachments to place had to be continually cultivated throughout these various moves. My second aim is to assess how each transmission environment developed its own unique site-specific expressive ecology. Here, I explore how each transmission center setting allowed for different aspects of *madang* discourse to shine through, with respect to shifting social, cultural, economic, and political climates. In this way, I explain how these practices intersect with differing agendas (personal, political, economic) in unpredictable ways. Based primarily on locational moves, the history of Pilbong *p'ungmul* transmission

TABLE 1.2 Pilbong *P'ungmul* Transmission Center Phases

PHASE DATES	LOCATION	DESCRIPTION
Phase 1 1970–1983	Pilbong village, Gangjin township, Imshil County in North Jeolla province	Informal instruction, taught at Yang Sunyong's home or at the *maŭl hoegwan* (village assembly building), small numbers of students accommodated.
Phase 2 1984–1994	Hobokdong village, Bojeol township, Namwon County, North Jeolla province	Classes led by Yang Sunyong. Had use of several village homes to house students, medium numbers of students accommodated.
Phase 3 1994–2000	Rural school in Namwon county in North Jeolla province	More structured instruction, whole school and grounds used for instruction, larger numbers of students accommodated.
Phase 4 2000–present	Pilbong transmission center complex, adjacent to Pilbong village	Instruction expanded and formalized, new buildings constructed so that larger numbers of students can be accommodated.

falls into roughly four phases: phase 1 (1970–1983), phase 2 (1984–1994), phase 3 (1994–2000), and phase 4 (2001–present) (see table 1.2). I will save the bulk of the discussion on the fourth phase of transmission for chapter 2, which will further situate Pilbong's current state of transmission and take the reader deeper into a week-long experience at the transmission center.

Phase 1 (1970–1983): Beginning in Pilbong Village

Starting around 1970, the charismatic lead gong player (*sangsoe*) and Intangible Human Cultural Asset Holder, Yang Sunyong (1941–1995), began teaching substantial numbers of visiting students with no prior connection to the village. This was a significant departure from pre-folk revival modes of transmission, where skills were transmitted more often in close proximity: from parent to child or from one villager to another. Yang Sunyong's reputation and the ensuing popularity of Pilbong *p'ungmul* grew in tandem with a revival and upsurge of interest in Korean folk culture. This folk revival atmosphere helped to bring increasing numbers of "outsider" students in contact with the Pilbong *p'ungmul* style, thereby increasing their exposure at a very critical juncture. Because of this, they were able to establish and build relationships with influential individuals and groups from all over the country relatively early on. This is important, because once a student or community group has established a connection with a particular form (such as Pilbong *p'ungmul*), they tend to stay with this form, thereby ensuring a continuous stream of new students for years to come.

Long before Pilbong *p'ungmul* or *nongak* was officially recognized as Important Intangible Cultural Property No. 11-5 in 1988, Yang Sunyong's reputation had begun to spread by word of mouth. From the 1970s on, students, researchers, and artists began to seek him out for instruction by visiting him where he lived in Pilbong village. One of the reasons for his popularity, aside from his level of skill and artistry, was his ability to articulate the subjectivity of a farmer or the "mind-spirit of a farmer" (*nonggunŭi maŭm*). At the core of his farmer-oriented view was a conviction about what it means to play *p'ungmul* in the context of village-based *kut* (ritual). These thoughts can be encapsulated in the popular Pilbong catchphrase, "abundant *kut*, abundant life" or *p'ujin-kut, p'ujin-salm*. Drawing on the words of Yang Sunyong, what this means is that "in order to create a life for everyone that is full of *shinmyŏng* (spiritual catharsis, joy), one must play *kut* abundantly" (Yang Chinsŏng 2000, 74). Another aspect of this is the idea that there is no separation between the act of living life and playing *kut*.

It is important to note here that while *p'ungmul* rituals are performed according to a Korean shamanistic worldview, they should not be confused with shaman rituals that are conducted exclusively by either spirit-appointed shamans or ritual specialists, usually called *mudang* in Korea. Even so, Peter Park asserts that "*p'ungmul-kut* . . . are an essential part of the Korean *mu* religion" (2014, 100). Because not all Korean "shamanistic" rituals are actually performed by shamans, Peter Park argues that the term "Korean shamanism" is misleading; he therefore prefers to use the term *mu*, a religion that he and Maria Seo argue is devoted to maintaining harmony between the three main elements of the cosmos (called *samjae* in Korean): heaven, earth, and humans (Park 2014, 90–91; Seo 2002, 3).[8] Another possible term for *mu* might be animism, but most *mu* scholars do not use this term, perhaps because the *mu* pantheon and accompanying philosophy includes much more than the spirits of nature.

Yang's emphasis on *p'ungmul* as *kut* ritual was appealing to democratization movement students and scholars, because *p'ungmul* presented a mode of expression that could be seen as both natively Korean (and therefore anti-colonial) as well as spiritually and politically transformative. What made *p'ungmul* additionally compelling was its highly experiential nature. Though this initial phase corresponded with one of the darker periods of recent Korean political history (the Yushin era), the practice of *p'ungmul* offered temporary moments of light, during which participants could experiment in what was seen as a democratic or communal form of expression.

Yang Chinsŏng (Yang Sunyong's son, b. 1966) sees this first phase as a period that could not have happened without the sincere devotion and commitment of the younger generation to learn the way of life of *p'ungmul* (2000, 78). What made Yang Sunyong unusual among his peers was his receptiveness to the aspirations of the younger generation and his ability to galvanize them. According to Yang Chinsŏng's account, instruction did not occur during this period in a systematic and intensive class format. Instead, when students arrived, they attuned themselves to the lives of the farmer-teachers by working alongside them during the day. Interestingly, this early phase was strikingly similar to early *nonghwal* except that, during their free time, students listened to the teachers talk about *p'ungmul* and learned what they could by playing along (2000, 78). In a sense, this method was probably much closer to earlier village-based modes of transmission.

Even though many people left with a positive experience of their visits to Pilbong, the harsh political climate of the Yushin-era in the early 1980s was such that it was becoming more and more difficult for the villagers to accommodate students. As mentioned previously, the government came to believe that political activists had taken refuge in folk culture organizations, especially those dedicated to mask dance drama and *p'ungmul*.[9] It follows that the government began to ban the playing and/or teaching of *p'ungmul* in villages on the grounds that it encouraged organized opposition and protest. According to Yang Chinsŏng, by the beginning of the 1980s the government had become so suspicious of young *p'ungmul* players that "just being caught playing a *soe* or *changgo* was enough to be taken away by the government" (Yang Chinsŏng interview, October 5, 2003). To make matters worse, Pilbong was popular with activists and even counted prominent *minjung* figures such as artist Kim Pongjun and actor Kim Myŏngkon as students (Kim 2011, 204). While the Pilbong *p'ungmul* troupe did not yet have recognition or support from the government as an Intangible Cultural Property, the government certainly knew about Pilbong and even conducted surveillance on the Yang family and their *p'ungmul* teaching activities (Yang Chinsŏng 2008, 30).

The combination of these factors made it very difficult for Yang Sunyong to stay in the village of Pilbong. As a result, in 1984, he took advantage of an invitation to move to a much smaller village called Hobokdong in the Bojeol township, where he had developed a good reputation as their guest *sangsoe*. Although he did not formally move his teaching to Hobokdong, eventually students sought him out there (Yang Chinsŏng interview, October 5, 2003). Relatively speaking, the Hobokdong villagers were very welcoming. It also helped that the village was quite small—only ten to fifteen houses total—and as such, it is said that Yang Sunyong was able to continue playing and teaching without much consequence (Oh Mi-ae interview, October 7, 2002; Yang Chinsŏng 2000, 79).

Phase 2 (1984–1994): Hobokdong Village as a Space of Kut *Education*

During his stay in Hobokdong in phase 2, Yang Sunyong was able to realize one of his main dreams—that the Pilbong style be named an Important Intangible Cultural Property (No. 11-5). This dream came to fruition in 1988 when it was recognized as a representative of *p'ungmul* (also termed *nongak*) from the Honam Jwado region. That same year, Yang Sunyong was also bestowed the status of Human Cultural Asset holder (*ingan munhwaje poyuja*) for the form. Given how difficult it was for Yang Sunyong to uproot himself from his hometown, it is ironic that by moving away he was able to pursue his dream of putting himself and Pilbong on the map of folk culture in Korea. Yang Chinsŏng characterizes this phase as significant because it was a time when they were able to really cultivate a "space of *kut* education where students could fully immerse themselves" (Yang Chinsŏng 2000, 80).

In reality, this "space of *kut* education" or *kut kyoyukt'ŏ* consisted of a humble assemblage of three or so empty homes in Hobokdong, a tiny, tucked-away mountain village. With Yang Sunyong's family already occupying one of the houses, there were only two other homes for the students to live in. The open space by the water reservoir and the shady area underneath one of the trees served as practice "rooms." Because of the limitations of space, each group of ten or so students had to share one room for the duration of their stay. When I interviewed Oh Mi-ae, now a *chŏnsu kyoyuk chogyo* (literally "transmission education assistant teacher") of the troupe, she recounted how shocked she was on her first visit to Hobokdong in 1988 when she learned that she had to share a room with her male fellow students. Still a first year in college and a devout Christian, she laughingly admitted that she could not bring herself to continue at that point in time and came promptly back home. Fortunately, she managed to muster up the courage to go the following summer break to become one of the few female students to be invited to join the performing group under Yang Sunyong.

During the years that Oh Mi-ae went to *chŏnsu* at Hobokdong (late 1980s to early 1990s), as many as seven or eight teams of ten people each may have attended per session. Each session lasted a week, with sessions continuing throughout the university breaks. These numbers demonstrate that the interest was high relative to the capacity at the time. Because of the circumstances of the *chŏnsu*, each participant had little choice but to pull their weight in taking care of basic needs such as preparing food, cooking, and cleaning. In general, each team was responsible for their own food, preparing it in camping fashion on portable gas ranges in their own rooms. Yang Chinsŏng described the Hobokdong *chŏnsu* as an experience where just the act of eating and living in an agricultural setting gave the participants the opportunity to get a closer and more embodied understanding of the challenges, physical difficulties, and artistic sensibilities that stem from the life of a farmer (2000, 80). Oh Mi-ae noted that the whole experience was incomparable to the way *chŏnsu* is run now (Oh Mi-ae interview, October 7, 2002).

The teaching style of Yang Sunyong was also markedly different from what people encounter today at *chŏnsu*. Oh Mi-ae explains:

> At that time, the teacher [Yang Sunyong] did everything . . . but there was no specific thing that he taught us. When the teacher entered the room, he would just say "play the rhythms." So then we would play *sa-ch'ae, o-ch'ae, yuk-ch'ae, hohŏgut*, and when we were done playing all the rhythms in this way, he would just go. Sometimes he would tell us a few stories about *kut*, but he would never say "play the *kkwaenggwari* like this" or "play the *changgo* like this." There was no deliberate teaching method like there is now. Why? Because we were supposed to watch him and try to play like him, this was the most original way to learn . . . To the students that were closest to him, he might tell them things. But even so, the highest praise he might give from time to time was "oh, you play well," but this meant he was really, really giving you high praises . . . it meant that you had gained his recognition. (Oh Mi-ae interview, October 7, 2002)

When Oh Mi-ae did receive specific instruction or help, it tended to happen in a manner more integrated with daily life.

> When I was living with the teacher . . . I worked with his wife all the time helping out in the kitchen. One morning, while I was practicing my steps for *changgo*, I had the experience of being personally taught by him. Of course I was really moved . . . because he doesn't normally give personal attention to teach so specifically like that. When people started to live and become a little bit closer, there were those times when he did take an interest in you. There was a time when I had gotten up around 6 a.m. I had to light the fire to make breakfast, in the *kamasot* [traditional cast iron pot and kiln]. But you have to have done it before to know how to do it. So I was just standing there, not being able to light it, all the while smoke was getting everywhere. The teacher came by and said "that's not how you light it, look here, Mi-ae," and so the teacher stood by my side, showed me how to do it and even stayed to cook. Those are the times that make up my best memories . . . because they speak to the quiet warmth of humanity that was inside him. (Oh Mi-ae interview, October 7, 2002)

Hobokdong was unique among the various *chŏnsu* locations because it provided a welcoming, intimate village environment where students could learn *p'ungmul* through a philosophy of experiential immersion and emulation. By extension, they were also able to live and play in an intimate village *madang* setting, which helped create a physical frame of reference in creating their own "*madangs*" back at school. For Yang Chinsŏng, this was a phase where students could try to live by the saying, "to be a *turŏngsoe* [a proficient *p'ungmul* player within the *ture* cooperative farming system], one must act like a *turŏngsoe*" (personal communication). Because they were able to live side by side with the Hobokdong villagers, they also had the opportunity to have more meaningful contact with people who made their living from farming, and therefore left with a more realistic sense of this lifestyle. From Oh Mi-ae's account, it appears that students were recognized for their efforts in helping around the village and were sometimes even rewarded with special attention.

As students continued to have positive experiences in Hobokdong, the popularity of Pilbong *p'ungmul-kut* increased to the extent that they needed to find a larger place to accommodate more students. Eventually, they found a nearby empty school that they could use, still somewhat hidden away in the countryside but closer to the city of Namwon. This became known as the Namwon *chŏnsugwan*. As a side note, shortly after Pilbong had received their Intangible Cultural Property status, the government helped to build an "official" transmission building next to the village of Pilbong in 1989.[10] This later became the cornerstone for the transmission center complex that sits there today.

Phase 3 (1994–2000): The Namwon Chŏnsugwan

While the Hobokdong location could accommodate about seventy to eighty students at a time, the Namwon school could easily house up to 200 or more students per week. Located away from the main road and surrounded by farmland, the school had an atmosphere of remove from urban life. Despite this, it was not a typically quiet and peaceful rural haven by any means. When I visited for the first time in 1999, I remember being surprised by the "trot" music that was blasted periodically on the loudspeakers for the benefit of the older-generation farmers working in the nearby fields. Add to this the noisy hum of summer cicadas and frogs, not to mention the ubiquitous sound of students practicing *p'ungmul*. The entrance of the school opened up into a large *madang* or playground covered with fine reddish dirt. Directly behind the *madang*, concrete steps led up to a long building consisting mostly of classrooms. Smaller structures for restrooms, bathing, office space, and private living quarters were located on both sides of the building. Inside the main building, the largest rooms were used for instruction and other large gatherings, while the rest were used to house the students. Usually, they designated one team to a room, depending on the size of the group and space availability. Since the school had limited kitchen facilities, people often cooked, ate, slept, and socialized all in the same room. When it was not raining, the outdoor field was regularly used as a practice space.

Due to many factors, this phase was very much a time of transition for Pilbong *p'ungmul-kut*. Most palpably, Yang Sunyong passed away in August of 1995, just a year after the move to the larger facility. Still in his fifties and relatively robust in health, his passing was very unexpected, and the group was left extremely unprepared for his loss. While there was an outpouring of support from the larger community and students continued to come in large numbers to Namwon, his death opened a considerable gap. There were very few practitioners of his generation in their late forties, fifties, and sixties who were prepared to lead. Exceptions included Yang Sunyong's brother, Yang Sunju, who played the *taepyŏngso*, and Pak Hyŏngnae, the other Human Cultural Asset holder, who both, for various reasons, were not able to assume the performance and teaching responsibilities of Yang Sunyong at the Namwon transmission center.

Pak Hyŏngnae did teach at the smaller Pilbong *chŏnsugwan*, but he could not accommodate a lot of students at one time. This left the duties of transmission at the Namwon center almost exclusively to the younger generation, led by Yang Sunyong's sons, Yang Chinsŏng and Yang Chinhwan. With most of the teachers now in their twenties and thirties, many did not have a comparable lifetime of knowledge and experience playing *p'ungmul* within the context of farming. Although some teachers like the Yang brothers had grown up in village households, most of them had attended university. In this way, they at least had the advantage of being able to relate to the students' perspective of learning. Their family history coupled with their ability to bridge the gap with students helped bolster their authority and authenticity in the wake of Yang Sunyong's passing.

As the Yang brothers and other younger teachers began to take charge of the Namwon transmission center, they interpreted what they had learned from Yang Sunyong and other older members of the troupe and developed their own teaching styles and philosophies. After Yang Sunyong's death, it was likely more difficult for students to learn primarily through anecdote or emulation. In adjusting to these new circumstances, some of the new generation of teachers began to bolster their teaching by articulating how to master various aspects of *p'ungmul* practice, such as instrumental technique, or the incorporation of movement and breathing. In interpreting Yang Sunyong's teachings and style in their own way, the teachers developed and implemented their own pedagogical methods and strategies.

Though the transmission session was becoming more structured, there was an openness to the *madang*-related elements of *kut* (ritual), *shinmyŏng* (spiritual catharsis), and *nanjang* (chaos) that was unique to the Namwon center. One of the main reasons for this had to do with the location itself. For the first time, the teachers and students were able to have complete control of the place. Since they were not living as part of an actual village community, they did not have to be as attentive to the nearby residents as they did in Hobokdong and Pilbong in the earlier phases. As a result, college group practices became more dominant, intermingling to create a new *p'ungmul chŏnsu* culture. In addition, since the school was already in a state of abandonment and disrepair, they were not overly concerned about the inevitable wear and tear of things getting a little wild, which was often the case during the height of *chŏnsu* season. One example of the liberties students could take was in the tradition of writing on the peeling papered walls. Over time, the walls of the rooms read like an overflowing testament to the streams of students who had breathed a second life into the previously closed-down school.

Another factor that added to the intensity of Namwon was the rough and crowded camp-like atmosphere. When I visited in the summers of 1999 and 2000, approximately 200 students had to make do with using outhouses for restrooms. Bathing took place in a humble building that was equipped with a large tub and hoses attached to the walls that provided mostly cold water. With only one such room, men and women had to alternate according to a pre-planned schedule. Because there was no air conditioning and the windows did not have screens, it was also necessary to make peace with the teeming insects (especially mosquitoes) that thrive in South Korea's hot and humid summer season. Going in the winter had the advantage of fewer insects, but it was also much colder. In sum, these experiences had the effect of pushing the predominantly urban students outside of their comfort zone, contributing to a more emotionally charged atmosphere.

In comparison to playing *p'ungmul* at college, Namwon was a new and different experience. It gave students the opportunity to be in close proximity to nature and to a similar rural village environment as that of Pilbong. And though the school was not technically part of a village, it was easy to encounter village residents during walks outside the school's walls. One time while I was walking with some friends to the nearest market to get some refreshments, I had a friendly encounter with a living *turŏngsoe*, an older farmer who had grown up playing *p'ungmul*. He asked us which rhythms we had learned so far, and he seemed as impressed with our progress as we were surprised about his knowledge of the Pilbong rhythm names and ordering.

In addition to the intense conditions, I noticed that the students and teachers approached the *madang*-related notions of *kut* (ritual), *shinmyŏng* (spiritual ecstasy), *nori* (play), and *nanjang* (chaos) in very specific ways. This was apparent from the first day of class during an informal shamanistic ritual or *kut* that the students had organized to pray for a blessed session. With large containers of locally made *makkŏlli* (a milky rice beer) delivered almost on a daily basis, the presence of alcohol also played a role in fueling the participants' perceptions and experiences of *kut*, *shinmyŏng*, *nori*, and *nanjang*.

In terms of cultivating *nori*, the Namwon *chŏnsu* incorporated game-playing into their program. This is significant because it was unique to the Namwon *chŏnsu*, so much so that students who had gone to Namwon often recall how much they liked this part of the program. When I was at Namwon, I remember reacting privately to the prospect of having to spend an afternoon playing schoolyard games with a certain mixture of disbelief and annoyance. When I asked Ch'oe Ho-in, one of the more philosophical teachers, about this, he replied in his own cryptic fashion that there was a reason behind the game-playing and that we should think about it while we played. I never got a direct answer from him about why he thought game-playing was necessary, but I did have fun and it was an effective way to bond with others and get over one's physical inhibitions. In a way, this set up a genial atmosphere of play that fed into the next day's performance.

Though students mainly drank in the evenings, there was one time during the summer of 2000 when our class was encouraged to drink alcohol in the middle of the afternoon during practice on a hot summer day. Choosing to go with the flow, I went along and immersed myself in this fieldwork experience. Strangely enough, this was one of the most emotionally potent and disorienting experiences I have ever had playing *p'ungmul*. It all began when Mun Ch'anggi, one of the guest teachers, decided to drop by and bring us some special, locally made *kimch'i*. As quaint as it sounds, this was quite a moving gesture given that teachers do not often go out of their way for students. While we were practicing our steps, playing and dancing in the large outdoor *madang*, our current teacher immediately told some of the students to bring some *soju* (distilled Korean liquor) to have with the *kimch'i*. As we made our way around the *madang*, volunteers fed us little bites of *kimch'i* followed by shots of *soju*. Pretty soon, everyone was playing in a relaxed and inebriated state.

As we continued, I remember being overcome by two major feelings. On the one hand, as people collectively lost their inhibitions, the feeling of connection to one another became more apparent in the expressive interactions among the players. One thing that one often hears while learning *p'ungmul* is to "smile and look into each other's eyes." In that moment, I remember being extremely moved by the expressions of joy and goodwill that lit up everyone's faces. This was probably the first time I realized what *shinmyŏng* is supposed to look and feel like in the *p'ungmul madang*—where individuals are said to appear to glow or "shine with the spirit" (the literal meaning of *shinmyŏng*). While one could interpret this as just an instance of group intoxication, the alcohol did mark a turning point in the *chŏnsu* session by amplifying the aesthetic ideals and emotions of *p'ungmul*, which carried over into the remainder of the session.

The other feeling I had was more private in nature. It happened while I was trying to grasp the aesthetics of stepping in the *madang*. I remember trying to feel my weight give into the malleable ground with each step. It is said that the action of carefully stepping in the *madang* purifies the space and discourages bad spirits and energy and contributes to a more aesthetically desirable stepping movement. While I was doing this, I was suddenly overcome by a spiritual presence that I intuited as somehow ancestral. It was as if the connectedness I felt with the group suddenly blurred into a connectedness with the spirit world. This spurred an emotional release during which I found myself crying uncontrollably as I continued to play. As strange as this sounds, no one seemed to notice, and I did not have to explain myself to anyone. To this day, this remains one the most emotional and disorienting experiences I have ever had in the *madang*.

In my subsequent efforts to process this experience, I have been especially drawn to Tomie Hahn's work that radically re-interprets "sensually extreme" field experiences. Asserting that researchers "are often cautioned not to 'go native' and to keep extreme, *extra*-ordinary 'illusions' out of their work," Hahn bravely re-defines these disorienting experiences as having the potential to "catch ethnographers off guard and bring to the surface extraordinary cultural insights, as well as personally transforming orientations" (Hahn 2006, 89). By situating these fieldwork experiences within what she calls the "realm of the sensually extreme," Hahn highlights the role of the body in developing a "sensational understanding" of how a community or culture "constructs and makes sense of their environment and lives" (2006, 88–89). In citing Arthur Frank, she points to a need to "apprehend the body as both a medium and outcome of social 'body techniques,' and society as both medium and outcome of the sum of these techniques" (Frank 1991, 48, cited in Hahn 2006, 88).[11] In light of this, I realized that performing the "body technique" of stepping in the *madang* had summoned a volley of "sensational understandings," simultaneously aesthetic, social, spiritual, and personal. By performing this action, I was able to know and feel—on a bodily level—how the mastery of the up-and-down stepping movement is also dependent upon being in synchrony with the rest of the group. Aesthetically and socially speaking, learning to move gracefully in step with others is one of the cornerstones of *p'ungmul*. The spiritual significance of stepping, in terms of stamping out bad spirits, is tied to the social, in the sense that it must be done in a group with a unified sense of intention.

On a personal level, this experience helped me get in touch with the spiritual dimensions of *p'ungmul* practice. More specifically, it was an outlet for me to mourn the loss of my grandmother who had passed away a few years earlier. By extension, the emotion I was feeling made me come to terms with the depth of my desire to connect with my cultural "roots," which I previously suppressed as an invalid reason for conducting fieldwork. In a way, I think I was also mourning the life I could have lived had I grown up in Korea. In retrospect, conducting fieldwork in Korea has helped me work through and let go of some of the holds that Korea has had on my psyche having grown up in the United States as a second-generation Korean American.

My own personal revelations aside, I share this incident because it reveals something about the energy of the Namwon center and how the *chŏnsu* community drew on the "sensually extreme" to push *p'ungmul*'s "culturally defined boundaries" and "performative limits" in the continual process of defining the genre's identity (Hahn 2006, 88). In this way, the consumption of alcohol was one avenue through which students were able to push the boundaries of *p'ungmul*, especially in the way that it heightened the experience of *shinmyŏng*. CedarBough Saeji similarly interprets the consumption of *makkŏlli* at transmission camps as a means through which participants experience a Turnerian state of liminality and communitas (2013, 78–79). They were able to do this because of the strong influence of college culture on the atmosphere of this *chŏnsu*, removed as it was from the supervision of the elder generation, especially after Yang Sunyong passed away.

Given that alcohol is usually encouraged in *p'ungmul* settings, I was surprised to find one scholar-practitioner, Kim Samt'ae, come out in criticism of how alcohol consumption has come to be so closely associated with the expression of *shinmyŏng* in *p'ungmul* (2001b, 140–48). Kim Samt'ae sees the compulsory consumption of alcohol as a recent phenomenon that was promoted by the younger generation college students. Kim asserts that this practice "quickly spread and soon became regarded as central to the expressive identity of *p'ungmul*" (2001b, 141). He maintains that before, when alcohol was consumed, students were more often in the company of elders and therefore drank moderately, more in the spirit of sharing than to get drunk. And while I agree with the tenor of Kim's critique, alcohol was certainly a factor that helped enable some students at the Namwon transmission center to explore the sensually extreme boundaries of *p'ungmul*, perhaps in a search to derive more visceral meaning from a genre whose relevance in modern society was more difficult to ascertain. Despite the passing of Yang Sunyong, Pilbong *p'ungmul* continued to thrive in Namwon. Not only did the Namwon transmission center continue to have a high attendance rate, but their annual Lunar New Year Full Moon Ritual, which was then held in downtown Namwon, drew huge crowds of enthusiastic people.

CONCLUDING THOUGHTS

As the political climate and related problems of being situated in Pilbong eased by the late 1990s, it was inevitable that Pilbong's core practitioners would eventually bring the center of their activities back "home." By 1999, the leaders of the IPNPA began making ambitious plans to expand from the single transmission building built across from the Pilbong village in 1989 into a diversified complex with multiple buildings and cultural spaces or *madangs* (figure 1.2). As the transmission center activities were moved and consolidated in Pilbong later in 2000, the stage was set for Pilbong to again become the central hub of activities for the organization, including transmission activities and large-scale events such as the much-touted village-based Lunar New Year ritual (see chapter 4). Bringing the center back to Pilbong also made it easier for those more locally connected to Pilbong to take part again. Regardless of the many paths that have led participants to Pilbong, the current center is now equipped to serve a larger sector of the population, including seniors, families, and children alike, as well as a growing number of professionally minded students. While I was there in 2001–2002, it was common for the center to have as many as 300 students in attendance at any given time during the *chŏnsu* season.

During my primary fieldwork year in 2001–2002, the teachers were still in the process of developing their programming in accordance with the expanded goals of what the planners proposed as a "twenty-first century *p'ungmul* village" (see chapter 2). Inevitably, students took stock of the differences and changes between the Namwon and Pilbong *chŏnsu* programs. Though most accepted the changes as a trade-off, some lamented a decrease in the feeling of community (*kongdongch'e*) and noted that there were fewer opportunities to meet and bond with the other groups present. Though most acknowledged the convenience of not having to prepare meals, this shift placed more of a focus on class-time instruction and practice, and less on the experience of working and contributing to a community. In addition, because the facilities were nicer and therefore could accommodate groups from a wider sector of society, the culture of college-style socializing, drinking, and game-playing could not take over to the extent that it did in Namwon. When I was there, evening drinking was confined to the large cafeteria, and groups were no longer allowed to drink in their rooms. Though groups theoretically could intermingle in the cafeteria, because of the tables and loud atmosphere it was difficult for groups to sit in a circle and have the same intense level of engagement. When talking with the Daejeon university group, they noted that the game day was omitted and replaced with the Pilbong village *tapsa* or fieldtrip. In addition, the students did not conduct their own ritual of blessing in the beginning of the week. Though I will go into more detail about the specific structure of the transmission week in the next chapter, the changes I have mentioned contributed to a very different *chŏnsu* experience.

In summary, this historical trajectory reveals that the Pilbong group demonstrated a remarkable resilience in sustaining their practice while maintaining a fluid, and yet regional, sense of place through site-specific performance and transmission. As Pilbong adapted from one transmission setting to the next, different discursive practices of the *madang* and village came to the fore to define each *chŏnsu* experience. Although the most recent incarnation of the Pilbong transmission center as a "twenty-first century *p'ungmul* village" may be a far cry from the actual village of Pilbong, its very existence does tell us something about the power of expressive culture to materially impact the production of space as well as the overall ecology and economy of the surrounding region. Not only was the transmission center complex built (creating local jobs along with it), but as more and more people traveled to Pilbong, transportation routes have improved. These include direct bus routes from Seoul and the expansion of the main road into a high-speed highway. Regular, site-specific performances all but ensure that the village of Pilbong and surrounding natural areas continue to be well maintained and cared for, including its sacred sites and other important objects therein. While the proximate ecology of Pilbong benefits, it is also possible that the increased construction, highway, and resulting traffic have negatively impacted the environment.

Environmental impact aside, this struggle to sustain both the culture and place of Pilbong did not happen overnight. The volatile politics of the 1970s, '80s, and early '90s in South Korea made it very difficult for farmers and *p'ungmul* practitioners alike, but these challenges only temporarily dampened the activities of young people who sought to learn folk expressive culture as an oppositional practice through *chŏnsu* or help farmers through *nonghwal*. At the same time, more and more Koreans in the 1990s and beyond were becoming more interested in regional culture, including site-specific cultural artifacts, architecture, rituals, and festivals. As this chapter has shown, place is anything but stable, and while Pilbong *p'ungmul* is mostly a success story, it still had to actively cultivate a sense of place and continues to do so. In the next chapter, I will focus on *how* the site-specific transmission experience engages people in place and space through intermodal transmission techniques.

FIGURE 2.1 *above* Empty *madang* in the village of Pilbong (2002). Photo by the author.

FIGURE 2.2 *right* Full madang in the village of Pilbong. FIGURES 2.1 and 2.2 are from the same *madang* (2002).

TWO

"Becoming One" through Site-Specific Intermodal Transmission

It was a cold winter's day in 2002 when I first observed *p'ungmul* (percussion band music and dance) performed within the context of a Lunar New Year ritual in the village of Pilbong. What made it an even more rarefied experience was that it was also the first time the Lunar New Year ritual took place in the village of Pilbong in fifteen years.[1] I was looking forward to this event all year because it was my first opportunity to experience the communal philosophy of "becoming one" in the actual village of Pilbong. For someone who had only heard about the *madang* as a metaphor for a more participatory kind of performance space, it was truly staggering to see an actual courtyard of an otherwise quiet village home (figure 2.1) transform into a sea of bodies, all moving up and down and swaying their arms back and forth perfectly in sync with the music (figure 2.2 and video 2.1 🔊).

At first glance, the communal "way of being" in the *madang* pictured in figure 2.2 may seem remarkably natural and spontaneous to an outsider, as if all of the participants had grown up together in the same village.[2] In actuality, many of these performers and audience members came from other towns and cities, and the vast majority of the younger participants made a conscious choice to learn how to move and interact in a Pilbong *p'ungmul* event, mostly likely through an intense process of cultural transmission. Korean ritual specialist Pak Hŭngchu observed that "Pilbong's events are unique because so many people have developed an intimate knowledge of their *kut* (ritual performance)" (personal communication). I argue that this high degree of coordinated participation and cultural familiarity evident here would not be possible without the ability to attend intensive week-long sessions of site-specific instruction (called *chŏnsu*) at transmission centers called *chŏnsugwan* (also called *chŏnsuhoegwan*).

My fellow members and teachers at the Korean Youth Cultural Center in Oakland, California first told me it was possible to attend *chŏnsu* at transmission centers that specialize in various Korean genres of expressive folk culture. One of the constant refrains that I heard from people who attended *chŏnsu* was the idea that in order to truly learn a style, one had to go to the actual place and learn in person, a sentiment that echoes the philosophy of *tapsa*. When I visited the Goseong Ogwangdae mask dance drama transmission center, the managing director at the time, Hwang Chonguk, said that one of their main goals was for students to leave with a strong sense of the local *mat* or "distinct flavor" of the mask dance style and region (personal communication). This was achieved through the integration of fieldtrips and visits to local landmarks and restaurants. As a result, many returning students developed meaningful attachments to the place of Goseong and often came to view it as a second hometown.

Although I detailed the history of the Pilbong *chŏnsugwan* in the last chapter, here I will go further to situate this center within the larger field of Korean transmission and beyond. These centers were originally built to support Korean forms that were designated as Intangible Cultural Properties by the South Korean government and, as such, deserve special attention as an alternative cultural institution in South Korea. While most of these centers strive to establish cultural continuity with earlier modes of transmission, they can never truly recreate the traditional rural settings of the past. At the same time, most of these centers do not conform to the more modern institutional models established by standardized performing arts schools or conservatories.

In keeping with the other chapters in part 1, I continue my case study on Pilbong *p'ungmul* and focus on the ways in which South Korean transmission centers structure the experience of an expressive folk culture form by emphasizing site-specific instruction and employing intermodal pedagogical techniques that heighten an awareness of the body in both place and space. In her ethnography of Japanese dance transmission, *Sensational Knowledge: Embodying Culture Through Japanese Dance*, Tomie Hahn writes that "systems of transmission structure experience so that, within the social group, the world appears similarly constructed and members know how to interact within it" (2007, 5). I am inspired by Tomie Hahn's assertion that Japanese systems of transmission can convey a "Japanese sensibility" (2007, 5). Given Hahn's focus on the senses, her word choice of "sensibility" is well warranted. In my case, I decided to play with this idea by using the word "subjectivity" as an alternative, in order to highlight personal experiences, perspectives, and the potential for agency. In addition, this links nicely to a later discussion of Thomas Csordas's ideas on the body and intersubjective experience (1999). In this way, I contend that the Pilbong *p'ungmul* transmission center cultivates the embodiment of an alternative Korean subjectivity that is expressed through music, dance, and other social activities, but is further enhanced by situating the body within the iconically Korean spaces of the rural hometown, village, or *madang*. I argue that this center cultivates an alternative subjectivity that is characterized by a more participatory, *madang*-oriented way of being, which contrasts with the more competitive mindsets that drive many contemporary urban Koreans. Most crucially, the *madang* way of being encompasses both performers and audience members and ideally works to blur the boundaries between the two.

Implicit in this chapter is the notion that modes of transmission are significant, not only because they help to effectively pass down musical content from one individual or set of individuals to another, but because they can also figure powerfully into the transmission and re-negotiation of various forms of cultural knowledge. On one level, I see the cultivation of a *madang* way of being as an effective way of nurturing "community" (*kongdongch'e*), which I interpret as coming from a democratization movement–inspired cultural politics of de-colonization — both of space and the body.[3] This is important given that these transformative feelings can be interpreted to signify the possibility of social and political mobilization on a larger scale. As discussed in chapter 1, this *madang* way of being can also lead to intense feelings of individual transformation, which can play out in the re-negotiation of identity in terms of class, ethnicity, gender, or sexuality.

This chapter links to the book's central thesis in demonstrating how integral transmission processes are to sustaining a site-specific expressive ecology in Pilbong. Following a contextual discussion on transmission, I pursue this line of inquiry by examining some of the theoretical and pedagogical processes involved in creating a communal way of being in the *p'ungmul* transmission center that informs the expressive ecology of Pilbong. Some of these include processes of internalization, embodiment, and the development of certain Korean subjectivities. Because many of these processes are oriented toward interacting within the *madang* setting, I argue that the *madang* serves as an iconic frame for the transmission center community — just as the stage may serve as an important frame for other types of expressive communities. I will demonstrate these points by delving into the world of the transmission center complex and the adjacent village of Pilbong. Specifically, I will focus on the practice of *tapsa*, or "fieldtrips," to the actual village of Pilbong, as well as the culminating leader competition and performance. Lastly, I will analyze some of the unique pedagogical techniques that specifically target the body, transmitting a sense of groove that is unique to the Pilbong style of *p'ungmul*.[4] In sum, I argue that site-specific transmission works through the spatial philosophy of the *madang* by privileging the phenomenological experience of the body, bringing expressive attention to the local features of space and place, and providing opportunities to develop a more dynamic range of social relations and interactions that can engender increasingly meaningful articulations of people, place, and time.

SITUATING KOREAN TRANSMISSION

The notion of vitality and agency existing within a government-driven system of intangible cultural asset preservation—such as the one that was developed in South Korea—contradicts the widespread belief that this type of policy contributes to the "freezing" of "tradition." As in most contemporary societies, however, the transmission of older cultural forms is an area where discourses, institutional structures, and practices collide—often in messy, conflicting, and unpredictable ways. While the Ministry of Culture set the terms of the discourse of cultural preservation through the Cultural Property Protection Law in 1962 (*Munhwajae pohopŏp* Law 961), it was not necessarily enacted at the institutional level in a centralized, top-down fashion. Although there are some national institutions that serve as obvious centers for the cultural preservation of certain Intangible Cultural Properties—such as the National Gugak Center for court-related genres in particular—most expressive folk culture forms were granted government support to build their own transmission centers, or *chŏnsugwan*, to support their local base and maintain regional identity (Yang Jongsung 1994, 70–72).[5]

As stated previously, the *chŏnsugwan* represents a relatively new type of cultural institution: one that is sanctioned by a national government mandate but nevertheless maintains some local autonomy. As such, most of these centers are run by local practitioners, and because of the flexibility this entails, they tend to be managed differently from location to location. Some transmission centers have been extremely successful in eliciting the participation of college students and members of the community, many of whom were active in the cultural arm of the

1970s and '80s political democratization movement or *minjung munhwa undong* (literally "people's cultural movement"). This movement spurred a grassroots and college student–driven folk revival that generated alternative discourses and ensuing debate about the role and function of expressive folk culture in contemporary Korean society.[6] To put it simply, the government was primarily concerned with preservation, "authenticity," and the fostering of regional and national identity, whereas those involved in the grassroots movement were much more interested in making folk culture relevant as a means of social commentary, political protest, and community building. While the Pilbong *p'ungmul* transmission center has had a long history of attracting those involved in folk revival politics, it has also benefitted from government support.

Due to their decentralized location, relative degree of autonomy, and influence from a range of cultural ideas and policies about folk culture, transmission centers like the one at Pilbong do not follow the model of a standardized arts institution. This may be because there is more flexibility in the way that these *chŏnsugwan* structure experiences to accommodate different kinds of individuals and groups—from young children, to politically minded college students, to those pursuing more of a professional or academic track in the arts.[7] These various groups inevitably mix and give rise to a more diverse range of practices that are not necessarily bound by the dominant discourses that inform each group or even the transmission center. Drawing primarily on Pierre Bourdieu's theorization of practice theory (1977), Ingrid Monson writes that "practices can take many forms—musical, economic, sexual, ritual and so on, but key to their difference from discourse is their stress on embodied knowledge and action" (Monson 2007, 26). What transmission centers, such as the one at Pilbong, do so well is emphasize this embodiment of practice—not just in terms of aesthetic expression, but also more critically in the realm of social life and action. For example, in addition to teaching aesthetic content, the teachers highly encourage activities that promote leadership as well as a robust work ethic of community service, activism, play, and volunteerism.

While there are many studies in Asian music that focus on elite music institutions (Sutton 1991, Brinner 1995, Sumarsam 1995, Wong 2001, Witzleben 1994, Lau 2008), it should be apparent that this is not a top-down study of transmission where the central point of inquiry might be the National Gugak Center or the Ministry of Culture and Tourism's Intangible Cultural Property system.[8] Rather, I am interested in bringing attention to the regional practices of transmission that happen on the ground, with an eye toward documenting the incremental changes that demonstrate how a group flexibly adapts to new realities, even while adhering to a government mandate of preservation. Along these lines, this book joins a large body of work that focuses on regional forms of Korean folk expressive culture, including major studies in English on regional forms of Korean shamanism (Park 1985, 2003; Howard 1989; Seo 2002; Lee 2004; Mills 2007), rural *p'ungmul* (Hesselink 2006, 2011; Saeji 2013), regional folksong (Maliangkay 2017), and mask dance (Saeji 2012).

While regional genres are well documented and explored in Korean music studies, this chapter explores a less traveled path in its attention to the micro-practices of transmission and the role of embodiment in particular.[9] In the broader field of ethnomusicology, however, this chapter intersects with several recent threads of inquiry on transmission. As noted earlier, I draw much inspiration from Tomie Hahn's work in considering the body as a conduit of "kinesthetic transmission" and drawing on her multi-sensory approach in the transmission of dance movements and cultural knowledge (Hahn 1996). Although I do not methodically explore all of the senses in this chapter, I do consider the powerful role of the senses in heightening the transmission process. In addition, my interest in looking at the role of techniques of transmission across multiple domains resonates with Timothy Rice's attention to what he calls aural-visual-tactile pedagogy as well as Benjamin Brinner's landmark work, *Knowing Music, Making Music: Javanese Gamelan and the Theory of Musical Competence and Interaction* (1995). Interestingly, Brinner draws on cognitive science and cognitive musicology to systematically identify and theorize multiple domains of musical competence.

Gina Fatone furthers Brinner's foray into cognitive musicology in her interdisciplinary study of the use of intermodal imagery in Scottish classical bagpiping (2010). Specifically, Fatone revisits Brinner's notion of cross-domain or cross-modal cognitive processes and defines them as "mental operations involving the transfer or interaction of counterparts between different domains of experience (i.e., visual, motor, auditory, vocal, imagined)" (2010, 397). However, by her conclusion, Fatone favors the term "intermodal" over "cross-modal" in order to emphasize that certain pedagogical techniques encourage more of an interactive back-and-forth process, rather than a unidirectional movement from one domain to another (2010, 415). My research and experience concur with Fatone's, so I have opted to use the term "intermodal" as well to describe this process. Lastly, this chapter also intersects with Fatone's sophisticated discussion of embodied cognition theory, which she aptly summarizes as "based on the idea that our thought processes are fundamentally rooted in bodily experience" (2010, 413).

While she does mention a few limitations of this theory in explaining certain aspects of her research on transmission, I have found it to be especially relevant in *p'ungmul*, especially given that it is a highly embodied form of expression. By focusing on site-specific, intermodal techniques of the body, I shed some light on how musicians learn how to play with the characteristic sense of "groove" associated with the Pilbong regional style. In this way, I hope to demonstrate that these techniques are not only embodied, but emplaced.

PEDAGOGY, EMBODIMENT, AND THE PILBONG NONGAK TRANSMISSION CENTER

The Imshil Pilbong Nongak Preservation Association (IPNPA) is one of many folk culture organizations in South Korea that preserve and continue their tradition through the practice of *chŏnsu* or intensive site-specific transmission. As mentioned in chapter 1, a typical *chŏnsu* program is typically one week long and is attended as part of a larger group that has already learned the basics of the style. While this norm is changing, the Pilbong transmission center stands out in terms of diversifying their programs to reach a wider spectrum of participants. Because of this, students travel from all over South Korea and even abroad to experience *p'ungmul* being taught in close proximity to the village of Pilbong.

The current Pilbong transmission center not only cultivates a distinct local environment in which participants are able to hone their skills, but it provides a place where students can learn how to interact more effectively, both socially and musically, in *madang*-type settings. Physical *madangs* are integral to villages such as Pilbong. In addition to the house courtyard *madang* pictured in figures 2.1 and 2.2, *madangs* can also be found at important village sites such as the main water source or spring and the tutelary spirit tree (*tangsan namu*). Larger and more public *madangs*—also called *p'ans*—might also be cleared in a village common area or in an adjacent field. Inspired by these types of spaces, *madangs* and *p'ans* were strategically placed throughout the transmission center complex (figure 1.2), which is adjacent to the village on the other side of a road that has recently turned into a major thoroughfare.[10]

In my research, I have found that encouraging *madang*-type interactions is achieved through the use of pedagogical techniques that emphasize *madang*-related discourses (table 0.1). These discourses help to strategically transmit Korean expressive folk culture by encouraging the "internalization" of a communal "way of being" in the *madang*, often in a relatively short span of time and in a transformative manner. According to Anna M. Gade, "internalization is a process by which social messages and meanings are felt, thought and experienced in ways that affect how people make themselves and their worlds" (2002, 328). In this way, I assert that the "internalization" of a *madang* way of being may play a role in facilitating feelings of transformation, in a manner akin to what may occur in ritual or religious settings.[11]

Following Gade's suggestion that the "keys to understanding internalization processes . . . often emerge within processes of learning" (2002, 342), my goal here is to analyze how a *madang* way of being is "taught" and therefore "internalized" in ways that explicitly involve the body. For this reason, I find it important to examine this phenomenon from a participant's perspective as part of a process of "embodiment." According to Thomas J. Csordas, an anthropologist who has synthesized several strains of thinking on the body, a theory of "embodiment" entails situating the "body" as the "subjective source or intersubjective ground of experience" (1999, 143).[12] Given that transmission centers are usually very intense and isolated environments, they can be especially conducive to the cultivation of intersubjective experience and the embodiment of certain alternative Korean subjectivities. These Korean subjectivities stand in relief to the hyper-competitive mindsets that many South Koreans espouse in order to succeed in a neoliberal capitalist society. More specifically, these subjectivities tend to align with the philosophy of community participation (*kongdongch'e*). In the world of the Pilbong *p'ungmul* transmission center, I have observed that what constitutes a "good" *p'ungmul* player is very much intertwined with what constitutes a good "subject." Because of this link, the transmission center can be a powerful place to learn and negotiate the various modes of behavior, social interaction, and attitudes that are associated with *p'ungmul*-oriented subjectivities.[13]

Although the assemblage of people who occupy a transmission center is always changing, there can be a remarkable sense of community that persists from week to week. I argue that this has to do with the fact that the transmission center creates community through a constancy of intention. In this way, the participants of each session must work to recreate this intentional community. In the case of Pilbong, participants of this intentional community then form a network of people who share an interest in Pilbong *p'ungmul*. In the words of a member of *Aekmaegi* (literally "bad luck blockers") from Ewha University:

> When our group comes here like this, we're all living together. We experience the life of community (*kongdongch'e*), and then as we receive instruction, we

get a taste of what *p'ungmul* is like and then this makes us feel *kongdongch'e* more strongly. When we play on our own, we can't get a sense of this actually. No matter how well our older sister members teach us, it's really important to witness it directly. You have to try to see what it's like to play in a *p'an* with others, and get a feeling of that atmosphere. When this new group of people comes together, we create a new culture—that is what the experience of *chŏnsu* is all about. (Kim Namhŭi interview, August 10, 2002)

A Twenty-First Century Traditional P'ungmul Village

In 1999–2000, the leaders of the IPNPA initiated ambitious plans to construct what has become one of the most comprehensive transmission centers in South Korea of its kind. The plan consisted of expanding upon the small building that was built in 1989 as part of the process of receiving recognition and support from the Korean government as an Intangible Cultural Property. According to the plan proposed in the early 2000s, the new transmission center complex would include additional buildings for instruction and practice, a traditional residential area for the teachers, a memorial/performance hall, an office/resource center, a museum, and a large residential hall with an adjoining cafeteria. In the last decade, additional spaces of performance, recreation, and lodging were built with a more traditional Korean architectural design.

These developments to the transmission center complex have made it much easier to accommodate increased programming for a wider diversity of students. Though a majority of *chŏnsu* students used to come from college-based *p'ungmul* clubs or circles, increasingly, students include middle-aged amateurs from community organizations, grade-school children and their families, and a growing number of seniors. While I was there during the 2001 and 2002 sessions, it was common for the center to have as many as 300 college students in attendance at any given time during the *chŏnsu* season. Since the 2010s, fewer college students and young people have been attending the week-long sessions in *p'ungmul* (Saeji 2013, 70). Interestingly, the shorter weekend programs now attract large numbers of families, children, and youth seeking a more general introduction to Korean arts and culture. In addition to *p'ungmul*, other Korean performing arts and crafts are taught, including mask dance, mask-making, *kanggangsullae* (women's group play with movement and song), folksong, egg-basket making, and traditional cloth-dyeing. When I asked Yang Chinsŏng, Pilbong's leader, what was behind some of these recent developments, he replied that it grew out of a desire to make Korean traditional culture fun and easy to integrate into the *saenghwal munhwa*, or "culture of everyday life" (Yang Chinsŏng interview, May 20, 2012).

Much of the appeal of the current center is due to its overall design that highlights the aesthetics of traditional culture while working in harmony with the natural beauty of the region. Many of the buildings that were added later were built on terraces carved into the hills that afford picturesque views of the Pilbong village and surrounding scenery. From one vantage point, the distinctive Pilbong mountain provides the perfect natural backdrop for the traditional open-air stage that is situated on an upper terrace of *hanok* or Korean-style buildings (figure 2.3). While many of the buildings are constructed in a more modern, institutional style with brick exteriors, the residential areas for teachers and special guests are constructed in the *hanok* style typical of older Korean homes. Though some of the materials were recycled from older structures, the buildings were completed with newly plastered walls and freshly papered screens on the windows and doors, resulting in intimate, clean, and airy living areas. Though the *hanok* have their own *madang* courtyards and traditional floor plans

FIGURE 2.3 View of Pilbong mountain from the Pilbong transmission center open-air stage (2016). Photo by the author.

that require going outdoors to reach the bathroom, they are all equipped with the modern conveniences of cable TV, high-speed internet, modern plumbing, machine laundry, and *ondol* floor heating.

Apparent in the design of the transmission center was an intention to push the concept of transmission in new directions. In a brochure for the 2001 Pilbong *P'ungmul* Festival, they proposed their vision of the complex as a "traditional *p'ungmul* village." In keeping with this, some of the goals they listed include: (1) "to preserve and develop Pilbong *p'ungmul* in an inventive manner and increase the cultural artistry and manpower of the organization"; (2) "to promote the traditional *p'ungmul* village into the twenty-first century"; (3) "to enliven local traditional culture and develop an appropriate course of cultural tourism"; and (4) "to create a model of Korean cultural work and offer a cultural resting place to appreciate the region's beauty" (Imshil Pilbong Nongak Preservation Association 2001, 6–7). In this way, this Pilbong organization has combined their goals of preservation and transmission with a vision to expand upon *p'ungmul*'s potential to sustain the expressive ecology of the village and transmission center as well as stimulate local tourism and contribute to its economy.

"BECOMING ONE": INSIDE A WEEK-LONG SESSION AT THE PILBONG TRANSMISSION CENTER

> Yang Chinsŏng said something about how when you are playing in the *p'an* or *madang*, it's not about showing off one's skill, it's about being aware of each other and *becoming one*. He said that it is more important to be thinking about what kind of spirit or soul you are going to play with, than anything else . . . You have to think about one's *chŏngsŏng* [one's true heart, sincerity, devotion] or feeling.
>
> *Ewha University student interview, August 10, 2002*

In the words of another *chŏnsu* participant from the Ewha University group, *Aekmaegi*, a typical week-long program at the Pilbong transmission center is structured toward the goal of coming together or "becoming one" in the *madang*-setting of the final *p'ungmul* performance. The daily classes provide the training and insight to inspire students to fully interact expressively in this culminating *madang* event (whether as a player or audience member). In the evenings, students congregate in spirited social gatherings called *twip'uri* where the participants can theoretically develop the "spirit" and "sincere feeling" to play

TABLE 2.1 Winter 2002 Pilbong *P'ungmul Chŏnsu* Schedule

MONDAY	TUESDAY	WEDNESDAY	THURSDAY	FRIDAY	SATURDAY	SUNDAY
	9–12 a.m. *P'ungmul* lecture (*iyagi p'an-kut*)	9–12 a.m. Class	9–12 a.m. Class	9–12 a.m. Class	9–12 a.m. Class	9–11 a.m. Class
						11 a.m.–12 p.m. *Sangsoe* contest
	2–4:30 p.m. Class	2–4:30 p.m. Class	2–4 p.m. Pilbong fieldtrip (*tapsa*)	2–4:30 p.m. Class	2–4:30 p.m. *Sogo* dance class	Practice and clean-up
6 p.m. Arrive, group-run orientation			4:30–6 p.m. Folksong	4:30–6 p.m. Environment class	4:30–6 p.m. Folksong	
	7–9 p.m. Group or individual practice	7–9 p.m. Group or individual practice	7–9 p.m. Group or individual practice	7–9 p.m. Group or individual practice	7–9 p.m. Group or individual practice	6 p.m. Final performance
	9 p.m. Social *twip'uri**	9 p.m. Social *twip'uri**	9 p.m. Social *twip'uri**	9 p.m. Social *twip'uri**	9 p.m. Social *twip'uri**	9 p.m. Social *twip'uri**

*Note: *Twip'uri* literally means "after-party" and refers to informal gatherings that follow a significant event, but in this case, they occur almost every night of *chŏnsu*.

meaningfully together.[14] Along with this, the participants of the camp must also collectively choose a *sangsoe* who will lead the final performance in a contest called the *sangsoe ppopki* or "picking the *sangsoe*."

The format of the *chŏnsu* program is somewhat similar to what one might encounter in music camps in the United States. The *p'ungmul*-oriented program does vary from session to session as the teachers have experimented with adapting existing activities or fitting in other types of classes and activities. These include anecdotal *p'ungmul* lectures called *iyagi p'an-kut* (roughly "story showcase"), *sŏlchanggo* (solo *changgo* playing), *minyo* (folksong) classes, *sogo* dance (dance classes with the handheld *sogo* drum), fieldtrips to the Pilbong village, and presentations on the environment and other topics (table 2.1).

Another key to the popularity of Pilbong's *chŏnsu* programs may be its relatively low individual cost, especially compared to other well-known Korean transmission programs and music camps around the world. For example, during my fieldwork period in 2001–2002, Pilbong only charged 40,000 *won* (roughly $40) per adult, and 30,000 *won* ($30) for high school age students and under for the whole week. Eating at the cafeteria cost an additional $6–9 per day. When I interviewed students about why they chose this particular transmission program over others, many of them did indeed mention its affordability. When I told Yang Chinsŏng this, he laughed and responded in this way.

> In Korea, among all the transmission centers, there's no other place that attracts as many students as we do. Really. In terms of us being the cheapest, I actually think this is a really beautiful thing. Don't you think? Actually, we never thought about it as a way to have a lot of students come here. (Yang Chinsŏng and Ch'oi Ho-in interview, August 10, 2002)

Social Organization

Although I spent a good amount of time at the Pilbong transmission center by myself, I did arrange to attend as part of a group twice, once in the winter and once in the summer. While one of the reasons I did this was to organize opportunities for others to come, I also felt it was beneficial to participate as part of a group, because the group dynamic is so integral to the way the *chŏnsu* experience is structured. For example, immediately upon arrival, the first mandatory activity we had to participate in was a *chŏnsu*-wide group orientation. No matter how many times I have gone to *chŏnsu*, I have always found myself somewhat unprepared for the high level of interaction and coordination that is expected among the various groups. During the winter *chŏnsu* (January 2002) group orientation, I remember being in a crowded room as each group was asked to come up, introduce themselves, and perform some type of skit or song. Despite the absence of preparation time, every group, including ours, had been miraculously ready for this and managed to put on reasonably entertaining performances.

Following this, we had to elect a *p'aejang* or "group leader," who would act as a liaison between the teachers and the students as well as a coordinator for all student-led activities. We also elected a treasurer/manager who was responsible for gathering donations for any drinks and food not provided by the cafeteria and helping coordinate the logistics for the final performance. Lastly, each group had to elect their own representatives who were then responsible for attending daily meetings with the other representatives.

Whether one regards the *madang* of the transmission center as a space of work, play, ritual, or performance, it is important to note that this social organization of the *chŏnsu* community plays an underlying role in the way participants interact in the *chŏnsu*. Most basically, the representatives, group leader, and treasurer become part of a student governing body that assists the teachers in running the center smoothly. Early in the meetings, it is decided which chores will be conducted by whom and when. Chores include sweeping and cleaning the various practice rooms, cafeteria, showers, and bathrooms, as well as garbage maintenance and helping with the dishes. Another major responsibility is the coordination of *chŏnsu*-wide events, such as the final *madang* performance. In this way, the students are able contribute to the communal atmosphere in a more meaningful way. In addition to lending a hand in various chores, they also take part in the social governance of the *chŏnsu*. This in turn encourages leadership and increases substantive interaction between the various groups. For example, the student governing body decides who does what in the final performance. Not everyone can be a member of the *ch'ibae* (those that perform an instrument or character role) and so the governing body makes sure that each group is equally represented.

In terms of gender representation, the highest positions tend to go to men, although women are very active as treasurer/managers, representatives, and helpers at *chŏnsu*. The majority of teachers are also men, although this has changed as more women have become prominent in the organization. Despite some inequality in terms of gender representation, the teachers try to nurture a cooperative environment of equal participation, inspired by the ideals of *kongdonch'e* and cooperative farming (*ture*). Even so, there is a tacit social hierarchy of authority that is assumed and rarely challenged. In this social hierarchy, the teachers are undoubtedly at the top, with certain teachers carrying more authority over others, such as the director and lead *sangsoe* player, Yang Chinsŏng. One example of the way this hierarchy works is in the practice of extreme deference and gift-giving to the teachers. Typical gifts include refreshments or juice, boxes of fruit, nuts, and alcohol.

This hierarchical element usually goes unmentioned or is de-emphasized in discourses on the *madang*. This may be because it goes against the grain of *madang*-related concepts such as *kongdongch'e* (community), *nanjang* (topsy-turvy chaos), and *shinmyŏng* (spiritual ecstasy). During one of the week's programs, one of the teachers, Han Chaehun, voiced his sense of conflict between asserting his own authority and promoting the ideals of *kongdongch'e*.

> Don't just think about how to play the *changgu* or *kkwaenggwari*. What we call Pilbong-*kut* is actually a person . . . [or] a song that a person sings or a story that a person tells. If there are no people, *kut* doesn't have any meaning, right? . . . When you go back to the *chŏnsugwan* [transmission center], it's the same thing. In your life at the *chŏnsugwan*, think about how you go about living the life of *kut*. Once in a while, we talk to you about cleaning more, and actually it's very uncomfortable. It's easier just to go around telling people what to do, but I don't really want to do that. Why? Because if we are trying to create the life of *kongdongch'e* together. You should be able to take care of the cleaning yourselves. When you have a free moment, even if it's not your job, do it anyway. I really think it is important to develop this attitude. (Han Chaehun recording, January 17, 2002)

In actuality, community does not just happen, it requires work; it comes about through a dynamic process of tension and struggle. As I listened back to Han Chaehun's closing words that day, I realized that the emancipatory power of creating a good *kutp'an* (or, a "participatory ritual space-time") in Han Chaehun's words is equal in proportion to the effort and struggle that participants put in every week at *chŏnsu*.

> Every time you fight, every time you play, every time you cry, and so on, it is possible to create a *kutp'an*. Likewise, at the *chŏnsugwan*, think about creating a *kutp'an*. Take care of your neighbor, take care of your other friends. Go to other rooms and talk and play. Don't just play when you drink . . . When I go around, you play amongst yourselves but hardly anyone has been going around to visit other groups in their rooms. This is not a *kutp'an*. I don't want you to play that kind of *kut* (ritual). I want you to create a real *kutp'an* . . . Well, your expressions tell me that you are thinking about what I said, I guess we'll see tonight, or tomorrow. (Han Chaehun recording, January 17, 2002)

Just as he was ending his speech, the sun suddenly broke through the clouds, and as the teacher exclaimed, "ah, the weather just got better," I noticed everyone look around with a mixture of humility and hope in their eyes.

Environmental Awareness, Tapsa, and Maintaining a Sense of the Hyŏnjang

Chŏnsu is an intensely physical and sensually stimulating experience for many of those who attend. One of the reasons for this is that many of the discursive practices of the *madang* that are emphasized during *chŏnsu* specifically target the body. This is especially evident in the way some students throw themselves into the spirit of community, carrying out various laborious chores with little complaint. A gentler manifestation of this can be seen in programs that are designed to impart an embodied awareness of the place of Pilbong or the "actual location or moment" (*hyŏnjang* in *madang*-related discourse). These programs have included a Pilbong *tapsa* or fieldtrip as well as a geographic demonstration on the surrounding environment.[15]

During the Pilbong *tapsa*, students not only develop an embodied understanding of the sights and sounds of Pilbong village, but they can also walk through the *madangs* and places that are associated with various *p'ungmul*-related rituals (table 3.1). For example, one of our first stops was the main bridge that must be traversed in order to enter the village. Han Chaehun, who was our guide when we went, explained that villagers used to have to cross on a bridge made of stepping stones called a *jingŭmdari*, or what is known more locally as a *nodi*. To pray for safe crossing over the course of the year, the village *p'ungmul-kut* group would perform a ritual called the *nodikosa-kut* on the fifteenth day of the Lunar New Year (Yang Chinsŏng 2000, 131). Since crossing by way of the current bridge is much more practical than the *nodi*, the *nodikosa-kut* is no longer played regularly. Even so, this practice brought students in close contact with historically important locations throughout the village, providing more nuanced, ritual meaning to the place of Pilbong.

In addition to targeting the body by taking the students on a journey through the village, the *hyŏnjang* (actual location and time) concept also contributes to an effective pedagogy of on-site learning. This technique is particularly effective in cultivating cultural memory by bringing past people and events into clearer focus in the present. For example, on one of these fieldtrips our guide walked with us up the road toward the village, stopping at a grassy mound up on the hill where the previous *sangsoe* leader was buried. This served as a departure point for our guide to introduce us to Yang Sunyong (the previous leader or *sangsoe*). Here, Han Chaehun was able to effectively segue into describing the life of this particular *sangsoe* in this location-specific story:

> After a *kut* [ritual] is finished, there is this thing called the *sangsoe taejŏp* [*sangsoe* reception].[16] First they prepare a table of food and call for the *sangsoe* to come. On this really big table, they put meat, soup, fish, side dishes... and then all the village elders come and talk [give their evaluation]. First, they say thanks and then ... they might say "when you played *morigut*[17] the *toen samch'ae*[18] was too slow," and so they pick up one of the side dishes and take it off the table. "When you did the *panguljin*[19] you spiraled in the wrong direction," and so they take off the meat. "During the *p'ungnyu-kut*,[20] it was too... brazen, bold," and so they take something away. If it's decided that the *sangsoe* really didn't play well that day, they take everything away, and so the *sangsoe* has no choice but to eat his rice with some water and soy sauce. If he plays well, then they let him eat and tell him what parts he played well. And in the event that the *sangsoe* really didn't play well, then the next day they tie him to a tree... When the *kut* doesn't go well, then the one who receives all the anger and punishment is the *sangsoe*. (Han Chaehun recording, January 17, 2002)

In this way, Han was able to convey both the essence of community aesthetic assessment as well as the weight and gravity of being a *sangsoe* as some of us, no doubt, contemplated the possibility of being tied to a tree all day.

As we made our way toward Yang's residence, Han Chaehun spoke movingly about how Yang's life as a *sangsoe* also affected his family life:

> The teacher's house is right here. His wife lives there now. If you look at it one way, his wife also had her share of hardships. Of course, the teacher did too ... The *sangsoe* needs to be taken care of. Though he lived here originally, when the *sangsoe* was invited to Namwon, they had to take care of the *sangsoe*. They had to decide how much money to give, how much land, and how much rice. This is called the *sangsoe moshigi* ... In this way, even if he was working, he would drop everything at the sound of a *kut*, he would just go. His wife had to worry about eating and surviving. But [Yang Sunyong] would work, then play *kut*, work and then play, which had the potential to cause a lot of problems. But, even so, it's largely due to the teacher that Pilbong has come so far. And as much as Pilbong has grown, his wife always has worked just as hard. Whenever there is a large *kut*, she always takes care of all the food on her own ... this is the way she has spent her whole life. (Han Chaehun recording, January 17, 2002)

Although the contributions of women are often left out of *p'ungmul* narratives, being in the *hyŏnjang* of the village seemed to help trigger the filling of these gaps,

Site-Specific Transmission **73**

thus providing a fuller picture of *p'ungmul* practices. From one perspective, this story could serve to perpetuate the idea that a women's place in *p'ungmul* is to serve and not play. At the same time, however, Han conveys his deep respect for his wife's contribution by putting it on equal footing with that of Yang Sunyong's. In sum, the various locations of the village provided an anchor for the students to get a more tangible sense of the people, sounds, and stories of Pilbong.

Sangsoe Ppopki *(Picking a* Sangsoe*) and the Final Performance*

A longstanding tradition of the Pilbong *chŏnsu* has been to hold a contest to pick a *sangsoe*, or lead small gong player, who will then lead the final performance. Held on the morning of the last day of programming, the contest takes place in the main *madang*. Cut into a hill, one side of the *madang* is graduated into steps that serve as seats for viewing. Normally, about eight to fifteen people participate (figure 2.4). Whether these young men and women win or not, the contest gives them an opportunity to prove their ability to embody the *sangsoe* role with all the attendees and teachers as witnesses (figure 2.5). Practically speaking, the person who is chosen is the one who can best negotiate the various elements of a *p'ungmul madang*. According to the current *sangsoe*, Yang Chinsŏng, these three main elements include the people, the artistic features (music and dance), and the space of the *madang* itself (2000, 39).

In order to evaluate mastery of these three elements, the contestants proceed through several rounds of competition that are judged by representatives from the various groups participating in a given training session. In the first round, each contestant plays a passage of their own choosing. From here, the judges select the three most promising contestants to compete in three more stages in which they demonstrate their skills by: (1) playing the challenging *kaenjigaeng* rhythm, (2) dancing with a *sogo* drum, and (3) displaying their knowledge of Pilbong *p'ungmul* by answering a set of questions that often explore how one might handle a given spatial, temporal, or social situation in the *madang*.

In the first stage, the contestant must display their mastery in playing *kaenjigaeng*, a fast, rolling 12/8 cyclical rhythm that is characteristic of the Pilbong style (table 2.2). This rhythm is felt in four major pulses with a downward emphasis of the body on the first, fourth, seventh, and tenth beats. *Kaenjigaeng*'s emphasis in the competition makes sense given that many Pilbong practitioners say that if one can play *kaenjigaeng* well, then one can play anything in the Pilbong repertoire well. In table 2.2, *kaenjigaeng* appears deceptively simple

FIGURE 2.4 *Sangsoe ppopki* ("picking the sangsoe") contestants (2002). Photo by the author.

FIGURE 2.5 Female *sangsoe ppoki* ("picking the sangsoe") contestant (2002). Photo by the author.

and repetitive. In practice, *kaenjigaeng* is elusive for many *soe* players because it requires a facility and speed that can only be achieved through much practice, coupled with a relaxed but controlled technique. It also requires a solid sense of embodied groove that can be described as having a cyclical, sinking, and rising feeling. Like an embodied fractal, this sinking and rising pattern correlates with the various movements that go along with this rhythm and can be felt within each major pulse, the cycle as a whole or even across a grouping of cycles. Good players must be able to play subtle variations while carefully etching patterns of emphasis that can stretch over one to four cycles of the rhythm. The most basic pattern of emphasis involves accenting the first beat of every major pulse (1, 4, 7, 10), all the while sinking the most emphasis on the first beat and building up energy through beats 7 to 9 and releasing it during beats 10 to 12. This conforms to the aesthetic of "produce-heat up-tighten-release" (*naego-talgo-maetgo-p'ulgo*) that is quoted so often when describing the proper expressive flow and rhythmic groove of many Korean folk music genres (Kim Inu 1987, 119).

In the second stage, the three contenders must demonstrate their ability to dance and play *sogo* (two-sided handheld drum). Although the *sogo* makes very little sonic impact in the *p'an* (entertainment-oriented word for *madang*), the inclusion of this activity attests to the importance with which the Pilbong teachers view the *sogo* player's role. At a basic level, playing the *sogo* gives a good indication of how an individual moves in the *madang* and attests to the widely held view that movement is critical to being a good *sangsoe*. As Kim Inu has noted, it is widely accepted that "*p'ungmul* is played with one's heel!" (Kim 1987, 113). Because *sogo* players are free to dance and play without worrying about playing complicated rhythms, this round also highlights the individual's personality; it is ultimately a test of one's ability to connect with the audience and control the overall mood or spirit of the *p'ungmul p'an*.

In the final stage, the teachers ask each contender a separate question about Pilbong *p'ungmul-kut*. Some questions are obviously meant to test the thoroughness of a contender's knowledge and memory of Pilbong rhythms and ordering. For example, in one of the *sangsoe* contests I attended, the teachers asked the following questions: (1) in the *ap-kut* (front series of Pilbong *p'ungmul-kut* rhythms), describe the different connecting rhythms (*iŭmsae karak*) that are used, and (2) list the different types of rituals that are performed in Pilbong *p'ungmul-kut* and describe the order of actions and rhythms in one of them. Other questions test an individual's ability to adapt to different situations by asking, for example, "If you only have eighteen minutes to play a *kut* (ritual performance), what series of

TABLE 2.2 Basic *Soe* Part of the *Kaenjigaeng* Rhythmic Cycle

KEY. The numbers represent the beats of the cycle, while the syllables represent different onomatopoetic strokes on the *soe* instrument. The gong is generally held with the left hand and is struck with a wooden mallet with the right hand. Fast 12/8 meter.

Kaen: A long sound of medium loudness.
Ji: A short sound of specific duration, and in faster tempos it functions as an ornament to the following sound.
Gaeng: A short sound of medium loudness.

1	2	3	4	5	6	7	8	9	10	11	12
Kaen	ji	gaeng	Kaen	ji	ng	gaeng		ji	gaeng	Kaen	ji	gaeng

rhythms would you play and in what order?" Other questions were more open-ended and philosophical. During one contest, one of the newer teachers posed, "What does it mean to 'live life in the way of *kut*'?" Another asked a more specific, theoretical question: "How does one maintain the concept of 'produce-heat up-tighten-release' (*naego-talgo-maetgo-p'ulgo*) in a *kut*?" In addition to serving as a necessary component of competition, this round is a unique educational forum at *chŏnsu*. Even after the contenders have given their answers, *chŏnsu* participants often talk amongst themselves and insist that the teachers follow up and reflect upon the answers themselves. The multiplicity of skills tested in the *sangsoe* competition demonstrates that artistic proficiency on the *soe* (handheld gong) is not enough to become *sangsoe*. For example, a contestant with strong musical skills may be perceived as being too absorbed in their own playing and would therefore elicit much discussion about whether he/she possesses enough maturity to truly be attuned to everyone else in the *madang* (Kwon 2005, 251). Depending on a given session, debates about who should become *sangsoe* can become quite heated and conflicted, especially as women have become more prominent practitioners of genres previously dominated by men (Chin 2010, 77–90). The *sangsoe* competition remains a fascinating forum in which to gauge how the core values and aesthetics of *p'ungmul* are evolving and continually being negotiated in relation to changes that are occurring in South Korean society.

For the winner, the chance to embody the *sangsoe* and lead people from a multitude of teams can be regarded as a kind of "ultimate" experience for an aspiring *p'ungmul* player. The final performance that results from the *sangsoe* competition serves as the culminating, and often most cathartic, event of *chŏnsu*. From start to finish, the final performance is completely run by the

Site-Specific Transmission 77

students, largely through the leadership of the student governing body and the newly chosen *sangsoe*. Though the format is somewhat open depending on the *chŏnsu*, this event is modeled upon a village ritual festival or *kut*, much like the one Pilbong organizes for Lunar New Year, but on a smaller scale. Depending on the season and the participants, the format can take either a ritual or more entertainment-oriented direction. In addition to practicing for the performance, important tasks include preparing a bonfire (necessary to provide warmth and light in the evening), buying and cooking the food, and cleaning up afterward. Although not everyone can play an instrument or character role (*chapsaek*) in the final performance, the idea is that everyone should contribute in some way.

Since this event takes place within the concentrated context of transmission, it is a unique opportunity for students. Although not exactly spontaneous, the event challenges the students to embrace being in the moment or *hyŏnjang*, an important aspect of *madang* discourse; for example, they must make the most of what resources and circumstances are present in the space, time, and social milieu of a given *chŏnsu* session. These include the people, the chosen *sangsoe*, the weather, the friendships that were forged, the songs or stories that were shared, any unfolding drama among the participants, and the food that was available at market that day. In addition to the *hyŏnjang*, the participants have the potential to embody several other *madang*-related discourses such as *kut* (ritual), *kongdongch'e* (community), *shinmyŏng* (spiritual catharsis), *nori* (play), and even *nanjang* (chaos) (table 0.1). When I asked Yang Chinsŏng why he thought it was important for people to come directly to Pilbong to play, he replied:

> Even though people come to Pilbong, playing the Pilbong way is still hard. The easiest thing to do is teach Pilbong as a composed set of rhythms . . . But we are not here to teach a composition, we're here to teach Pilbong as a ritual or *kut*. Well, what is *kut*? . . . *Kut* is not a problem of instruments, it is a problem of people . . . It also has to do with the social environment that people live in. This is something we have to create continuously together. So, to do Pilbong *kut* the right way, you have to meet each other and think about it, and as you play . . . then that feeling comes, right? . . . Students come knowing this, they come because they want to learn about *kut*. (Yang Chinsŏng and Ch'oe Ho-in interview, August 10, 2002)

TRANSMITTING THE GROOVE: A MICROANALYSIS OF MUSIC, MOVEMENT, AND THE BODY

Though Yang Chinsŏng often tells students that mastering *kut* is more a "problem of people" than a "problem of instruments," one look at the schedule suggests that this is meant to be more rhetorical than literal. In fact, day in and day out, students may spend from four to eight hours per day learning, playing, and rehearsing Pilbong rhythms and movements on the *changgo* or *soe* (small gong). While the culminating final performance serves as an important macro-level structuring device that defines one's experience at *chŏnsu*, the micro-practices of class instruction are just as significant and deserve further attention. Specifically, I am interested in analyzing the pedagogical techniques that highlight an awareness of movement and the body in the transmission of a distinctive Pilbong style or microrhythmic groove. Many of these techniques are intermodal in nature and effectively draw attention to the body, working to draw its participants into a social and musical groove that has been defined by Charles Keil as a "participatory discrepancy" (1994a, 96) or in the somewhat less loaded phrasing of Steven Feld as a state of being "in synchrony, while out-of-phase" (1994, 119).

My ultimate goal here is to better understand the relationship between the processes of embodiment, mastering the Pilbong groove, and the internalization of a communal way of being, all crucial to sustaining the underlying expressive ecology of Pilbong. These elements are also critical to the development of transformative feelings of group cohesion ("becoming one"), so highly valued in Pilbong *p'ungmul*. Nathan Hesselink explores similar concerns in a chapter that analyzes Pilbong's rhythmic "structure and organization at the micro and macro levels" (2011, 265). While Hesselink's concerns do not delve deeply into Pilbong's distinctive microrhythmic tendencies, his demonstration of how Pilbong's rhythms are structured and performed in order to embody communal awareness is highly resonant here. I further this mode of inquiry by focusing on the actual experience of learning these techniques, to give a sense of their phenomenological texture and significance. In doing so, I will highlight some of the intermodal pedagogical techniques of two teachers: Mr. Kim and Ch'oe Ho-in.[21]

Mr. Kim: Multiple Approaches to Embodying the Rhythm

One of the common methods of engaging the body in reproducing a particular sound, employed by both Mr. Kim and Ch'oe Ho-in, is by vocalizing the rhythms through *ipchangdan* (literally "mouth rhythms").[22] *Ipchangdan* are vocables (vocalized syllables) that correspond, in this case, to various drumstrokes. This common intermodal technique—spanning the vocal, auditory, and rhythmic motor domains—serves several purposes. One is that this technique encourages the player to connect or translate the expressive potential of the embodied voice to an instrument that is technically "disconnected" from the body of the player, not to mention limited in some ways that the voice is not. This technique extends the expressivity of a student's playing, thereby enabling the student to better capture the "feel" of a rhythm. How does this work exactly? I used to think that performing vocables served first as a mnemonic learning device and second as a guide for where to place the accents in a rhythm. Later, I realized that the prominent use of vocables indicates that the teachers think of the rhythms with a centrality usually afforded to melodies. For example, vocables are employed to get students to soften their playing. In one class, we were in the midst of learning the *pan-p'ungnyu* rhythm (audio 2.1 ◀⇧). Getting the moderate-tempo feel of *pan-p'ungnyu* is especially crucial because it is one of a handful of rhythms that facilitate maximum openness and audience participation in the Pilbong *p'ungmul madang* (table 2.3). In helping us to capture the relaxed feeling of this rhythm, he called on students to repeat back the first four vocables, "Tŏ Tŏ—ng, Tŏ Tŏ—ng." After a split-second of reflection, his response was that our "Tŏ—ng" was not long enough to fill the empty space of the third beat.

In other words, the underlying purpose of singing the rhythms is to help a player give more weight and articulation to the empty spaces of a rhythmic cycle. By extension, the practice of vocables may also reference an underlying dynamic "tonal" quality that is associated with the different drumstrokes. In this case, intonational patterns not only indicate the presence of "tones" such as the "sinking and rising" lilt that he gave to the longer "Tŏ—ng" vocable, but they also signal durational length, which may help students better articulate emptiness. According to Mr. Kim, playing *p'ungmul* with *mat* or "taste" is all about how one articulates through this "emptiness." In this way, the vocables facilitate the embodiment of a rhythm, and in the process, help a student develop a better expressive command of both the "full" and "empty" spaces of a rhythm so that they may negotiate or play with the groove with more ease and finesse.

Another favorite intermodal technique that Mr. Kim employs to build bodily awareness across the auditory, visual, and motor domains is to instruct half of the class to play while the other half dances along and vice versa. Because he is known as a particularly animated and distinctive dancer, most students enjoy watching Mr. Kim demonstrate how to dance what is called the *ŏkkaech'um* or "shoulder dance" (figure 2.2 and video 2.1 🔊). A relatively simple movement, *ŏkkaech'um* involves articulating the shoulders slightly while dropping or swaying one's forearms to the left and right. One can do this while standing or bobbing in place or by coordinating this motion with one's steps. Mr. Kim makes sure to demonstrate that since stepping in the Pilbong style of *p'ungmul* always begins with the left foot, it follows that you also sway your arms to the left first, otherwise it looks funny. The main point of this exercise is to bring movement and the body into the forefront of one's awareness while playing. Another is simply to teach students how to synchronize their movements to the music.

These exercises can also be seen as facilitating entrainment, which Martin Clayton, Rebecca Sager, and Udo Will define as "a process whereby two rhythmic processes interact with each other in such a way that they adjust towards and eventually 'lock in' to a common phase and/or periodicity" (2004, 2). In this way, this simple shoulder dance exercise points to the occurrence of mutual entrainment between the dancers and players. It is also important to note that the concept of entrainment—whether social or self-oriented—is by its nature an intermodal process, because one is entraining one process to another and vice versa.

This process carries with it implications that are practical, musical, aesthetic, and social, and as such, contributes greatly to the success of a large *madang* event. For example, when a large *madang* performance opens up to the audience members and becomes filled with people, the musicians sometimes have to rely on entraining to the movements of arms swaying back and forth in a synchronized manner, especially when the sonic atmosphere becomes dispersed and chaotic. This process can only work if the majority of participants know how to perform the shoulder dance in a uniform manner. Mr. Kim warned that the most annoying thing in the *madang* is when the rhythm is played well, but the dancers are not matching either the rhythm or each other. In this way, processes of entrainment do have a direct bearing on the aesthetics of the *madang*. These processes of entrainment are further connected to aesthetics in the way that students are encouraged to play not just in "sync" with the dancers, but also with the right dynamic expressivity to encourage people to dance in the *madang*. By the same token, Mr. Kim tells his students that one should dance to "inspire" and give energy back to the musicians playing.[23]

While the shoulder dance exercise is an example of *social entrainment* (defined as occurring interactively between at least two individuals), Mr. Kim's emphasis on coordinating one's playing to one's own breathing or *hohŭp* is more indicative of what Clayton, Sager, and Will call *self-entrainment* (2004, 7). More broadly, *hohŭp* refers to the regular process of breathing and respiration. Practitioners also use the term to refer to one's inner pulse. In this way, the emphasis on *hohŭp* in Korean drumming hints at the importance of self-training to one's inner bodily rhythms. Mr. Kim further embodies this process by linking *hohŭp* to a bodily movement called *ogŭm*: a sinking and rising motion performed by bending the knees. Even when not performed by bending the knees (sitting down, for example), the sinking and rising motion of *ogŭm* is often translated to other parts of the body (head, shoulders, upper torso).

Going back to the concept of breath for a moment, Clayton, Sager, and Will categorize respiration as an example of an *endogenous* rhythm, meaning that it occurs naturally within the living body (2004, 3). Kim Samt'ae (2001a) argues that *endogenous* rhythms, like breathing and the heartbeat, are fundamental to *p'ungmul* and proposes that this theory helps explain the derivation and prevalence of triple subdivisions in *p'ungmul* and Korean music in general (Hesselink 2011, 264). In practice, I do not think that *p'ungmul* players "entrain" their playing to these endogenous rhythms all the time. However, coordinated breathing certainly comes into play at certain points—for example, during the first articulation of a new rhythm. In my view, these endogenous rhythms serve effectively as rhythmic templates that help a player tap into a more embodied feeling of a rhythm.

Given that Mr. Kim often stressed that mastering the feeling of *hohŭp/ogŭm* is more important than knowing the actual rhythms, it is worth taking a closer look at the motion of *ogŭm* itself. In his view, it is not enough to bend one's knees down and up. One must also replicate the speed and the quality of the motion so that it seems natural and perpetual. This means that the movement must be continuous, flowing, and most of all—not too jerky. At the same time, I have observed that this movement is not perfectly continuous and even. Rather, the sensation of *ogŭm* has to do with sinking with the force of gravity and then rebounding or rising back up from this force. In addition, one cycle of this motion is imagined as being subdivided into three beats, with the first beat coinciding with the downward sinking motion and the rise peaking on the third beat. Practically speaking, working with the force of gravity produces a motion that is less constant in speed but more efficient.

Many *p'ungmul* practitioners claim that when a player plays *p'ungmul* in good coordination with *ogŭm*, the movement is so efficient that they never get tired, even after playing all day long. Some even speculate that the roots of this type of efficient motion may lie in *p'ungmul*'s role coordinating the movements of farming labor (Kim Inu 1987, Yang Chinsŏng 2000, Kim Samt'ae 2001a). Whatever the reasons or roots, there is no question that this motion is somehow embedded within the aesthetic feel of the rhythms. For Mr. Kim, mastering *hohŭp* and *ogŭm* is not just a matter of movement style, it is a kinesthetic sense that must be internalized in one's playing so that it can be imagined and translated sonically and visually even in situations of limited movement. Based on my personal experience, playing in a rural environment surrounded by farms does help one gain a more labor-informed groove and kinesthetic sense of playing *p'ungmul*.

 Playing that is deeply entrained to *hohŭp* and *ogŭm* (whether externally or internally) is characterized by patterns of accent and intensity that correlate with *ogŭm*'s distinctive sinking and rising motion. Sometimes these patterns of accents are articulated in the yin/yang-influenced aesthetic of "strong/weak" or *kangyak*, where the stronger accents tend to coincide with the downward sinking motion. Another effect of this is that drum strokes are placed less metronomically and more with a swinging or lilting feel. This feeling is accentuated by the dominance of triple subdivisions found in a majority of Korean *p'ungmul* rhythms (Komodo and Nogawa 2002, 571–73). Even in extremely fast rhythms, such as *ich'ae*, the pulse is still subdivided into three in the Pilbong style of *p'ungmul*. In slow to medium tempo 12/8 rhythms such as *pan-p'ungnyu* in table 2.3, the swing translates in the discrepant timing of the third eighth note of a three-beat grouping that coincides with the correlating upward motion of *ogŭm*. Based on a spectrogram analysis (figure 2.6) of Mr. Kim playing *pan-p'ungnyu* on the *changgo*, it is clearly evident that the third eighth note of a three-beat grouping is often delayed. For example, the third eighth-note beats articulated by the *changgo* on the ninth, fifteenth, eighteenth, and twenty-first eighth-note beats are delayed by more than the average margin of discrepancy (table 2.3).[24] This phenomenon is somewhat analogous to the delayed timings of swing in jazz (Keil 1994b, 61; Prögler 1995, 26).

I also discovered from the spectrogram analysis that the three-beat durations demonstrated a pattern of expansion and contraction where the first, third, fifth, and seventh of the larger durations are significantly longer than the others (they are bolded in the last two rows of table 2.3). This was especially evident in the longer suspension of the accented beats of 7, 13, and 19. It follows that this pattern

TABLE 2.3 *Pan-p'ungnyu* Rhythm on the *Changgo*

KEY. The numbers represent the beats of the cycle, while the vocables represent different onomatopoetic strokes on the *changgo* instrument. The *changgo* is a two-headed hourglass drum that is struck with a mallet-like stick with the left hand and a thin bamboo stick with the right. 12/8 meter.

Tŏng: A sound of longer duration made with both heads of the drum being struck at the same time.
Tŏ: A short sound made by both heads of the drum being struck at the same time.
Tak: A sharp, slapping sound made with thin bamboo stick striking the rim of the right drumhead.
Kung: A sound made with the mallet striking the middle of the left (or right) drumhead.

1	2	3	4	5	6	7	8	9	10	11	12
Tŏ	Tŏ—	ng	Tŏ	Tŏ—	ng	Tŏng		Tŏ	Kung	Tak	
13	14	15	16	17	18	19	20	21	22	23	24
Tŏ—	ng	Tak	Kung	Tak	Kung	Tŏ—	ng	Tŏ	Kung	Tak	

DETAILED TIMINGS OF INDIVIDUAL DRUMSTROKES AS PLAYED

0.0	0.255		0.792	1.103		1.544		2.228	2.379	2.61	
3.082		3.758	3.933	4.164	4.433	4.558		5.201	5.354	5.573	

REGULAR (METRONOMIC) TIMINGS OF THE BEAT FOR REFERENCE

| 0 | 0.252 | 0.505 | 0.757 | 1.009 | 1.262 | 1.514 | 1.766 | 2.019 | 2.271 | 2.523 | 2.775 |
| 3.027 | 3.280 | 3.532 | 3.784 | 4.037 | 4.289 | 4.540 | 4.794 | 5.045 | 5.297 | 5.549 | 5.801 |

TIMINGS OF EACH THREE-BEAT DURATION

0.792	0.752	0.835	0.703
0.851	0.625	0.796	0.700

NOTE: Timings are noted in seconds rounded to the third decimal point. Due to the brevity of this sample, I elected not to employ other systems of microrhythmic analysis such as Jairazbhoy's system of NUTS, or "Nominal Units of Time."

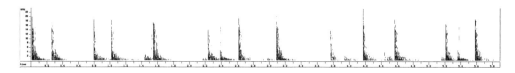

FIGURE 2.6 *Pan-p'ungnyu* rhythm spectrogram. Created by the author.

of expansion and contraction would also be reflected in the *ogŭm* movements with an alternation of longer/deeper knee bends with shorter/shallower ones. While it is difficult to determine whether this tendency first arose in the music or the body, I can speculate that this alternation of effort produces an easier and more efficient bodily motion. This pattern of expansion and contraction can also be seen as reinforcing the aesthetic of alternating strong and weak accents (*kangyak*). Christiane Gerischer has also found patterns of expansion and contraction across several styles of samba (2006, 106–10). Despite similarities with genres such as samba and jazz, however, I posit that this particular combination of embodied sonic elements contribute to Pilbong's characteristic heavy groove or, in Mr. Kim's words, "*tto-bak tto-bak*" quality of simple clarity and "chunky" regularity akin to the rhythm of walking.[25] This contrasts with other *p'ungmul* styles whose sounds are more polished and elegantly ornamented. While it is possible to learn this groove without setting foot in the village of Pilbong, the site-specific *chŏnsu* experience goes a long way in helping students embody this regional "*tto-bak tto-bak*" quality.

Ch'oe Ho-in: Drawing Out "Somatic Modes of Attention"

Of the younger generation of teachers, Ch'oe Ho-in taught at the Pilbong *p'ungmul* transmission center with a remarkable steadiness and resolve, despite the challenging lifestyle. Like Mr. Kim and many other teachers, Ch'oe Ho-in also emphasizes *ipchangdan* (vocables), *hohŭp* (breathing), and *ogŭm* (knee bending). In one memorable class, Ch'oe Ho-in made use of all three of the above techniques, while also drawing upon what Thomas Csordas calls "somatic modes of attention." According to Csordas, somatic modes of attention involve a "culturally elaborated attention to and with the body in the immediacy of an intersubjective milieu" (Csordas 1993, 139). In this way, Ch'oe Ho-in used techniques that were particularly effective at eliciting a culturally elaborated form of somatic attention. I quote here from my fieldnotes:

> Today Ho-in took us out to the main *madang* to practice outside. Spreading out, we were instructed to stand at random and not in a line. First, he broke down the motion of *ogŭm* by telling us to incorporate *hohŭp*. We did this for a long time, in what seemed to be an excruciatingly slow pace. It wasn't long before I started to get really tired. Then he told us to say the *ipchangdan* (vocables). After repeating the vocables a few times, I remember him expressing his dis-

satisfaction by asking, "Why is it that everyone can sing a folksong but no one can say the *ipchangdan*?" Later, he explained that a rhythm is like a song that no one can really sing. After fine-tuning the inflections of our vocables, we continued to practice while doing *ogŭm* knee bends—for what seemed like forever! Finally, he let us get our instruments and actually play while bending our knees at a faster pace. After spending most of the class time performing *ogŭm* so slowly, playing with our instruments at the normal tempo suddenly made it seem so easy and natural. (August 10, 2002)

Even though the delayed gratification of the class was frustrating, in retrospect it was extremely effective in enabling students to experience that magic, intense moment when the music locks in perfectly to make a previously labored movement suddenly seem easy. Though I had experienced this kind of coordinated ease before, I never had my attention drawn to it in that kind of methodical manner. In citing Marcel Mauss, Thomas Csordas explains that a somatic mode of attention "associated with the acquisition of any technique of the body" often "recedes into the horizon once the technique is mastered" (1993, 139). Given that we were in an advanced class and most of us were already accustomed to performing *ogŭm*, the discomfort of slowing and breaking down the process made us re-focus our attention to the body in a way we would not have had it been more automatic.

From another perspective, Ch'oe Ho-in was, in effect, having us re-enact a classic "scene" in the stories people tell about *ture*, or the cooperative farming style of *p'ungmul*: that is, the discovery that it is easier and more effective to work in the fields in conjunction with the rhythms of a *p'ungmul* band. When I related my thoughts about how the class conjured for me what it might have felt like to perform *ture p'ungmul* in the fields, he smiled knowingly and said that this was indeed his intention in pacing the class so slowly. With muscles still sore from that afternoon, I think this was his way of keeping *p'ungmul*'s connection to labor close at hand. All of the intermodal pedagogical techniques that I have described in this section—*ipchangdan* (vocables), *ŏkkaech'um* (shoulder dance), *hohŭp* (breathing), *ogŭm* (knee bends), and "somatic modes of attention"—can be seen as inter-related in the way that they seek to help students embody and reproduce an aesthetic groove central to the Pilbong style of *p'ungmul*. While these techniques can be effectively applied elsewhere, learning to entrain these rhythms at Pilbong is crucial because it ensures that the many dispersed groups that are learning this style are able to check in periodically and entrain with each other so that the distinctive groove of the Pilbong does not stray too much from one group to another.[26]

CONCLUSION

By looking at the programming and embodied pedagogical techniques of transmission center culture, I have investigated how Pilbong *p'ungmul* teachers work to transmit more than just musical or stylistic content. In this vein, I have argued that by shaping the social structuring, programming, and pedagogical methods of *chŏnsu*, the teachers and participants have created a site-specific intentional community of cultural transmission. As part of this process, I have also focused on *chŏnsu* as a place where students develop a communal way of being in the *madang*. This includes participating in various discursive practices of the *madang*. In addition, I have argued that *chŏnsu* serves as an experimental environment where participants can practice and push the boundaries of various roles and subjectivities (such as the influential *sangsoe*) with a flexibility that does not exist in the realm of sanctioned Pilbong *p'ungmul* performance.

In summarizing my thoughts on transmitting a sense of groove in *p'ungmul*, I would like to echo that the value of groove extends beyond the sonic realm. For example, groove in *p'ungmul* helps us to connect space with time by encouraging us to embody space more fully in time. In addition, grooving together musically can enhance feelings of *community* togetherness. More specifically, a good groove in *p'ungmul* theoretically should elicit increased embodied participation from audience members, thereby cultivating an inclusive atmosphere. The embodied qualities of grooving as exemplified in *hohŭp* or *ogŭm* also link with *p'ungmul*'s history as part of *ture*, a pre-industrial system of cooperative agricultural labor. Lastly, groove can also be seen as guiding the transformative, ritual, or dynamic phases of the *madang* and is absolutely essential to cultivating the experiential qualities of spontaneous engagement and play in the *madang*.

Ultimately, these site-specific techniques do much more than transmit the musical content; in fact, most of the students come to *chŏnsu* having already learned the rhythms that comprise the "original form" or *wŏnhyŏng*. Instead, the Pilbong teachers place much more focus on conveying a region-based sensibility, sound, and philosophy of making expressive folk culture relevant in everyday life. In addition, I posit that the Pilbong teachers are involved in a particular brand of post-colonial cultural politics by helping to articulate culturally specific ways of being and socializing in Korea; these then contribute to the bodily inscription of indigenous cultural spaces and encourage the development of cultural memories associated with certain geographic places or locales. In the following chapters, I will delve into these processes of site-specific bodily inscription at work in the actual village of Pilbong as members of the Pilbong community work to prepare the village for the Lunar New Year ritual festivities in chapter 3 and participate in it in chapter 4.

THREE

Cultivating the Village, Preparing for Ritual

For most students and visitors who come to Pilbong, the transmission center complex—with its mix of modern and traditional indoor and outdoor spaces—serves as *their* de facto village. From here, the "real" village of Pilbong beckons from across the valley, close enough to be visible and yet too far away to hear or see anything going on there in crisp detail (figure 2.3). For some, the transmission center and village are situated at a comfortable, safe distance from each other. For the serious *p'ungmul* student and fan, however, exploring the village's nooks and crannies is a rite of passage. The most likely reason for this can be traced back to the popular mantra that the Pilbong style of *p'ungmul* should be understood first and foremost as village ritual, or *maŭl-kut*.[1] In order to live up to this mantra, the Imshil Pilbong Nongak Preservation Association (IPNPA), together with the residents of Pilbong, carry the somewhat unusual burden of maintaining the expressive ecology of the village. Furthermore, their popularity and status as an Important Intangible Cultural Property (No. 11-5) has heightened expectations among participants, giving rise to competing notions of what a village with ongoing ritual traditions should be.

For me, the concept of expressive ecology brings together the dual mandates of preserving and protecting a cultural heritage form as well as the place and community in which it is situated. In South Korea, these two mandates do not always go hand in hand, but in the case of Pilbong, the practitioners of the IPNPA have staked their lives on it; they have worked incredibly hard to cultivate the expressive ecology of Pilbong in a time when village life in Korea is steadily eroding. Throughout this book and especially in this chapter, I define expressive ecology as the sum and relations of all the human and non-human elements that sustain a given place-based expressive cultural form, including its participants, its supporters, development and infrastructure of the location (buildings, roads, bus routes, topography, etc.), and the surrounding environment (geographic features and living things). In the following, I will convey a facet of these efforts—how Pilbong practitioners prepare the village for ritual each year—hoping that it will bring into focus what it really means to cultivate a village-based ritual or *maŭl-kut*.

The emphasis of Pilbong *p'ungmul* as village ritual or *maŭl-kut* was initially part of a conscious effort to promote *p'ungmul* as something more than "just entertainment." While these tensions have subsided, during the 1990s and early 2000s, this move was an implicit critique of Korean drumming groups who focused mainly on the entertainment-oriented *p'an-kut* format, or the more recently developed staged genre called *samul nori*. In most *nongak* or *p'ungmul* traditions, *p'an-kut* can be thought of as a showcase of rhythms, choreography, and other more spectacular elements that define a particular regional style of *p'ungmul*. For Pilbong practitioners, reducing *p'ungmul* to *p'an-kut* signifies a profound erasure of a whole set of ritual expressive practices that are wedded to different sites within the village. Even more significantly, focusing on *p'an-kut* suggests to students that *p'ungmul* can be approached as a musical composition set to choreography, where the goal is to master the rhythms, movements, and other skills. Instead, many of the Pilbong teachers repeatedly stressed the conceptualization of *p'ungmul* as a living, village-based practice, with a philosophy that is embedded within the ideals of a cohesive community.

Interestingly, the *maŭl-kut* that the IPNPA has performed in the village of Pilbong since 2002 is also a condensed version of prior ritual practices. According to the IPNPA director and leader, Yang Chinsŏng, several smaller rituals performed around the Lunar New Year used to take place over a two-week period (table 3.1). For maximum drama and effect, however, these rituals were collapsed into one event and performed typically on the Saturday closest to the first full moon of the Lunar New Year; this was then re-presented as *Chŏngwŏl Taeborŭm-kut* or the "Lunar New Year Full Moon Ritual." At least one member of the IPNPA has expressed ambivalence about the increasing "production" of the ritual as a "show, show, show," implicitly geared more for outsiders than village residents. Despite this change, the concept of *maŭl-kut* remains pivotal to the very identity of Pilbong *p'ungmul*. In fact, Pilbong teachers often make the claim that they are one of the few *p'ungmul* groups to have preserved their form of village ritual in

TABLE 3.1 Types of Pilbong *P'ungmul-kut* Rituals

TYPE OF RITUAL (*kut*)	DATE PERFORMED (lunar calendar)	PURPOSE
Madangbalbi	Performed sometime during the first ten days of January	Praying for good fortune in the New Year, chasing away bad spirits
Mae-kut	Last day of December	New Year's Eve village ritual
Tangsanje	Ninth day of January, in the evening	Village Guardian Spirit ritual
Ch'albapgŏtki p'ungmul-kut	After the fifteenth of January (after the New Moon of the New Year)	Gathering of boiled sticky rice to brew rice liquor to drink toward the end of the Lunar New Year festivities
Nodikosa-kut	Fifteenth of January	River stepping-stone ritual
Kŏlgung-kut or *Kŏllip-kut*	After the fifteenth of January	Fundraising ritual, troupe plays for another village
Ture-kut	Various times annually	To alleviate repetitive agricultural tasks such as weeding or rice harvesting. Also performed after the final weeding, called *homisshishi* or "hoe-cleansing" holiday

NOTE: Based on Yang Chinsŏng's book, *Honam Jwado Imshil Pilbong-gut* (2000, 114–37).

such a continuous manner. While this is not exactly true, this is one of the ways in which the IPNPA has distinguished themselves from other *p'ungmul* groups that are recognized as Important Intangible Cultural Properties.[2]

Given *maŭl-kut*'s importance to the very identity of the IPNPA, anticipation ran high back in 2002 when the IPNPA was getting ready to hold its annual *Chŏngwŏl Taeborŭm-kut* back in the village of Pilbong for the first time since 1987. In retrospect, I was very fortunate to be there during this key time in 2002 and again, fourteen years later in 2016. Although I did not know this before I went, 2016 turned out to be another important juncture for reasons I will later explain. By any measure, both events required hard labor, not to mention continual cultivation in the intervening years, to produce and maintain Pilbong village as the cultural and spiritual center of the Pilbong *p'ungmul* style. In the next section, I will share some of these scenes of labor from 2002; while I focus mostly on the physical aspects of labor, I also reflect on how participants prepare their "heart/mind/soul," or *maŭm*, for ritual. I will then follow this up with my observations of preparing for the ritual in 2016.

Cultivating the Village

SCENES OF PREPARATION: LUNAR NEW YEAR IN PILBONG IN 2002

Scene 1: Contemplating "Open Emptiness" on the Bus

In the weeks leading up to and following the Lunar New Year in 2002, I found myself traveling (mostly by bus) up and down the South Korean peninsula racing from one *kut* ritual to the next, while also alternating between the transmission centers for Pilbong *p'ungmul* and Goseong Ogwangdae mask dance drama. One of my guides on some of these excursions was a fellow scholar, friend, and interlocutor named Cho Ch'unyŏng. During a visit to a smaller shamanic *kut* ritual at a shrine in Jeonju, Yi Chongjin (another scholar and friend of Cho's) recounted the folk saying (*sŏkdam* in Korean), "if you go to a *kut*, you should at least eat some rice-cake."[3] The mildly sweet and wonderfully chewy rice-cake called *ttŏk* in Korean is a staple offering of shrines for ancestor spirits or gods. While it would be rude to grab some *ttŏk* before or during a ritual, it is generally acceptable to partake in the shrine delicacies that are shared with participants after the conclusion of the ritual in a gesture of communal blessing. In this light, the saying seems to suggest that if you attend a *kut* ceremony—even if you are a non-believer—you should at least be open to receiving such blessings. Yi and Cho's ensuing conversation suggested that in the larger picture, a good *kut* should always be open and welcoming so that anyone would feel welcome enough to have some rice cake.

As we continued this discussion on the bus trip back up to Seoul, Cho connected this folk saying to what he believes is a core quality of the *madang*: a *yŏlyŏitnŭn piyŏissŭm* or a "state of open emptiness." Expanding his theory, he explained that this open emptiness replicates tropically—in a fractal-like fashion—within and across different domains. Physically, the *madang* can be seen as an empty space that is repeated all throughout the village: at the foot of the tutelary spirit tree, in front of the village spring and the village community building, in the upper field, not to mention the multiple locations within each house. Metaphorically, Cho expressed that this open emptiness of space can also be extended to the spirit, the mind, the stomach, etc. According to him, "the emptier one is beforehand, the more capacity it has to be filled" (personal communication). At first, I had trouble grasping what he was getting at because my vision of the *madang* was much the opposite—a space always brimming over with life, people, sounds, and activity.

Scene 2: Arriving in Pilbong

Approximately a week later, my return to Pilbong gave me the perfect opportunity to reflect on the concept of "open emptiness." In an excerpt from my field notes, I describe my initial reactions to my experience of Pilbong in the flurry of preparations.

> We arrived in Pilbong via Jeonju on Wednesday around 6 p.m., just a few days before the ritual was to begin on Saturday. Strangely, tonight was the best quality time I have spent with Pilbong folks in a long time—Ch'unyŏng was right. When I expressed apprehension about being a bother to the teachers during such a frenzied time, he assured me by saying that "people are busy, but their hearts are always open." Sure enough, their attitude was not as crazy, closed, or busy as I thought it might be had I been in their shoes. I am not sure how they pulled it off, but my guess was that their relaxed attitude is perhaps due to experience and that their openness goes hand in hand with the community spirit of the proceedings.
>
> Even though the transmission center was in full session when we arrived, things seemed relatively calm. This may be because student attendance was much lower than usual. When I talked with some of the students in the session, they told me that everyone knows that attending the week of the Lunar New Year ritual is a trade-off. Since the teachers are busy with preparations, it is not the best time to learn. Given the participatory nature of the transmission center (discussed in chapter 2), students are also expected to help. Most students who choose to come during this time understand that it is a unique service and experiential learning opportunity, or in the discourse of the *madang*, it is a meaningful way to practice *kongdongch'e* (community spirit). In my initial observations of Pilbong, Cho's theory did seem to ring true. The fact that Pilbong's Lunar New Year ritual is more of a "show, show, show" did not make this any less so; on the contrary, witnessing the communal attitude toward the mammoth amount of work that needed to be done only seemed to amplify Cho's theory.

Scene 3: Zones of Labor

As an independent ethnographer working alone, it is difficult to attain a bird's-eye view of all the aspects of preparation and production going into this event. Aside from not being able to be in multiple places at once, I quickly discovered that many of the work activities are divided into zones by gender, age, level of experience, or role within the Pilbong village or *p'ungmul* organization. As a woman, there were certain activities that I had more or less access to than others. For example, in my fieldnotes, I note that I only became aware of the male activity of slaughtering a pig or *twaeji-chapki* (literally "pig-catching") by talking with Ryu Han-p'il, one of the male teachers in residence:

> Ryu Han-p'il shared a lot of interesting stories about growing up in the country, and how *twaeji-chapki* always reminded him of the atmosphere of a village festival. I guess there is a male camaraderie that develops around the killing of a pig. He described how right after the pig is slaughtered, the men go around sharing parts of the raw meat, often the liver, while washing it all down with *soju* liquor.

Had I not talked to Han-p'il personally, I may have never learned of *twaeji-chapki* as a mode of male bonding.

In general, preparing food for the hundreds of people that come comprises a large chunk of the workload. In comparison to *twaeji-chapki*, the women of the village were much more visible in their roles preparing, cooking, and serving the food. In the days leading up to the event, one could see the women in front of the village center building (*maŭl hoegwan*), cooking in front of huge steaming cast-iron bowls heating over wood fires. Though this job is overseen by the women of the village, I did see some of the male teachers lending a hand along with the some of the female students who helped with chopping, serving, and clean-up. Though the women were more visible in this area, I learned from a staff meeting that certain men also had important roles, such as Yang Chinhwan, who was in charge of ordering all the food, beverages, alcohol, and other materials. Even so, this is somewhat suggestive of a patriarchal division of labor where men order the food and women do the cooking.

Other major responsibilities were divided among the main teachers/staff of the transmission center. In 2002, Han Chaehun oversaw communications and publicity. Han Chaehun and Ch'oe Ho-in took care of teaching at the transmission center, while Ch'oe Ho-in spearheaded the preparation of all the *madangs* in collaboration with their director, Yang Chinsŏng. As the IPNPA's leader, Yang Chinsŏng delegated these responsibilities and supervised most of the other work that was going on. His family, of course, worked in coordination with village elders who held their own meetings and took care of things such as preparing the *tangsan* (tutelary spirit) shrine for the ritual that would take place there, taking care of spinning thread from plant fibers by hand, and preparing other sacred sites in the village.

Another group of individuals who shoulder much of the work at the Pilbong transmission center are jokingly called *baeksu* (literally "white hand"). These self-proclaimed *baeksu* are generally young adults who are in between school, military, or job obligations and reside at the transmission center as unpaid apprentices. In exchange for free tuition, lodging, and food, they work and help out with running the center. Sometimes, this dedication leads to greater performance and teaching opportunities. The idle, "good for nothing" connotation of the *baeksu* term is ironic given that they are usually extraordinarily hardworking and devoted. Because of the ephemeral nature of their employment, *baeksu* often remain "behind the scenes" and do not receive as much credit for their work. Even so, the common progression of *baeksu* into teachers and performers is a testament to an apprenticeship process where the ability to work selflessly within a community is valued as highly as one's playing skill.

Scene 4: Preparing the Madangs

Since the Lunar New Year ritual had not been performed in Pilbong for many years, the physical *madangs* themselves needed an extraordinary amount of work. In order to accommodate the hundreds of people who would come that year, the *madangs* had to be emptied of debris, weeds, and excess vegetation, and the ground needed to be leveled and surfaced with fine gravel. The smaller sacred sites had to be decorated or demarcated with handmade straw rope that was interwoven with fluttery white paper. On Thursday afternoon before the performance, I was able to take part in the process, but as noted here in my fieldnotes, I had to bend the rules and stray out of my gendered work zone order to do so:

> In lieu of the *tapsa* (fieldtrip) to Pilbong, the male students were called on to go to the village to work and help clean while the female students were told to engage in individual practice (*kaein yŏnsŭp*). I decided to tag along with the male students and take pictures. Later, I found out that many of the women were resentful of being left out of this chance to help. When I walked up to the village, men whom I recognized as players in the troupe were riding around in tractors and dumping big piles of earthy reddish gravel onto the *tangsan madang* (tutelary spirit tree *madang*) and *sanjŏng madang* (mountaintop *madang*) sites. The *sanjŏng madang* where the evening *p'an-kut* was to take place needed a

lot of sand to cover its large surface area, which then needed to be compacted down (figure 3.1). They also assembled bamboo poles and hay into a huge teepee shape, to be burned in a bonfire after the *p'an-kut*.

The neglected village spring also needed a lot of work and that's where I ended up. The brush and debris needed to be cleared away and all the garbage and plastic burned (that was my job). There were probably many more things being done that I was not aware of. It was raining lightly throughout the day and though we all got pretty muddy, it was kind of soothing to hear the pretty, delicate sound of the raindrops falling on the yellow grass around us.

In the actual 2002 Lunar New Year ritual, the site of the village spring proved to be a pivotal site of Turnerian drama, so it was gratifying to have contributed to its preparation (figure 3.2).

Scene 5: Sacred Ropes and Flower Hats

On Thursday evening, the transmission students and apprentices worked on making the paper *kokkal mojas* or "flower hats" for the performers to wear during the event. On Friday during the day, I learned how to make some more of the straw rope, called *kŭmjul* (literally "prohibitive rope"), that was used to delineate the *madangs* by tightly winding pieces of straw together by hand. Practically speaking, once they are put in place, people are forbidden to enter the site before the ritual is to take place. They are also believed to ward off negative energy and bad spirits. Lastly, they help demarcate a space as clean and sacred (figure 3.2). In helping out and witnessing various stages of physically and spiritually clearing away space, I thought repeatedly of the appropriateness of Cho Ch'unyŏng's *madang* theory of "open emptiness." In addition, lending a hand in the clearing of these spaces made me feel bodily connected to them in a way I had not anticipated. Even though the number of actual villagers is dwindling, there are now communities of students, apprentices, and IPNPA members and staff who have forged similar attachments to places in Pilbong over the years.

Scene 6: Mae-kut — The Night Before

Friday evening, the night before the big event, about ten of the male members of the troupe went out in their regular clothes and played an informal *kut* at most of the major sites in the village. They also played in the homes of those who

FIGURE 3.1 Entertainment-oriented mountaintop *madang* (called the *sanjŏng madang*) for *p'ungmul* played in the *p'an-kut* format (2002). Photo by the author.

FIGURE 3.2 Village spring ritual site, cleared and marked off with sacred rope (2002). Photo by the author.

would host the *madangbalbi* (literally "stepping on the *madang*") portion of the ritual. I followed along to watch and take pictures. The people who attended were mainly people from the village. I wondered if perhaps they were doing it for the benefit of the television video crew from KBS who had been there all week to feature Pilbong's *Chŏngwŏl Taeborŭm-kut* for a show called *Event in Korea*. The reason for this is that they may have wanted to show that they were adhering to "tradition" by performing *mae-kut*, a ritual said to be performed on New Year's Eve to give thanks and set the mood and spirit for the larger Lunar New Year rituals to follow (table 3.1).[4] Regardless, I appreciated the opportunity to observe them play informally in a more intimate ritual setting, where, despite the rolling of cameras, there was much less pressure to put on a "show." It also served as a dress rehearsal for the next day's events, which must have helped to prepare the hearts, minds, and bodies for what would come the next day.

While they were playing, I could not help but notice that the transmission center's little white dog was gleefully following the troupe from one *madang* location to another. Even when she was barking, no one seemed to mind. This reminded me of a moment I had with Cho Ch'unyŏng while discussing his *madang* theory of "open emptiness." When I challenged him by saying that "open emptiness" could just as easily apply to the concert hall as it could the *madang*, he amended his definition by saying that "the *madang* is so open that even a dog would be welcome" (personal communication). Though dogs are perhaps the most familiar of domesticated animals, they also embody the wild, chaotic, noisy, and ludic qualities of nature. At a basic level, welcoming the dog into the *madang* represents a belief in humankind's connectedness to nature. It also signals an openness to the potential of noise. As Jacques Attali put it, with "noise is born disorder and its opposite, the world . . . It is at the heart of a progressive rationalization of aesthetics, and it is a refuge for residual irrationality; it is a means of power and a form of entertainment" (1985, 6).

COMING BACK TO PILBONG IN 2016

Although I have visited teachers at the Pilbong transmission center several times since 2002, I was not able to observe the Lunar New Year Festival again until February of 2016. While dogs were still very much part of the soundscape in 2016—not to mention their companions in chaos, disorder, and noise—much of the village had changed. As I made my way through its narrow paths, my natural inclination was to try to reconcile what I was seeing with what I remembered of

FIGURE 3.3 Older home in Pilbong village in a state of disrepair (2016). Photo by the author.

Pilbong circa 2002. Although I could easily pick out certain landmarks such as the tutelary spirit tree (*tangsan namu*) at the head of the village and the village center (*maŭl hoegwan*) just above it, much of what I saw was nearly unrecognizable. While I have long since accepted the high turnover of development in Seoul as par for the course, I naïvely expected Pilbong to have been preserved in somewhat the same manner as the art form for which it is known. Perhaps what struck me the most was Pilbong's dramatic state of uneven development. Not only was I surprised to see several abandoned older homes leaning over in a state of disrepair (figure 3.3), but there were just as many newer homes in brick and concrete that did little to blend in with older homes (albeit this trend began before 2002). To cap it off, several new ostentatious homes had cropped up nearby, one of which was constructed in a hybrid "log-cabin" style (figure 3.1 ⊙). When the subject came up over lunch, one of the main staff members and performers of the IPNPA explained that the reason for the abandoned homes is that as the older villagers have passed on and their children have moved to larger cities, they have neither the motivation to sell the properties nor the resources or motivation to maintain or renovate the homes. Meanwhile, new people with

Cultivating the Village 99

resources are moving into the village and building new properties, and the worry is that they will not be supportive of the IPNPA's activities.

These developments have eroded the expressive ecology of Pilbong by reducing the number of villagers who support and truly understand the IPNPA's activities. Perhaps in response to this, the IPNPA put in motion a plan to transform Pilbong into a "*p'ungmul* village" that was implemented in 2015–2016. These changes are impossible to miss, as the first thing one encounters upon entering is a large wooden sign that announces that this is the "original location of Pilbong-*kut* that is recognized by UNESCO as an Intangible Cultural Heritage of Humanity and designated as Important Intangible Cultural Property 11-5 by the South Korean government" (figure 3.2 ⊙). Smaller signs dot the village, marking and directing visitors to important sites throughout. Some of the ritual sites only received upgrades, while other sites have been completely reconstructed. In addition, several new cultural landmarks, buildings, and other outdoor structures were constructed specifically for this event (figure 3.3 ⊙).

For context, the main sites of the Lunar New Year ritual (at least from 2002) were the village center *madang*, the tutelary spirit tree, the stone prayer cairns, the spring, several homes within the village, and a large *madang* for performing the evening *p'an-kut* and bonfire. In terms of upgrades, the walls around the "grandfather tutelary spirit tree," or *harabŏji tangsan namu*, and stone prayer cairns have been fortified and now have new hardscaping that further define this area (figure 3.4). Up the hill and toward the rear of the village, they created another site for a new grandmother or *halmŏni* tutelary spirit tree that was ostensibly cut down for lumber during the Japanese colonial era (1910–1945). The new site boasts several newly planted trees and an accompanying set of stone prayer cairns.

By far, the most controversial change was the construction of a new village spring situated near grandmother *tangsan* spirit tree at the top of the village. The spring was essentially a square stone structure with no natural water flowing from a well or spring (see figure 3.5, compare with older spring in figure 3.2). While I will go into the specifics of how this played out in performance in the next chapter, suffice it to say, the IPNPA received many negative comments about the new "spring." Interestingly, the most vocal critics were the many photographers who came expecting to photograph a more "authentic," or at least older-looking ritual site. When the subject came up, the IPNPA director, Yang Chinsŏng, noted with some exasperation that the new spring was actually constructed at the site where the original spring used to be. They also recreated a grain and rice pound-

FIGURE 3.4 Grandfather Guardian Spirit Tree (*haraboji tangsan namu*) located near the entrance to Pilbong village (2016). Photo by the author.

FIGURE 3.5 New village spring with Pilbong mountain in the background and marked off with sacred rope (2016). Photo by the author.

ing mill (*tidilpang-a*, traditionally powered by steps) that also used to be located close to the original spring.

Another surprise for repeat visitors was the construction of a beautiful brand-new Korean-style residence with courtyard and gate that is supposed to represent the home of the *sangsoe* or leader of the ensemble. According to Yang Chinsŏng, they had received a grant to build multiple residences that would form a sort of a *p'ungmul*-village-within-a-village (personal communication). However, they did not receive enough funds to complete this plan so they were left with just one house. From talking with IPNPA staff, I surmised that the main reasoning for doing this is that the number of households who can host the Lunar New Year ritual in their home is quickly disappearing. In 2016, the only "real" home that they visited was that of the mother of the current leader and *sangsoe* Yang Chinsŏng.

While the village center *madang* remained much the same, they did create a brand-new outdoor performance *madang*, located just a few steps away from the representative *sangsoe* residence. This circular *madang* performance space was surrounded by a tiered stone seating area and framed by a multi-paneled granite backdrop etched with narrative text and representations of Pilbong *p'ungmul* performers, characters, and several generations of leaders or *sangsoe* going back to the late nineteenth century (figure 3.6). They also had to clear a large additional field on a terrace just behind this performance space for the bonfire. In 2002, they performed the *p'an-kut* and bonfire in more or less the same large field, but the new performance *madang* was too small to accommodate playing around a large bonfire safely.

Finally, they finished off the *p'ungmul* village area with additional park-like structures and spaces to better enable the festive public nature of the event. These included an additional barbecue pit area and a transitional area to conduct educational activities and sell food and other market goods. Down below, there was another multipurpose terrace with public restrooms, facilities for cooking, and space to accommodate tables and tents for dining. All the *madangs* needed to be finished off with a layer of fine reddish gravel, both to enhance their rustic look and also to prevent excessive mud. Due to unavailability, however, they were unable to secure the gravel in time for this event.

Because of the addition of these new spaces, there was more work to do but fewer people to do it. As in 2002, this included preparing all the sacred spaces and decorating them with the handwoven "prohibitive rope," or *kŭmjul*. On Friday, many of the male apprentices and students were busy mounting huge

FIGURE 3.6 New outdoor performance space called the *kut madang* in the Pilbong village. The bonfire area made of bamboo and straw is visible on the upper field on the left (2016). Photo by the author.

flags on poles. While the most important flag is the one that was mounted in the village common near the village center building where they begin the event with a *ki-kut* or "flag ritual," many other flags were mounted in prominent places around the main performance area. In general, flags are an important part of the visual material identity of *p'ungmul*, so much so that at least two players are designated to hold flags throughout the entire ritual. Although there were enough younger IPNPA members and apprentices around to complete these preparations, involvement from college and high school students attending the transmission center in the week preceding the Lunar New Year ritual paled in comparison to earlier years. It used to be that helping with the ritual preparations was highly valued as a communal, educational experience, but now it seems that students tend to avoid coming the week preceding Lunar New Year.

Cultivating the Village **103**

Food preparation worked in much the same way as it did in 2002. While the whole Yang family contributed to securing all the special sacrificial foods for the tutelary spirit tree shrine, a small group of women took care of most of the food preparation to feed all of the participants during the day-long event. As in 2016, the cooking was still directed by Yang Chinsŏng's mother and consisted of a mixture of relatives, women from the village, and female IPNPA members. The director, Yang Chinsŏng, must be very accustomed to assigning people participatory roles, because when I arrived, he asked me if I wanted to "play the *sogo* drum, or maybe . . . wash dishes?" I demurred by saying that I would be taking pictures and video. I did end up helping with the cooking. The free dinner they provided for everyone consisted of a spicy pork and vegetable soup with rice and two vegetable side dishes. When I arrived on the scene on Friday, the women were working in a large vinyl greenhouse, finishing up the second side dish consisting of reconstituted dried zucchini in a garlic sesame sauce. In a change from 2002, some of the women were also preparing simple foods to sell as snacks, such as fish cake patties on sticks or *odeng*, a popular Korean street comfort food. Interestingly, they were very concerned about pricing things at cost or below, so as not to be perceived as trying to make a profit. Other available foods included fried savory pancakes, drinks like *makkŏlli* (milky rice beer), rice cakes, tea, roast chestnuts, and sweet potatoes.

The sum of these preparatory physical changes that they implemented over the course of one year (2015–2016) prove to me that the IPNPA is truly entering a new era. While I am sure it was a few years in coming, I believe that it represents a shift that is of equal consequence to what I saw in 2002 when the IPNPA brought the ritual back to the village for the first time in many years. At the very least, it appears that the Lunar New Year ritual has become even less oriented toward serving the residents of the village and more toward serving the public. In fact, it is telling that they only visited one living household in 2016 for the *madangbalbi* portion of the Lunar New Year event. They also did not perform *mae-kut* the evening before the big event, which would have been intended to serve the village residents in a more private setting. Despite all these changes, the spirit with which the IPNPA throws their heart, bodies, and soul into preparing for the ritual remains unchanged.

STRAINING TO SUSTAIN THE EXPRESSIVE
ECOLOGY OF THE VILLAGE

Yang Chinsŏng's back decided to give out just days before the 2016 Lunar New Year ritual as he was working on prepping the enormous bonfire that concludes the event. His strained back greatly impacted the flow of the ritual and served as a visceral reminder of the precarity of the expressive ecology of Pilbong. Just as the back bears the weight of the body, the village in Korea carries the weight of a lot of cultural baggage. In other words, the village (much like the *madang*) operates as a cultural trope with powerful, nostalgic connotations as a repository of "authentic" Korean culture or as a symbol of an idealized pre-modern, pre-colonial past. A publicity document from the 2003 "Pilbong New Moon" or Lunar New Year festival provides a telling picture of the kinds of statements IPNPA practitioners make about the village and its relation to *p'ungmul* ritual.

THE PERFECTLY PRESERVED PILBONG NEW MOON FESTIVAL

Due to its geographic exclusion from the "outer world," Pilbong Village has remarkably preserved its traditional forms of celebration.[5]

P'ungmul as a form of social communication and wish-making

The eroding of community-based values and ways of living is no longer a problem at the individual level: it is a problem we now have to face as a people, as a society. The Lunar New Year Full Moon Festival at Pilbong is significant in that it gives us a chance to enliven the values of sharing and giving that lies at the back of all our hearts. (Hwang Sunju 2003)

Toward the end of the document, it implies that due to the efforts of the previous leader Yang Sunyong, village *kut*, or ritual, has survived "in a time when modernization [is] cutting off our ties to our traditional heritage" (Hwang Sunju 2003). In contrast to the modern city, the village is portrayed as a communal utopia—an all-too-familiar designation that finds resonance in many parts of the world. The persistence of such imaginings and the complex sedimentations of thought and practice that are deposited in such places have led theorists like Foucault to reconsider the meaning of utopian spaces in recent times. Just as Pilbong is not a utopia in real life, Foucault argues that civilization has produced "counter-sites" or "effectively enacted utopias," which he refers to as *heterotopias*. Just as the village is seen as "other" to the spaces most modern-day Koreans inhabit—namely, cities—heterotopias are "outside of all places" and "have a function in relation to all the space that remains" (1986, 24–27).

Foucault's heterotopias are resonant with villages like Pilbong in other key ways. First, Foucault sees heterotopias as somehow privileged, sacred, and often equipped with "a system of opening and closing that both isolates them and makes them penetrable" (1986, 24–26). This principle certainly applies to the marking off of sacred sites within the village during ritual times. In addition, the village is much more open to guests during Lunar New Year or other public events, and less welcoming at other times. Second, he writes that "society, as its history unfolds, can make an existing heterotopia function in a very different fashion" (1986, 25). With the full-fledged *p'ungmul* transmission complex located within walking distance and the recent construction of the "*p'ungmul*-village-within-a-village," Pilbong is transforming into a cultural attraction that already draws tens of thousands of students and cultural tourists who visit during certain times of the year. Lastly, Foucault sees heterotopias as capable of juxtaposing different senses of space and "slices in time" (1986, 25–26). This is made possible through bodily, sensory experience. For example, by stepping into Pilbong, we know we are in the present. And yet the sights, smells, and textures of the village trigger associations of the past that make us feel "as if the entire history of humanity reaching back to its origin were accessible in a sort of immediate knowledge" (1986, 26).

While provocative, Foucault leaves the question of the larger significance of heterotopias somewhat open. Here, I turn to social scientist Satish Deshpande, who redefines heterotopias (in relation to nation-space and Hindu communalism) as follows:

> Heterotopias are very special kinds of places because (and here I depart from Foucault's formulation) they mediate, in a mirror-like fashion, between utopias and ideological subjects. In other words, heterotopias enable—incite, compel, invite—people to see themselves reflected in some utopia. They function as an ideological hinge, linking social subjects (people) with a possible political-moral identity (utopia) that they could assume (inhabit). (Deshpande 1998, 24)

In this fashion, a village such as Pilbong is invested with more than the survival of a *p'ungmul* ritual; it is a link to a utopian vision of a specifically Korean communal cultural identity. Just as Foucault stipulates that a heterotopia is an "effectively *enacted* utopia," Pilbong offers the possibility for people to embody and experience this identity in a powerful way—whether in acts of cultural transmission (chapter 2), preparation (chapter 3), or performance/ritual (chapter 4). This process contributes to the cultivation of both site-specific cultural spaces and certain kinds of "social" subjects.[6] Ultimately, I argue that these expressive practices contribute to how various group identities (national, regional, political, class, gender) come to be deeply embodied and mapped onto places such as Pilbong. Crucially, it is Pilbong's *effectiveness* as a *utopia* that is *enacted* through various acts of transmission, preparation, and performance/ritual that differentiates it from other historic areas designated for preservation such as the Bukchon Hanok district in Seoul and Yangdong village in Gyeongju. This puts Pilbong more on track with developments in Hahoe village in Andong, famous for its ritualized mask dance drama called Hahoe *Pyŏlshin-kut T'alnori*. However, because Pilbong does not quite compare to Hahoe's natural beauty and more cohesive state of preservation—with its uniform thatched roof construction and stunning riverside cliff views—its connection to *p'ungmul* will likely remain its main draw.[7] In the end, only time will tell whether the continuing heterotopian transformation of Pilbong will be worth all of the strain and ultimately succeed in sustaining the expressive ecology of the village.

FOUR

"Abundant Kut, Abundant Life"
The Place of Ritual P'ungmul

Yang Sunyong, the previous leader of Pilbong, is often credited for promoting the concept of *p'ujin-kut, p'ujin-salm*, roughly translated as "abundant *kut* (ritual), abundant life." One could see this as a distillation of the many stories he liked to tell about how to play *p'ungmul*. In one passage, he is quoted as saying that "*kut* must be played abundantly, you have to put the whole of life into it in order to create a world flowing with *shinmyŏng* (spiritual catharsis)" (Yang 2000, 74). As his son and current leader, Yang Chinsŏng, put it: "life is *kut*, and *kut* is life" (Yang 2000, 74). In other words, ritual *p'ungmul* is best played and experienced as part of daily life. During the Lunar New Year, Pilbong beckons with the narrative that by participating in a long-running "traditional" *p'ungmul* ritual, it is possible to make it (or at least pieces of it) part of one's own daily life. The underlying social or spiritual message is that all participants (performers, staff, volunteers, ritual attendees) should give as abundantly as they hope to receive.

During the earlier period of my fieldwork in the early 2000s, "abundant *kut*, abundant life" was central to the Imshil Pilbong Nongak Preservation Association's philosophy. Another important aspect of the IPNPA's identity is its government-recognized status as a representative example of a well-preserved village-based *p'ungmul* ritual. On the cover of the 2016 brochure for Pilbong's *Chŏngwŏl Taeborŭm-kut*, or Lunar New Year Full Moon Ritual, these sentiments have been condensed into the English homonymic phrases of "*Kut* is Good!"[1] or "Feel so Good! Pilbong!"

The subtle shifts in this discourse can be seen as a mostly successful response to changing times. In the late 1990s and early 2000s when I first began interacting with Pilbong teachers, they were already used to drawing large numbers of people from other areas to their transmission camps and events. For example, the Lunar New Year ritual drew around 500 to 600 people in 2002, more than 75 percent of whom were not from Pilbong. This number has only grown since then; in 2016, I estimated about 1,500 in attendance. When calculating the total number of visitors who come to Pilbong annually for all of their programs, the number of visitors has grown to approximately 60,000 (IPNPA brochure 2016).

In the approximately two decades that I have been researching the IPNPA, I have wrestled with how to ethnographically interpret these changes in the field. Do I interpret this discourse as simply a manifestation of the authoritative local voice of Yang Sunyong? Or is it being woven into a promotional story of cultural heritage that appeals to domestic tourists looking to experience or affirm their own distinctive regional and/or national identity? In another vein, is it becoming part of what anthropologist and cultural tourism scholar Edward Bruner might call a "pretour" or "master narrative" that is used to attract an array of regional, national, and international visitors? In *Culture on Tour: Ethnographies of Travel*, Bruner suggests that the lines between these interpretive possibilities have long been blurred:

> Tourist tales are not fixed, self-contained entities. Our stories merge with theirs, genres become blurred, the border between tourism and ethnography becomes porous, and the line between subject and object becomes obscure. (2005, 23)

For Bruner, "tourist tales" align closely with what Bruner calls the "trip as told," which he differentiates from the trip as lived or experienced.

In a nod to Bruner's blurred realm, I aim to investigate Pilbong's Lunar New Year ritual as simultaneously a village ritual, a heritage performance, and a cultural destination woven together with the master narrative of "abundant ritual, abundant life." One of the main goals of this chapter is to document how this idea plays out in this ritual event, as well as in the lived reality and experience of its participants. The way that the master narrative compares, then, to the lived reality and experience of this event is critical to understanding what it takes to sustain Pilbong as a site-specific expressive ecology. Another goal is to analyze how this event—and by extension the place of Pilbong itself—is produced through *madang*-related discourses (table 0.1). By comparing how this ritual was performed in 2002 and later in 2016, I hope to provide a picture (however incomplete) of how this narrative, lived reality, and experience has shifted over time.

While acknowledging the blurring of ritual and cultural tourism, it is important to highlight Pilbong's unique position within this broader phenomenon. For example, I argue throughout this chapter that one of the ways in which Pilbong differs from other cultural tourism destinations is the degree to which it fosters a high degree of participation through performative ritual and bodily engagement, *madang*-based practices, improvisational gender play, and Turnerian social drama. These participatory strategies help contribute to a more open-ended socio-temporal engagement—or that feeling of living in the moment—that I argue is crucial to the continued relevance of the form. Whether as a destination for cultural transmission and education, ritual, performance, or cultural tourism, Pilbong's status as a representative example of village-based *p'ungmul* continues to draw people to the expressive ecology of Pilbong. The IPNPA's emphasis on cultural transmission and education is critical because it helps foster more informed participants for their events. In this chapter, I shine a light on this signature event and examine the power of ritual performance to spur people to engage with Pilbong's expressive ecology in a memorable, if highly directed way.

BRINGING LUNAR NEW YEAR BACK TO PILBONG IN 2002

During the week of preparations prior to the Lunar New Year ritual (detailed in chapter 3), the weather was mostly cloudy and rainy. But on Saturday, February 23, 2002, the day that the IPNPA had decided to perform the ritual for the first time in Pilbong since 1989, the sun came out clear as a bell, cutting through the cold. As I walked toward the village, I was greeted by volunteers and invited to sign a guestbook at the registration tables. Even back in 2002, the event had outgrown its humbler "abundant ritual, abundant life" beginnings to become more of a production that embraced outsiders in numbers that greatly outweighed the villagers. Glossy, professionally designed programs were made available and included information about the troupe's history, accomplishments, mission, and personnel list, as well as a schedule of the day's events:

1:30   *Ki-kut—Tongch'ŏng madang* (Flag ceremony—Village common *madang*)
2:00   *Tangsanje* (*Tangsan* ritual)
2:30   *Saem-kut* (Spring ceremony)
3:00   *Madangbalbi* (literally "stepping on the *madang*," referring to visiting individual homes)
6:00   Dinner

7:00   *Taeborŭm p'an-kut* (Full moon *p'an-kut*)
11:00 *Taljip t'aeugi* (Bonfire)

As guests walked into the center of the village, they were greeted by another table where participants could donate and take a piece of white paper and write down their New Year's wish to tuck into the sacred ropes around the prayer cairns or perhaps burn in the bonfire later that evening. This small invitational gesture of asking people to include their personal wishes is a common and effective method of eliciting participation because it appeals to an individual's hopes and then symbolically binds these hopes into a community expression as they are displayed, collected, and/or burned in the bonfire.

Though the participants trickled in and out, by the end of the day there were as many as 600 people in attendance. The residents of Pilbong and the troupe itself comprised about eighty people. Interestingly, the troupe that year included at least one White female American member who was in Jeonju studying *p'ungmul* and teaching English. In addition, there were a modest number of residents from the nearby town of Gangjin and other neighboring villages. The majority of participants, however, consisted of hundreds of students and former students of Pilbong *p'ungmul-kut*. There was also a small contingent from Japan, a handful of Americans, and several regional and national television crews. While it has not been uncommon to see some non-Korean enthusiasts at Pilbong's Lunar New Year, this has occurred primarily through word of mouth and not through tourist agencies, guides, or brokers.

Ki-kut *and* Tangsanje: *Beginnings*

It became clear that things were going to begin soon when the *nabal* (long-necked valveless bugle) was sounded, signaling the players to finish their lunch and gather in full dress, transforming the wintery, muted colors of the village common into a riot of color. Whenever I see *p'ungmul* players wearing their characteristic white garments called *minbok* overlaid with vests and sashes in blue, yellow, red, and black[2]—complete with the colorful hats (*kokkal moja*) topped with large paper flowers in white, yellow, and magenta—I cannot help but think about the aptness in the saying that "*p'ungmul* is the flower of the *minjung*," or "common people." I first heard this from Yang Chinsŏng. Though this saying exudes a certain dreamy idealism, Yang managed to bring it down to earth by pointing out that most of the year, farmers would work in the fields, often with their legs knee-deep in the rice paddies and their bodies and clothes in constant contact with dirt and mud (personal communication). In this context, even the act of wearing colorful, clean garments was a rare pleasure and source of joy. Ultimately, Yang's message is that *p'ungmul* should be seen as a precious and positive form of expression that "blooms" from the otherwise difficult life of the *minjung*. I am not sure how much "pleasure" today's players derive from wearing their outfits, but the colorful, traditional outfits do have a transformative effect on the body and the *madang*, and everyone tried to look their best. When most of the performers had gathered in the village common (*tongch'ŏng madang*) with their instruments tied around their bodies or held in their hands, Yang Chinsŏng somewhat unceremoniously signaled everyone to start playing the flag ritual or *ki-kut* (figure 4.1 ⊙).

Pilbong performances almost always begin with a series of "warm-up" rhythms called *kutnaenŭn karak*.[3] Today's event was no exception. The main purpose of *kutnaenŭn karak* is to give the players a chance to synchronize their sense of time, movement, and breath with one another. Since this ritual is meant to honor the flags of the village, the flags were placed in the center of the *madang* while the troupe rotated in a circle around them. While they played the rhythms associated with the flag ritual, the participants gathered around and the *chapsaek* characters made their entrances. The *halmi* or grandmother character, played by Cho Yun-mi, wasted no time in getting attendees involved by urging them to wave their arms back and forth to the music. I was surprised to see how the participants became so easily engaged this early in the performance and I realized that this was also a time for the participants to warm-up and synchronize with the performers. Another surprise was the entry of Mr. Kim,[4] who was dressed as the young woman (*kakshi*) character, especially given his usual role of playing the *sogo* drum. Dressed in a dark purple *hanbok* (Korean traditional dress) with fake pillow-like breasts tied onto the outside of the bodice for all to see, Mr. Kim's entrance caused a chain reaction of shock and laughter throughout the crowd. Before moving on, they bowed three times to the flags in the center of the circle while playing a series of beats, called *ŏrŭm karak*, that speed up progressively with each bow. In keeping with tradition, one of the *chapsaek* characters (in this case, Mr. Kim) made sure to pour three cups of rice alcohol (*makkŏlli*) at the base of the flags. After the bows, they played some connecting rhythms and made their way toward the next location: the *tangsan namu*, or tutelary (guardian) spirit tree.

Had *Tangsanje* (a rite specifically to give offerings to the village tutelary tree spirits) been performed separately, as outlined as traditional practice in Yang

Chinsŏng's text (2000, 125–29), they would only need to perform a simpler ritual called *tangsan-kut* at this juncture. However, they elected that year to fold the *Tangsanje* into the *Chŏngwŏl Taeborŭm-kut*. Interestingly, this move gave the participants more to experience in this part of the ritual, and therefore offered more possibilities for the participants to engage in *madang*-related discourses. For example, the elements of rituality, community, and embodied participation were all brought to the fore because of this change. At the same time, it also propelled a normally private *Tangsanje* into a more public activity (video 4.1 🔊). In 2002, this change did not proceed without a few snags.

Whether a full-fledged *Tangsanje* or simpler *tangsan-kut*, the mode of entry into the *tangsan* area near the entrance of the village is the same and quite effectively demonstrates some key characteristics of the *madang*-type space such as: (1) the sense of entering a space marked as "other," special or sacred; and (2) a symbolic and dynamic reversal of movement and flow (connected to the cyclic notion of yin and yang). In 2002, when the troupe arrived at the base of the hill where the tutelary spirit tree is located, two of the flagholders immediately formed a gate by tipping their flagpoles into an inverted V-shape. After the group had assembled and the rhythmic series had been played to completion, the troupe members began a new rhythm as they proceeded one-by-one underneath the flagpole gates—only this time, they processed in reverse order, with the *chapsaek* characters first, then the *sogo*, *puk*, *changgo*, *ching*, and *soe* instrumentalists last. Similarly, they also proceeded around the tutelary spirit tree in clockwise motion, which is a reversal of the counterclockwise motion they normally move in.

Although the flagpole mode of entry is used in other sections of the ritual (i.e., to symbolize acceptance to enter the home of a host during the *madang-balbi*), here it is used to convey respect to the tutelary spirits and to signal the entry into a differentiated realm. The feeling of suspension from "normal" life is further accentuated by the reversal of direction and order. The initial entry of the *chapsaek* characters may also have a practical function as a way of facilitating their more pronounced role in the *Tangsanje*. It is important to point out that these techniques are particularly effective precisely because they are performed *in situ*—in the *hyŏnjang*—with an actual, historically recognized and deeply rooted *tangsan* tree. It would be difficult to recreate the same sacred sense of place in any other location or in front of any other tree.[5]

After circling the tutelary spirit tree several times, the troupe gathered in front of an altar at the base of the tree that was filled to the brim with an elaborate arrangement of sacrificial food items. Here, they paused in their playing to allow a village elder in a dark robe to begin conducting various ritual actions at the altar. Then the members of the troupe were given the opportunity to bow and offer monetary donations to the tutelary spirits. Though the attendees seemed engaged enough as observers, some of the *chapsaek* characters (especially the *taep'osu* or hunter character) began to encourage several people to participate in the ritual by bowing, donating some money, and making personal wishes. At this point, the elder who was conducting the *tangsan* ritual became mildly upset as he expressed his disapproval about the direction the ritual was taking. His discomfort became especially obvious as the attendees started taking the food from the altar to share with one another. Although it is customary to share this food after the ritual is over, some participants did not wait long enough and started grabbing the food in a manner that was perceived as disrespectful.

Although the *chapsaek* were trying very hard to create an atmosphere of inclusion and community, it was clear at this point that community coherence should not be so easily assumed. At no time was the lack of connection between the ritual intentions of the village community and the general ritual attendees clearer than when members were asked to declare their wishes; instead of tailoring them to the needs of the village, most answered in a more individualistic vein, hoping for a boyfriend or girlfriend. Although these individuals were most likely being true to their innermost desires, had they been more attuned to the village community purpose of the tutelary spirit ritual, they may have wished for something more appropriate to the occasion. In terms of *madang* discourse, it made sense that the troupe tried to create community by including the attendees through ritual and embodied participation. However, this was one of those moments when the *madang*-influenced discourse of inclusion did not play out smoothly in practice, exposing a rift between the villagers and outsiders. However, just as the troupe reversed directions (counterclockwise around the tree) before moving on to the next site, the moment of conflict soon dissipated.

Saem-kut: Hyŏnjang, *Social Drama, and Performative Misfirings*

The *saem-kut*, or spring ceremony, opened up a discrepancy of another, more obvious, nature. In this case, the water's dubious and unused state ran against the ritual's main premise of blessing the spring as an active, pure, and generously flowing water source (figure 3.2). As a result, this made everyone rethink what this ritual was for. Though moments of chaos or crisis (*nanjang*) can disrupt the flow of an event, they also open the *madang* to the possibilities of play, improvisation, and what Korean scholars such as Im Chint'aek and Pak Hŭngchu refer to as the *hyŏnjang*, or the quality of "being in the moment."[6] When moments like these happen, they often elicit strong emotions—fear, anger, joy, and laughter. In the case of the spring ceremony, this crisis gave rise to one of the more spontaneous and interactive moments of the whole day (video 4.2 🔊).

Much of this was played out in the *tŏkdam*, a form of stylized speech or oral verse that usually performs some type of performative ritual action (i.e., blessing or establishing approval). *Tŏkdam* is an important, though often overlooked, component of *p'ungmul* practice that is initiated primarily by the *sangsoe*, or leader of the group. Performing *tŏkdam* requires great skill, wit, charisma, and presence of mind. In the Lunar New Year Full Moon ceremony, aspects of *p'ungmul* such as singing, eliciting *ch'uimsae* (responsorial shouts), and *tŏkdam* can make a huge difference in the atmosphere of the event and are therefore very important skills for a *sangsoe* to master. Though good *tŏkdam* incorporates improvised speech, it also relies heavily on stylistic conventions and rhythmic delivery. In the Pilbong style, the pattern of rhythmic emphasis in the *tŏkdam* often correlates with the rhythms that are played either before or after the *tŏkdam*. According to Yang Chinsŏng's book (2000, 117), the conventional verses given for the spring ceremony are short and simple.

Atta kŭ-mul chok'una	Oh, this water is really good!
Adŭllak'o, ttallak'o	Give birth to a son, give birth to a daughter
Miyŏkkuge pammalse!	Mix your rice with your seaweed soup!

The choice of "seaweed soup" at the end is significant because it is said to help women recover after giving birth, and rice is key because it is considered the main carbohydrate staple of the Korean diet. In this way, this verse links the water of the spring not only to general nutritional health, but also to female fertility, and by extension, the continued health and survival of future offspring in the village. This and other verses are often accompanied by a stylized call and response. For example, when the leader calls out "*Hwadong!*"[7] everyone follows with an enthusiastic "*Ye-i!*" Thus, *tŏkdam* often includes call and response, and is integrated with the practice of responsorial shouts (*ch'uimsae*), elicited from members of the troupe or attendees.

The ritual function of blessing the spring also includes the act of drinking the water in conjunction with the performative speech of the *tŏkdam*.[8] In 2002's spring ceremony, the doubtful drinkability of the water was the cause of a much-expanded and highly interpolated *tŏkdam* (video 4.2 🔊). To better understand the social dynamics of what occurred, I turn to Victor Turner's four phases of "social drama" or what he calls "public episodes of tensional irruption" that consist of "units of aharmonic or disharmonic process, arising in conflict situations" (1974, 33–37). Here, Turner proposes four "processual units": breach, crisis, redress, and re-integration, or alternatively, a schism (1974, 38). In the transcription and analysis that follows, it is evident that this *tŏkdam* corresponds easily to these four sections.

The first section represents a breach of convention in the way that the *sangsoe* leader tries to immediately defer drinking the water and later seems to lose his resolve. The others respond with a round of repetitive remarks, exclaiming repeatedly that the water is good, until finally, someone yells out the truth.

> ***Sangsoe (Soe 1): Hwadong!***
> Participants: Ye!
> ***Sangsoe: Ah, hunter (taep'osu), come over here.***
> *Taep'osu* (Hunter): *Aigo, aigo, aigo*, this water, I just drank some. Since I already drank a cupful, now it's the *sangsoe*'s turn to drink . . . [random comments, laughter]
> Soe 2: *Atta* that water is good, *A-tta* this water is really good!
> *Taep'osu: Atta* that water is really good!
> Soe 2: The water even *looks* good.
> *Taep'osu*: That's right!
> *Ch'angbu* (Male entertainer): [Scooping up a bowlful of water] Ah, you can see everything, in here you can see all there is to see.
> *Taep'osu*: Uh-huh, look at how clean that water is.
> Soe 2: *A-tta*, you know the water is good, you're just using this as an excuse to say how good it is. [laughter]
> **Soe 3: That broth is like undiluted soy sauce, *chinguk*!**[9]
> ***Sangsoe: All of a sudden, my wits have left me.***
> *Ch'angbu*: Wait, wait, wait . . .
> *Taep'osu*: You were about to make me drink.
> *Ch'angbu*: [He makes a motion to strain the water of debris with his hands, after which everyone squeals.] After I've strained it, this water is okay. [gives water to *sangsoe*]

This is a rare occurrence of being in-the-moment (*hyŏnjang*) where the performers go way off script, which prompts the *sangsoe* leader to slip and say, "my wits have left me."

116 *Local Transmission and Ritual Performance*

In the next section, the situation escalates to the second stage of *crisis* (albeit a mild one). Here, it reaches a point where, in Turner's words, it is "least easy to don masks or pretend there is nothing rotten in the village" (Turner 1974, 39). In this unit, the *sangsoe* leader tries to perform the verse as he is supposed to, but instead, he ends up departing from established practice by making the hunter (*taep'osu*) drink first. The situation also reaches a point of no return when the *sangsoe* publicly acknowledges the problematic state of the water by saying that they need to play their instruments a much longer time in order to remedy the situation. Though this statement demands some suspension from reality, it does attest to the integral role of music-making in the overall ritual practice.

> *Sangsoe*: **Hwadong!**
> Participants: Ye-i!
> *Sangsoe*: **Ah, today, umm, we're here to play *saem-kut* [random shouts of affirmation]**
> *Sangsoe*: **These *chapsaek* have strained the water, helped themselves already, and *now* they want to turn it over to the *sangsoe*!**
> **Now that I look at this water, *Ya-tta*, it actually looks good enough to drink!** [laughter]
> *Taep'osu* (Hunter): He's going to taste it and see!
> Soe 4: Since people have drunk cleanly, today, you just have to do it.
> *Sangsoe*: **Anyway, today I have to play *a lot* for *saem-kut***
> **Because if I drink from here, then I'll be full . . .**
> **This time though, it's . . . the hunter's turn!** [participants respond in agreement]
> *Taep'osu*: I drank just a second ago, see, look at how wet my beard is!
> *Sangsoe*: **Ah, come on, even if you've drunk, what's the big deal?**

The *sangsoe* leader begins to take *redressive* actions in the third phase by historically re-framing the situation by personally attesting that the water used to be very refreshing in the past. The hunter's act of drinking can be seen as a form of embodied redress, symbolizing an acceptance of the water's condition.

> *Taep'osu* (Hunter): [He finally drinks.] Okay, now it's the *sangsoe*'s turn to drink, I'm going to take out all the nonsense, until it's clear and clean.
> *Ch'angbu* (Male entertainer): Here, I'll make it clear. [pretends to spit onto his hands while attempting to strain the water]
> *Sangsoe*: **Don't do that.**

Ritual P'ungmul 117

Taep'osu: It's done . . . ya, ya ya! [The *ch'angbu* makes another move to spit.]
Ch'angbu: Yup, now it's clear.
Soe 4: Ahh, you're making such a scene.
Taep'osu: Ah, the *sangsoe*'s throat must be thirsty, c'mon now.
Sangsoe: *Atta*, since I have drunk this water before
I mean, a long time ago, our spring
Our spring's water is really tasty
Why doesn't Mr. P. D. (project director for television) have a cup?
 [offers to others, but no takers]
Sangsoe: Seeing that I have drunk this water from ages ago.
Participants: *Olshigu*! (a typical shout of encouragement, or *ch'uimsae*)

In the last phase, the situation heads toward *reintegration*, as the *sangsoe* is forced to come to terms with the water. As he tries to say the proper verse again, it is interesting that no one will let him get away with it unless he actually drinks the water himself.

Sangsoe: *Atta*, this water is so good, give birth to a son, give birth to a daughter, mix your rice with your seaweed soup! [muddled response from the participants]
Ahhh . . . how come there is no response?
Ch'angbu (Male entertainer): You gotta drink it first and then do it, drink.
Taep'osu (Hunter): How come you keep on mixing your rice? [After a moment, the *sangsoe* quits stalling and finally drinks the water.]
Sangsoe: *Atta*, this water is so good, give birth to a son, give birth to a daughter, mix your rice with your seaweed soup! [short *ch'uimsae* from participants]
***Atta*, this water is so good, *pŏlkŏk, pŏlkŏk*,[10] drink it up!**

Finally, the *tŏkdam* sticks the second time around and the situation resolves as the troupe launches into a particularly robust and celebratory bout of rhythms that mirror the *tŏkdam*. Interestingly, the playing intensifies later with the inclusion of *tchaktŭrŭm*, which is an optional variant in the *hwimori* rhythm that features fast hocketing between the *soe* players. Before *tchaktŭrŭm*, the *soe* players drop out, heightening the drama. This also opens up a sonic space for other participants to interpolate their responsorial shouts or for the *changgo* players to improvise their own rhythmic variations (video 4.2).

Based on my observations of the spring ceremony in other villages, the end of the ceremony would have been marked by a gathering of participants around the spring so that they could also taste the water before moving on. I imagine that the water's state was the main reason this did not happen in 2002. Otherwise, this would have been another good opportunity for participants to engage in the *madang* through embodied participation. Even so, I would argue that this spring ceremony was still effective in creating place-based attachments or memories, even if laced with a wry nostalgia.

Thinking about this 2002 episode as a Turnerian social drama is effective in identifying critical moments in this rupture from established practice. Of course, it is only one of many modes in which we can analyze this episode. Take, for example, the theories arising out of performativity and ritual. According to J. L. Austin, a performative utterance can only truly be successful when said within the appropriate circumstances or context; otherwise, it may fail or "misfire" (1961, 223–25). Within the spring ceremony context, the *tŏkdam* functions as a performative utterance in the way that its very utterance performs the ritual action of blessing the water. In 2002's *saem-kut*, one could say that the performative *tŏkdam* "misfired" because the context was skewed; not only was the water in terrible condition, but it was obvious that the spring was no longer in use. This called into question the larger ritual and cultural relevance of the whole ceremony. Amy Hollywood, whose article "Performativity, Citationality, Ritualization" I draw on heavily here, concludes that the misfiring of the performative should not be seen as a failure or source of danger, but rather as a possibility that "opens room for improvisation and resistance within the very authoritarian structures (e.g., of child rearing, education, and religion) in which subjects are constituted" (2002, 115). Following this, I contend that the misfiring of the performative spurred the players to improvise, which led the participants to find new meaning and relevance in the ritual. In line with Judith Butler's notion of ritual as a "reiterative" process (1993, 10), it seems significant that the players made great use of repetition. Instead of abandoning the conventional *tŏkdam* altogether, they repeated fragments of it, using it as an opportunity to insert their own contemporary observations and jokes.

Even though they followed through with the ritual in the end, I argue that the ritual function of the spring ceremony was trumped by a desire to be present in the moment and place (*hyŏnjang*), and to ultimately create a more meaningful *madang* in the sense of coming together as a community. Other *madang*-related discourses such as *nori* (play) and *kondongch'e* (community) were also evident throughout this ritual. For example, *nori* was on full display in the teasing banter and playful behavior, as well as in the high quality of verbal and musical improvisation. The element of community was evident in the way the characters jumped in to take a larger role in salvaging and resolving the situation. In this way, I argue that *madang* discourses can play an especially pivotal role in updating outdated rituals and sites, thereby helping to sustain the expressive ecology of Pilbong.

Within the repetitive structure of the ritual, subjects and communities were constituted in a new way. For example, when the hunter and the leader finally drank the water, they were, in effect, forced to come to terms with the muddy, brackish taste of their own modernity; in other words, they could no longer act as if they were in an idyllic village that had remained somehow unchanged. As the participants bore witness to this realization, the ideological tendency to define the Pilbong community in terms of an ideal past was irrevocably disrupted. Power relations among the players were also articulated in a new way in this episode. I have always thought that the imbalance of power among the players—with the *sangsoe* leader at the top—conflicted somewhat with the philosophy of *kongdongch'e* (community). However, here the relationship between the *sangsoe* and some of the other key players became somewhat more equalized. This was evident in the way that the *sangsoe* allowed more space for the other players to contribute performative dialogue. As the other players assumed more control, one can say that the *sangsoe*'s power became subverted when he gave up his right to drink first. What is important about this *madang* event is that it allowed for multiple identities and "ways of being" to collide and gradually be redefined.

Madangbalbi: *A Question of Ownership*

"The owner (*chuin*) of a ritual (*kut*) is the guest, not the performer." This is a contemporary phrase that I heard repeatedly from *p'ungmul* practitioners where the notion of an "owner" or *chuin* is akin to the patron in Korean expressive folk culture. In the context of *madangbalbi* (literally "stepping on the *madang*"), a practice in which the troupe visits individual village homes to perform a set of rituals, the head of the household would undoubtedly be considered the patron, host, and owner, at least while the troupe was visiting the home. However, what happens when too many outsiders stream into the owner's home to witness *madangbalbi*? Is the head of household still the owner or does ownership (read as power) shift to the spectators? And if it does tilt in the spectator's favor, should we still consider this event a ritual or is cultural tourism the better frame? Given the intimate nature of encounter that occurs in the *madangbalbi* between the owner, villagers, performers, and spectators, I investigate this issue by examining how this shift impacted the dynamic relations between the various actors involved.

Although the term *madangbalbi* can also be used to refer to the name of a comprehensive village ritual, in this context it refers to the section of the ritual devoted to visiting personal *madangs* or homes in the village (figure 2.1). In either context, *madangbalbi* can last many hours, even days; in 2002, however, the Pilbong *p'ungmul-kut* troupe squeezed four home visits into a span of two to three hours. Due to their condensed schedule, they were not able to perform all the specified rituals at any one home. Still, for perspective, I provide the full order of the smaller ceremonies that are supposed to be performed at each individual home (Yang Chinsŏng 2000, 114–24).

1. *Mun-kut* (gate ceremony, performed before entering the gates of the home)
2. *Madang-kut* (*madang* ceremony, performed as the group circles the inner courtyard)
3. *Sul-kut* (alcohol ceremony, usually followed by a break for food and refreshments)
4. *Chowang-kut* (kitchen ceremony, performed inside or in front of kitchen)
5. *Ch'ŏllyung-kut* (storage jar ceremony)
6. *Saem-kut* (a ceremony for the home's water source)
7. *Nojŏk-kut*, also *Kotkan-kut* (storage shed ceremony)
8. *Sŏngju-kut* (tutelary spirit ceremony, takes place on front porch)

The traditional home is like a microcosm of everything that can happen in the *madang*; it is a space of work and daily life, but it also hums with the possibilities of ritual, play, community, and chaos (table 0.1). My observations suggest that the material conditions of a home as well as the social status of the family have a direct impact on how a ritual is performed in each *madang*. In fact, each *madangbalbi* was conducted differently to suit each home. All four homes were pre-determined and the order in which the homes were visited seemed to proceed in terms of the relative size and status of the household, with the most important house last.

In addition to this ordering, there was also a distinct pattern in the way the activities flowed from one house to another (table 4.1). This pattern appeared to be modeled on the dynamic of tension and release (yin and yang), which is also articulated by folklorist Kim Inu (and many other Korean music practitioners) as *naego-talgo-maetgo-p'ulgo* or "produce-heat up-tighten-release."[11] The first

TABLE 4.1 *Madangbalbi* Ritual Order

HOUSEHOLD 1	HOUSEHOLD 2	HOUSEHOLD 3	HOUSEHOLD 4
1. *Mun-kut*	1. *Mun-kut*	1. *Mun-kut*	1. *Mun-kut*
2. *Madang-kut*	2. *Madang-kut*	2. *Madang-kut* with *chapsaek* play	2. *Madang-kut*
3. *Sul-kut*	3. *Chowang-kut* with song	3. *Chowang-kut* with songs	3. *Chowang-kut*
4. *Chowang-kut*	4. *Saem-kut*	4. *Madang-kut* with group play	4. Played on roof
5. *Saem-kut*			5. *Saem-kut*

household was conducted in the most straightforward fashion, cohering with the initial "produce" phase of the pattern of tension and release. The second household warmed up the energy put forth in the first house by adding songs for interest. In the third household, there was a high degree of expressive interpolation with the added character play, songs, and group play. These interpolations contributed a great deal to the sense of climax or "tightening" that occurred toward the end of the third household. Interestingly, although the last destination may have been the most important in terms of status (as the home of the Yang family), it was the calmest of the four. This contributed to the feeling of the *madangbalbi* coming to a point of rest or release.

From my experience observing *madangbalbi* in other villages, it is not all that abnormal for the sequence of rituals to be altered from one house to another. This depends on the needs of the homeowner, the discretion of the *sangsoe*, and the overall mood of the participants. In comparing the actual sequences at each house in table 4.1 with the prescribed order of *madangbalbi* according to Yang Chinsŏng, it appears that the ceremonies for the storage jar (*chŏllyung-kut*) and the storage shed areas (*nojŏk-kut*) were routinely omitted. By contrast, the rituals that were performed the most consistently across the four households were *mun-kut*, *madang-kut*, and *chowang-kut*. Of these, *mun-kut* (gate ceremony) was performed with the most consistency. In *mun-kut*, the troupe stops just outside the home while the flagholders form a symbolic *mun*, or gate, by crossing their long poles. As the *sangsoe* shouts the *tŏkdam* verse, "owner, owner, open your gate, if you don't open your gate, then we will go," the troupe seeks approval from the homeowner to enter and proceed with the ritual.[12] While they wait for approval, the troupe plays a short rhythm that mimics the rhythmic accents of the gate ceremony chant (Yang Chinsŏng 2000, 118). When approval is granted, the flagholders open their poles and the troupe can then pass through and enter the home. Without much variation, this is how the gate ceremony was performed at every household. However, since approval was granted beforehand, this was an interesting moment in which the performative force of the chant was pre-emptively rendered moot. Although I argued in the previous section that performative misfiring could be a source of spontaneity and drama, here the clear expectation of approval made the *tŏkdam* more a matter of following custom.[13]

After entering the gates, it became apparent that it would be difficult for everyone to enter the first household and participate comfortably. Perched higher up in the village, this home had a lovely view but at the same time, the *madang* itself was relatively small and narrow. As the troupe entered and proceeded to play *madang-kut* by performing a series of rhythms while in a circular formation, the participants did their best to squeeze into the small space or find a higher spot from which to watch. In the process, it became obvious that when space is tight, the local villagers tend to get pushed out and displaced, while the "outsiders" were generally more motivated to muscle their way in. Interestingly, this was one of the more substantive criticisms of the event that was mentioned during their evaluation.

Sometime later in this first *madang*, the owners put out a small table of food and drink in the center of the circle. This signaled to the troupe that preparations had been made for the *sul-kut* (alcohol ceremony). Soon thereafter, the leader gave the spoken signal to the players that it was okay to have a drink and take a break. Though the troupe took breaks to drink in the other households, the leader only performed the alcohol ceremony *tŏkdam* (verse) in the first home. After the break, they proceeded to the kitchen ceremony, or *chowang-kut*. The kitchen ceremony is perhaps one of the more important rituals in *madangbalbi* because it is one of the few times the leader directly addresses both the human owners and spirit occupants of the home. He does this in an extended *tŏkdam* that performs the function of acknowledging some of the major deities of the household, including the "outer" or *daeju* spirit and the "inner" or *chowang* spirit associated with the kitchen. The *tŏkdam* continues by wishing for great fortune and luck to come into the lives of the occupants. Finally, the *tŏkdam* closes with a declaration of chasing away the bad spirits while hoping for the good. In this first household, the leader was faithful to the established script as documented in his book (Yang Chinsŏng 2000, 121). In addition to performing the *tŏkdam*, the act of "stepping" on the *madang*, by the players, is also associated with chasing away the bad spirits. This may explain why the heavy stepping movements of *p'ungmul* players are so highly emphasized. Before heading to the next house, the troupe visited the home's personal water source to perform a quick spring ceremony. Since there were no doubts about the water's condition, everything proceeded smoothly.

The second *madang* was performed much like the first, save for a few exceptions. The *sangsoe* leader omitted the alcohol ceremony and proceeded directly to the kitchen ceremony. Then, the players took a break to eat and pour each other shots of *soju* liquor, while some opted for a bottle of Bacchus, a popular Korean energy drink. The kitchen ceremony was somewhat muddled in that the *tŏkdam* (verse) was not articulated in full. Instead, the *sangsoe* opted to sing a song called "Sŏngjupuri," which was followed by the popular folksong called "Jindo Arirang." Because the *sangsoe* did not stand on the porch of the house, it was difficult to see him as he was singing. To make matters worse, the various television camera crews crowded in on the *sangsoe*, and their obtrusiveness was the subject of much criticism. This issue raises the question of ownership, and more specifically, for whom the ritual is being performed. In this moment of conflict, the *sangsoe* opted to give a "show, show, show" for the benefit of the spectators by singing instead of delivering a carefully considered *tŏkdam* to the homeowner. At the same time, this choice opened the *madang* to a different mode of vocalized participation, as the spectators enthusiastically sang along with the songs that they knew.

While the second household "heated up" the energy "produced" in the first, the third household "tightened" it by allowing for more participation. This household is also centrally located and boasts a spacious *madang*. Unique to the way *madangbalbi* was conducted in the third household was the addition of character play (*chapsaek nori*) at the end of the first *madang-kut*. Character play occurs when the *sangsoe* signals one of the characters to come out and dance solos. Because of its improvisatory nature, it is here where the *chapsaek*'s skills of being in the moment truly come into play.

Among students of the Pilbong style, *chapsaek* characters are looked upon as ideal role models of how to act in the *madang*. Although *chapsaek* clearly represent archetypes of Korean society, the question of whether they represent "ideal" Korean subjects is a complex one. For the most part, the aesthetic expression of the *chapsaek* tends to foreground the comic foibles and pathos of a given character's class, profession, personality, and gender. The most unequivocally ideal subject is most likely the heroic hunter, or *taep'osu*. *P'ungmul* practitioners often talk about the hunter as the most important *chapsaek* character. The reason given for this is that the hunter is supposed to have the most authority to govern the flow of the players and overall shape of the event. Displaying great vigor and masculine authority, Pilbong's *taep'osu* wears a red satin jacket, sports an unruly beard, carries a gun, and dons a dramatic brass crown (video 4.3 🔊). In keeping with the hunter's image and importance, it is fitting that the leader called the hunter into the *madang* first, followed by the *kakshi*, or young woman.

The *sangsoe* leader sets the mood of each solo by establishing a medium tempo 12/8 rhythm played by the full *p'ungmul* ensemble. Character-play solos are structured so that the character improvises through a series of rhythms (usually three), each one a little faster than the last. Solos almost always end on a fast 4/4 *hwimori* rhythm. Though the *t'aep'yŏngso* (conical double-reed) weaves in and out throughout the entire ritual, it plays a particularly key role here in providing a dynamic musical soundscape for the character's movements. The hunter provided a narrative structure to his solo by acting as if he were on a hunt. In the first part of the solo, he made great use of the circular *madang* by "searching for prey" and turning in all directions. The intimate setting of the inner courtyard *madang* was particularly advantageous because the deft facial expressions that the hunter employed could be more fully appreciated. I was struck by how his eyes darted around the *madang* and conveyed fierce, piercing expressions. Other features of his dance included open-leg, bent-knee stances, the whipping and twirling movements of his gun, and the jerky, popping articulation of his shoulders and arms. As the rhythms shifted, the hunter began to use his gun to shoot at imaginary targets. At one point, he even shot at the *kakshi* (young woman) character—presumably to capture her heart—after which he tried to pull the *kakshi* into the *madang* to join him. After the *kakshi* rejected his advances, the hunter finished his solo (video 4.3 🔊).

When the *kakshi* was called in, the leader started the mood with a slightly slower 12/8 rhythm (called *kutkŏri*) that better suited the coquettish nature of the character. Because Mr. Kim, who usually plays *sogo* (handheld drum), did not have that much experience playing the *kakshi*, his solo lacked stylistic definition. What he lacked in finesse though, he made up for in his brazen interpretation of the village "hussy." Like the hunter, Mr. Kim also made great use of facial contortions that ran the gamut of coy seduction to orgasmic ecstasy. Although he waved his arms in the manner of typical woman's movements as portrayed in Korean dance, he also incorporated atypical movements in the hips in order to portray a more overt sexuality. Perhaps the most prominent feature of his solo, however, was the provocative use of his "breasts" as props. He also incorporated a move found in many mask dance styles where the female character pretends to urinate in the *madang*. In addition to its comedic shock value, this move also signifies sexual desire in Korean mask dance narratives (Jang 2013, 17). Toward the climax of his solo, the *kakshi* proceeded to tempt various characters including the hunter, another *soe* player, and finally, even the *sangsoe*.

When I asked Yang Chinsŏng about his last-minute decision to have Mr. Kim play the part of the young woman, he explained that he thought it was appropriate given that Lunar New Year used to be the only time when women could participate and release some inhibitions. Although this is reminiscent of a Bakhtinian "carnivalesque" moment with its suspension of social norms, it also corresponds with the notion of *nanjang* or chaos. Taking this into account, the *kakshi*'s character is symbolic of the potential of *nanjang* or the topsy-turvy ability to transform and rise out of one's station in life. Although the hunter presents a clear-cut example of the ideal male subject in terms of vigor and authority, in this performance, the *kakshi* character represents something more complex. Instead of representing the ideal feminine, I would assert that the *kakshi* stands in for a gendered freedom from societal restraint.

As much as I understand the symbolic implications of Mr. Kim's performance, I am left with a feeling of unease. First, there are few specifically female roles for women in Pilbong's *p'ungmul* ensemble, so to choose a man for a part that has been played by a woman—at least since the 1980s—has a significant impact on the female representation of the group. Prior to *p'ungmul*'s revival in the 1960s and '70s, most troupes were segregated by gender, with a predominance of male groups.[14] In the all-male troupes, even the female character parts were played by men, so while there is historical precedent for this, Mr. Kim's performance went against contemporary trends where women had been increasingly represented in *p'ungmul*. While not on the vanguard, the Pilbong troupe had steadily increased their inclusion of women, and by 2002, there were approximately five women who performed regularly with the troupe. More specifically, two women played *changgo*, one played *ch'aesang sogo*, and two performed the female character roles. In addition, it is notable that the other female character, the grandmother (*halmi*), was never given a chance to perform a solo. Ultimately, I see Mr. Kim's *kakshi* performance as more of a symbolic gesture to women. As such, it does succeed at destabilizing social norms, but it does so at the expense of disembodying the specificity of the female experience. We are left then with a comedic and hyper-sexualized projection of female resistance coming from the male perspective that I doubt many female performers would feel comfortable emulating. While I have never witnessed it myself, I have heard of women cross-dressing as men in other *p'ungmul* groups while making similar use of baudy props and gestures.

If this were the case in Pilbong, I may modulate my interpretation, but thus far I have not seen any evidence of this. In general, male-to-female cross-dressing is common in Korean expressive folk culture, especially when including mask dance drama. If this phenomenon was expanded so that female to male cross-dressing was just as normalized, I think this practice could potentially expand the norms of gendered performance in South Korea.

Looking at this *madang* as a heterotopic space as defined by Foucault and Deshpande, the *chapsaek* characters are visible embodiments of "social subjects" who then negotiate a utopian world defined by inverse power relations. Although I am in sympathy with Pilbong's efforts to reclaim and redefine Korean subjectivities that are in line with a more democratic worldview, it is a world that has been largely dominated by a male perspective, even if this continues to change in the new millennium. Based on past footage of the troupe when it was led by Yang Sunyong, it is important to note that women were very effective at playing the *kakshi* and *halmi* (grandmother) roles and were much admired for their skill. In any case, the *chapsaek* characters are very effective in inspiring others to act and move in the *madang*. A former *chapsaek* member, Hwang Sunju, told me that the key to being a good *chapsaek* is to act so foolishly that it helps people let go and enter the *madang* without any self-consciousness (personal communication). In the third household, the energy of the *chapsaek* solos increased the level and quality of participation, functioning as a climax of the *madangbalbi* portion of the ritual. In particular, the solos of the hunter and *kakshi* demonstrated how one might truly inhabit one's character and establish presence in the *madang*.

In addition to the solos and attendee participation, the third household gained from well-performed *tŏkdam* (stylized speech). Unlike some of the others given during the kitchen ceremony, this *tŏkdam* was personalized, delivered with a generosity of spirit, and interpolated with a short song. Here the *tŏkdam* began strongly with the *sangsoe* calling out "*Hwadong!*" to which the participants readily called in unison "*Ye-i*." After commenting on how well the participants answered his call, the *sangsoe* immediately proceeded to name the owner of the household, mentioning that he used to play the large gong (*ching*) in the ensemble. He also proposed that perhaps the reason why the family had been blessed with extraordinary fortune was because they had been visited more than once by the troupe. He used this as a pretext to recount the recent achievements of several family members and ended his praise by mentioning how the family had produced a long string of sons. Then he transitioned into the standard verse, but instead of ending it by saying "now it's time to play a *kut* (ritual)," he added his own spontaneous twist by saying, "before we play a *kut*, I'll have to sing a song." With a show of modesty, he claimed that he was doing this not because he wanted to sing, but because this was how it was done long ago. After the attendees responded with a few laughs, he launched into a song that he wrote himself in the Jeolla regional folksong style.

The singing gave way to the second *madang-kut*. Since the participants were energized by the character play, verses, and singing, it took very little time for them to completely take over the *madang*. Soon, they were moving in a remarkably coordinated fashion to the rhythms that were provided by the drummers, now standing on the sidelines. In scenes like this, it really did feel like ownership belonged to the spectators. In one moment, all eyes were on the *sangsoe*; in the next, all one could focus on was the way everyone was waving their hands in sync with the rhythm (video 2.1 🔊). Though the feeling of community was obviously strong here, the element of *nanjang* or chaos was also evident in the way the scene shifted abruptly from the performers to the participants. This *nanjang* quality of transformation can activate multiple subjectivities and multiple owners, but it can also lead to conflicts that can "break the *p'an*" (*p'an kkaejida*) or *madang*.

The last or fourth household was the Yang household, where the mother of the current leader and *sangsoe*, Yang Chinsŏng, resides. Given this, I was surprised that the *madangbalbi* ceremony here was not more exciting. It could be that the players were just tired and hungry. From my observations of the Yang family, his mother's hardworking and yet humble nature may have also been a factor. Perhaps all of this was taken in account and was planned so that the energy climaxed in the previous household was released in the final *madangbalbi* location.

Although the *sangsoe* elaborated his verses a little bit, I was expecting a higher degree of personalization, given that this was his family's home. However, the lack of personal interaction between the homeowner and performers was not exclusive to the last household. In general, I observed that the Pilbong homeowners were not very present and engaged as the beneficiaries of the *madangbalbi* rituals, especially in comparison to other Lunar New Year rituals that I have observed. For example, in other places, the owners were usually addressed more directly. In addition, they often took a more active role in expressing themselves and their wishes. The main reason for the more subdued behavior in Pilbong probably had something to do with the sense of being "on display," especially with the large numbers of outsiders and the ubiquitous presence of television crews. Another interpretation may be that the owners were just very busy hosting the event with so many "guests." When I brought up this issue, Yang Chinsŏng responded by saying:

> I think it's the responsibility of the spectators or *kugyŏngkkun* to make room for the villagers. At the same time, the spectators shouldn't just expect that the villagers will be "playing" and "dancing" all the time . . . For example, if the villagers play around, then who's going to make dinner? Our villagers do want to play but according to the Korean concept of *chŏng* [love or affection], part of what it means to "play" is to feed people, care for them, welcome them . . . When people come and eat well and then turn around and complain that the villagers did not "play," something just seems very wrong. (Yang Chinsŏng interview, October 5, 2003)

In revisiting the saying, "the owner of a ritual is the guest, not the performer," there is no question that the IPNPA and the Pilbong villagers put in a great deal of effort to please all the guests. However, the difficulties that surfaced in the event suggest that the question of who comprises Pilbong's "guests" is quite complex. What is clear from this *madangbalbi* is that Pilbong's *Chŏngwŏl Taeborŭm-kut* was not being performed *exclusively* for the well-being of the villager-based guests who live there. Furthermore, the fact that the flow of the four homes conformed to the Korean aesthetic formula of *naego-talgo-maetgo-p'ulgo* ("produce-heat up-tighten-release") reinforces the notion that *madangbalbi* was conceived more as a production for the pleasure of the communal whole, rather than for any individual home.

Dinner: An Interlude of Food, Drink, and Shinmyŏng

Dinnertime in the village center was an important *madang* in and of itself. In writing about *madang* theater (*madanggŭk*), Namhee Lee suggests that "we stop focusing primarily on the privileged duration of the performance itself and consider the potential and unanticipated effects in everyday life" (2003, 577). The same is true for *p'ungmul*. As I was making copies of my videotapes of the performance for the Pilbong teachers, I asked them whether they wanted me to include my footage of the dinnertime revelries and they said, "of course, this is the fun part." While it was playing, they continued to watch with genuine amusement. As I discussed earlier, providing food for everyone was more than just a necessity, it was a way in which the village could convey their welcoming spirit.

It was obvious that they put a great deal of care into the food. With the help of many volunteers, everybody was able to share in the same meal, which I would argue is a form of communal bodily engagement. Furthermore, the spicy stew was the perfect sustenance for being out in the cold all day.

After the guests had eaten and had a few drinks, one group of students began to sing. It only took a few seconds for more people to join in, and before long, the whole village common was a commotion of bouncing bodies and heterophonic voices. They began with a newly composed folksong called "Sarangga" (literally, "love song"). Because of this song's ubiquity among folk culture groups, it was the perfect choice to get everyone going. Soon they switched to a more uptempo, slightly bawdy song about a girl's wedding night called "Kakshi Bang'ae" ("In the Bride's Room"). The last song that I was able to record was "Miryang Arirang," which is a popular folksong from the Miryang area. It is interesting that, even while letting loose, the guests stayed within the realm of the Korean folksong repertoire. To me, this indicated a desire to contribute to the *madang* sociality in a manner coherent with the event as an expression of Korean heritage. What was special about this interlude was that it was the only moment in the entire event that seemed to belong solely to the attendees, and as such, it unfurled with an unfettered sense of joy. College-age students may have initiated it, but the sense of sociality soon spread to the children and older adults in the crowd. Although several elements of *madang* discourses were evident here, such as community, *nanjang*, openness, and play, the concept of *shinmyŏng* (spiritual ecstasy, joy) seems to best capture what happened in this particular *madang*.

P'an-kut *and* Taljip *t'aeugi: Evening Entertainment*

After dinner, the attendees followed the performers up to the "mountaintop *madang*" (*sanjŏng madang*) to participate in the evening *p'an-kut* and *taljip t'aeugi* (bonfire). A *p'an-kut* (literally *p'an*-ritual) is an entertainment-oriented format that showcases all the best aspects of a given style and is performed in the *p'an*, a term very similar in concept to the *madang*. Situated on a high, open plateau surrounded by a ring of hills, and freshly laid with fine reddish gravel, the IPNPA worked hard to create a picturesque space expressly for this occasion (figure 3.1). True to the event's name, a full moon hovered just above the bamboo bonfire that was set up on the eastern edge of the *madang*. For both Yang Chinsŏng and Yang Chinhwan, the image of the moonlit *madang* holds special significance. Yang Chinsŏng explains:

> From when I was young, I was exposed to [*p'ungmul* under] the natural lighting of the moon. Under this moon just floating by itself, eternal, what I saw was the *madang*. Lately, I have also been exposed to the bright and colorful culture of artificial lighting. And though the culture of moonlight is not as bright, the kinds of things that happen . . . by the light of the full moon is what I have come to see as truly beautiful (Yang Chinsŏng interview, October 9, 2002).

In addition to the aforementioned moonlight, they also added four sets of electric lights and several bonfires to give some additional light and warmth.

Though I observed the Pilbong troupe perform *p'an-kut* in many other types of locations, what I witnessed that evening was markedly different from these other performances. I think what made it unique was the confluence of such a large, enthusiastic, and well-informed community, the historic circumstances, and the freedom to conduct the *p'an-kut* to its fullest capacity. Too often, *p'an-kut* performances are confined to hour-long slots of time and therefore tend to settle into fixed choreographies and reduced spontaneity.

Given that the *p'an-kut* is a showcase of a given style's rhythms, distinctive characteristics, and choreography, the way that the participants interact and utilize space within this format is very different from most of the preceding rituals. First, the physical space of the *p'an-kut* needs to be spacious enough to accommodate both choreographed "formations" and free-flowing movements of people. It helps if the space is either circular or square, with just enough room for the participants to stand and not much larger, otherwise the sound and energy dissipates. Along these lines, Pilbong's "mountaintop *madang*" was ideal and even benefitted from having a hill on one side that spectators could climb to get a better view.

As a result of the shift from ritual to entertainment, there was also a corresponding change in the discursive practices of the *madang* that were present. Perhaps the most prominent element of *madang* discourse that I observed here had to do with the influence of "cosmological patterns" in the choreography. These can be identified most readily in the predominance of circles and spiraling movements in space but can more comprehensively be understood in terms of "yin-yang five element" (ŭm-*yang ohaeng*) theory. Scholars, such as Chŏng Pyŏngho, see many of the movements of *p'ungmul* as representative of "the transmigration between yin and yang, heaven and earth, this world and the next world, sacred and secular . . . tension and harmony" (1992, 494–95). The "five elements" are sometimes represented with respect to the "five" directions (east, west, south, north, and center), or perhaps more visibly in the choice of the corresponding five colors (blue, white, red, black, and yellow) that are employed heavily in their costumes and flags.[15] Socially speaking, *p'ungmul* participants apply the concept of *yin-yang* in the reciprocal "give and take" relationship between the performers and spectators. For Yang Chinsŏng, a truly exciting *p'an-kut* is when this give and take between the spectators and performers happens with tacit understanding and ease (2000, 40). In 2002's evening *p'an-kut*, I was struck by how strongly etched these "cosmological patterns" were, both in the choreographed movements of the performers and in the free-flowing movements of the participants.

Few *p'an-kut* performances rival the one that comes at the end of Pilbong's Lunar New Year Full Moon Ritual, especially in terms of how many participants flow so enthusiastically in and out of the *madang*. The leader mentioned that he had to elongate the time and insert more rhythms just to accommodate the participatory mood of the attendees. Even so, in analyzing my field videos, I was astounded by how the order of the rhythms and corresponding formations of the *p'an-kut* seemed to lend themselves so well to the give-and-take interactions between the attendees and the performers. This is not as evident in my videos of other Pilbong *p'an-kut* performances, because the spectators are rarely as active throughout the whole performance as they were here. Often, participation is relegated to the *twip'uri* or "after-party" that happens at the end of the performance.

In a full *p'an-kut*, a performance can last several hours and is usually divided into the "front ritual" (*ap-kut*) and "back ritual" (*twi-kut*). In general, the front ritual features more formal choreographies while the back ritual features improvisation, participation, singing, and individual solos. In the process of analyzing this *p'an-kut*, I discovered that the rhythmic formations were sequenced in such a way that the participants could alternate coming in and out of the *madang*. I categorized rhythmic formations that welcome the influx of participants as "open" and those that work when the audience members exit the *madang* as "closed." I use the term "rhythmic formation" to describe a set of rhythmic cycles and movements that are bound together in a pre-determined order, set of signals, choreography, and sometimes even function. These rhythms that comprise a rhythmic formation commonly proceed in order of tempo, from slow to fast, often ending with the duple *hwimori* rhythm. Each of these series of rhythms have a corresponding directive in terms of movement, such as to simply move in a circle in the counterclockwise direction. This common circular formation is what I would call an "open" rhythmic formation because it is stable enough to allow for people to come into the center of the circle without disrupting the

TABLE 4.2 Order of Rhythmic Formations in the *Ap-kut* (Front Ritual)

RHYTHMIC SERIES	MOVEMENT FORMATION DESCRIPTION	OPEN OR CLOSED
Ch'ae-kut	Counter-clockwise circular formation	Open
Hohŏ-kut	The group splits into two lines and moves in opposite directions to form curved, wave-like shapes similar to the yin-yang symbol. They soon come together to form two parallel curved lines facing in the same direction. Then they proceed in the opposite directions again.	Closed
P'ungryu-kut	Counter-clockwise circular formation	Open
Pangŭljin-kut	The group spirals into the center of a circle and then switches directions and unwinds like a corkscrew and proceeds to make another spiral on the other side of the *madang*.	Closed or open
Mijigi	After coming out of the previous formation in a zig-zag pattern, the group forms two long lines and moves back and forth in these two lines. Spectators are free to mimic their movements on both sides.	Open

choreography. "Closed" rhythmic formations have more complex choreographies that work better if the performance space is emptied out or "closed" to participants (table 4.2).

The way the participants flowed in and out of the *p'an* in the front ritual was remarkably smooth. Generally, it is the *chapsaek* character's responsibility to encourage people to come in, but on this night, they barely had to do more than make a welcoming hand gesture to fill up the *madang* with people. When the *madang* was full, bodies moved in perfect synchrony with the music, even those who had the extra burden of children on their shoulders. From the higher vantage point that I had while videotaping, the performers' bright costumes and the more pedestrian clothes of the attendees contrasted with each other in a striking balance. The front ritual ends with *mijigi*, and while not a dazzling formation by any means, somehow, seeing the mass of people move back and forth swaying their arms to the music was beautiful in its simplicity (video 4.4 🔊).

After a short pause, the *twi-kut* (back ritual) began with a rhythmic series called *kajin yŏngsan*. One of the more complex rhythmic patterns, it also features a high degree of responsorial rhythmic improvisation between the *soe* players. Although I cannot go into too much detail here, improvisation *within* the rhythmic cycle, or *changdan*, is a perfectly acceptable practice within *p'ungmul* (Hesselink 2011). In fact, rhythmic variation or improvisation within the cycle helps greatly to add new spark to rhythms that are repeated a lot over the course of a performance and add an element of spontaneity to the *madang*.

After going through a series of transitional rhythms, the *sangsoe* then proceeded with the individual solo section, or what is called *kaeinnori* (literally "individual-play"). In *kaeinnori*, individuals are motioned to come in and give a solo while the rest of the ensemble accompanies. On this occasion, the *sangsoe* chose the *kakshi* (young woman) and *taep'osu* (hunter) characters again, the lead *changgo* (hourglass drum) and *ch'aesang sogo* (handheld drum with twirling streamer hat) players, as well as a *soe* (small gong) player who came out with his wife. The individual play began with the *kakshi* character, and though the young woman had been carrying on with various antics in other parts of the *p'an-kut*, it was here that the *kakshi* began to steal the show and really began to exert a lot of influence on the overall mood of the *madang*. While it is hard to imagine how much further the *kakshi* could take things after his performance in the *madangbalbi*, he managed to top himself by performing a striptease. Although it was relatively tame in terms of how much skin was shown, it did effectively disrupt the expectation of showcasing virtuosity in this section of the *p'an-kut*. Even after he had performed, he remained a hilarious presence throughout the rest of the individual solos as he would yell things like, "remember that you're mine!" to the lead *changgo* player after a particularly virtuosic sequence, or "don't go away, don't show your stuff to anyone else," to the same player as he turned in the other direction. He similarly lightened the mood when he did an intentionally poor imitation of the acrobatic barrel turns that the *ch'aesang sogo* players perform while twirling streamers from their hats. By the end of the evening, he prompted comments from *p'ungmul* veterans such as "yah . . . today the *kakshi* (young woman) was really good," or "today the *kakshi* became the *sangsoe*." And though the *kakshi*'s influence was temporary, it was a memorable moment of topsy-turvy chaos, or *nanjang*.

Following the solos was a series of rhythmic formations that highlighted a great deal of embodied participation. Coming out of the "high" that the solos induced, the participants rebounded into the *madang* with a kind of riotous energy. This was then channeled into a rhythmic formation called *norae-kut* that features call-and-response singing. The final rhythmic formation was *subakch'igi*, which is performed to a series of participatory pattycake-style games that the attendees perform facing each other while bouncing and squatting into progressively lower stances until one falls or collapses. After the *subakch'igi*, the group played a long bout of rhythms that everyone could enjoy and dance to, eventually making their way over to the bonfire (video 4.5 🔊).[16]

The performers then bowed three times before lighting the bonfire. I took one last look at the unlit bonfire of tall bamboo poles and could not help but notice that many people had faithfully entwined their paper wishes into the ropes that held the structure together. The *sangsoe* then allowed some time for people to voice their wishes verbally. The first up was Ch'oe Ho-in, who is one of the principal teachers of the transmission center. As he is a popular teacher, people yelled that he should get married that year, and in reciprocation he wished that the New Year would bring health and good luck. Interestingly, he also added that he hoped that Pilbong would make their money back from this event, which I suppose was his way of reminding people to contribute and do their part. When it was Yang Chinsŏng's turn, he made a big point of thanking the residents of the Pilbong, mentioning that he knew how much *kosaeng*, or "hardship or effort" they had gone through during this event and that he sincerely hoped it could be held in Pilbong again next year.

Another interesting gesture was turning the microphone over to village elder and *changgo* player Pak Hyŏngnae, who stayed in Pilbong and temporarily ran the transmission center after Yang Sunyong left for political reasons.[17] As Pak acknowledged that "today, he had shed tears like rain," it was an unexpectedly heartwarming moment of reconciliation after a long period of Pilbong *p'ungmul* activity being split amongst various locations. This was followed by a wish for all the Pilbong *p'ungmul-kut* players who had passed away. Finally, Yang Chinsŏng reiterated Yang Sunyong's words of "abundant *kut* (ritual), abundant life," emphasizing their intentions to play *kut* as generously as you live life and live life as generously as you play *kut*. For me, the combination of these shared words and gestures conveyed a deep sense of community and drove home the desire to frame Pilbong *p'ungmul* as a ritual that everyone can experience and apply to their daily lives.[18]

REVISITING THE LUNAR NEW YEAR RITUAL IN 2016

The new construction and other physical changes that were implemented as part of the project of turning Pilbong into a *p'ungmul* village in time for its 2016 event greatly impacted the Lunar New Year ritual in ways that will continue to play out in the years to come. The morning after the event, I distinctly remember the leader, Yang Chinsŏng, asking me, "so, you didn't regret coming all the way from the United States for this, did you?" Still aching from a strained back that kept him from performing at his fullest capacity, it was his way of acknowledging that things were not perfect. I assured him that I felt extremely fortunate to have witnessed what I believe will be remembered as a landmark year of change for Pilbong. While 2002's event was considered pivotal for being brought back to Pilbong, 2016 was notable for being produced just as Pilbong is making a more visible transition into a new era as a heritage site. Although some of the ritual events were performed at sites within the village that have some continuity with the past, others were staged at new locations and buildings that form a sort of mini village within a village (figure 3.3 ⊙).

In keeping with the past, the event began with the flag ceremony (*ki-kut*) that was performed in the exact same location and in much the same manner as it was in 2002. Upon hearing the three sustained blares from the *nabal* (long-necked bugle), the performers began to play in the village common in front of the old village center building (figure 4.1 ⊙). Of all the ceremonies that took place that day, this one seemed the most unchanged from 2002. It helped that not that many people were watching at this point and therefore the photographers and videographers were still able to maintain a respectful distance. From here on though, things began to take a more dramatic turn as the troupe began to make their way down to the *tangsan namu* (tutelary spirit tree) where more people were waiting to participate in the *tangsan* ceremony. The greater numbers of people coupled with the reduction of available open space (due to the increased hardscaping and new construction) made it even more difficult to maneuver. What made things somewhat worse was the increased presence of cameras of all kinds: phones, DSLRs, and video equipment. As the flagholders crossed their flags to make a gate formation before the troupe entered the sacred space of the tutelary spirit tree, the photographers rushed in, even going so far as to pull participants out of their way so that they could have an unobstructed shot (figure 4.2 ⊙).

Once the flags were raised and the flag gate was lifted, the performers began to enter the tutelary spirit area in reverse order, and only then did the photographers move out of the way. The troupe proceeded to play in a tight clump near the tutelary spirit tree as onlookers gathered around them. When they stopped playing, the leader, Yang Chinsŏng, made an announcement telling people to "play, don't just watch, play with no regrets." Perhaps this was his subtle way of telling people to put the cameras down and be present, in the moment. From here, people lined up to take part in the ceremony, which took place at an altar that was placed at the foot of the tree. Compared with 2002, the ceremony itself seemed to have fewer ritualistic steps conducted by village elders. Instead, they focused their attention on the participants who lined up to pay their respects, make wishes, and receive blessings by making cash donations, pouring rice wine, and bowing three times. Although there was a little more of a presence from village elders in 2002, this time around it seemed clear that the ceremony was serving the needs of the spectators. What surprised me here was the enthusiasm with which the participants seemed to own and embrace this ritual. The fact that this *tangsan* tree was likely not one that they grew up with did not seem to diminish people's desire to pay their respects to the tutelary spirit of Pilbong. Of all the ceremonies that are sequenced together in the Lunar New Year Full Moon Ritual, this one seems to carry the most meaning for participants and was consequently one of the more crowded events. As in 2002, as soon as the ceremony concluded, the participants scrambled to quickly distribute and eat the sacrificial altar foods. Interestingly, it is the only older ritual site that was incorporated into the new mini village area.

From here, the troupe traveled to the site of another tutelary spirit tree, which they termed the *halmŏni* or "grandmother" tutelary spirit tree. This was a new development in 2016 and unlike the "grandfather" or *harabŏji* tree at the foot of the village, the grandmother trees were recently planted to replace the original tree that had been cut down long ago. Due to the newness of this site, the ritual conducted here was simpler and more subdued. This was mostly likely because the *sangsoe* or leader of the group, Yang Chinsŏng, left the ensemble unexpectedly due to his strained back, leaving the ritual direction under the charge of another elder *soe* player.

As mentioned in the previous chapter, the most controversial addition to the *p'ungmul* village was the new spring that was ostensibly constructed in the approximate location of the original one (figure 3.5). Although the previous site of the *saem-kut* did have water flowing from a natural spring (figure 3.2), they opted to abandon it due to its inconvenient location in the middle of a field. Despite its historic underpinnings, the new spring did not have any naturally flowing water and had an unmistakably "fake" quality that many people complained about (especially the photographers). I am not sure whether it was just coincidence that the *sangsoe* opted to be absent, but the resulting *saem-kut* was conducted in a competent but perfunctory manner and lacked any spontaneous banter that may have addressed and resolved any issues with the new spring.

The *madangbalbi* portion of the 2016 ritual was a hybrid of ritual and entertainment. While there was some ritual continuity with what I witnessed in 2002, it also included several radical departures that will have significant implications for the future of the Lunar New Year Full Moon Ritual. If 2002's event already reduced the number of village homes visited to four, 2016's event reduced this to one (well, two if you include the pretend home that was part of the mini village). The one actual home that remained on the roster was the Yang residence where the mother of the current *sangsoe* lives. Even in the Yang residence, the smaller ceremonies that address various parts of the home were reduced, eliminated, or altered. Instead of proceeding through a set of smaller ceremonies that address different parts of the home, they basically performed the *mun-kut* ceremony at the front gate before entering, played a brief *madang* ceremony, and more informally addressed the owner at her front door before launching into introductions, banter, jokes, and songs. As in 2002, Mrs. Yang did come to the door and took the time to thank people for coming but did not appear to like being the focus of attention beyond that. Given this, the *chapsaek* decided to hold court in her place and told some stories, jokes, and sang a few songs before departing. One particularly memorable moment was when one of the *chapsaek* (the *hwadong* character) reminded everyone that the purpose of *madangbalbi* is to "step on the *madang*": to come together as a community to stamp out the bad and usher in the good.

From here, they proceeded to the gate of the mini village. My ethnomusicologist radar acted up as soon as I saw several young female IPNPA members waiting on the other side of the gates wearing wireless microphones and dressed up in colorful clothes resembling what a stereotypical village woman would wear. After a robust gate ceremony, the troupe was allowed to enter the generous interior *madang* of the newly constructed village home. Given the ample space, the participants had more room to dance to the rhythms than in the previous home. After being absent for several ceremonies, Yang Chinsŏng returned to resume his duties as *sangsoe*. He proceeded to interact with the women and other participants by performing the established *madangbalbi* ritual verses and launching into singing "Sŏngjupuri," which is appropriate given that it addresses the tutelary spirit of the home. From here, they launched into a playful series of playing and dancing, singing, and semi-improvised comedic banter. What made this iteration of *madangbalbi* so different is that these women were clearly not actual villagers, but performing the role of villagers, complete with dialect mastery, singing skills in both older popular and traditional genres, and semi-prepared comedic routines and props. While the IPNPA has been developing various dramatic productions for other programs throughout the year, this was the first time I was aware of them incorporating this mode of performance into their Lunar New Year ritual. While many of the spectators were still enthusiastic about the opportunity to dance along in the *madang* while the ensemble played, I sensed some hesitation and confusion in terms of what to make of this dramatic turn of events. Like the previous visit, the various rituals that used to make up *madangbalbi* were stripped down to the bare bones, giving way even more to communal play and spectacle.

After the *madangbalbi*, everyone went to have dinner, which consisted of a free meal of spicy pork soup, seasoned zucchini, radish, and kimchi, which was very similar to what was offered in 2002. For those wanting other options, there were various Korean snacks and drinks available at very reasonable prices, such as savory pancakes called *pajŏn*, fish cakes, and *makkŏlli* (rice beer). Despite the cold wind that intensified at nightfall, dinner was a calm and orderly affair, even if it lacked some of the spontaneous singing and carousing that occurred in 2002. The sense of order may have had something to do with the ample new dining terraces that were constructed as part of the mini village to accommodate larger numbers of people.

After dinner, the troupe performed *p'an-kut*, which took place in the brand new *kut-madang* (as it was called in the program) that was constructed expressly for the performance of *p'an-kut* (figure 3.6). Although *p'an-kut* used to be held on a terraced field a short distance away, the new *kut-madang* was situated in the center of the mini village. Given the tighter confines, I heard one prominent member deem it too small for *p'an-kut*. However, in practice, the size and layout — with its rounded concrete panels, cushy circular floor, and surrounding stone steps — lent itself well to concentrating the focus and energy of the participants while still providing visibility and adequate room to move around in. In form and content, the *p'an-kut* was performed much as it was in 2002, with its division of rhythmic formations into the *ap-kut* (front ritual) and *twi-kut* (back ritual). As in 2002, participants flowed in and out of the *madang* with ease, with some help and encouragement from the *chapsaek*.

The crowd was more diverse than I remembered in 2002; while there were still large numbers of college students and people in their twenties, there were also groups of older Korean women and men in their forties and fifties, families with kids, older folks who relish showing off their stylish dance moves in the *madang*, as well as more than a handful of non-Korean enthusiasts and tourists.[19]

In keeping with this diversity, the movement of the participatory dancing was not as synchronized as I remembered. For example, there were several artsy, college-age participants who expressed themselves by putting a more individual spin on their movements instead of opting to synchronize with the performers' rhythms and movements. Surveying the *madang* from above, the cumulative effect was less cohesive, but no less fervent (figure 4.3 ⊙). With its warm lighting and bowl-like structure, the new *madang* proved to be quite cozy and intimate. Although the location afforded a wonderful view of the full moon that evening, the manufactured quality of the *madang* did not feel as connected to its natural surroundings. The culminating bonfire, however, did take place on an adjacent field and had a more natural feel; as people gathered around the bonfire, they could feel the dirt under their feet, smell the burning straw and bamboo, and sense the searing heat coming from the enormous bonfire. The troupe did play as the bonfire began to burn, but due to the *sangsoe*'s strained back, they ended early instead of extending into a longer *twip'uri* (after-party). As the bonfire continued to burn and throw off sparks, the 2016 Lunar New Year sputtered to an anti-climactic end (figure 4.4 ⊙).

CONCLUSION: RITUAL, HERITAGE, TOURISM, AND NATURE

In preaching the philosophy of "abundant *kut* (ritual), abundant life," Pilbong has cultivated an ever-growing community of people in South Korea and beyond. In terms of how this narrative has played out in the lived reality and experience of participants, I found that the integration of ritual with daily life has decreased, and the sharing of work has become less evenly dispersed over time. In 2002, a strong spirit of generosity, dialogue, and service could be discerned in the interactions between the people who were producing the Lunar New Year ritual (the villagers, IPNPA members, and assorted volunteers) as well as in the give and take between the performers and participants. For example, in preparing for the ritual, more people shared in the work, many of them volunteers. In the actual ritual itself, there was more of a spontaneous back-and-forth dialogue that served to resolve real-life tensions or discrepancies, as evident in the spring ceremony. In 2016, the activity of giving abundantly and sharing the workload had shifted considerably as more responsibility had been placed on paid staff at the transmission center, some villagers, and higher-level IPNPA members. In addition, the number of transmission students that the IPNPA could count on to volunteer declined significantly. In the 2016 event, there was also much less space for spontaneity, as certain aspects of the ritual have become more entertainment oriented. While there were still several key, long-time village residents who were physically capable of and spiritually invested in hosting the ritual in 2002, this was no longer the case in 2016, simply because many of them had passed away. From my conversations with IPNPA members, the construction of the *p'ungmul* heritage village is a clear response to this reality.

Despite these trends, the number of non-village residents who have gained an intimate knowledge of Pilbong's ritual life and expressive ecology has increased to include more and more diverse sectors of the population, due in large part to the IPNPA's continued outreach and transmission activities. It is important to note that for many repeat visitors, the knowledge gained—while it cannot replace that of a native resident—goes beyond text-based knowledge. Through learning how to play *p'ungmul* and by participating regularly in performances and rituals, this is knowledge that is deeply entrained, embodied, and emplaced. While the more spontaneous moments of engagement that have occurred during Lunar New Year may be on the wane, the feeling of communal participation remains strong. When I attended in 2016, I expected the quality of open participation to be more limited and prescriptive in nature. And while this was the case in certain rituals such as the tutelary spirit tree ceremony and the spring ceremony, this was not so in the evening *p'an-kut*. Here, I was pleasantly surprised to find people—young and old—defy expectations and express themselves and interact with each other in the *madang* in astonishingly individual ways. In general, *madang*-related discourses and practices continue to be instrumental in the way people participate so wholeheartedly in the moment, as well as in the overall expressive ecology of Pilbong. As I have argued elsewhere, one key to this process is the privileging of the body. Throughout the comprehensive ritual, there are numerous opportunities to experience the ritual through the body—by sampling the sacrificial foods, partaking in the traditional foodways of the Pilbong region, bowing at the tutelary spirit tree shrine, and dancing in the *madangs*.

Even despite this emphasis on bodily participation, I can only conclude that participants and practitioners produce, experience, and interpret the narrative meaning of the Lunar New Year Full Moon ritual in multiple ways. For many, it is first and foremost a *kut* ritual—and while the event is not conducted by shamans, it is based upon shamanic beliefs and spiritual cosmology. For those open to shamanism, this event provides the opportunity to seek out the blessings of spirits and come together to stamp out their bad or mischievous tendencies.

The popularity of certain activities—such as bowing at the tutelary spirit tree ceremony and writing one's prayers on strips of paper and tucking them into the sacred ropes around the stone cairns or bonfire—attests to the enduring ritual draw of Pilbong's Lunar New Year event. Equally serious are the Korean music and dance students and aficionados—often students and friends of higher-level IPNPA members who teach in various settings—who come expecting to experience high-quality *p'ungmul* performed in a more idealized spatial, spiritual, and robust participatory context. Viewing this activity within the larger framework of cultural heritage production and tourism, what sets Pilbong apart is the extent to which the community invests in educating their participants.

Given the IPNPA's dual recognition from both UNESCO and the South Korean government, viewing Lunar New Year at Pilbong within the frameworks of cultural heritage and heritage tourism—and not just an isolated ritual—has several advantages. First, it allows us to link with a broader range of worldwide cultural phenomena and engage with developing theories in the heritage and tourism literature. For example, according to Laurajane Smith and Natsuko Akagawa, heritage is increasingly being theorized as a "cultural practice, rather than simply a site, place or intangible performance or event" (2009, 6). They continue to write that several authors (Urry 1996, Dicks 2000, Graham 2002, Peckham 2003, Smith 2006) have "examined heritage as a body of knowledge and as a political and cultural process of remembering/forgetting and communication" (2009, 6). While these statements are certainly relevant, I do think that the emphasis on practice overlooks the ways in which heritage practices are inextricably linked with the tangible, more material aspects of culture, place, and the environment. In my broader theorization of Pilbong as an expressive ecology, I have been especially interested in the ways in which IPNPA practices have driven the production of space and place, in both conception and physical manifestation. We have seen this repeatedly in the realization of the transmission center complex as well as the more recent mini village within the village of Pilbong. One could also see this at work in the shaping of the actual physical contours of place (landscaping, pathways, roads) and in the ways in which humans have interacted with nature-related features and landmarks such as trees, stone cairns, and shrines—from careful cultivation to re-siting and even to purposeful neglect and/or destruction.

More than twenty years ago, Barbara Kirshenblatt-Gimblett theorized "heritage" as "a new mode of cultural production in the present that has recourse to the past" (1995, 39). She also wrote that "heritage produces the local for export" and explains that the pull of heritage is one of the ways in which tourism "imports visitors to consume goods and services locally" (1995, 373). The combination of national cultural preservation, political cultural revival, and the so-called "*tapsa* boom" created a solid foundation for the success of domestic heritage tourism in South Korea. Site-specific events such as Pilbong's Lunar New Year have been well positioned to benefit from these trends and have enabled more people to engage with the expressive ecology of Pilbong.

The increased popularity of heritage tourism in Pilbong coupled with the declining village population, however, does carry serious implications in terms of the sustainability and future health of this expressive ecology. For example, if left unchecked, construction as well as increased human waste and pollution could negatively impact the surrounding environment. Perhaps more importantly, as the older villagers pass away, their way of life cultivating the surrounding land for farming also suffers. In 2016, there were already signs of abandoned farmland in Pilbong, which is unsightly but could also lead to erosion as well as decreased ecosystem fertility and diversity if not dealt with properly. Another fear is that the land will continue to be sold to people who have little stake in Pilbong's cultural legacy. The potentially devastating impact on the expressive ecology of Pilbong would be twofold: environmental degradation as well as the loss of any connection to the living community that once sustained Pilbong *p'ungmul* rituals and practices. On the one hand, this result, if it did occur, would probably happen over a long period. Due to its location, the land in Pilbong is not especially valuable for development purposes, and as a result, most of the current property owners do not seem to be in any hurry to sell. On the other hand, the pressure to move out of the village to live in larger cities remains strong and any current village property owners and/or their descendants continue to have little reason to stay and maintain this way of life. Meanwhile, more properties are falling into disrepair as their departed owners work somewhere else hoping to make enough to rebuild the homes later.

Time will tell how the IPNPA is able to manage these issues, but it is my humble opinion that they need to do more than just focus on hosting their events in the newly constructed mini village of Pilbong. In the future, I hope that they will be able to cultivate more of a healthy, living community of residents and business owners (e.g., organic farmers, traditional Korean homestay managers) who are interested in not only maintaining the expressive ecology of Pilbong but who are also willing to further develop it to appeal to families and nature-lovers as well. While still just an idea, Yang Chinsŏng did tell me that now that the mini village is in place, they may alter the way they condense many of the Pilbong rituals into one day during the Lunar New Year and instead, spread them out more traditionally over the course of the calendar year. This is a positive signal that they are thinking more about cultivating the daily life of residents as well as the year-round sustainability of Pilbong.

In bringing part 1 of this book to a close, it is important to emphasize that the Imshil Pilbong Nongak Preservation Association has consistently brought increasing numbers of people in closer contact with the expressive ecology of Pilbong, especially since 2002. In so doing, they have been remarkably successful continuing a legacy that began well before it was officially recognized by the South Korean government in 1989. In continuing to cultivate important ritual sites within their village, they provide visitors with a vision of humanity's relationship to nature—one that stems from an older, Korean, village-based shamanic world view. In so doing, they acquaint people with the animistic spirits of the Pilbong village and bring them in direct contact with the places in which they dwell, such as the tutelary spirit tree, the village home, or the nearby springs. The pounding, synchronized rhythms serve as a sonic reminder of *p'ungmul*'s connections to the movement of cooperative agricultural labor or *ture*. While there is not a lot of direct sonic imitation or representation of nature in Pilbong's style of *p'ungmul*, nature references can be found scattered throughout the oral verses or stylized speech (*tŏkdam*) and song lyrics that have been passed down as part of the form.

Similarly, many visual and kinesthetic aspects of Pilbong *p'ungmul* are imbued with nature symbolism. For example, the costumes utilize colors (black, red, blue, white, yellow) that represent the five natural elements (water, fire, wood, metal, earth), corresponding to the "five-element" philosophy of *wu xing* in Chinese or *ohaeng* in Korean. This *ohaeng* theory also corresponds to the five directions or *obang* (north, south, east, west, and center), which play a role in some of their choreographic formations (Hesselink and Petty 2004, 274–78). In addition, cloth or paper flowers are used to adorn the heads or hats of nearly all the instrumental performers, which serve as a constant visual reminder of the saying, "*p'ungmul* is the flower of the people." The costumes not only represent the five elements of nature and are seen as a protection from bad luck, but they also represent the kind of beauty that can only spring from a life toiling in the elements (figure 4.1 ☉). The bonfire that crackles from the burning of bamboo and straw also links with the elements of wood and fire and is a multi-sensory symbol of the sacred power of nature.

All these nature connections aside, perhaps what Pilbong does best is to facilitate bodily connections to the earth, in ways both physical and metaphysical. In tempos fast and slow, Pilbong's characteristic rhythms and heavy groove (discussed in chapter 2) facilitate the entrainment of intensely embodied up-and-down motions that bring a participant's feet in constant, repeated contact with the earth. During the Lunar New Year, the IPNPA has consistently drawn people together to step on the grounds of Pilbong—in various *madangs* and pathways, all over the village, all day long. Read in a ritual context, bringing this many people to the village goes a long way toward collectively stamping out bad spirits and ensuring good fortune for its residents. As performers and participants bend their knees down toward the ground and rebound up to the sky while dancing and playing, the body becomes a living fulcrum between the three elements of heaven, earth, and humans called *samjae*. Maintaining balance between these three elements is one of the central tenets of Korean shamanism (Seo 2002, 3) and playing *kut* is widely considered to be a mode of restoring harmony to *samjae* (Seo 2002, 3; Park 2014, 164).[20] In a more secular context, this event is significant in demonstrating the importance of site-specific ritual and performance.

PART II
Articulating Regional, National, and Transnational Connections

FIVE

The Madang on the Move

While part 1 of this book explores how a *site-specific* expressive ecology is supported locally through historical trends (chapter 1), transmission practices (chapter 2), communal labor (chapter 3), and ritual performance (chapter 4), part 2 examines what I would categorize as mostly *site-oriented* or *madang-oriented* expressive ecologies at the regional (chapter 5), national/urban (chapter 6), and transnational (chapter 7) levels. For context, the continuation of grounded ritual performances like the one based in the village of Pilbong is quite remarkable given how much the Korean music landscape has changed. Even well before the twentieth century, talented *p'ungmul* performers moved beyond the village to play with itinerant performance troupes—such as *namsadang*—in villages, marketplaces, town squares, temples, and courtyards of wealthy aristocratic patrons.[1] In the early to mid-twentieth century, many Korean performing arts were adapted to the proscenium stage. Later, in the cultural heritage and preservation era beginning in the 1960s, performances began to proliferate in a number of venues, including sports arenas, schoolyards, parks, festivals, multi-purpose rooms, and even specially designed outdoor *madang* performance areas. Given this proliferation of performance spaces and opportunities, I argue that the *madang*—both as a mobile conceptual frame and as a material performance space—serves as a fulcrum of cultural continuity in response to these changes. In this context, this chapter examines how the *madang* continues to inform site-oriented performances of Korean expressive culture at the regional level.

The main line of inquiry that drives this chapter is whether *madang*-type performances can still forge "resonant" connections between people, place, and the environment when a regionally based group goes on tour or performs at another location or venue not exclusively associated with their tradition. Here, I draw inspiration from ethnomusicologist Marié Abe's insightful theory on "resonance" (*hibiki* in Japanese) that she defines as "a simultaneously acoustic and affective work of sounding that articulates latent socialities, the acoustic environment, and sedimented histories" (Abe 2018, 29). While the effects of resonance can be varied and ephemeral, I argue that these performances still have the potential to be site-oriented and, as such, can contribute to one's experiential knowledge. In addition, through the tropic force of the *madang*, I argue that these performances can also create "integrative maps" and "patterns" that help connect people to place, the environment, and to each other (Turino 2008, 3). In this way, these performances provide avenues for participants to engage with place at the regional level, even going so far as to define what is considered "regional" in new ways. It is important to pay attention to these types of performances, given that they comprise the majority of what is offered in terms of traditional music and dance in *madang* settings. I argue that site-oriented expressive ecologies, while less stable, must still be produced or cultivated. In general, the results are less lasting and more historically layered, less private and more public, and yet because of their ubiquity, I would argue no less important. I begin this chapter by providing an overview of the development of the *madang* as material culture to better understand the development of how folk expressive culture was configured to represent both region and nation. Then, I explore how region, history, memory, and changing demographics are woven together by examining several contrasting regional case studies.

THE EVOLUTION OF PERFORMANCE SPACE AND THE *MADANG* AS MATERIAL CULTURE

As described in part 1, the quintessential spatial image that the *madang* conjures to mind is the intimate courtyard of a Korean village home. Traditional Korean village dwellings are usually made up of several small buildings that are constructed around a centralized open area or *madang* (figure 2.1).[2] Although *madangs* tend to be associated with intimate gathering areas, this does not mean that they do not also exist in more densely populated towns. For example, a town square or even an open street corner could be called a *madang*. More often, however, these more public spaces tend to be called by the related term *p'an*. *P'ansori* scholar and performer Chan E. Park defines the *p'an* as a "space of wholehearted gathering" where itinerant *p'ansori* (musical storytelling) entertainers

FIGURE 5.1 Marketplace *madang*. Moran Market, Seoul (2001). Photo by the author.

are said to have performed in the late Chosŏn dynasty (2003, 1). Entertainment *p'ans* are often set up in busy marketplaces and can still be found today (figure 5.1). Beginning in the late seventeenth century in Korea, mask dance drama performers were especially drawn to marketplace culture and were known to set up temporary outdoor *t'alp'ans* (mask *p'ans*) in scenic locations (on a riverbank for instance) close to the periodic regional markets of the time (figure 5.1 ◉).

Permanent theaters or performance spaces began to appear at the turn of the twentieth century and, according to Yi Hyejin, were the single-most influential factor that led to the "interruption" of *madang*-style performance and expression (Yi Hyejin 1998, 22). The most noteworthy of these early theaters was the *Hyŏmnyulsa*, which was built in 1902 for the fortieth-anniversary celebration of King Kojong's ascension. Interestingly, this theater is said to have been modeled on the Colosseum in Rome[3] but on a smaller scale and made in a circular shape with seating on three sides. After closing in 1906, it later reopened as the *Wŏngaksa* in 1908 (Killick 1998, 54–61; No Dongŭn 1995, 661; Pihl 1994, 46–47; Song Bangsong 2000, 33). With the opening of other theaters in 1907 and 1908 such as the *Kwangmudae, Dansŏngsa, Changansa,* and *Yŏnhŭngsa,* entertainers

Madang on the Move 151

from all over the country were said to have flocked to Seoul to perform diverse genres (Song Bangsong 2000, 35).

With the ensuing Japanese colonization of Korea (1910–1945) and the Korean War (1950–1953), the culture of theaters and concert halls developed in fits and starts throughout the next several decades. Even so, the development of these theaters set up a fundamental dichotomy between the concept of the stage, or *mudae*, and the *madang*. In the most basic terms, what sets the *mudae* apart from the *madang* or *p'an* is its more fixed and closed-off nature. However, this basic difference bears enormous ramifications. According to Jacques Attali in *Noise: The Political Economy of Music*, the concert hall or theater stage promotes the channeled representation of music.

> As we have seen, charging admission for representation presupposes the sale of a service . . . This idea of the exchangeability of music is disruptive, because it places music in the context of abstract, generalized exchange, and consequently of money . . . Representation requires a closed framework, the necessary site for this creation of wealth, for the exchange between spectators and productive workers, for the collection of a fee. (1985, 57–58)

In this way, this "commodification" of music presupposes a separate relationship between the spectator and the performer, the consumer, and the producer. In *Musicking: The Meanings of Performing and Listening*, Christopher Small discusses how the architecture of the concert hall and the structural flow of a symphonic event enhances the feeling that attendees are "spectators rather than participants" (Small 1998, 44). In this way, the stage not only changed the nature of performance and what it means to be a performer, but it also radically changed the nature of audience engagement.

Because of the global hegemonic power of the stage format in the context of Korea's modernization, the *madang* format and its associated genres were at risk of disappearing by the middle to late twentieth century. This was compounded by the fact that several forms of *madang*-oriented expressive folk culture were targeted for suppression during the Japanese occupation (1910–1945). One of the reasons for this was that large-scale, group-oriented events that promoted the gathering of crowds of people were banned, including Lunar New Year ceremonies and tug-of-war games (Yi Hyejin 1998, 23). In addition, village life, culture, and shamanist beliefs were increasingly undermined during the Japanese colonial period. Even after the country began to rebuild after the Korean War (1950–1953), village customs and landmarks continued to be targeted as "backward" and "superstitious" (*mishin*) by the economic reform-minded officials of the South Korean Park Chung Hee [Pak Chŏnghui] regime (1962–1979). For example, in one of Park's signature reforms called the New Village movement (*Saemaŭl undong*) that began in 1970, the government removed tutelary spirit trees and other ritual sites in an effort to "improve" roads and enlarge the entrances to villages (Park Shingil 2000, 64).

Some Korean expressive genres that existed prior to the advent of stages passed fairly smoothly into the stage format. These tended to be the genres that were cultivated at court or in aristocratic chamber settings. Others branched into new forms that were adapted more toward the stage: most notably, *ch'anggŭk* derived from *p'ansori* and later, a virtuosic form of drumming called *samul nori* developed from *p'ungmul* (percussion band music and dance) and other genres such as the varied entertainment traditions of itinerant troupe performance called *namsadang* (Hesselink 2012). In terms of discourse, one of the facile ways in which young people differentiated *samul nori* from *p'ungmul* was to assert that *samul nori* was adapted to the stage or *mudae* and that *p'ungmul* was oriented toward the *p'an* or *madang* (Park Shingil 2000, 188–90). In actual practice, however, there was more overlap between these two sensibilities. For example, Katherine Lee notes that the original performances of "Kŏllipp'ae p'ungmul" by the founding group SamulNori were performed around a pagoda in the *madang* courtyard of the Space Theater in 1980 (2018, 26–27).

Despite the popularity of newer genres like *samul nori*, this does not mean that older forms such as *p'ansori* or *p'ungmul* ceased to exist. These genres either were presented on stage in ways congruent with their earlier contexts, when possible, or were alternatively adapted to modern outdoor spaces, such as large open fields or sports stadiums. Yang Sunyong, an influential *p'ungmul* practitioner, called this trend the "mass game effect" (Yang Sunyong, quoted in Yang Chinsŏng 2000, 86). The establishment of government-sponsored regional and national folk arts competitions that often took place in stadiums was especially instrumental in this process. Participating or earning a prize at the National Folk Arts Competition, instituted in 1958, was considered especially pivotal to a group's national recognition, especially within the Intangible Cultural Property system (Park Shingil 2000, 67). As a result, many groups adapted their performances to be more competitive in these more expansive conditions.

As practitioners and participants became increasingly critical of these formats, an interconnected web of discourses centering on the keywords of the *madang* and *p'an* began to form (Kwon 2005, 53–124). These discourses were heavily influenced by the oppositional stance of the *minjung* movement in the 1960s and '70s and were most intensely realized in *madang* theater (*madanggŭk*). Eventually, these discourses began to manifest in the material culture, design, and presentational practices of theaters. For example, theaters became influenced by the *madang* in various ways. In the late 1970s and 1980s in *ch'anggŭk*, this influence even became known as the *madanghwa* ("madang-ization") phase and was marked by a simplified stage design, closer and more intimate proximity between the performers and audience members, and the cultivation of increased audience interaction and participation (Killick 1998, 298–99, 453–55). In the genres of *p'ungmul*, mask dance drama, and *madanggŭk*, outdoor and indoor spaces were oriented to the *madang* format where the performance area would be located in the center with the audience surrounding in a circle or semi-circle.

Perhaps the most tangible material manifestation of *madang* discourses can be seen in the development of circular, open-air arenas called *norimadangs* ("play-madangs"). Beginning in the early 1980s, these unique structures were designed explicitly to present Korean folk performing arts in a more multi-regional and celebratory fashion (rather than in a competitive arena). For example, in 1982, the National Korean Theater (*Kungnip Kŭkjang*) set a new national and cultural standard by adding a *norimadang* to its performing arts complex (Hŏ Kyu 1988, 69). Soon after, the Seoul Nori Madang was built in 1984 to become one of the more stunning examples of *norimadang* architecture through its incorporation of "traditional" and "natural" elements such as the gravel-paved earthy performance area, the surrounding Korean-style buildings, and tree-lined park setting (figure 5.2).[4] It quickly became a very popular venue for its highly varied programming of regional performing arts. Outside of Seoul, other places followed suit, such as the Jeju Island Cultural Promotion Center's Norimadang in 1988 (Yi Hyejin 1998, 89) and the Andong International *T'alch'um* Festival's Norimadang in 1997. In 1998, even the country's most revered "traditional" music institution, the National Gugak Center (*Kungnip Kugakwon*), amended their performing arts complex by adding an outdoor semi-circular open-air *madang* now called the Yŏnhŭi Madang (called the Pyŏlmaji't'ŏ prior to 2013, figure 5.2 ◉).

All of these material manifestations of *madang*-influenced architecture are proof that expressive culture can influence the production of space. Moreover, it reflected a national desire to see and interact with folk performing arts in urban settings. I will offer more analysis of how folk performing artists adapted their performances in the new millennium in venues like the Yŏnhŭi Madang in chapter 6, but in what follows, I will focus more on regional *madang*-style events.

FIGURE 5.2 *Twip'uri* ("after party") in the Seoul Nori Madang, Seoul (2001). Photo by the author.

AMPLIFYING REGION AND HISTORY: FROM THE *TONGHAK* MOVEMENT TO THE TURTLE SHIPS

Despite its small size, South Korea possesses several distinct regional dialects, culinary traditions, and other cultural characteristics. In the Korean expressive folk culture world, I soon learned that many of my interlocutors took immense pleasure in sharing, embodying, and performing their regional culture with others. This attention to regional culture has figured prominently in South Korea's intangible heritage program and more recently has come to the fore with the emergence of festival culture. Here I focus on events where the "region" or "location" becomes just as much a defining feature or locus of attraction as any particular performing group. I will look at two contrasting regional festival events: the *Tonghak* Peasant Uprising Baeksan Revolt 108th Year Commemoration and the Goseong Ogwangdae Mask Dance Drama Annual Performance, both of which the Imshil Pilbong Nongak Preservation Association (IPNPA) had varying degrees of involvement with in 2002.

Madang on the Move 155

"The Mung Bean Flower Blooms Again: Finding Hope in History"

> This is Baeksan. In our history, it's a place we cannot forget.
> It's a very important place. This is where the peasants' revolution started.
> In terms of the fight for Korea, the fight for liberation . . . this is where
> it all started. Everyone, right now you have all come into this *hyŏnjang*
> (actual scene). You are all sitting here right now, can you not feel its power?
> Can you feel it? For those who can feel it, give a little shout! . . .
> In our history, 108 years ago, the farmers of this area gathered here . . .
> this is where you become one with these farmers. But more importantly,
> this is where our history comes together and becomes one.
> So, with this energy, as we go forward with reunification, with
> democratization, I hope you will connect it to your lives.
>
> *Kim Anju, Tonghak event speaker, April 28, 2002*

On the sunny spring day of April 28, 2002, members of the IPNPA got off the bus to perform at the *Tonghak* Peasant Uprising Baeksan Revolt 108th Year Commemoration[5] in Baeksan township. As soon as they finished getting dressed in their outfits, they made their way up the base of a hill called Baeksan, or "White Mountain," where the trail was marked by a banner that read "The Mung Bean Flower Blooms Again: Finding Hope in History." Here, the troupe began to play the rolling *p'ungnyu-kut* rhythm series, serenading an array of participants—school children in uniform, young and middle-aged adults, and some seniors—as they made their way up the hill to attend the event. I soon found out that this was the site of a Paekche kingdom (18 BCE–660 CE) fortress where rebels chose to gather during the *Tonghak* Peasant Uprising of 1894,[6] led by the famous "Mung Bean General" Chŏn Pongjun (1855–1895).[7]

This desire to engage more directly with history, evident in the title ("The Mung Bean Flower Blooms Again: Finding Hope in History"), is often theorized within the context of the *minjung undong* (democratization movement) that began in the 1960s and peaked in the late 1980s. According to Nancy Abelmann, the *minjung* movement can be considered "as a particular postcolonial engagement with history" (1996, 20). Namhee Lee further characterizes this historical engagement as a process of "reconstituting *minjung* subjectivity" (2001, 156). Lee explains this as a response to a "crisis of subjectivity" induced by the perception of modern Korean history as a failure: embodied as injured, broken, ravaged, fractured, or otherwise less than whole (2001, 159). Within this context, the

Tonghak Peasant Uprising has been widely regarded as the "genesis" of the nationalist and *minjung* movements, or more abstractly, what Abelmann refers to as "*minjung* consciousness" (Lee Namhee 2001, 174; Abelmann 1996, 20). From this perspective, the *Tonghak* Peasant Uprising has been "heralded as a true example of Korean people making their own history" (Lee Namhee 2001, 171).

In this light, the *Tonghak* Peasant Uprising Baeksan Revolt 108th Year Commemoration event offered an engagement with history and place that was carefully ritualized and embodied. In 2002, the IPNPA played a crucial role in this process. To begin with, the creative participation of the IPNPA was anything but incidental given that cultural expression has long been seen as pivotal to the *minjung* movement as the "repository of such *minjung* consciousness and practice" (Abelmann 1996, 26). In addition, *p'ungmul* is the quintessential expression of "peasant" culture, especially in Jeolla province. Abelmann even goes so far as to say that for the student activists of the democratization movement in South Korea, "peasant" cultural forms such as *p'ungmul* became almost synonymous with protest and dissent.

This commemoration was unusual in that it was intentionally organized across multiple spatial and temporal fields (table 5.1). There was not only an emphasis on place, but on movement between places. This movement between various sites (whether traversed by foot or by bus) helped recreate and reinforce the sensation of physical, social, and political mobilization within the body. In Abelmann's theorization of *minjung* discourses, mobilization works in tandem with history and memory in narratives of collective or individual transformation (1996, 21). From this perspective, the event facilitated a kind of interplay of history, memory, and mobilization that then became enacted upon the body. For Abelmann, this process is dual in that "memory posits a repository from which mobilization draws, and mobilization comprises the repository of memory" (1996, 21). The IPNPA's role was pivotal in this process because they not only played and facilitated bodily movement through historically significant sites, but they also dramatized the theme of mobilization in their performances.

With audiences that were primarily Korean and local, the emphasis of the event seemed to be about engaging and educating nearby communities (especially youth) about regional history, rather than attracting high numbers of people from far away or protesting a particular contemporary cause. Brightly colored bandannas reminiscent of the ones worn by the *Tonghak* rebels were handed out in abundance and soon everyone could be seen with them tied somewhere on their body. As folks were making their way up the hill, the IPNPA

TABLE 5.1 108th Commemoration of the *Tonghak* Peasant Uprising Baeksan Revolt, Schedule of Events (April 28, 2002)

EVENT	TIME	LOCATION	IPNPA ROLE
Memorial ceremony	10–10:30 a.m.	Baeksan Mountain stronghold	Performed for the procession up to the top of Baeksan Mountain (more like a hill).
All-participant walking assembly	11 a.m.–12 p.m.	Baeksan Mountain → Chŏn Pongjun's old house	Performed alongside the participants as they walked for about twenty-five minutes to Chŏn Pongjun's old house.
Battleground fieldtrip	12–1 p.m.	Malmok Market → Mansŏkbo Yujibi → Hwangtojae Battleground	N/A
Student writing and drawing competition	2–4 p.m.	Hwangtojae Memorial Hall	N/A
Battleground fieldtrip	2–4 p.m.	Old Gobu District → Lotus Pond and Pavilion → Gobu School and Shrine → Sabal Tongmun and Tonghak Uprising Pagoda	N/A
Cultural *madang p'ungmul-kut* performance	4–5 p.m.	Hwangtojae Memorial Hall	Performed a newly arranged *p'an-kut* on the Tonghak theme.

NOTE: The information in the first three columns is translated from the event brochure printed by the Tonghak Peasant Uprising Commemoration Society. In the fourth column, I have provided my own description of the IPNPA's role, where applicable. Movements from one location to another are indicated by the → sign.

even tried to engage more playfully with participants, drawing them into a moment of *madang*-style interaction by asking them to sing a song before being allowed to pass.

Once at the top of Baeksan, participants sat down and listened to the memorial proceedings, where speakers, such as Kim Anju (excerpted above), gave inspirational speeches and thanked various community members and groups. From here, the organizers had planned the event in such a way to allow for a greater emphasis on more interactive modes of memorializing. Even the act of climbing up and down Baeksan, or "White Mountain," was a potentially moving experience. It is from here that the rebels once gathered and proclaimed that "if you sit, it's Bamboo mountain, if you stand, it's White mountain!" What they meant was that while the masses of rebels were sitting, the mountain was covered with bamboo spears being held at the ready, but once standing up, the mountain would become white from the bodies of peasants wearing *minbok* (traditionally white peasant clothing). Despite Baeksan's small size, the sensation of being at the top is unexpectedly exhilarating, because it is one of those geographical formations that juts up out of nowhere. Instead of an expanse of rugged territory typical of the Korean countryside, the surrounding land is unusually flat in comparison, and as a result, the rebels were able to survey much of the surrounding territory from this vantage point.

After the ceremony, the IPNPA troupe played in formation as the participants traveled by foot from Baeksan to Chŏn Pongjun's reconstructed home. Marching together with the rest of the participants to the rhythms of the *p'ungmul* was effective in engaging the dual processes of memory and mobilization. For example, walking along the path that the rebels may have taken not only stimulated and instilled memory but was also, in itself, an act of mobilization. The walk was lengthy enough to register what it might have felt like to march in the *Tonghak* movement.

From here, the IPNPA proceeded by bus to the Hwangtojae Battleground and Memorial Hall. Hwangtojae is the site where the peasant rebels won their first battle against the government forces on May 11 of 1894. Today, Hwangtojae looks less like a battleground and more like the grounds of a temple, with nicely landscaped terraces, memorial buildings constructed in "traditional" Korean architecture, a memorial pagoda, and well-kept lawns.

Of all the IPNPA performances I have seen, this one stands out for its level of creative engagement with a particular event's purpose. In 2002, it was one of the few times I observed the IPNPA focus primarily on telling a political narrative—in this case, a narrative of the mobilization of *Tonghak* rebels—as expressed through *p'ungmul*.[8] Along these lines, this event was a catalyst for both political and creative engagement. Although it was officially sanctioned by the IPNPA, many of the actual performers were not regular members of the IPNPA. Here, they drew upon a pool of talented younger players who would be more open to creating and rehearsing a newly arranged entertainment-oriented *p'ungmul* performance or *p'an-kut* on the *Tonghak* theme.

The story was organized into five movements or *madang* (in the temporal unit sense of the word used in *p'ansori* and mask dance). Each *madang* was dedicated to memorializing different aspects of the *Tonghak* experience.

1. First *Madang*: The Sound of the *Puk* (barrel drum) Fills the Sky
2. Second *Madang*: *Sabal T'ongmun* ("round robin" document)
3. Third *Madang*: Farmer's Training
4. Fourth *Madang*: Hwangtojae, Hwallyongchon, and Jeonju Fort Battles
5. Fifth *Madang*: The *Tonghak* Peasant Uprising Battle Cry Sounds Again

Even though they did not compose new rhythms specifically for the event, they did fashion fresh arrangements and choreographies that were startlingly different from the IPNPA's *p'angut* (entertainment) or other ritual formats I had observed. Performing in an open grassy area, the first *madang* began with the blowing of the *nabal* bugle. This was swiftly followed with a formation of just the *puk*, or two-sided barrel drummers. They proceeded through the following *madangs* in a dizzying array of choreographies, often splitting into two groups to portray opposing sides. In addition to the new arrangements and choreographies, another striking feature that really differentiated this performance was that all the percussionists played while also performing *sangmo* (the twirling of streamers or feathers attached to special hats). Though normally the province of the *soe* and *sogo* players, here the *changgo*, *puk*, and *ching* players all performed while manipulating their twirling headgear. The addition of *sangmo* for instrumental players is not considered "traditional" practice for Pilbong and is the direct result of increased physical virtuosity. Though some participants may have viewed this as off-putting and excessive, others may have appreciated its resonance with the event's emphasis on revolutionary movement and mobilization that was subtly apparent in the military roots of the additional *sangmo* headgear (Hesselink 2006, 68–74). The *chapsaek* dramatic characters were the exception and did not perform *sangmo*. This may explain why they often seemed shut out of the *p'an*, struggling to find their places within this new milieu.

Although the emphasis on "site" and situated practice was not always articulated in terms of the *madang*, there were some key ways in which aspects of *madang* discourse intersected with this event. First, there was an awareness of shared space as vital to community. More prominently, the notion of being in the *hyŏnjang* or "actual spot or moment in time" was at the very heart of the event's strategy. It was through this commitment to the *hyŏnjang* that the participants were able to experience the historic resonance of the location, thereby helping to engage the construction of memory and locality in tangible ways. Even though the participants may have not been able to experience the actual historic events that were said to have taken place in these locations, they were able to create their own experience of physical and political mobilization as they moved from site to site. Despite some unevenness in the IPNPA's performances, they helped imagine and produce a historically informed and embodied ontology of space and place that participants were able to experience and remember.

"In the Smile of a Mask, Coming Together as One"

> This is a festival-*madang* for all of us. Everyone is a performer, and everyone is a participant. We are all owners and we are all guests. So please feel free to yell out or dance as much as you want! We have provided a diverse *madang* for you: face painting, food, photography, totem pole making, mask making, so please enjoy!
>
> Chŏn Kwangnyŏl, Goseong Ogwangdae member and announcer, July 28, 2002

Goseong Ogwangdae (literally "five entertainers," *ogwangdae* is the regional term for mask dance) is a style of Korean mask dance drama that was first developed by practitioners from Goseong, a town located on a craggy stretch of the southwestern coast in South Gyeongsang province. With its characteristic combination of strong stances and fluid movements, Goseong Ogwangdae received its status as Important Intangible Cultural Asset No. 7 in 1964. Musically, the sound of Goseong Ogwangdae is similar to *p'ungmul* in that it uses many of the same percussion instruments—*changgo*, *puk*, *ching*, and *kkwaenggwari*—although in smaller numbers. It also employs the conical double-reed called the *t'aep'yŏngso* that is heard in *p'ungmul*, but in Goseong Ogwangdae, this singular melodic instrument plays a larger role in creating a melodic flow that is crucial for the dancers.

During my fieldwork year in 2001–2002, I spent a good deal of time following the activities and performances of the Goseong Ogwangdae Pojonhoe or "Goseong Ogwangdae Preservation Association" (hereafter GOPA) because I wanted to get a more dance- and drama-oriented perspective on *madang* performance. Most importantly, they are a group that really understands how important it is to cultivate the social and community-oriented aspects of the *madang*. As the above quote attests, the *madang* was a central concept that served as an "integrative map" that helped guide how they produced their annual 2002 performance in the spatial, temporal, social, or experiential realms.

For this event, GOPA chose the theme of "In the Smile of a Mask, Coming Together as One," encapsulating the hopeful and now familiar theme of "becoming one." While the notion of "becoming one" was also used in the *Tonghak* event, in this context, the phrase takes on added significance given Goseong Ogwangdae's desire to express solidarity across regions by inviting representative folk expressive culture groups from strategically distinct areas. For example, two of the groups that were invited represent Hwanghae and Hamgyeong provinces, both now a part of North Korea. The group that represents Hwanghae province is a mask dance group called Eunyul T'alch'um and has been designated with the national status of Important Intangible Cultural Property No. 61. The other group that represents Hamgyeong province is a "song and dance" group called Tondollari that has been recognized locally as the Hamgyeong province Cultural Property No. 1.[9] They also opted to invite the Imshil Pilbong Nongak Preservation Association (IPNPA), even though they could have easily chosen well-established groups from within their own province. Given that Goseong is located deep in South Gyeongsang province, the selection of Pilbong is particularly significant because they hail from a province that has long been regarded as a rival. According to Goseong Ogwangdae's manager, Hwang Chonguk, the tacit vision behind the inclusion of Pilbong was to bring together two culturally contrasting and historically antagonistic areas: Jeolla and Gyeongsang provinces, or what are otherwise respectively known as Honam and Yeongnam (personal communication).

In addition to the *madang* concept, Goseong's regular annual event was also clearly influenced by the "festival" or *ch'ukche* phenomenon. According to their manager, Hwang Chonguk, the rise of festivals in South Korea has gone hand in hand with the rise of regional tourism. Despite his acknowledgement of the excessive display of festivals in South Korea, Hwang still sees the *ch'ukche p'an* or "festival format" as a more suitable setting for the presentation of their performances to contemporary audiences, the development of which he sees as the direction of the future (Hwang interview, September 13, 2002). In light of this view, the group has experimented considerably by incorporating festival-like themes, formats, and programming. For example, in their 2002 event, they organized an extensive activity area, including totem pole carving, mask making, face painting, and the writing of wishes to burn in the bonfire.[10]

For several years, GOPA has created events that go beyond the affirmation of their own style to offer something new to local audiences. This can also be seen as a strategy to give their event an added edge to attract audiences from further afield to develop a more national or even international reputation. They have also enhanced the festival-like atmosphere by choosing geographically or historically significant locations.[11] In 2002, GOPA chose the Danghangpo Tourist Site as the location for their event. Aside from being a picturesque bay surrounded by hills, Danghangpo is also the site of a successful maritime battle against the Japanese in June 1592 led by Admiral Yi Sunshin, a renowned Korean naval commander. Seen as one of Korea's greatest heroes, Yi Sunshin was a pivotal leader in resisting the Japanese invasions of Korea led by Toyotomi Hideyoshi (1592–1598).[12] By choosing this site, they were able to draw upon regional history as an interactive backdrop for the performances. As mentioned previously, the performance groups were also chosen to "represent" various regions, contributing to an event that displayed a subtle inter-regional reflexivity.

The Goseong Ogwangdae Preservation Association cultivates *madang*-style events similarly to the Imshil Pilbong Nongak Preservation Association in several ways. Most notably, they know how to draw support and strength from various communities. In particular, they both build upon the spirit of *kongdongch'e* (community) cultivated at their respective *chŏnsugwan*, or "transmission centers." Unlike the IPNPA however, GOPA did more than just employ the *chŏnsu* students as volunteers, they also gave them opportunities to perform the *kibon ch'um*, or "basic dance sequence," at the very beginning of the event.

Both groups also have a keen sense of how to best create the atmosphere of the *madang* through the careful configuration of space, time, and people. The GOPA's 2002 event at Danghangpo was no exception. It helped that the Danghangpo Tourist Site is already equipped with an informal outdoor stage that is situated on one end of a rectangle-shaped plaza (figure 5.3). Other facilities included some rustic booths that were originally set up to display historic artifacts but served as the perfect backdrop for the event's totem pole carving and other hands-on activities. In front of this area, the GOPA set up around a dirt gravel *madang* where they placed a teepee-shaped structure of bamboo and other grasses to burn later for the bonfire. White plastic chairs set up in rows framed the performance area in front of the stage. On the floor, right in front of a raised stage, the GOPA set up an altar upon which they arranged pre-established offerings for the *t'al kosa* or "mask ceremony," performed in honor of all the ancestors that have helped to propagate the Goseong style of mask dance. Although the GOPA, IPNPA, and Eunyul T'alch'um groups performed in the central performance area paved with light gravel, Tondollari performed on the stage.

Natural elements also served to frame the area. To one side of the stage, a hill served as part of a natural enclosure. On the other side, the GOPA provided some visual balance with colorful banners mounted on tall bamboo poles (figure 5.4).

FIGURE 5.3 Danghangpo outdoor stage and plaza, Goseong Ogwangdae Regular Annual Performance, Goseong (2002). Photo by the author.

FIGURE 5.4 Danghangpo outdoor stage and plaza with bamboo on one side and a hill on the other, Goseong (2002). Photo by the author.

Beyond the cultural center, the audience members could glimpse a sliver of ocean in the distance. During the day's festivities, many of the participants took the opportunity to explore this watery expanse where Yi Sunshin's ships are said to have once sailed. Spatially, the area was set up to encourage many of the qualities espoused in *madang* discourse: openness, community, and audience participation, as well as a sense of ritual and play (video 5.1 🔊).

Temporally and socially, however, the *madang* was not always configured well to bring out these qualities throughout the whole event. The arts and crafts and other pre-program activities began earlier in the afternoon, which worked well, but the opening events suffered somewhat when the "official" program began at 5 p.m. with the opening of the mask ceremony.

PRE-PROGRAM

1. Arts and crafts activities
2. Goseong Ogwangdae students perform *kibon ch'um*

CEREMONIES

3. *P'an Shissŭm* (playing *p'ungmul* to "cleanse the *p'an*")
4. *T'al Kosa* (mask ceremony), 5 p.m.
5. Banner painting ceremony

PERFORMANCES

1. Pilbong Nongak (IPNPA)
2. Eunyul T'alch'um
3. Tondollari
4. Goseong Ogwangdae (GOPA)

Being the first to perform, the IPNPA had several factors working against them. When they came out to play around 6 p.m., the sun was still beating down oppressively. Afterward, Yang Chinsŏng (the IPNPA leader and *sangsoe*) commented that he could not remember ever having to perform in such sweltering heat (personal communication). They also had the unfortunate position of performing right after the ceremonial section of the program. Despite the importance of the *t'al kosa* (mask ritual) in particular, these types of ceremonies tend to drag and bring the overall energy of the event down. When I asked Hwang Chonguk about the GOPA's group evaluation of the event, they all acknowledged that the *t'al kosa*

Madang on the Move **165**

was too long, causing the event to temporarily "lose steam" (Hwang interview, September 13, 2002). Most significantly, their position as first in the program meant that their performance was limited: not just in terms of time but also in terms of their overall role. For example, even though they may have technically had enough time to bring the audience into participatory play in the *madang* following the conclusion of their performance, it would not have been appropriate given their position as first in the event. In a related vein, because it was still daylight, their performance suffered in terms of ambience. In comparison, the later acts enjoyed the focusing effect of professional evening lighting and the added atmospheric effect of the brazier fires.

Given these circumstances, the Pilbong *p'ungmul-kut* troupe did their best to represent their style in an energetic manner. Even so, their performance was very standard and considerably less dynamic than they are capable of. For example, their rhythmic ordering showed very little variation except for the fact that they took more breaks than normal and allotted more time to individual solos. The group played together for about thirty minutes with a solo section of twenty minutes. Although there were many audience members who knew how to participate in the *madang*, I was surprised by how few chose to come in during their performance. Interestingly, the Pilbong *p'ungmul* troupe also seemed less open to the audience as well. For example, when an elderly gentleman came into the *madang* to dance with the *kakshi* (young woman) character, he was swiftly escorted out by the *yangban* (aristocrat) character after he began to get too close to the *kakshi*.

Since the Pilbong group normally concludes their performances with a robust *twip'uri* or participatory group play, the lack thereof would have made their performance feel incomplete to those who knew their performances well. This could have been remedied had the troupe decided to stay until after the Goseong Ogwangdae closed the program to join the final *twip'uri*. However, they opted to leave shortly thereafter because they had a long drive home (about four hours). Although GOPA opened up a nice space for the IPNPA to perform, the Pilbong troupe was not ideally situated on the program. Because of this, the IPNPA's participation fell a little short of the symbolic ideal of coming together, but it probably could not have been avoided given the challenges of logistics and scheduling and the vicissitudes of the weather.

The next two groups who performed represented Korea's northern provinces (now in present-day North Korea): Eunyul T'alch'um (mask dance drama) and Tondollari folksong. They performed as darkness fell, which helped focus the audience's attention on their performances. Eunyul T'alch'um features a vivacious and supple lion character (typically performed by two dancers) who spontaneously responded to the heat by feigning exhaustion, which served as a comedic prompt for the audience to come out into the *madang* and try to revive the lion. After several unsuccessful tries, a member of the Goseong troupe eventually came out and helped appease the lion out by bowing and offering the fantastical beast some *makkŏlli*. The Tondollari folksong group followed by performing on the well-lit stage, accompanied by drums, water gourds, and unique vertical flutes. Aided by the cooling evening temperatures and focusing effects of lighting and sound amplification, the audience seemed very attentive and receptive to these northern manifestations of Korean folk culture.

When the Goseong Ogwangdae group finally took the stage, the ambience and sense of intimacy was heightened with the help of the central bonfire and raised brazier fires that lent a warm and exciting glow to the performances. Like the Pilbong group does back in their home village ritual, Goseong also went out of their way to use natural illumination over artificial lighting, even going so far as to have individuals hold torches at pivotal locations around the *madang*. Given the open-air setting of a *madang*, this is one of the most effective ways to create natural atmosphere and drama in mask dance.

The performance that evening went much like others I had seen from the group, but the special effort that they had put into every detail did create a dramatic and ritualistic atmosphere. In this context, each scene of the play seemed more defined, expressive, and vivid. For example, the first scene that highlighted the wordless exertions of a solitary, wandering leper seemed even more poignant. Here, the leper (*mundungi*) finds redemption by finally being able to wield the drum with his gnarled hands and find catharsis in dance. The second scene dramatically highlighted the sweeping but powerful motions of the five nobles dressed in robes of different colors, their shadows flickering in the moonlight. This entrancing scene was then punctuated by the entrance of the horse groomsman (*malttugi*) character, who cleverly mocked them with his witty banter and strong movements. The third scene is the *Pibi Kwajang* or "Play of Pibi the Beast," where the Pibi figure dominated the large space by chasing around nobles to eat. Here, the characters interacted a lot with the audience by traversing across from one edge of the *madang* to the other, with the Pibi monster even hiding amongst unsuspecting audience members and sitting on their laps at one point. The fourth scene features a mysterious apostate monk who attempts to attract two young maidens, their long sleeves billowing in the air. The fifth and final scene documents the travails of an older wife searching around for her husband who has run off with a younger concubine. In this performance, the older wife was especially good and using various comedic antics to involve the audience. The play ends with the funeral of the older wife, where many of the performers return to carry a colorful funeral bier and sing songs while audience members are invited to mourn along with them. Given that the Goseong group was in their hometown, audience and community members were especially enthusiastic in wanting to take turns climbing up on the bier, tucking money into its ropes as donation. This flowed into an energetic *twip'uri* or "after-party," where accompanying Korean rhythms are played while the remaining audience members are all invited to join the *madang* to dance with the performers (video 5.1 🔊).

What is apparent from the way that the event unfolded is just how crucial the social element, or more specifically, the orientations of the participants are in creating a *madang*. Although many of the elements of a *madang* are important, I would suggest that it is the people that are the critical "glue" that holds these elements together. Further, it is in the hands of all the participants to shape whether a *madang* becomes more intense in a given realm (such as the social/relational, transformative/dynamic, or experiential, table 0.1).

In sum, the GOPA extended a gesture of goodwill to other nationally recognized groups by inviting them to perform at their own annual festival. As was evident in this 2002 GOPA annual event, these situations are much like a delicate balancing act that, if swayed in the wrong direction, can potentially have an adverse effect on the character of the *madang*.[13] Although the GOPA event did not quite live up to the promise of "coming together as one" in the "smile of a mask," it was a success because fundamentally, I think all of the groups understood that it was essentially a Goseong event. Although the event was planned in order to attract outside attention to Goseong,[14] in actuality, most of the audience was either local or had some connection to Goseong Ogwangdae through the transmission center. In this way, the GOPA exposed local audiences to styles they may have not otherwise been able to see, and at the same time contributed to the circulation of Korean expressive folk culture groups.

For both the IPNPA and GOPA, these events only present a small piece of what they do regionally. In choosing to focus on these two events, however, I have demonstrated how different types of agendas can come into play in the articulation of the region. While both events drew attention to the importance of site and place-based history, the IPNPA's creative engagement celebrated grassroots politics through the performative embodiment of mobilization. They did this by creating a map of events through which participants could actually walk in the footsteps of the *Tonghak* rebels, thereby providing ways to experience place and imagine its connection to history. In contrast, GOPA's selection of Danghangpo for their annual event that particular year was less explicitly political in this sense. Rather, this decision worked to strengthen its place within the regional culture by strategically aligning itself with famous regional and national markers such as Danghangpo and the renowned military commander Yi Sunshin, and encouraging multiple avenues through which to engage with regional culture (mask making, looking at Danghangpo artifacts, strolling alongside the water, for example). The goal of "coming together as one" was also woven into articulating the national through their invitation of performance groups from very different provinces. Their selection of two teams who represent North Korea also indirectly gestured toward a progressive politics of reunification. Although these events were free and open to the public and therefore not driven solely by the logic of capital gain, they were influenced by the forces of regional culture and heritage tourism and supported in part by national Korean entities such as the Ministry of Culture, Sports, and Tourism. Because of this, these events were inevitably entangled with mainstream efforts to foster regionalism as a mode of strengthening national identity. At that juncture in time in the early 2000s, this expression of nationalism was more aligned with the legacy of the democratization movement (*minjung undong*). However, nationalism in Korea can also take on more authoritarian, conservative, and even xenophobic directions. In the following section, I will explore how groups like the GOPA have tried to counteract these tendencies by embracing diversity and supporting disenfranchised migrant workers in Korea.

FORGING ALLIANCES WITH MIGRANT WORKERS

Just one week after this 2002 annual performance, Goseong Ogwangdae was invited to perform for a starkly different occasion: closing night of the Equality Summer Camp for Migrant Workers that took place at the Handong school on Geoje Island. I highlight this event because Korean groups like GOPA are not often seen as having a role in the emergent discourses of multiculturalism and globalization in South Korea. In fact, a Korean cultural anthropologist, Geon-Soo Han [Kŏnsu Han], implies in his article that "traditional" Korean culture has a very limited role in the discourse of multiculturalism and in contemporary society in general. Looking mainly at the mainstream media, Han argues that Korean traditional culture is mainly trotted out during holidays such as *Ch'usŏk* as a vehicle for the assimilation of marriage-based migrant women, migrant workers, and other foreign residents (Han 2007, 32–33).

While this may be true of the mainstream media, my ethnographic observations of this event and of the younger generation of performers that followed in these footsteps suggest a more nuanced story. From as early as 2002, groups such as Goseong Ogwangdae have been responsive to the struggles of multicultural populations and have even radically altered their performances in order to better speak to their needs. While this particular event was not as site-oriented as the previous examples were, it did draw on *madang* discourses to build new connections to people, place, and time in a meaningful way. In a slightly different vein from the Danghangpo performance, I posit that this event was part of an effort to frame rural regions differently. As opposed to thinking about them as havens of Korean traditional culture, this event acknowledged that rural regions such as Gyeongnam province are on the forefront of a dramatic reckoning with changing demographics and diversity. Perhaps more importantly, the increasing number of migrants to Korea makes it imperative to query the meaning and impact of *madang*-oriented events for those who have very little power to claim a site or space as their own.

Over the past decade, the multicultural population in South Korea has grown tremendously. Korea has developed from a more ethnically homogeneous society to a more multicultural one in a relatively compressed period. From 2006 to 2015, the number of foreign residents in South Korea grew from 537,000 to more than 1.7 million, making up 3.4 percent of the total population (Eum [Ŭm] 2015). It has been widely reported that 14 percent of all marriages are international marriages; much of this is due to the phenomenon of rural bachelors marrying other Asian women in a society where various factors have contributed to Korean adult men slightly outnumbering women (Onishi 2007) in a society where Korean women are focusing more and more on work and career advancement.

In rural areas that typically struggle with the exodus of its citizens to urban centers, the influx of migrant workers and marriage migrants has altered the social landscape in increasingly visible ways. In Gyeongnam province alone, where Goseong is located, there are as many as 70,000 migrant workers (Gyeongnam Migrant Community Service Center, n.d.). When I observed the Equality Summer Camp organized by the Gyeongnam Migrant Community Service Center in 2002 (hereafter GMCSC), the camp was already in its fifth year with 300 participants coming from diverse countries such as India, Bangladesh, Sri Lanka, Pakistan, Indonesia, China, Uzbekistan, Russia, and the Philippines. As of 2017, the GMCSC has grown and gained visibility with its multi-day Migrant Arirang Multi-Cultural Festival, which included a parade and was attended by as many as 3,000 foreign residents (Un 2017).

Back in 2002, Goseong Ogwangdae took part in a more grassroots event that was scheduled outdoors in the school courtyard. In order to be more inclusive, the program also involved the camp participants in an open mic, the lighting of a bonfire, and a talent show that consisted mainly of karaoke singing and dancing. Given the degree to which they creatively adapted to this unique situation, it was apparent that the Goseong Ogwangdae leaders cared more about facilitating an open and meaningful experience for the participants than about showcasing their form. Most significantly, they dramatically reduced their usual performance content from five acts down to one. They also opened up several opportunities for their younger trainees and transmission students to participate in ways that enhanced the transitions and dynamic flow of the event and maximized engagement. For example, they began their entry into the performance space by leading their younger mask dance trainees in a parade throughout the courtyard called *kilnori* (literally "road play"). The percussion band for the *kilnori* also accompanied several female singers as they sang traditional Korean folksongs. Their earthy vocals really engaged the camp participants as several of them began to rise and interact more with the performers by performing a dance that involved alternating steps of the feet in a backward criss-crossing motion. Given that men originally performed all the roles in this form (even the female characters), I was impressed by their decision to give women a chance to sing in this multicultural arena. When I asked them how they decided what to perform that day, the managing director, Hwang Chonguk, told me that they quickly surveyed the scene and figured out what would work best in the moment.

After the folksongs, the percussion band segued into opening act of Goseong Ogwangdae: the *Mundung Pukch'um*, or "Leper Drum Dance." Although the "Leper Drum Dance" constitutes a relatively short episode in the five-act drama, it makes perfect sense that they chose to focus solely on presenting this scene. Firstly, it is one of two acts in the whole play that does not rely on dialogue to convey the gist of the narrative and can more easily translate to a diverse audience. Secondly, of all the dramatic material that is covered in the five acts, the story of a marginal figure in society transcending adversity relates perhaps most closely to the migrant worker experience. Just as the leprosy that the character suffers is not the result of his own sins but payback from an ancestor's wrongdoing, the hardship of a migrant worker often stems from issues of one's class and status at birth or other forces beyond one's immediate control. The lesson of this character is that by overcoming small challenges, little by little, one can regain strength and achieve moments of ecstatic joy, or *shinmyŏng* in Korean. While the brown, pock-marked mask serves as a prominent identifying marker for the leper character, it also serves to mask the individual actor's identity so that the viewers can more easily identify themselves with the character on an abstract symbolic level. The power of the mask lies in its ability to enable the viewer to project his or her own personal experience onto the character and understand themselves and their own bodies as possible agents of change and transformation.

In watching this performance, I was moved by how well the audience reacted to the gradual shift from despair to ecstasy (*shinmyŏng*). This shift is usually signaled through changes in the music, dance movements, and gestures with the drum and stick as props. Sensing the power of the handheld drum that was laid out on a straw mat, one of the camp participants was so drawn in that he tried to take it and play it himself. In a spontaneous moment of interaction, the leper called attention to the missing instrument and the drum was gently retrieved and put back in its place. As mentioned previously, being able to pick up the drum is considered a major achievement for the leper and is therefore a signal of increasing power and strength. Retrieving the handheld drum from the audience member added to the drama of the evening as the leper was finally able to move and master the drum. Eventually, the leper took the drumstick and pointed it up in the air in a triumphant extension of the body, twirled the end in a small circle, and cued the drummers to switch to the faster *chajinmori* rhythm. Spurred on by the faster rhythm, the leper character began to cover more space and move more animatedly, eventually moving in close to a cluster of camp participants located in one corner of the courtyard. Many of the audience members responded by clapping, synchronizing their movements, and even getting up and dancing. Although the rest of the performances shifted to the camp participants as they performed in a talent show, the embodied expression of *shinmyŏng* cultivated toward the end of the leper dance seemed to linger until the camp participants ended the evening by dancing in the warm glow of a bonfire.

Although Goseong Ogwangdae did not radically alter their repertoire, I think they succeeded in making this event less about themselves and more about the camp participants. What I found significant was that they created a *madang* that was open enough to allow individuals to respond with their own cultural movement vocabularies. For example, toward the end of the evening, I witnessed groups of people exchanging moves and dance styles as the musical styles on the karaoke machine shifted from Korean pop to American disco, techno, and even a spirited rendition of "La Bamba."

Through their flexible ability to read and adjust to the event, GOPA was able to create a *madang* that dynamically transformed an ordinary schoolyard into a resonant articulation of music, movement, space, bodies, voices, and sociality. In this way, I build upon Marié Abe's definition of resonance as "a simultaneously acoustic and affective work of sounding" (Abe 2018, 29) to include bodily movement as well. Rather than sound as the primary medium of "affective" communication, I would argue that the affective work can also reside in the elicitation of embodied responses through sounding *and* moving. While the effects are ephemeral and indeterminate, as Abe critically notes, the success of such affective work speaks to the expressive power of sound and movement to transcend linguistic, cultural, and other barriers. In order to gauge the lasting impact of these kinds of exchanges, much more work needs to be done and requires interviewing migrant workers more directly. However, I offer these preliminary ethnographic observations to make the point that while groups like Goseong Ogwangdae are normally associated with a more homogeneous regional identity, I would suggest that these types of groups can contribute meaningfully to supporting a more plural regional identity in South Korea. Although they may not get as much public recognition for doing events like this, they have set an influential model for the next generation of performers to follow. In fact, several groups have already been following in their footsteps, which will be the subject of the next chapter.

SIX

Creative Korean Performing Arts in National Urban Spaces

> Now, concrete times have rhythms, or rather are rhythms—and all rhythms imply the relation of a time to a space, a localized time, or, if one prefers, a temporalized space. Rhythm is always linked to such and such a place, to its place, be that the heart, the fluttering of the eyelids, the movement of a street or the tempo of a waltz.
>
> *Lefebvre 2004, 9*

In the midst of dramatic demographic changes taking place in twenty-first century Korea, this chapter addresses the efforts of creative traditional performing arts (*ch'angjak yŏnhŭi*) teams to adapt to the evolving rhythms of this increasingly diverse urban South Korean population. In doing so, I am interested in examining how they continue to draw upon on *madang*-based concepts to reach out to different audiences in a range of national urban spaces—from public urban *madangs* to intimate senior centers, palatial grounds filled with tourists to bustling city streets, utilitarian stadium entrances to open apartment complex grounds. Many of the sites I focus on in this chapter are in the metropolitan area of Seoul and serve as highly visible representative markers of the nation. Using an arsenal of different expressive modes—music, sound, dramatic dialogue, movement, dance, and other expressive skills—these performers are constantly on the frontlines of creating site-oriented expressive ecologies in urban spaces by eliciting bodily and social participation from various groups of people who reside in or visit South Korea. In meeting diverse members of Korean society where they are today (rather than in an idealized, receding past), they are re-imagining and re-configuring Korean folk culture in the process. As will be seen in this chapter, the effects of their work are unpredictable. Each performance is contingent, indeterminate, and ultimately ephemeral, but when things come together, they do encourage people to embody older forms of Korean folk culture, thereby making it more present and meaningful in their lives. Through this, a sense of social cohesion, community, and belonging can develop, and perhaps even a temporary sense of place in a rapidly evolving cityscape.

CONTEMPORARY SOUTH KOREA IN THE NEW MILLENNIUM

When I first began investigating Korean performing arts traditions that take place in the *madang* in the early 2000s, Korean music institutions were enjoying an upswing in support. No longer were they a somewhat marginal object of preservation and revival and, even worse, a vilified mode of cultural protest. Rather, they were on their way to becoming a regular feature of the national curriculum and cultural landscape. Those in power from 1998 to 2008 such as former Presidents Kim Dae-Jung [Kim Taechung] (1998–2003) and Roh Moo-Hyun [No Muhyŏn] (2003–2008) were actively involved in the democratization movement and understood the value of Korean cultural forms. I distinctly remember a conversation in 2002 that I had with the leader of the IPNPA, Yang Chinsŏng, where he emphasized how much things have changed since *nongak* or *p'ungmul* drumming was seen mostly as the oppositional protest medium of choice of the democratization or *minjung* movement of the 1970s and 1980s. Noting the dramatic increase of government federal and regional support and gesturing toward Pilbong's greatly expanded transmission center, Yang pointed out that the *minjung* politicians were in power and that it was a completely different world due to the increased public acceptance and support for *p'ungmul*. I nodded and had every reason to be optimistic that the future of Korean traditional performing arts would continue along this trajectory into the new millennium.

The way it played out over the next decade, however, would prove to be much more complicated. In the political realm, the cultural tides changed course dramatically with the more conservative presidencies of Lee Myung-bak [Yi Myŏngbak] (2008–2013) and Park Geun-hye [Pak Kŭnhye] (2013–2017), who were both more proactive in supporting "culture industries" over traditional arts (Jin 2016, 32–37). In the economic realm, the new millennium in South Korea was punctuated by financial upheaval. It was presaged by the 1997 Asian financial crisis (referred to in South Korea as the IMF crisis) and crashed in the aftermath of the global 2008 financial crisis. Both had lasting impacts, precipitating several neoliberal changes that have led some Korean youth to liken contemporary Korea to a living hell, which they call by the somewhat irreverent and trans-lingual nickname of "Hell *Chosŏn*." *Chosŏn* refers to the last dynasty (1392–1910) of Korea and is associated with Confucian values and a more rigid social hierarchy; it is also a backward-looking synonym for the nation and is even the preferred name of "Korea" in North Korea. In terms of employment, the IMF bailout that was negotiated in response to the 1997 Asian financial crisis was granted under the condition that various austerity measures would be put in place.

This paved the way for the neoliberal restructuring of labor in South Korea. As a result, it was easier to fire workers and the number of stable and secure jobs dwindled while lower-paid and irregular employment (*pi'jŏng'gyujik*) increased. Somewhat analogous to what happened in Japan in the 1990s, educated, middle-class Korean youth could no longer rely on the prospect of decent employment in the professional sector upon graduation from a reputable university. With prospects dimming for these young adults, the fertility rate has plummeted to one of the lowest in the world at just 0.78 births per woman in 2023 (Ahn 2023). At the same time, the Korean population is aging "faster than any other advanced economy on Earth" with a median age that has risen to 41.2 from 19.6 between the years 1975 to 2015 (Larmer 2018). Meanwhile, there is a labor shortage in blue-collar jobs in manufacturing, agriculture, and construction. These jobs are generally not seen as desirable by educated young people and are increasingly being filled by migrant workers. This phenomenon has contributed to a persistently high domestic unemployment rate of just under 10 percent among younger Korean workers (Larmer 2018). Many Korean women are also opting to prioritize work over having a family, and if they marry, they often do so at a later age. This has contributed to the rise of "marriage migrants," who are mostly Chinese and Southeast Asian women. As mentioned in the previous chapter, South Korea is becoming more multiethnic, which is challenging the notion of the Korean nation being based upon a singular ethnicity.

Meanwhile, South Korea's efforts to become increasingly global in its cultural, economic, and technological reach—perhaps most visible in the success of K-pop—has attracted higher numbers of foreign tourists, longer-term foreign residents (exchange students, teachers, scholars, etc.), as well as increased numbers of consumers of Korean products worldwide. Just as more people from abroad are coming into South Korea, there are also more Koreans seeking to "escape" "Hell Chosŏn," either temporarily as exchange students, and/or later as more permanent workers or residents.

As a result of these changes, the trajectory of Korean traditional performing arts did not quite pan out in the way that I was expecting in the early 2000s. With fewer opportunities for advancement within the rigid Intangible Cultural Asset system, the pool of younger people studying traditional performing arts has become less balanced in terms of age and gender and has now become more dominated by women who have more flexibility to pursue the arts in contemporary Korean society (Yeo 2018, 30–31; Choi 2014, 51). By contrast, as the economic and employment situation has tightened in the new millennium, men have experienced more economic pressure to find more lucrative and stable employment, as opposed to pursuing the arts (Yeo 2018, 32–34). Meanwhile, as the state shifted from the preservation of traditional arts and culture to supporting "culture industries" with the rise of *hallyu* or the "Korean wave" (Jin 2016, 28–35), more and more of the younger generation of traditional performers have chosen to pursue more creative and contemporary avenues of Korean performing arts, often by fusing together Korean genres with a host of other cosmopolitan genres—from jazz and classical to pop, hip-hop, rock, and more.

An important part of this backdrop of creative fusion is that the twenty-first century has seen several surges of K-pop success, partly fueled by capitalizing upon social media digital technologies such as YouTube, eventually leading to the international breakout hit of Psy's "Gangnam Style" in 2012 and the recent successes of girl and boy groups such as Blackpink, BTS, Twice, and Stray Kids. Contributing to the spread of K-pop in Asia, the US, Europe, and South America was the collaboration of corporate and state actors to promote K-pop as a medium of South Korean "soft power" globally (Jin 2016, 32–37).

In part due to the spectacular success of the K-pop industry and the prevalence of women in Korean performing arts, one creative avenue that some female performers have gravitated toward is a genre called "fusion *gugak*," which usually consists of all-female groups like Queen, whose members were trained in Korean traditional music or *gugak* but play music hybridized with other styles, often moving while performing in appealing hanbok-derived contemporary costumes. Fusion *gugak* groups have been heavily criticized by the Korean elite music community for "playing commercialized easy listening music, mostly covers of various types of popular music" (Yeo 2018, 144). Other hybrid groups have scorned the term and have actively tried to disassociate themselves from the genre. For example, one well-known group named Jambinai (featured in the 2018 Winter Olympic closing ceremonies) firmly stated on their Facebook page at one point that their "genre" should be called "post-rock, metal, dark, traditional, avant-garde, but NOT fusion *gugak* ever."[1]

Despite this criticism of fusion *gugak*, the experimental melding of Korean traditional music with popular genres has continued to ebb and flow, with a noticeable uptick in success in the early 2020s with alternative groups such as Leenalchi and Ak Dan Gwang Chil, but also with K-pop groups such as Ateez, Oneus, Kingdom, and BTS's own Agust-D (Suga) with his critical 2020 hit "Taech'wita." While all of these examples warrant attention, I return now to *ch'angjak yŏnhŭi*, a creative performing genre that I have chosen to focus on because it continues to be aligned with the *madang* concept, the subject of my initial research.

CH'ANGJAK YŎNHŬI (CREATIVE KOREAN PERFORMING ARTS)

Since the mid-2000s, young and creative performers in "traditional performing arts" or *yŏnhŭi* have turned increasingly toward exploring the *ch'angjak yŏnhŭi* realm. Korean scholar Son T'aedo has even referred to the period from 2007 until the present as "the era of *ch'angjak yŏnhŭi*" (Son 2021, 126). *Ch'angjak* means "creative" or "newly composed" and *yŏnhŭi* serves as an umbrella term for various types of Korean traditional performing arts that would normally be performed outdoors in *madang*-style spaces. Along these lines, *ch'angjak yŏnhŭi* commonly draws from the *yŏnhŭi* genres of mask dance theater or *kamyŏn'gŭk*, *p'ungmul*, *p'ansori*, *namsadang*-related performing arts such as puppet play (*kkoktugakshi norŭm*) and spinning disks (*pŏna*), and shamanic *kut* (Jeong 2015, 86–97). In the 1980s and 1990s, the more common route for a serious performer within these genres would be to stay within one's lineage or school and wait to ascend the hierarchy as older members retire or pass away. However, in the 2000s, many young performers realized that viable opportunities for advancement were few and far between. At the same, Korean society was changing and many of these performers wanted to boldly adapt Korean performing arts in ways that would speak more directly to contemporary audiences. In genres that are designated within the South Korean Intangible Cultural Heritage system, making these kinds of changes to the art form is an uphill battle.

Also contributing to the draw of *ch'angjak yŏnhŭi* is all the support it has received from cultural institutions, organizations, and state agencies to revitalize the Korean performing arts. It also helps that several universities such as the Korea National University of the Arts, Chung-Ang University, Sehan University, and Wonkwang Digital University all developed competitive *yŏnhŭi* major programs that trained students and encouraged creativity in this area. In addition, competitions such as the Creative *Ch'angjak Yŏnhŭi* Competition that began during the First *Yŏnhŭi* Festival in 2007 have been especially influential. Since then, the Ministry of Culture, Sports, and Tourism has continued to organize *Ch'angjak Yŏnhŭi* Festivals and/or competitions. As a result, those featured in these festivals have enjoyed critical success and economic benefits from these events, including two groups that I will be focusing on in this chapter: Yŏnhŭi Chipdan The Kwangdae (2013 Grand Prize) and The Greatest Masque (2010 Grand Prize) (Son 2021, 126).

For many groups working within this somewhat new genre, the creative element of *ch'angjak* may simply involve the artful mixing or novel arrangement of elements from multiple genres. Given that multiple elements from diverse genres are not usually performed together by the same troupe, this, in and of itself, can seem fresh for some viewers. However, most *ch'angjak yŏnhŭi* groups do adapt these elements to create theatrical works that tell new stories or present them in creative new ways in order to speak to contemporary audiences. In this way, *ch'angjak yŏnhŭi* shares some similarities with earlier hybrid theatrical forms such as *madanggŭk* but is driven more by an artistic motivation to connect to audiences by engaging with contemporary social issues. In contrast, *madanggŭk* was driven more by a radical desire to transform political consciousness through art, although there is some overlap. Research on *ch'angjak yŏnhŭi* is still very minimal but this work is critical because these groups are actively testing the relevance of Korean folk culture for contemporary millennial audiences in deep and creative ways.

The groups I focus on in this chapter are Yŏnhŭi Chipdan The Kwangdae, Norikkot, The Greatest Masque (Ch'ŏnha Chaeil T'algongjakso), and Norikkundŭl Todam Todam. While a steady stream of *ch'angjak yŏnhŭi* teams debut every year, very few manage to succeed and persist beyond the first year or two. Given this, the groups I focus on here were selected for their persistence, talent, and creativity. They also represent different sectors of this burgeoning but highly fluid category of performance in Korea, although they all hail from a branch of *ch'angjak yŏnhŭi* groups that Son T'aedo sees as developing out of the university-based *yŏnhŭi* programs (Son 2021, 116). The two longest running of these groups are The Greatest Masque and Yŏnhŭi Chipdan The Kwangdae. Both were formed in 2006 and have a strong theatrical sensibility, with many of their core members coming from Korean mask dance drama backgrounds. Although both groups consist of male and female contributors, the main performing members tend to be mostly male. In contrast, Norikkot features all female performers and tends to highlight content that reflects women's experiences and stories. Formed in 2008, Norikkot performers have a slightly more musical sensibility with various members trained in genres such as *p'ungmul* and *samul nori* drumming, Korean instruments like the *haegŭm*, and *p'ansori*. Norikkundŭl Todam Todam was formed most recently in 2012, and perhaps because of their relative youth, they possess the refreshing ability to deconstruct genres and a willingness to take risks in order to speak to the younger generation.

Due to the global COVID-19 pandemic, not all of these groups have remained as active as they were prior to 2019, but even so, I aim to document their extraordinary ability to negotiate social space in performance. As in chapter 5, Marié Abe's wonderful analytic of resonance or *hibiki* as a "dynamic and indeterminate articulation of sound, space, time and sociality" (Abe 2018, 29) is especially instructive here. Abe writes that "soundings of resonance can move, lift up, pick out, recall, activate, and amplify historical meanings, practices and memories in a particular location, or in people's sentiments—including the deviant, the residual, and the subversive" (2018, 191). Since I can only explore a fraction of the creative output of the *ch'angjak yŏnhŭi* groups featured in this chapter, I highlight those moments where these groups have "lifted up" interactions with the marginalized, forgotten, or otherwise "residual" sectors of a changing Korean population while also contributing to urban expressive ecologies in their own unique ways.

Yŏnhŭi Chipdan The Kwangdae: Pied Pipers of Touristic Space

I first became aware of Yŏnhŭi Chipdan The Kwangdae through my work with the Goseong Ogwangdae mask dance drama association, as several of their founding members were trained in Goseong Ogwangdae. It is fitting then that their name includes the term *kwangdae*. This is the same word used in *ogwangdae*, just differently romanized; *kwangdae* is often translated as "clown" in English but it really is more of a versatile folk entertainer within the context of Korean expressive culture. Formed in 2006 by Goseong Ogwangdae members An Daech'ŏn, Hŏ

Ch'angyŏl, and Sŏn Yŏng'uk, shamanist *kut* musician Hwang Minwang and others, this group is considered one of the more established *ch'angjak yŏnhŭi* groups today; they have developed many new works including *Tonŭn Nom Ttwinŭn Nom Nanŭn Nom, Good Morning Kwangdae-kut, Kŏrŏsan, Hwangŭm Kŏji, Chara,* and *Hollim Nakkshi*. On their webpage, they write that "unlike groups that only perform a prescribed, fixed form, Yŏnhŭi Chipdan The Kwangdae aim to become leaders in the field by tapping into the flow of contemporary society and breathing new life into tradition by constantly creating new works based upon the spirit of experimentation."[2] In developing and workshopping new work, they not only are able to ascertain what themes speak to current audiences, but they must also anticipate what might appeal to future audiences. Along these lines, they have inserted modern themes into their work, such as critiquing the mindless consumerism and the unending drive to keep up with others in society, as well as revisiting enduring themes in the theatrical arts such as poverty, religion, and death. In my observations, they have become skilled at adapting spontaneously to diverse audiences and contexts, interacting with audiences in the *madang* in creative ways.

Many of these skills were on display one warm day in early September 2015 in the busy, well-known tourist district of Insadong in Seoul. A crowd was gathering as the percussion-based musicians for Yŏnhŭi Chipdan The Kwangdae began playing as they strolled down several blocks on the main avenue—pied piper-like—drawing the attention of people browsing the art galleries, traditional street food stalls, teahouses, cafés, and souvenir shops. In doing so, they extended the spatio-temporal field of performance for their popular show *Tonŭn Nom Ttwinŭn Nom Nanŭn Nom* (loosely translated as "Spinning Guy Running Guy Flying Guy / I'm a Guy"), clearly drawing upon *madang*-based notions about the openness of performance space and how it should be integral with daily life. The eventual destination of the musicians was the relatively new Naminsa Madang (built in 2009), a circular *madang* space located on the triangular southern tip of Insadong (figure 6.1 ⊙). After playing briefly in the *madang*, the musicians promptly went to the side so that the MC could enter, make some announcements, and even teach the audience members how to participate in the *madang* by yelling out *ch'uimsae*, or shouts of encouragement like "*Chot'a!*" (Great!).

Soon thereafter, the percussion band immediately began playing accompaniment rhythms for the masked dance character named *Imae* (performed by Hŏ Ch'angyŏl), who made a startling entrance by moving his way through the audience with his shirt open and belly on full display. *Imae* is a foolish servant character with slurred speech and a limping walk who comes from a village-based ritual form of mask drama called Hahoe Pyŏlshin-kut T'alnori from Andong in North Gyeongsang province. After commenting on the weather and addressing the audience, *Imae* is urged on by his musicians to go find someone from the audience to "dance and play" with. This inducement to participate is central to the embodied participatory spirit of the *madang*. Setting his sights on the opposite end of the performance area, *Imae* immediately honed in on a white man, who—after multiple attempts—adamantly refused. Then, he tried to entice a young Korean woman who also gestured that she was too shy to dance. Finally, on the other side of the *madang*, he was joined by an older Korean man in a plaid shirt who was eager to jump in. He was quickly joined by another older Korean man in a utility vest. After dancing raucously together to a robust and rollicking set of *chajinmori* and *hwimori* rhythms, the man in the plaid shirt left the *madang*, having received the cue to end. The man in the utility vest, however, was reluctant to leave the *madang*, appeared to have a disability and missed the cue entirely. After *Imae* politely complimented him on his dancing, he was gently coaxed to exit, although he continued to dance on the margins. When I asked Hŏ Ch'angyŏl, the performer who played *Imae* for this performance, whether this kind of thing happens often, he confirmed that it does. When I asked him to continue, he said that he thinks about these issues a lot because mask dance characters, including *Imae*, often portray characters who are marginalized in society. He said that it is even more important to be sensitive and kind in these interactions, and that characters like *Imae* are crucial because their foolish and unabashed nature is meant to make others feel less self-conscious in comparison.

The next scene featured a supple white lion character from the Eunyul T'alch'um mask dance drama style. This lion is animated through the movements of two performers, one in front manipulating the head and the other in back. This character is popular with children and families and in keeping with this, they even tried to spontaneously "cast" a few children to try it out themselves and perform in the lion costume. However, in this particular performance, the "casting" did not go so well, as one of the children that they selected decided not to do it at the last minute and the one that was left was somewhat uncooperative.

With varying degrees of success, Yŏnhŭi Chipdan The Kwangdae made concerted efforts to reach out to different sectors of people in the audience: tourists, young Korean women, older Korean men, and children. While everyone except for the older Korean men showed some ambivalence about participating in their targeted role in this newly arranged folk play, you can see the group exploring a range of strategies to elicit participation from people of different ages and backgrounds. With the austerity measures that were implemented as part of an IMF bailout that was negotiated in response to the 1997 Asian financial crisis, employment for the working class has become increasingly precarious and irregular. Given this, I found it especially moving and comforting that they managed to bring some joy to some older working-class men in such a public, touristic space.

In another street theater piece in their repertoire called *Hwangŭm Kŏji* (Golden Beggar), featuring Sŏn Yŏng'uk as the beggar, they address the issue of precarity head on. Performing outside well-known public spaces such as Tongdaemun History and Culture Park and Boramae Park in Seoul, the piece is about a "beggar who is not afraid of poverty."[3] Over the course of the show, the beggar entertains the audience with a multi-use white bowl that he spins impressively high up in the air with a stick. He also uses the same bowl to make percussive sounds as well as "beg" for snacks from the audience, which he then redistributes to other audience members. With the assistance of his fellow guitar and *puk* drum accompanist, they also sing songs and even teach them to the audience, asking them to repeat lines like "I am a beggar, and I have many dreams." It quickly becomes clear that the subtext of the show is to put audience members in the position of being a beggar, eliciting empathy and encouraging them to not be afraid of those in the precarious position of being homeless. Such efforts—even if unsuccessful—communicate that public urban spaces in Seoul should be welcoming to people of all abilities: Korean and non-Koreans, young and old, rich and poor.

Norikkot: Engendering Space and Millennial Participation

The next group I call attention to is the all-female *yŏnhŭi* group called Norikkot. It was formed by Kim So Ra [Kim Sora], Kim Jungwoon [Kim Chŏngun], Pang Ayang, Pak Sua, and others in 2008 to become one of South Korea's premier all-women's *ch'angjak yŏnhŭi* (creative traditional performing arts) groups. Their name, Norikkot, plays on the homonym meanings of "no-ri" (노리), "nol-i" (놀이), and "norida" (노리다), and is described in their brochure as meaning "a blossom that blooms or matures in the *norip'an*." Here, the *norip'an*, which literally means "play-*madang*," is analogous to the more common term *norimadang* and references Korean performing traditions that are normally performed in *madang* spaces. Their representative works include *Norikkot P'ida* (Blooming

Norikkot) and the more theatrical *Pae-ŭi Pam-i* (Night on a Ship). *Norikkot P'ida* chronicles the journey of life from birth, growing up, falling in love, getting married, and having children as conveyed through traditional Korean performance styles such as *p'ungmul*, *p'ansori* (musical storytelling), *pŏna* (spinning discs), *pukch'um* (barrel drum dance), and instrumental music. *Pae-ŭi Pam-i* is a story based on the Japanese "comfort women" (women forced into sexual slavery during World War II) and employs traditional performance modes to tell a story of a woman's last night on a ship on her way back to Korea from Japan. While the members of Norikkot remain committed to preserving tradition, they are very interested in figuring out how to "create a *norip'an* [or a cultural expressive space] that fits the current generation" (Norikkot brochure, 2015).

In a 2015 performance in the popular Namsan Hanok Village park in Seoul, *Norikkot P'ida* employed several techniques that seemed targeted toward reaching out to an audience that was seated rather far away from the main stage (video 6.1 🔊). Like Yŏnhŭi Chipdan The Kwangdae, Norikkot drew upon spatiotemporal *madang* concepts by blurring the boundary between the audience and the performers, often going back and forth between the stage on one end, across the open area, and, on several occasions, into the audience stands. Interestingly, while the Namsan Hanok Village does not have a dedicated *madang*-style performance space like the Naminsa Madang at Insadong, the Namsan Hanok Village does lend itself well to *madang*-style performance, in part because of the more wide-open performance space that is afforded within the park. In addition, the picturesque *hanok*, or Korean architecture that pervades the area, provides a conducive frame for Korean traditional performance, much like the traditional associations of Insadong afford a cultural ambience to Insadong performances. However, because Namsan Hanok Village feels calmer due to its insulated park-like surroundings, it becomes subtly gendered as an archetypically feminine space, especially within the context of a Norikkot performance (figure 6.2 ⊙).

Similar to other *yŏnhŭi* groups, Norikkot also encourages participation by teaching *ch'uimsae*, which are shouts of encouragement as well as a *Norikkot*-themed song in the style of a Korean folksong. Fittingly, the *ch'uimsae* or shouts of encouragement they taught were gendered as well. Instead of the gender neutral "*Chot'a!*" ("Good!"), they taught everyone to say "*Ippŭda!*" which means "You're so pretty!" The song that they taught everyone to sing was also more feminine in nature with lyrics that go "*ŏyadwiya, ŏgiyach'a, kkotp'iuse, norikkot hwaltchak!*" which loosely means "it should be the flowers blooming, the flowers that bloom in the *norip'an*" (video 6.1) 🔊.

The most interactive feature of their performance, however, was a routine that features Kim Jungwoon going into the audience with her spinning disc on a stick called *pŏna* to find a potential suitor who can successfully spin the disc back to her (figure 6.3 ⊙). This segment has a transformative, dynamic, and topsy-turvy quality that is valued in *madang*-based arts because it turns a random person from the audience into a pivotal, comedic, and even climactic "character" in the show. In the couple of times that I have seen her do this segment, I have noticed that she seems to enjoy playing with expectations and purposely reaches out to very different audience members in terms of age, nationality, and personality type. In the end, she often does not pick the person you think she will, although I have never seen her play with heterosexual norms by choosing a female suitor. After unsuccessfully receiving the disc back from an older Korean man, she ended up selecting a tall, dark-haired, white male who did spin the disc back to her (figure 6.4 ⊙). This gesture seems to speak to their desire to recognize the increasingly diverse and cosmopolitan make-up of audiences in Seoul and of Korean society in general. What I find interesting about this segment and the show in general is the way in which it implicitly addresses certain milestones—courtship, getting married, having children—all of which many Korean millennials are increasingly giving up on. In fact, this is such a common frustration among young Koreans today that some even refer to themselves as the *sampo sedae*, or the "three giving-up generation"—the three things being courtship, marriage, and childbirth. Perhaps this is their lighthearted way of encouraging young audience members not to give up on finding fulfillment and meaning through at least some of these means. By choosing different types of suitors, Norikkot uses humor to demonstrate that courtship can mean very different things for different people, at least within the heterosexual norms of Korean society (video 6.1 🔊). At the same time, through an original *p'ansori*-style piece on the excruciating pains of childbirth, they also acknowledge the difficulties that women go through in bearing children, inspiring both sympathy for mothers and also, perhaps, understanding for those who decide not to choose this path.

The Greatest Masque: Communicating with Seniors through Movement and Dialogue

Another noteworthy *ch'angjak yŏnhŭi* (creative traditional performing arts) group is The Greatest Masque, or *Ch'ŏnha Chaeil T'algongjakso* in Korean. They formed in 2006 with principal performing members Hŏ Ch'angyŏl (who is also a member of the first group, Yŏnhŭi Chipdan The Kwangdae) and Yi Chuwŏn, together with producers Shin Chaehun and Kim Sŏjin. Although they have produced original staged works, such as a Korean mask dance drama adaptation of Shakespeare's *Othello* called *Othello and Iago*, they also continue to highlight representative forms of traditional mask dance repertoire in a variety of spatial settings.

In the fall of 2015, I was fortunate to be able to follow them to a performance at the Hyosŏng Senior Cultural Center, located in the city of Incheon. They performed in a multipurpose space with a small low stage where the musicians set up; in front of this, they cleared a space in front of the stage to create an impromptu *madang* for the masked performers. Although this was a lower profile performance, it was the most moving and enthusiastically received one that I witnessed during that particular research trip to Korea. This production was billed as "Masterpiece Mask Dance" and instead of presenting a regional style of mask dance drama in its entirety, it showcased solo dances from different representative mask dance (*t'alch'um*) traditions such as the *Mokchung* apostate monk character from Bongsan T'alch'um, the *Miyal* grandmother from Gangnyeong T'alch'um, the *Mundung Pukch'um* (leper drum dance) from Goseong Ogwangdae, and *Imae* (foolish servant character) from Hahoe Pyŏlshin-kut T'alnori. Instead of assuming that the audience—even an older one—was familiar with Korean mask dance traditions, what was refreshing about this show is that immediately after performing, each character took off his or her mask, broke character, and generously explained the meaning and context of the dance to the audience.

While some of the dances were more dance-based like the monk and leper mask dances, two of the other characters engaged in a lot of banter, singing, and dialogue, even with the audience members. In the *Miyal* grandmother scene performed by Pak Insŏn, the premise is that she is looking for her "old man" (*yŏnggam*) who has purportedly run off with a younger mistress. Responding to her accompanist who told her to go look for her old man, she responded "First you tell me to call for him and now you are telling me to go look for him, why are you telling an old woman what to do?" Then, settling on a male audience member in the front row, she asked "Are you not my old man?" After a bout of laughter, she continued to jest, "How come you are just laughing and not answering?" After she repeated the question to an older gentleman with a blue jacket and a grey plaid cap, he hesitated for a moment, until the lady next to him dressed in a bright floral top said, "just say yes!" After a beat, he said yes, but not with much conviction, and the room erupted in more laughter. Not convinced, the *Miyal* grandmother retorted "You just said that because the lady next to you forced you to! Oh, where is my old man, all I see are other grandmothers here!" And indeed, the room was filled with more older women than men. Even so, after she took off her mask, the few men in the room asked her whether she found her old man. She quips that she would now look amongst the grandfathers in the room. As the sole female performer playing the only female character in the show, Pak deftly acknowledged the male respondents in the room while also taking note of the gender disparity. Most importantly, her tacit copresence with the women in the room speaks volumes about the pain and expressive power of the aging Korean grandmother with which many of the women in the room could relate (video 6.2 🔊).

In contrast, the next performer, Hŏ Ch'angyŏl, cultivated empathy primarily through the power of dance in his *Mundung Pukch'um* ("Leper Drum Dance"). Here, all his pain, frustration, and joy in overcoming his disability is expressed solely through movement. Hŏ Ch'angyŏl is an especially expressive dancer and performer, so it is not that surprising that a little more than halfway through his performance, he had inspired one of the senior male audience members to come up and dance with him. Waving a green 10,000-won bill (loosely equivalent to a 10-dollar bill) in his hand, which is a customary way to show appreciation to traditional performers, the man loosely mimicked Hŏ's dancing while also adding his own moves. Instead of trying to get him to leave the *madang*, Hŏ made him feel comfortable and graciously danced with him until the end of the performance. When Hŏ took his mask off to explain the leper dance, he made a point of saying that the dance is not meant to just imitate the movements of lepers for the sake of making fun of them, but rather to express their *han* (a Korean aesthetic concept that refers to pent-up sorrow) and demonstrate its sublimation into cathartic joy, or *shinmyŏng* in Korean. Similarly, the man who got up to imitate the leper clearly did not mean it to make fun, but rather to join in the experience of *shinmyŏng* (video 6.3 🔊).

The next and final character to perform was *Imae*, the same foolish servant character who also made an appearance in the Yŏnhŭi Chipdan The Kwangdae performance described earlier. This time, instead of being played by Hŏ Ch'angyŏl who was the leper in this performance, Yi Chuwŏn played *Imae* with his white top completely unfastened exposing his stomach, entering from the rear of the room and surprising the audience by immediately breaking the fourth wall. After embodying *Imae*'s unique style of arrestingly off-kilter dance, he proceeded to elicit participation from the audience by laughing ridiculously and

TABLE 6.1 *Imae*'s Dialogue with Seniors at the Hyosŏng Senior Cultural Center (Incheon, South Korea)

IMAE	AUDIENCE RESPONSE
Did you laugh? Did I laugh?	[clapping and laughing]
The *ajummas* [middle-aged ladies] really like it, look at that!	[clapping and laughing]
When you see me does it make you feel good?	It's good! [clapping and laughing]
Is it good?	It's good!
When you see me, is it good?	It's good!
Then look at me! [starts to take off his top to expose his belly and chest even more]	[clapping and laughing, whooping]
Aigo! The neighborhood *shinmyŏng* [cathartic joy] is amazing!	
But, this *shinmyŏng* is so good, wouldn't it be so boring to dance and play by myself?	
[He goes out into the audience and selects two women to dance with. One is tall and slender with her straight white hair pulled back in a clip and wearing a striped shirt. The other is shorter with dark permed curly hair and is wearing a leopard print shirt.]	[clapping and laughing]
I chose well, didn't I?	Yes!

posing a number of responsorial questions to the audience, all in the provincial accent of Gyeongsang province, where this style of mask dance drama originated.

As indicated in table 6.1, *Imae* did an excellent job of selecting two ladies who were more than happy to join him in the *madang*. The woman in the leopard shirt even launched into an opening dance gesture that got the room laughing right away. Picking up on this energy, he immediately turned to the woman in the leopard print shirt and said, "if you look closely at this woman, she actually looks a little like me." After a short pause he looked at her and yelled "Mama!" and gave her a hug as she happily played along. He continued by saying "let's dance and play together!" as the musicians played a rollicking *chajinmori* rhythm. Soon, another lady in a purple and black top and bright yellow sneakers joined them as they all proceeded to show off their individual moves. The *Imae* character then wrapped things up by saying, "Waaaa! If I didn't call them in to dance with me, it would have been tragic! Wasn't that fun? I had fun! I didn't eat but will my stomach be full? Now that we played and had fun, I'm going now!" (video 6.4 🔊) At the end of the performance, Yi Chuwŏn invited the other performers to come out for one last bow. He made a point of thanking the excellent musicians, who then played one last round while inviting all the audience members to come out and dance with them.

When thinking about addressing the changing demographics of South Korea, it is easy to overlook seniors. While they might not represent the future of South Korea, continuing to cultivate senior audience members in South Korea is critical because they are the living links to the past and occupy a large percentage of the population. In fact, South Korea is "aging faster than any other advanced economy on Earth" (Larmer 2018). While The Greatest Masque continues to earn recognition and awards for their other, more original staged plays, it is important to shine a light on how they draw on not only traditional repertoires, but also on distinctive ways of being in the *madang* to communicate meaningfully with various community groups, such as the lively group of senior citizens that they encountered at the Hyosŏng Senior Cultural Center.

Norikkundŭl Todam Todam: Attuning the Body to the Present and "Deviating from Daily Life"

The final group considered in this chapter is Norikkundŭl Todam Todam, which was formed in 2012. As one of the more newly formed groups to enter the scene, their name is apt, as it means something like "growing up well as *norikkun*." *Norikkun* is a Korean folk expressive culture term that refers to entertainers who excel at cultivating the atmosphere of play, or *nori*, in the *madang*. Their group consists of five core members, including representative Pak Insu and director Kim Chihun. Some of the main shows in their repertoire include a creative spin on mask dance drama characters called GTA *of Yŏnhŭi*, an educational show that presents different styles of Korean *yŏnhŭi* performance to new audiences and an experimental street theater piece called *Taedong* that incorporates audience participation in everyday life outdoor settings.

In GTA *of Yŏnhŭi*, they draw from a well-known *Saturday Night Live Korea* skit that parodies the video game *Grand Theft Auto*, but casts it within the setting of colonial Korea during the Japanese occupation. Incorporating similar *tŭrotŭ*-inspired theme music (a style of Korean popular music that was influenced by Japanese *enka*) used in the original skit, Norikkundŭl Todam Todam casts this video-game inspired scenario onto the world of Korean mask dance drama. Here, the audience follows how an archetypal mask dance drama character might fare in a battle against various types of mask dance figures, in this case, the lion, a stock figure in Korean mask dance drama, that is performed by two individuals. In this way, they cleverly present Korean traditional performing arts in a seemingly "choose-your-own adventure" format that younger people can relate to. They also bring in *madang* concepts in the spatial/temporal and social/relational realms (table 0.1).[4] For example, when I saw their show in the fall of 2015 in the National Gugak Center's Yŏnhŭi Madang, they began by blurring audience/performer boundaries, having the Korean percussionists process from starting positions in the audience and play while making their way to the center stage area. Instead of playing the all-too-familiar traditional Korean rhythms, they played deconstructed rhythms with some musicians playing slightly different percussion instruments than what would be expected in a Korean *p'ungmul* or *samul nori* drumming ensemble. The resulting sound was fresh and modern with a distinctive palette of percussive timbres. Overall, the musical introduction and accompaniment throughout reinforced a more youthful and playful sensibility. In addition, like the other teams, they also included participatory elements like teaching *ch'uimsae* (shouts of encouragement) and selecting a volunteer to learn and perform simple movements of the "idiot" or *Pabo* character. Here, the group transformed the volunteer into the *Pabo* character by simply putting a paper mask on him and teaching him how to say *hajima*, or "don't do that," while moving his right hand and leg up and down in a stiff gesture. While this might be perceived as distasteful or politically insensitive in some contexts, what I have heard from practitioners is that the point of these characters is not to make fun of them but to convey their humanity, elicit empathy, and provide an atmosphere where everyone feels welcome (Pak Insu interview, September 17, 2015).

Of all the shows presented in this chapter, the one that goes the farthest in incorporating the concepts of the *madang* to create a truly participatory experience is Norikkundŭl Todam Todam's somewhat more experimental work called *Taedong*, or "Group Play." *Taedong* is a street theater piece (*kŏrigŭk*) that re-imagines Korean *madang*-style performance by combining deconstructed Korean rhythms, the play of everyday objects, modernized mask dance drama elements, and participatory games. They have strategically staged *Taedong* in a variety of urban spaces, including plazas, train stations, busy streets, and outdoor parks. Instead of performing the same thing in each space, they greatly vary the form and content each time. This may be because this piece has gone through multiple phases of development, but the effect is that the piece seems to be re-worked according to the specificities of each space, context, and audience.

In one of its earlier iterations, *Taedong* was performed on the streets of Hongdae, which is known as a creative, trendy, and youthful neighborhood outside of Hongik University at the Seoul Fringe Festival in September 2013. Only about fifteen minutes long, this performance had the feel of a pop-up performance, consisting of a reimagined percussion-based *yŏnhŭi* piece where some of the Korean instruments in a typical performance are replaced with props from daily life, such as a metal noodle bowl replacing the *kkwaenggwari* gong and a large transparent blue water dispenser bottle replacing the *puk* drum. Added to this were two beverage bottles filled with grains utilized as makeshift shakers, a long steel pole that was tapped on by a stick, and a grooved washboard that sounded like a scraper. Dressed in everyday clothes, the performers began by playing a jaunty medium-tempo rhythm, alternating bent and upright postures, and stretching their bodies during the pauses, as if to represent waking up in the morning. They continued to pass each other, making turns at sharp angles, sometimes punctuating the pauses with notched knee bends and controlled jumps. The scene called to mind the rhythms of a random street in Seoul, conveying a sense of workers going about their everyday routine and not necessarily connecting with each other. This section continued to build in intensity, until eventually one of the performers broke their routine to ask the audience, "Do you like mask dance?" This was followed by the performers coming together to perform basic mask dance moves in the style of Bongsan T'alch'um, props still in hand. In keeping with the subtitle of this piece, "Deviating from Daily Life," the rest of the performance began to move away from the routine rhythms and random movements, and more toward complex rhythms and synchronized movements, drawing variously from mask dance, shamanic rituals, and *samul nori*. This progression was reflected in the way that each performer gradually transitioned from playing everyday objects to playing Korean percussion instruments. Although the final rhythms and choreography drew heavily from the upright and moving style of *samul nori*, they inserted their own contemporary dance moves as well, which injected a welcome dose of humor and youthful exuberance.

This process of adapting older and more rural Korean rhythms and movements to the contemporary urban environment is resonant with Henri Lefebvre's notion of "rhythmanalysis," whereby the *body* becomes the mode of analyzing the production of a new and different kind of space—in this case, a center of creativity in Seoul. In "Rhythmanalysis: Space, Time and Everyday Life," Lefebvre writes that the rhythmanalyst "listens—and first to his body; he learns rhythm from it, in order consequently to appreciate external rhythms. His *body serves him as a metronome*" (Lefebvre 2004, 29, my emphasis). In a later essay, he writes that the rhythmanalyst "is always 'listening out', but he does not only hear words, discourses, noises, and sounds; he is capable of listening to a house, a street, a town as one listens to a symphony, an opera" (Lefebvre 2004, 94). I argue that the creative members of *Taedong* drew on a process akin to this, metaphorically using their *bodies as metronomes* for ascertaining the rhythms of Hongdae, adjusting the tempo of the rhythms that previously served the needs of Koreans who lived in the villages and townships. In addition, they drew upon the energy and feel of these adapted rhythms and tempos as a foundation for improvising upon and even creating new rhythms and movements suited to the urban context. The result is more appealing and more "attuned" to the rhythms of city dwellers and the globalized and media-savvy denizens of Seoul, but, at the same time, it represents an adaptation to a space that is more intensely determined by capitalist, neoliberal forces.

Continuing along these lines, the next iterations of *Taedong* represented very different representations of people at work. Their commitment to continual variation here suggests that creative rhythmanalysis is a fluid process, yielding a variety of readings and interpretations each time. In a summer festival performance at Korea National University of Arts (video posted on July 11, 2015), the performers decided to wear the universal work attire of black pants and white dress shirts instead of the everyday student casual attire of their first performance. The ensemble began with the performers tethered to each other with neckties, each playing a different *p'ungmul* Korean percussion instrument, such as the *kkwaenggwari*, *changgo*, *puk*, and *ching*, with the addition of a Buddhist woodblock. Playing with exaggerated bent postures and awkward gaits, here the communal expression of *p'ungmul* was used to convey group submission and zombie-like fatigue, rather than community catharsis and joy. This continued until one performer, the *puk* player, untied his necktie to free himself from the group. He then tried to inspire the rest of the group to do the same, although they initially just followed him around robotically until they were all freed from their neckties and the rhythms converged into a careening chaos of drum rolls (called *ilch'ae*). This then gave way into a series of participatory elements that involved the audience in significant ways.

In an especially radical summertime version performed at the Seoul Fringe Festival on July 28, 2016, they dedicated about two-thirds of the show to participatory play. Still dressed in business attire, they included a fun chicken dance that gave way to a Korean-style chicken fight where audience members would hold one foot folded over one's thighs with both hands while hopping and getting others to fall, a game of *mugunghwa kkoch'i p'iŏtsŭmnida* ("The Rose of Sharon has Bloomed," similar to Red Light Green Light) and group jump-rope. What is remarkable is how Norikkundŭl Todam Todam managed to take these pedestrian schoolyard games and integrate them seamlessly into their show in a fresh way. The heavy use of participatory play or *nori* contributed to dissolving the audience/performer divide and resonated with multiple aspects of *madang* discourse (table 0.1). In a sense, the show is a reinvention of *taedongnori*, a group-play section that often happens at the end of *p'an-kut* performances, where the audience joins in and dances along to *p'ungmul* rhythms, but it is done in a way that is more relevant to the experiences of contemporary Korean youth. According to one of their principal performers Pak Insu, the goal is for audience members to have a cathartic (*shinmyŏng*) experience where they can "forget their jobs, release their stress and just play" (Pak Insu interview, September 17, 2015). In this way, this performance emphasizes the experiential process by bringing people "into the moment and place" (called *hyŏnjang* in Korean) of contemporary Seoul.[5]

Korean folk culture is rife with examples of play, from *subakch'igi* or patty-cake games to the large-scale, regional tug-of-war that takes place in Yŏngsan against the chaotic soundscape of competing *p'ungmul* bands. Both are examples of kinesthetic, intermodal games that require bodily strength, coordination, and the ability to respond to multiple domains (auditory, visual, motor, cognitive, etc.). In the parlance of video games, these could be considered proto-rhythm games, in that they involve haptic or kinetic interaction to audiovisual cues, just without the game interface.[6] By extension, chicken fighting, Red Light Green Light, and group jump rope are also proto-rhythm games. Just as video games do, rhythm games discipline the body, only here, the absence of the game interface means that social interaction and feedback occurs more directly and with more public consequences. In the first group game, members of Norikkundŭl Todam Todam selected random members by placing red rooster head pieces on their heads. The drummer then improvised some rhythms, and the audience members were gently coaxed to mimic the performers as they acted out chicken movements. This mimicry gradually morphed into a lively, synchronized chicken dance, where the actors and audience members performed a step dance with elbows flapping as they stepped back and forth. While the older members gamely followed along, one younger girl was left behind, standing frozen and refusing to be trained into play. This led into the more competitive chicken fighting where the object was to hop on one leg and show one's skill in making others lose their balance.

Although previous versions of the Red Light Green Light game section ("Rose of Sharon has Bloomed") involved playing rhythms on the *changgo* during the "green light" portion, this time the leader said the traditional *mugunghwa kkoch'i p'iŏtsŭmnida* phrase with his back turned and then turned around to face the players to signal them to freeze. No matter how it is played, this game is about training one's attention intensely on a leader figure to get a feel for his rhythms and anticipate his next steps in order to sneak up and win.[7] The last game required a greater degree of group bodily coordination as the volunteer audience members had to coordinate by jumping together on one large jump rope. The consequence for failing to do so was to lose one's turn. They transitioned out of this by doing some call-and-response rhythms on the various *samul nori* percussion instruments and ended by playing their version of a *samul nori* piece. Finally, it would not be a true *Taedongnori*, or "group play," without inviting all the audience members to join in and dance at the end.

While these rhythm games are all meant to be fun and inclusive, they also discipline the body to respond to audiovisual cues while practicing social skills such as paying attention, synchronization, anticipation, mimicry, and competitive play. In a sense, this is taking the "rhythmanalysis" of an urban, contemporary environment a step further by having the audience members perform these various rhythm games and interactions on their own bodies. By doing so, I argue that they are able to ascertain a closer read on the rhythms of the people in that particular time and place than the performers may have been able to interpret solely on their own. In various ways, Norikkundŭl Todam Todam has made concerted efforts to reach out specifically to today's Korean youth: not only by appealing to their sensibilities by drawing on video game and children's game culture, but also by responding to the stressful plight of youth today by providing a reimagined, playful release from the competitive, neoliberal Korean social conditions that many have dubbed "Hell Chosŏn."

CONCLUDING THOUGHTS

To conclude, I posit that these groups creatively draw on a range of participatory techniques—fueled by a range of *madang*-based practices—in order to better connect with diverse contemporary audiences in more urbanized environments.

Here, these creative adaptations are critical, because contemporary South Korean citizens and others who live in South Korea (including those who are not ethnically Korean) are not necessarily responding to the rhythms, songs, and movements of the past in the same way. I have even heard Korean musicians bemoan the fact that traditional Korean *changdan*, or rhythmic cycles, do not come naturally to modern Koreans. With the overwhelming popularity of K-pop and other forms of music in Korea, this is hardly surprising. Ethnomusicologist Thomas Turino writes that "in participatory settings . . . focal attention to synchrony becomes the most pronounced and important" (Turino 2008, 43). In this way, *ch'angjak yŏnhŭi* (creative traditional performing arts) groups are in a unique position to find a new synchrony, a new groove, or grooves even, between the rhythms of yesterday and today. As *ch'angjak yŏnhŭi* musicians and dancers poise themselves to perform in the streets, they have to listen to its urban sounds, and respond to the various people participating in their shows, ultimately, synchronizing themselves to the present intersection of people, place, and time. In other words, they are living links between an older repertoire of Korean music and dance and the rhythms of contemporary life. In trying to respond to the changing dynamics of various segments of the population—children, youth, seniors, firm and infirm, ethnic Koreans and others residing in or visiting Korea—they are ultimately conveying that there is a space of belonging and hope for everyone within the fabric of Korean society and that everyone has the right to contribute to it.

Unlike the Pilbong-based case study analyzed in the first half of this book, these projects are not necessarily focused on creating a site-specific expressive ecology in the city whereby a particular group is attempting to make a permanent claim or identification with a particular place or neighborhood. Even so, I would argue that these performances can produce site-oriented or *madang*-oriented expressive ecologies, in part because they are intentionally shaped to suit each location and occasion and contribute to experiential cultural knowledge. This would explain why no two performances of the same show are exactly the same and, in many cases, differ quite dramatically from one performance to another in form and content. Cumulatively, as *ch'angjak yŏnhŭi* performances are consistently programmed in certain locations—like the touristy, arts and crafts neighborhood of Insadong or Namsan Hanok Village—audience members and passersby can develop a more multisensory and historically layered sense of place. Furthermore, when audiences participate and are encouraged to embody the rhythms, movements, and music in a particular place, I argue that a deeper feeling of connectedness can develop, even if only for a short time. At the very least, these performances have the potential to alter how diverse urban dwellers experience public, shared spaces or *madangs*, developing stronger feelings of belonging and community over time.

SEVEN

The Politics of Sounding Space in the Korean American Community

Korean drumming and dance has become well known outside of Korea, due in part to the popularity of touring groups like SamulNori, but also because of the myriad efforts of Korean diasporic immigrants who fostered *p'ungmul* in Japan, China, England, the United States, and elsewhere. I cannot even begin to tell the story of how this happened in one chapter, but I will attempt to disentangle a strand that pertains to the politics of sounding space in the Korean American community. Along these lines, the central aim of this chapter is to explore how *p'ungmul* practitioners attend to site in the US, where claims to space and place cannot be taken for granted. As a marginalized ethnic group, Americans of Korean heritage are subject to the "perpetual foreigner" stereotype, and given this, playing *p'ungmul* in public is usually seen as an exotic curiosity at best. At worst, playing Korean drums in public spaces is more likely to be labelled and policed as excessive "noise." While many groups simply avoid these issues by playing in more private spaces, or by performing in sanctioned indoor venues, its loud volume, circular choreography, and mobile nature are not always conducive to these settings, and performances have inevitably spilled into the public. For some early Korean American political organizations, the intentional use of *p'ungmul* as part of a public demonstration, rally, or protest is considered its whole raison d'être and endures as one of the more significant manifestations of *p'ungmul* in the US.

Throughout all of this, I argue that Korean discursive ideas associated with *p'ungmul*—such as the *madang* and its historical legacy as a mode of political protest—continue to be influential for *p'ungmul* groups in the United States. Whether by conscious design or not, the *madang* has been an underlying presence as groups have adapted their rhythms and movements to a variety of spaces: indoor or outdoor, public or private, be it religious, educational, community-oriented, or commercial. I also posit that site-oriented performance practice (in some cases informed by the *madang*) has proven to be extraordinarily critical during historically challenging times (e.g., the Los Angeles Civil Unrest or 9/11). While my research is far from comprehensive, I aim to show how the politics of gathering, protesting, and performing in public spaces through *p'ungmul* in the United States diverge from South Korean practice, even as groups and practitioners in South Korea and the United States continue to be linked through transnational ties. As in chapters 5 and 6, I continue to explore the potential of *p'ungmul* to generate new meanings by paying attention to the dynamics of politicized drumming where ephemeral social interactions are enabled in the coming together of site, movement, and sound in a given time and place.

Drawing on Marié Abe's analytic of resonance, I argue that *p'ungmul* resonates differently in the US where there are very different histories and memories that are sedimented and potentially activated in each location. Furthermore, the stakes of sounding *p'ungmul* in the US are higher because its sounding is more dramatically otherized. Rather than being heard as belonging to a given public space, *p'ungmul* practitioners often must repeatedly assert their right to resonate in public spaces where competing forces are constantly working toward their exotic tokenization or silencing.

Ritual is a major focus of the first part of this book, and here I circle back to this theme in looking at how it has been adapted to forge political solidarity, community, and healing. I also link to earlier themes by assessing the power and limits of site-oriented performance to effectively achieve a sense of integrative wholeness and stronger connections to place and to each other when a group's claim to a given public space is tenuous at best. In looking at times of political unrest, I also examine the growing role of intersectional awareness and activism, as a potential response to the limits of marginality in the US.

P'UNGMUL IN THE UNITED STATES

Korean plantation workers who immigrated to Hawai'i were among the first to import or make Korean instruments to play during holiday feasts as early as 1907 (Sutton 1987, 103). These included percussion instruments, but it is unclear whether any *p'ungmul* groups were formed at this time.[1] According to music scholar Soo-Jin Kim, one of the earliest documented *p'ungmul* groups in the United States was the Nongak Troupe of the Eastern US (Midongbu nongakdan), who initially got together to perform in a New York City Fourth of July parade in 1976. They continued to perform in parades and festivals and eventually changed their name to the Peace and Unification Nongak Troupe (Pyŏnghwa t'ongil nongakdan) in 1998 (Kim Soo-Jin 2011, 134).

Between the years 1985 and 1989, a younger generation of Korean Americans were motivated by the energy of the *minjung* (democratization) movement in South Korea and formed a slew of new groups in the metropolitan areas of Los Angeles, Chicago, New York/Flushing, and San Francisco Bay Area (Berkeley and Oakland mainly). The earliest of these formed in 1985: Pinari in New York and Sori at the University of California, Berkeley. This younger generation was especially moved by the visits of several key figures, namely the *minjung* activist and artist Kim Pongjun (b. 1954) and political refugee Yun Hanbong (1947–2007). Kim Pongjun, best known for his iconic folk-inspired prints called *p'anhwa*, visited eight US cities in 1987, teaching the more comprehensive philosophy of *p'ungmul* as a way of life. He visited the Minjung Cultural Research Center (*Minjung Munhwa Yŏnguso*) that formed in 1986 in Los Angeles and met with individuals in Oakland who formed the Korean Youth Cultural Center (*Hanin Chŏngnyŏn Munhwawŏn*) in 1987. Their *p'ungmul* group was called Hanmadang (figure 7.1) (Jeanmann Park interview November 25, 2000; Jang Woo Nam interview, August 1, 2001).

Yun Hanbong first came to the US in the early 1980s and was a prominent South Korean activist and organizer in the May 18 Democratic Uprising in 1980 (also known as the Gwangju Uprising) (figure 7.1 ●). According to the New York–based *p'ungmul* player, Liz Chong Eun Rhee, Yun was blacklisted by the South Korean government for his activities and "had to be smuggled out of Korea on a boat, hiding in a bathroom until he landed in the US" where he sought asylum in 1981 (Rhee, personal communication). While in the US, he spoke from his own firsthand experiences to tell people about what happened in Gwangju and tried to raise awareness and support for the *minjung* movement in South Korea. Yun was instrumental in establishing a number of organizations that were initially affiliated under the umbrella organization Young Koreans United (YKU), which later became the National Korean American Service and Education Consortium (NAKASEC). Many of these organizations formed *p'ungmul* groups including Pinari (1985, figure 7.2) in Flushing, New York, and Ilkwa Nori (1988)

FIGURE 7.1 Hanmadang, Korean Youth Cultural Center in front of the entrance to their space (2001). Photo by Michael Hurt, used with permission.

FIGURE 7.2 Founding of Pinari, Minkwon Center for Community Action (1985). Used with permission of Jubum Cha.

in Chicago. Several of these organizations later changed their names; Flushing became the MinKwon Center for Community Action in 2009 and Chicago is now the Korean American Resource and Cultural Center in Chicago (Kim Soo-Jin 2011, 136–37; Kwon 2001, 42–45).

Another figure who also visited multiple organizations in 1990 and 1991 is Yi Chŏngun, who later became a minister. He focused on helping groups like Hanmadang improve both their technical and cultural foundation in *p'ungmul* and other related genres such as mask dance. He also assisted in the formation of one of the earlier collegiate groups, Kutkŏri at Harvard University (Kwon 2001, 42–45). While there are others who came from Korea as well, it is important to note that the personal testimonies and activities of these individuals cannot be underestimated. Although some of the more recently arrived, first-generation members of these early *p'ungmul* groups and organizations were politically active in South Korea before coming to the US, many who were already here (mostly 1.5 generation) were profoundly moved by these visits and became more politically engaged through these encounters.[2] In this way, the story of this period of Korean American *p'ungmul* was inevitably intertwined with the history of Korean and Korean American activism (Kwon 2001).

Although some of these organizations, such as those affiliated with NAKASEC, were not solely focused on *p'ungmul*, most had drums around to use during demonstrations and rallies. One of the reasons for this was that by the mid-1980s, *p'ungmul* had already cemented its position as a powerful index of protest in South Korea (Abelmann 1996, 61–62; Lee 2012, 180). However, given its emphasis on non-textual elements, *p'ungmul* has not received as much in-depth scholarly attention as a protest genre in South Korea compared to other genres, such as *madang* theater (*madanggŭk*) and protest songs (*minjung kayo*) (Lee 2012, 181–82).[3] Even so, ethnomusicologist Katherine Lee writes that "these sonic associations with dissent were understood not only by student activists, but also by ordinary citizens" (2012, 198). An extraordinary interview that Katherine Lee conducted with Lee Soobeen [Yi Subin], a musician/activist who participated in a memorial protest for fallen activist Yi Sŏkkyu on Geoje Island, illustrates how *p'ungmul* was strategically shaped to communicate effectively to others during a protest:

> *P'ungmul* wasn't just about the sounds or the *changdan* [rhythmic cycles]. By the time I started playing in 1984 and 1985, the sounds of *p'ungmul* had already acquired the associations [of protest]. Toward the end of 1986 we started to

seriously ponder this ... Because when you stage a protest, you're trying to say something, right? Various ideas can emerge or by playing, we can express our own opinions or deliver our messages. We thought very seriously about how to convey these messages the most effectively to people through *p'ungmul* and other kinds of genres ... So the more one heard and saw [*p'ungmul*], the people would understand what kind of message was being delivered. (Interview of Lee Soobeen by Katherine Lee 2012, 198)

As suggested here, Katherine Lee writes that "[c]ertain rhythmic patterns, when played, could activate choreographies of movement or channel collective energy in an efficient manner, all without the necessity for long-scripted dialogues" (2012, 198).

In general, *p'ungmul*'s adaptability, audibility, and effectiveness as a protest genre in South Korea's volatile democratization movement lent itself well to being used in various demonstrations in the US. Along these lines, I am interested in how Korean Americans grappled with similar issues but on new ground, eventually adapting the sounds, rhythms, and movements of *p'ungmul* to mobilize people and strategically move them through different kinds of spaces. College-based Korean drumming groups began to flourish and multiply from the 1990s forward, as well as many other types of special-interest groups (performance-oriented groups, church and Korean school-based groups, Korean dance schools, etc.). The late 1990s and early 2000s also coincided with multiple visits from more specialized teachers, including the Pilbong brothers, Yang Chinsŏng and Yang Chinhwan, among others, who were able to reach large numbers of students at regional or national *p'ungmul* camps. Interestingly, inviting Pilbong teachers made perfect sense for many of the groups who were active during this period because the Pilbong style was highly regarded by democratization activists due to their emphasis on community and ritual.[4]

THE COMPLEX DYNAMICS OF SITE-SPECIFIC PERFORMANCE AND THE EMERGENCE OF KOREATOWN *CHISHINPALPKI*

By the 1980s and 1990s, many Korean Americans had developed the resources to invest in their own homes and businesses, as well as community spaces, such as churches, senior centers, and community organizations. In a few cities, such as New York and Los Angeles, Korean businesses began coalescing into "Koreatowns." But even so, in comparison to South Korea, there were few public spaces that Korean Americans could call their own or that would be culturally identified as Korean that would be appropriate for a site-oriented performance. For example, there were no urban *madang*s (or *norimadang*s as they are called in Korea) or Korean American rural villages where it might be appropriate to perform a site-specific ritual performance of *p'ungmul*. Although there are Korean American–owned farms, it has not been common to host *p'ungmul* performances in these locations.[5]

Political events, such as parades and demonstrations held at targeted locations like Korean embassies, civic centers, or Korean community organizations, were among some of the first "site-oriented" performances conducted by early *p'ungmul* groups. For example, Jang Woo Nam, a longtime member of the Korean Youth Cultural Center (hereafter KYCC) recalls going down to Los Angeles to play with the group Uri Munhwa Kondongch'e to commemorate the opening of the Koreatown Immigrant Workers Alliance (KIWA) on March 1, 1992, just a few months before the Los Angeles Civil Unrest erupted. As KIWA evolved to serve a multi-ethnic coalition of workers in Koreatown in Los Angeles, they organized demonstrations that included Korean drums and other protest practices, often targeting exploitative businesses (even those owned by Korean Americans).

Despite the targeting of Korean businesses for their unjust treatment of workers in the case of KIWA, the majority of *p'ungmul* groups worked to forge mutually supportive relationships with Korean businesses through their activities. One of the main ways that they did this was by adapting the site-specific *p'ungmul* activity that is commonly called *chishinpalki* (literally "earth spirit treading") by Korean American groups. *Chishinpalki* is a regional term stemming from the Yeongnam area and is very similar to the *madangbalbi* ritual that is performed in the village of Pilbong on Lunar New Year.[6] Urban *p'ungmul* groups in South Korea first started adapting *chishinpalki* in Seoul as a popular fundraising activity in the 1980s.[7] This practice quickly spread to Korean American *p'ungmul* groups. According to Jang Woo Nam, the first *chishinpalki* in the mainland United States was performed by the KYCC's Hanmadang *p'ungmul* group in "Koreatowns" around the San Francisco Bay Area in 1988. Groups in the Los Angeles area followed in 1989.[8] In subsequent years, many of the NAKASEC-affiliated organizations began to implement *chishinpalki* into their annual activities in cities such as the New York, Chicago, and Washington DC/Baltimore areas. According to Ju Bum Cha, the resident *p'ungmul* group Pinari at the MinKwon Center for Community Action (hereafter MinKwon) began performing *chishinpalki* in 1995 in the New York area, often in collaboration with other groups such as New York University's NYURI.

Due to the high percentage of devout Christians in the Korean American community, *chishinpalpki* was not always received positively by Koreatown business owners or their customers. I distinctly remember the first time I performed *chishinpalpki* with Hanmadang in San Francisco and being loudly accosted by an elderly Korean man who followed us and yelled "*Mishin*!" (literally "superstition") in such an incriminating manner that one would think we were up to something much more nefarious than the promotion of Korean culture. And even if business owners were not religiously opposed to *chishinpalpki*, some were uneasy with *p'ungmul*'s activist associations, and others simply felt ill-prepared to host a group of loud drummers in their businesses or resented feeling "pressured" to donate to the *p'ungmul* group afterward. Because of this, Hanmadang (KYCC) began to notify businesses about two months in advance with a letter explaining the nature, purpose, and proposed schedule of *chishinpalpki*. Ideally, this would be followed by calling or visiting to talk directly with the business owners to see whether they would like us to visit or if they had any questions about the process. In my interview with Ju Bum Cha at MinKwon, I discovered that their group in New York had a very similar process.

> We don't just show up. We don't just visit them randomly. We go in advance and ask whether they would like to accept our *p'ungmul* groups or not. If they say "yes" then we visit. Some people are really welcoming! For example, there is a beauty salon that always sets up a nice shrine for us. There are about fifteen stores that said "yes, we would like to participate." Now these are the only ones we visit during *chishinpalpki*. (Ju Bum Cha interview, August 3, 2015)

In contrast to Koreatowns in Los Angeles or New York, many of the Korean businesses in the San Francisco Bay Area are very spread out. Because of this, KYCC's *chishinpalpki* involved visiting five locations in the Bay Area, including two neighborhoods in San Francisco, two in Oakland, and one in Berkeley. Even with the added assistance from nearby *p'ungmul* groups such as the college groups from Stanford University and the University of California, Berkeley, as well as Jamaesori [Chamaesori] (literally "Sistersound"), visiting them all can be exhausting. When I asked whether MinKwon visited multiple Koreatowns in the New York area, he replied that now they only visit Manhattan's Koreatown (near Midtown South). They like that they are appreciated and greeted warmly there, and over time the business owners have come to see *chishinpalpki* as a meaningful showcase of the warmth and freshness of *p'ungmul* and like its ability to connect with diverse customers in the area (figure 7.2 ⊙). Although there is also a high concentration of Korean businesses in Flushing where their office is, they have stopped playing there, in part because it is easier to sustain the practice by concentrating on one neighborhood, but also because they did not want to compete with a senior citizen *p'ungmul* group that began "going around to all of the Korean stores to ask for money" (Ju Bum Cha interview, August 3, 2015).

Although *chishinpalpki* differs from group to group and from one business location to the next, there are some common components that Korean American groups prepare, rehearse, and employ: (1) a series of rhythms and rhythmic series that are well known among the *p'ungmul* groups that they are collaborating with;[9] (2) stylized speech (*tŏkdam*) and responses (*ch'uimsae*); (3) Lunar New Year–themed folksongs or *minyo*; (4) ritual props (could include cups and a decanter to pour traditional *makkŏlli*, a portable shrine, etc.); and (5) banners and costumes for the *p'ungmul* musicians including *kokkal* hats topped with enormous tissue flowers, as well as individual costumes for all of the *chapsaek* characters. Although people from afar might interpret the rhythmic drumming to be the most important element of *chishinpalpki*, the leader's ability to perform various integrated duties (including stylized chants, impromptu banter, singing, etc.) is critically important in forging a festive intersubjective experience between the group, the business owner, and the audience. The better the leader can "read the room" and draw upon previous interactions and knowledge of the business and its owner, the more successful he or she will be in eliciting more generosity and mutual goodwill.

In a normative neighborhood *chishinpalpki* visit, a *p'ungmul* group generally starts by playing out in public on a nearby street corner or plaza to alert the store owners and help boost excitement for their arrival. *P'ungmul* groups typically begin with an introductory series of simple rhythms represented here in *changgo* drum vocables in table 7.1. After this, the group plays a medium tempo marching rhythm, such as the well-known *samch'ae* or *obangjin*, or maybe even *p'ungnyu-kut* or *kil-kut* (from the Pilbong style), and begins processing down the street toward their first destination.

Before entering the business, the group plays a bit more energetically to draw the attention of the business owner. When the business owner comes out, they pause so that the leader can ask permission to enter by calling out the series of *tŏkdam* and alternating responsorial chants and rhythms in table 7.2. The *p'ungmul* playing continues until the owner gestures for them to come into

TABLE 7.1 *Chishinpalpki* Introductory Rhythms

Insagut rhythm	1	2	3	4	5	6	7	8	9	10	11	12
	Tŏng	Tŏng	-	Tŏng	Tŏng	-	Tŏ Tŏ	Tŏng	Tŏng	Tŏng	-	Tak
	Ching											

This last stroke of "ching" is played on the large gong while everyone bows. Played at a slow tempo only once or twice. 12/8 meter.

| *Ilch'ae* rhythm | Tŏng | Tŏng | Tŏng | Tŏng | Tŏng | Tŏng | Tŏng | Tŏng | Tŏng | Tŏng | ... | |

Starts slowly and gets faster and faster, petering out into a roll (unmetered); played only once.

Ich'ae rhythm	1	2	3	4	5	6	7	8	9	10	11	12
	Tŏng			Tŏng			Kung		Tak	Kung		

Medium fast tempo and repeated cyclically. 12/8 meter.

the store. From here, the leader must evaluate the situation to see how best to proceed. If the store is busy, the leader may decide not to speak too much and cue the group to bow three times while playing *insagut* or *ilch'ae* and saying the traditional New Year's greeting of "May you receive many New Year blessings!" (*Saehae pok manhi padŭsaeyo!*) on the last gong stroke. If the owner is welcoming and relaxed, then the leader might give a more elaborate speech that is customized to the store owner, pour a drink of *makkŏlli* for the spirits while the owner bows at a makeshift shrine. All the while, the drummers will sing folksongs such as "Aekmaegi T'aryŏng" or "Sŏngjupuri" (about blocking the bad spirits and calling upon guardian spirits respectively). If the owner is in a festive mood, then the group can continue with more lighthearted popular folksongs such as "Sarangga" or "Jindo Arirang," before bowing and saying blessings. Finally, when the group has finished going to the designated businesses, they may take a break to eat and have some refreshments, or, if it is the end of the day, they might play a more entertainment-oriented set of rhythms or *p'an-kut* in a circular formation in a plaza or other open space to celebrate with the surrounding community. When KYCC played at San Francisco's Japantown, we made sure to visit the Korean restaurant last because they would always feed us a delicious hot meal for free in return for our efforts (see companion website for *chishinpalpki* photos ⊙).[10]

This Korean American practice of performing *chishinpalpki* in ethnic enclaves like Koreatown is a distinctly diasporic phenomenon. And while *chishinpalpki* has moved beyond the village *madang* and has been performed in more diverse and urbanized settings in South Korea, the site-specific nature of this practice

TABLE 7.2 *Chishinpalpki* Entry Rhythms and Verses

Leader	*Chuin chuin munyŏso, poktŭrŏgage, munyŏso* (Owner, owner, open your door, to usher in good fortune, open your door!)											
Members	*Chuin chuin munyŏso, poktŭrŏgage, munyŏso* (Owner, owner, open your door, to usher in good fortune, open your door!)											
Leader	*Chuin chuin munyŏso, mun anyŏlmyŏn kallayo* (Owner, owner, open your door, if you don't open them, we will go!) Followed by optional repetition by the members.											
Rhythmic response	1	2	3	4	5	6	7	8	9	10	11	12
	Tŏng			*Tŏng*			*Kung*		*Tak*	*Kung*		
	Tŏ-	*Tŏng*		*Tŏng*		*Tak*	*Kung*		*Tak*	*Kung*		
	Fast tempo 12/8 meter. Played after the leader and members recite the *tŏkdam* in call-and-response format. Similar to the *mun-kut* verse in Pilbong's *madangbalbi*.											

in the United States resonates differently because of the marginality of Korean Americans and others who inhabit these areas. Significantly, *p'ungmul* groups in both Los Angeles and New York City have made a point in recent years to use *chishinpalpki* as a way of embracing "the margin as a space of radical openness" as well as an inclusive site of resistance, "creativity and power," to evoke the words of bell hooks (1984, 145–52). For example, several groups such as MinKwon in New York and KIWA in Los Angeles have made a point to reach out to Black Americans and Latinx communities (figure 7.2 ⊙). In this way, the discourses of community, openness, and play that are associated with the *p'ungmul madang* have translated in very interesting ways in the US. For example, I posit that during *chishinpalpki*, *p'ungmul* groups employ these discursive and aspirational ideas of how to play in a *madang* setting and adapt them to the actual conditions and constantly shifting Koreatown neighborhoods that these *p'ungmul* groups have to negotiate. By forming relationships with business owners and encountering random customers and folks on the street, they also effectively draw a community of multi-ethnic "indefinite strangers" together into what Michael Warner and Nancy Fraser have called "counterpublics" (Warner 2002, 85–86; Fraser 1992, 123). Building upon Jurgen Habermas's theorization of a "public sphere," Warner and Fraser are primarily concerned with more oppositional or subaltern counterpublics that are formed through the circulation of texts. This links to Namhee Lee's theorization of *madanggŭk* (a form of political, experimental theater based on *madang* concepts) as a critical "counterpublic sphere" that she believed was not only oppositional but "integral to the development of civil society" in South Korea (Lee 2007, 9). Applying this to Koreatown *chishinpalpki*, I would argue that identity-affirming practices such as this could become a template and springboard for civic and political participation in the future.

In the realm of performance studies, Laura Levin and Marlis Schweitzer address how scholars "have turned to 'publics' to describe a performative relation between individuals—the ways that identities, identifications and ideologies serve to relate and differentiate people within the public sphere" in the context of performance (2011, 2). There are many performative relationships and effects that are enacted during *chishinpalpki*, and some are even spiritually antagonistic in nature. According to the ritual underpinning of this tradition, some of these performative effects include: (1) the stamping out of bad energy and spirits, and (2) ushering in good spirits and fortunes. In a more secular interpretation, one can also argue that: (1) mutually supportive relationships between the business owners and *p'ungmul* performers are performed and re-affirmed, (2) cultural pride and Korean identity is performed and strengthened, and (3) the right to exist in both the private and public spaces of Koreatown is claimed and blessed. It is no wonder then that during a 2015 *chishinpalpki* in LA's K-town, the leader, Han Kim likened his group to the "ghostbusters":

> It's you guys [who] bring out good fortunes of this year for our neighbors, for the whole entire world... Because we are ghostbusters in a sense. We're here to call in the good spirits, the good energy, and good fortune for everyone in our community. And we do it loud and proud, right?[11]

Because of *p'ungmul*'s "leftist" associations with the democratization movement in South Korea that peaked in the late 1980s, the reception of *chishinpalpki* has not always been positive. However, in the years following the April 29, 1992, Los Angeles Civil Unrest (or what has been called *Sa-I-Gu* by Koreans, referring simply to the date 4-29), the performative power of *chishinpalpki* took on even deeper meaning and significance. Jang Woo Nam explains:

> If you [went] to fifteen stores, only two or three would greet you. The others would say, "I'm not giving money to you, you commies." The [*chishinpalpki*] from '93 became a very community thing where they welcomed all these young Korean drumming folks, reminding Koreans of their Korean-ness and the Korean community. They realized that community does need to come together and celebrate its identity.[12]

For folklore and cultural studies scholar Timothy Tangherlini, *chishinpalpki* "serves to map the community . . . and simultaneously delimit the boundaries of this newly imagined village," which was especially welcome in Koreatown as they began to rebuild from the ashes (1999, 156). And while *chishinpalpki* did not quite have the same site-specific urgency in other "Koreatowns" in Chicago or New York in 1993, what happened in Los Angeles marked a turning point for Korean Americans who began to realize that they needed to better affirm, educate, and reckon with their place in American society.

1992 LOS ANGELES CIVIL UNREST AND THE KOREATOWN PEACE MARCH

In the 1993 documentary film *Sa-I-Gu* by Dai Sil Kim-Gibson, Christine Choy, and Elaine Kim, one can hear a thirty-second clip of *p'ungmul* being performed during the Koreatown Peace March that took place on May 2, 1992, three days after Los Angeles Civil Unrest broke out.[13] The familiar sound of the common 12/8 rhythm of *samch'ae* resonates against the harsh asphalt streets, with the higher *kkwaenggwari* and the lower *ching* gongs cutting through, followed by the muffled deep booms of the *puk* drum. Against this are the sharp whistles of the police and national guardsmen, the wailing sirens of the police escort vehicles, the honking horns of traffic, and toward the end of the clip, one can hear the chanting of "We Want Peace!" repeated asynchronously to the drumming as the family and friends of a Korean American victim, Edward Song Lee, process along the march route.

Despite the overwhelming desire for peace and justice expressed in the march, the truth is that Korean American responses to the Rodney King verdict and the civil unrest that followed were complicated, ambivalent, and raw. Ethnic studies professor and the co-producer of the film *Sa-I-Gu*, Elaine Kim explains how these sentiments are reflected in the way some Korean Americans chose to talk about what happened:

> Situated as we are on the border between those who have and those who have not, between predominantly Anglo and mostly African American and Latino communities, from our current interstitial position in the American discourse of race, many Korean Americans have trouble calling what happened in Los Angeles an "uprising." At the same time, we cannot quite say it was a "riot."

So some of us have taken to calling it [*Sa-I-Gu*], April 29, after the manner of naming other events in Korean history. (1993, 1–2)

During the Los Angeles unrest, Korean Americans were thrust into the national spotlight in what was largely framed by the media as a conflict between Blacks and Koreans. The reality was much more complicated. Although Korean merchants bore the brunt of about half of the total damages to material property, they only lost one life, that of 18-year-old Edward Song Lee. The rest of the fifty-four deaths were predominantly suffered by Blacks, Latinos, some Whites, and one other Asian American. While much is missing from a simplistic Black/Korean narrative—especially the story of Latinos—another is the larger history of racist, segregationist policies in Los Angeles that benefitted wealthier White communities and further exacerbated inequality. One emerging narrative was that the national guard and police failed to protect South LA and Koreatown, and instead prioritized wealthier (and more White) neighborhoods (Kim 1993, 5; Cho 1993, 201). Anthropologist Kyeyoung Park lends nuance to many of these issues in an in-depth monograph called *LA Rising, Korean Relations with Blacks and Latinos after Civil Unrest*, asserting that "race, citizenship, class, and culture were axes of inequality in a multi-tiered 'racial cartography' that affected how Los Angeles residents thought about and interacted with each other" (Park 2019, 4).

While it has taken time to understand the full legacy of the Los Angeles Civil Unrest, for Korean Americans it became clear that they needed to become more politically and civically engaged in order to better advocate for themselves. Many Korean political organizations pivoted from focusing solely on Korean domestic issues to addressing Korean American needs (Abelmann and Lie 1995, 185). These included improving the perception and understanding of Korean culture and people, and cultivating relationships with other groups with similar missions.

Although the Koreatown Peace March that took place on May 2, 1992 was certainly not the first time that *p'ungmul* was used in a demonstration in the United States, it was one of the more visible and documented occurrences. Part of this had to do with the sheer size of the event. The *Los Angeles Times* estimated the attendance to be around 30,000 (Chang and Krikorian 1992). Considering that the population of Korean Americans in Los Angeles County was about 150,000 in 1990 (Min 1990, 1), this was an unprecedented demonstration of Korean American civic participation.[14] Beginning at Ardmore Park (now Seoul International Park) and proceeding the length of almost thirty blocks, "the route of the march—west on Olympic Boulevard to Western Avenue, north to Third

Street and finally east to Vermont Avenue—was confined to Koreatown and went directly past many businesses that had been burned or looted during the riots" (Tangherlini 1999, 155).

While several sources documented the presence of Korean drummers at this event, few took note of the identity of these drummers.[15] Since most of the drummers were wearing white headbands and *minbok* (loose shirts and trousers) without the customary colorful sashes and vests that might help identify one group from another, observers likely assumed that the drummers were all from one contingent. An account by Brett Tam in UCLA's *Daily Bruin* newspaper notes that the UCLA *p'ungmul* group Han Ool Lim (literally "One Sound") "helped lead the march" and "performed traditional songs on Korean drums as the massive crowd followed and cheered them on" (Tam 1992) but there was no mention of any other groups. According to my interlocutors who participated playing in the Koreatown Peace March, the *p'ungmul* contingent was organized by Uri Munhwa Kondongch'e, but since they had very recently formed earlier that year after the closing of the Minjung Munhwa Yŏnguso (Minjung Culture Research Center), they did not have a lot of members, so they asked UCLA's Han Ool Lim to come, along with *p'ungmul* members from the Korean Resource Center.

None of the sources mention the specific rhythms that these drummers played for the duration of the march route. In the short clip from the *Sa-I-Gu* documentary, they played a rousing version of the 12/8 *samch'ae*. Since this is one of the most common rhythms played in marching formation, it might be assumed from the documentary that they played this one rhythm the whole time. According to the Uri Munhwa Kondongch'e member Yong Sok Chung, however, they actually played quite a variety of rhythms, including the *obangjin* and *chinobangjin* alternating series, *ich'ae*, *miryang haengjinkok*, and *kutkŏri* (personal communication). *Miryang haengjinkok* was not familiar to me, but Jang Woo Nam said that it was mainly used in rally and march-type settings and is similar to *obangjin*. It makes sense that they chose to play a variety of rhythms to adapt to the approximately thirty-block length of the march route. Other than this, it does not appear that the *p'ungmul* performers made any special modifications to play rhythms that conveyed strategic directions or messages, although there was some effort to synchronize the rhythms to the chanting whenever possible. This was challenging, however, because the soundscape of the march was especially dense with non-synchronous sounds from the whistles, honking, traffic, and chants of "We want peace!" from the marchers.

Some scholars have expressed some ambivalence on the meaning and effects of *p'ungmul*'s role in the peace march. Elaine Kim recounted that "[m]usicians in white, the color of mourning, beat traditional Korean drums in sorrow, anger, and celebration of community, a call to arms like a collective heartbeat" but later admits that she has also "been critical of cultural nationalism as detrimental to Korean Americans, especially Korean American women, because it operates on exclusions and fosters intolerance and uniformity of thought while stifling self-criticism and encouraging sacrifice" (1993, 15). Toward the end of her assessment, she concludes that if "Korean national consciousness is ever to be such a weapon for us, we must use it to create a new kind of nationalism-in-internationalism to help us call forth a culture of survival and recovery, so that our *han* might be released and we might be freed to dream fiercely of different possibilities." The notion of *han*—a Korean concept of unresolved sorrow and collective resentment that stems from historical oppression—comes up frequently in Korean performing arts discourse, but it has also been criticized as an essentialist and ethnonationalist concept (Kim 2017, 257). Perhaps sensing this, Kim's ultimate call to release and move beyond an ethnonationalist *han* is somewhat prophetic as many "different possibilities" have indeed been explored through *p'ungmul* in later decades.

From another angle, Timothy Tangherlini interpreted *p'ungmul* in this event as a folkloric performance whereby "Korean Americans began reasserting control of the contested spaces of Koreatown" (1999, 149–50). By literally marching around an imagined perimeter of a Koreatown still smoldering from the fires, Tangherlini viewed this as an effort to re-inscribe Korean cultural identity into the place of Koreatown, especially in the immediate aftermath of its erasure, as much of the Korean signage from the Korean businesses had burned in the flames. And while Tangherlini acknowledges that by drawing upon *p'ungmul*'s connections to South Korea's democratization movement, the demonstrators were also expressing implicit solidarity for the struggles of people of color in the United States, he ultimately states that this was "only accessible to audiences familiar with the history of *minjung* struggle in Korea" (1999, 156).

It is important to add that both the *Daily Bruin* and *Los Angeles Times* accounts note that more efforts could have been made to include other people of color in the march (Tam 1992, Chang and Krikorian 1992). Even so, Brett Tam observed that one Black American man in attendance was very moved to see signs that supported justice for Rodney King. Interestingly, Tangherlini wrote in a later article that there were "various African drill teams which also make use of drumming, as well as various Latino drumming groups" present at the Koreatown Peace March, although my sources were not able to confirm this (Tangherlini 2001, 111).

Despite what the actual composition of the drumming groups might have been, my response to Tangherlini's critique of this event as a nationalistic cultural inscription of identity is to direct attention to the more intersubjective moments that occurred in performance. When I asked members of Uri Munhwa Kondongch'e what they remembered most from the march, Yong Sok Chung responded that it was the outpouring of support from so "many different citizens around the community who marched alongside [us] to offer water when [we] were thirsty, while families even brought their babies in strollers despite the potential for danger" (personal communication). This level of support was especially meaningful and memorable for *p'ungmul* protesters because it signaled a broader recognition for the need for *change* in the way that the Korean Americans are understood by others in American society. While efforts to include more outreach to the Black and Latinx communities at the time were notably limited at the Koreatown Peace March, at least there were some in the community who understood that more needed to be done. In fact, these efforts were already underway elsewhere in California. According to Jang Woo Nam, who was a member of KYCC and a staff member of the Korean Community Center of the East Bay (KCCEB) in Oakland, California, there was a joint rally organized by these two organizations in Japantown Plaza in San Francisco that intentionally brought together Black and Korean American youth for a rally of speeches, music, and traditional Korean performances.

SOUNDING CULTURAL SPACE IN THE KOREAN AMERICAN COMMUNITY IN THE AFTERMATH OF 9/11

In the decade that followed *Sa-I-Gu*, Korean community and cultural groups shifted to focus more on Korean American domestic issues as opposed to Korean peninsular politics (Abelmann and Lie 1995, 185). For *p'ungmul* groups, educating the larger community about Korean culture became a priority, and some groups made a concerted effort to program more cross-cultural and multicultural events. At the same time, Korean American community organizations broadened their programming to serve different sectors of the Korean American community, including more women, seniors, children, Korean adoptees, non-binary people, and LGBTQ+ members.

To show how Korean American *p'ungmul* groups progressed in negotiating space and place in the United States, I fast forward to the activities of *p'ungmul* groups during the aftermath of the terrorist attacks of 9/11 in 2001, another significant period of national crisis. Just as site-oriented practices proved instrumental during the Los Angeles Civil Unrest a little more than a decade earlier, they were just as critical after 9/11 and beyond. Here, I examine how the Korean Youth Cultural Center (KYCC) in Oakland, CA coped with adjusting their fourteenth annual performance in the immediate aftermath of 9/11. Then, as a point of contrast, I also examine the site-specific *p'ungmul* activities that were organized closer to Ground Zero in New York by Pinari from MinKwon.

In August and early September of 2001, I was preparing for the KYCC's fourteenth annual fall performance scheduled for September 22. KYCC's annual fall performances usually draw heavily from Korea's folk expressive culture traditions including Korean drumming and dance (both in the *p'ungmul* and *samul nori* formats), mask dance drama (*t'alch'um*), and folksongs.[16] In addition, some newer practices have been incorporated, such as political movement songs (*norae undong*) and theatrical skits. In any given performance, these elements are usually arranged to highlight a pre-determined issue or theme such as the North Korean famine, reunification, or Korean American immigration narratives. Building upon recent activities that cultivated networking with other national *p'ungmul* groups as well as coordinating residencies with Korean master *p'ungmul* teachers from the Pilbong regional style, the theme for 2001 was to create a performance that would draw upon *p'ungmul*'s connection to village rituals called *maŭl-kut*. Along these lines, the performance was entitled *Taeborŭm Paraem-kut*, meaning "Gathering of Wishes Under the Full Moon." Clearly inspired by Pilbong's Lunar New Year ritual described in chapter 3, KYCC wanted to adapt this practice to the Korean traditional harvest moon holiday of *Ch'usŏk* (falling on the fifteenth day of August according to the lunar calendar), in part because KYCC's annual performances usually take place in the fall. In the original program order, the entire event was conceived as a large-scale *kut* ceremony in three sections:

SECTION 1
Paraem-kut (Gathering of Wishes Ceremony)
Ap-kut (Opening *p'ungmul* ceremony)

SECTION 2
Ch'um-kut ("Dance ceremony," teaching *kanggangsullae* group play
   with movement and singing)
Goseong Ogwangdae Mask Dance Drama

SECTION 3

Twi-kut (Closing *p'ungmul* ceremony)
Taedong-kut (Performing *kanggangsullae* group play with audience)

Conceptualizing the event as a large-scale *kut* ceremony rather than as a generic cultural performance necessitated several changes to KYCC's normal fall performance practice. First, it meant holding the event outdoors, as opposed to in an indoor multi-purpose room or theater. Even though KYCC members were aware of the importance of playing *p'ungmul* outdoors in the *madang*, it was still very much the norm to hold their annual performances indoors to accommodate other genres and audiences more easily. While KYCC had cultivated *madang* aesthetics into their previous indoor performances, they were ready to try to hold a *madang* event outdoors. Given that KYCC did not have exclusive access to an appropriate outdoor space of its own, it had to research and reserve a public space that could most closely elicit these qualities, preferably a natural green space with resonant properties and ambience. Second, conceiving the performance as a *kut* (ritual) also lengthened the overall program concept from a two-hour performance to more of a five-hour festival format. Set in a *madang*-style context, the shamanistic framing of the event came with associated discourses that define *kut* as a space of ritual transformation, a unifying community gathering and an event that is integral with everyday life.

In orienting the event as ritual, KYCC's primary aim was to emphasize various modes of audience participation. For example, in the "gathering of wishes ceremony," the plan was to unfurl a blank banner that audience members were encouraged to write their wishes on while KYCC performed shamanist songs in their repertoire.[17] Other participatory activities were incorporated into subsequent sections as well. For example, in the second section that was focused on the theme of dance or *ch'um*, the plan was to teach audience members the choreography involved in the women's group play with movement and song called *kanggangsullae*. Then in the third and final section, the plan was to end the event by having everyone perform *kanggangsullae* together.

Finding a space nearby for this newly imagined ritual would prove difficult. Throughout the 1990s and mid-2000s, KYCC was located in the Temescal neighborhood of Oakland, California within a few blocks of the Korean Community Center of the East Bay, as well as a handful of Korean restaurants and one Korean grocery store. However, these establishments were not enough to constitute a Koreatown and they did not have enough resources or space to host an outdoor

Korean cultural festival in that immediate area. Mosswood Park was about ten blocks away, and though KYCC often practiced there, it was not well suited for the ritual environment that KYCC was aiming for. For example, the park is adjacent to a large Kaiser hospital building and is also surrounded by dense urban and residential areas that would have been less than ideal for a large-scale *kut* ceremony. KYCC members also considered Lake Merritt, which is much larger and has several areas that would have been appropriate. However, a few months earlier, KYCC had a negative experience practicing there when residents in the area made noise complaints and had the police come to ask the group to stop playing (see companion website for Lake Merritt photos). This coincided with other similar incidents in the area that were later criticized as an unjust policing of people of color in public spaces through noise complaints, a dynamic that would continue to be an issue in future years (Levin 2015, Phillips 2021).

Eventually, KYCC settled on reserving a spot in the gently sloping green space of Marx Meadow, located in the heart of San Francisco's Golden Gate Park. And while KYCC rarely hosted their own performances in San Francisco, they chose it because it is a well-known location where one can enjoy a relaxed and beautiful natural setting. Another advantage was its unique acoustics that stem from its resonant, bowl-like shape, further aided by the mature pine trees and huge ghost gum eucalyptus that line the meadow to form an atmospheric, unique backdrop.

According to my interview and conversation with board member Helen Kim in 2005, the planning of the event prior to 9/11 already included many firsts for KYCC: (1) it was the first fall event to be held entirely as a *kut* ritual for the *Ch'usŏk* harvest holiday in an outdoor *madang*-style space with a focus on community participation; (2) it was the first year that we included a grassroots capital campaign; and (3) there was more of an effort to include other *p'ungmul* groups in the larger Bay Area, including UC Berkeley's *p'ungmul* group EGO, the all-women group named Jamaesori in the East Bay, Stanford University's Hwimori, and San Jose's HanUri in the South Bay. It is important to note that playing outdoors was critical because it made it possible to bring together all these groups. By contrast, it would be difficult to find indoor spaces that would accommodate so many percussionists, not to mention the audience; more importantly, the noise level would have been deafening. It is also important to note that KYCC's relationship to the master teachers of the Pilbong *p'ungmul* style was a catalyst for many of these changes: "The introduction to Pilbong had a big impact—they were introduced to the US, KYCC went there [to Pilbong] . . . that was the turning point" (Helen Kim interview, August 7, 2005).

Little did we know in our planning stages that 9/11 would become an even more critical turning point, not only in planning this event, but also in terms of KYCC defining itself as an organization. Although we were not located near the 9/11 attacks, KYCC's plans for the performance were irrevocably impacted. Ann Kwon, the president of KYCC at the time, recounts:

> Yesterday we escalated our discussion as to whether we should continue with the Fall performance . . . Reason being, I got a call from the Korean Consulate requesting that we don't have this program . . . We had a call from the Haninhwe in San Francisco [Korean American Business Association] . . . they wanted to talk to us. Several newspaper reporters called us requesting interviews wanting to know if we're going to continue with the performance and on top of that, we got three or four random phone calls left on our voicemail, very angry vociferous phone calls, just yelling at the top of their lungs, people asking us to stop our performance.
> So . . . they felt we were being disrespectful of the mood of the country. But then after a long discussion, people were like, what has the first generation [of Korean Americans] done for us in terms of supporting us? KYCC has a history of being in opposition with them because we were founded on the idea of [Korean] reunification, so we have a good relationship with the first-generation community but historically, we've also had . . . oppositional relationships because of our politics.
> After much discussion, we felt like we needed to continue, and I'm glad we're doing it . . . because we need to stand up for ourselves and our beliefs and show the first generation what our music is about . . . They don't really know what it's about because they only see the music as festive. [But] it is also used in times of mourning, funerals, and grieving . . . Yes, our music's loud . . . but if we properly set the tone of the performance, we felt like we could be successful. (Ann Kwon video interview, n.d.)[18]

In the end, all the other major Korean organizations cancelled their *Ch'usŏk* harvest holiday events except for KYCC. Intensifying the pressure from the community, one of the Korean language dailies in Northern California, the *Korea Times* (*Han'guk Ilbo*), ran an editorial by Mr. Son Su-Rak that ended with the line that "this is not the time to play *puk* or *changgo*," two prominent *p'ungmul* instruments (Son 2001). When pressed by Helen Kim, Mr. Son said this was just a figure of speech and denied targeting this comment directly at KYCC. However, it became clear that a consensus among mostly first-generation Korean immigrants in the Bay Area was to respond to 9/11 with a respectful silence. Helen Kim, an advocate of Asian immigrants' rights, interpreted this as a response that stemmed from the intensified atmosphere of fear of the potential scapegoating of all Asian "others" in the wake of this tragedy.

> I realized that there would be a lot of scapegoating with people of color, immigrants, South Asians, immediately harkening back to the Japanese American experience of the internment camps . . . people were so scared to speak up . . . People felt threatened so for the Korean community, they wanted to be ultra-patriotic, you know . . . And that is the tragedy of how insecure immigrants feel in this country. (Helen Kim interview, August 7, 2005)

Contributing to misunderstandings between KYCC and other Korean organizations in the Bay Area was the dominant perception of *Ch'usŏk* (harvest holiday) as primarily a celebration—a celebration that in the immediate aftermath of 9/11 would not have been appropriate. Even so, KYCC was adamant about reframing *Ch'usŏk* as a shamanist ritual, knowing that the first generation, many of whom are Christian, would have difficulty understanding this. Helen Kim links KYCC's thinking directly to their experiences with Pilbong teachers:

> When spending time in Pilbong, Yang *sŏnsaengnim* [Yang Chinsŏng "teacher"] said *kut* is a part of everyday life, [it's] not just a celebration . . . [it could be] a perfect vehicle to express so many different emotions. It could be a political statement without being overtly political. (Helen Kim interview, August 7, 2005)

The decision to proceed with the performance and go against the wishes of the Korean Consulate and the older Korean American generation did not come easily for some KYCC members. For those who grew up and had roots in the relatively small Korean American community in the Bay Area, it was akin to going against the wishes of one's own parents.

After several lengthy meetings of intense discussion, KYCC eventually came to a consensus to redirect the performance to "mourn loss of lives, build community spirit, and wish for peace." Their revised press document released on September 18 read that they would aim to:

> bring the community together through a traditional Korean drumming ceremony . . . The ceremony will allow individuals and the community to express our sorrow and wishes for a more peaceful society . . . As part of the rich cultural

diversity of the Bay Area, we believe it is important to continue to honor our cultural traditions in this time of growing intolerance and fear. The program will include a *Kosa*, a time to pay respects to those who have passed away, and a candlelight vigil to remember those who have died and their surviving loved ones. During our *Paraem-kut*, the gathering of wishes under the full moon, individuals can express their wishes for healing and peace. (Korean Youth Cultural Center 2001a)

Along these lines, each of the three sections was changed to reflect these new intentions (see changes/additions in bold):

SECTION 1
***Kil-kut* (Road Ceremony)**
***Kosa-kut* (Ceremony to Pay Respect)**
Paraem-kut (Gathering of Wishes Ceremony)
Ap-kut (Opening *p'ungmul* ceremony)

SECTION 2
Ch'um-kut ("Dance Ceremony," teaching *kanggangsullae* group play
    with movement and singing)
Song ("Eru-a, Eru-ŏlsa," HanUri)
Yeongnam *Nongak Samul nori* (EGO)
Goseong Ogwangdae Mask Dance Drama

SECTION 3
Twi-kut (Closing *p'ungmul* ceremony)
Taedong-kut (Performing *kanggangsullae* group play with audience)
Candlelight Vigil with *Chinhon-kut*

The first and third sections took on even deeper characteristics of ritual. In the first section, for example, the *kil-kut* and *kosa* ceremonies were added to the program. According to the new program, the *kil-kut* (road ceremony) "opens the event by bringing the performers to the 'Tree of Life' where the *Kosa* will take place. *Kil-kut* is traditionally a rhythm of travel from one space to another, both physically and spiritually" (Korean Youth Cultural Center 2001b). This led into the added *kosa* where participants could "share [a] sense of grief and loss and pay respects to those who have passed away by bowing in groups and lighting

Sounding Space in the Korean American Community 219

incense" (Korean Youth Cultural Center 2001b). KYCC members also followed traditional *kosa* protocol by reading and then burning a statement, called a *chemun*, and letting the ashes float up to the heavens. This flowed into the originally planned *paraem-kut*, or "wish ceremony," and concluded with the Pilbong-style *ap-kut* during which the opening series of rhythms were played by participating KYCC, Jamaesori, and EGO members.

The second section kept two pieces that were originally planned, the teaching of *kanggangsullae* group play, as well as the Goseong Ogwangdae mask dance. In order to build more solidarity with other groups, two additional performances were added by the Sacramento-based HanUri and University of California, Berkeley's EGO group. Still, *kanggangsullae* remained the centerpiece of this section and the program description left open the possibility of interpreting its meaning and applying its connotations of communal strength to the post-9/11 context.

> *Kanggangsullae* was born out of agricultural life but was specifically developed to provide a release of the tensions and "*han*" of women's life and work. *Kanggangsullae* is practiced particularly during the harvest moon *Ch'usok* holiday ... It is said that on Jindo Island, *Kanggangsullae* was performed on the mountaintops to ward off invaders who may have thought the island was vulnerable to attack during the Japanese Invasions in the late-sixteenth century. With this long history, we hope to continue this tradition of gathering strength and invite all to participate. (Korean Youth Cultural Center 2001b)

The third section kept the closing *p'ungmul* performance or *twi-kut* that was to be followed by the plan to have everyone now perform *kanggangsullae* together. The most significant change to the program here was KYCC's decision to end the day's events by adding a candlelight vigil during which dancer and KYCC member Dohee Lee performed a *chinhon-kut*, a shaman-inspired dance ritual that was performed to ensure the safe and peaceful passage of the spirits of people who have perished.

While the experiences of each performer and audience member were certainly diverse, the emphasis on inserting deep modes of participation into each section certainly contributed to the strengthening of existing affective alliances. To quote from my conversational interview with Helen Kim:

> DONNA: I think because I was so involved, being *sangsoe* [lead gong player] ... It was overwhelming, that space. And we had so many people as part of

the *p'an* and then we had San Jose who was playing with us, so I was really stressed a lot of the time, I had to really gather all those people. It's great that we had other events that gathered people like the candles, and the bowing. But I remember that parts of it were such a struggle.

HELEN: But it was executed really well.

DONNA: It was ambitious, there were certain things about it that were so different. Usually I connect *p'an-kut* [entertainment-oriented *p'ungmul*] to something bright and energetic, but here, the whole tone of it was so different. It was serious. When everything is serious like that, it's not quite the same *p'an-kut twip'uri* [after-release] feeling.

HELEN: That's why *kanggangsullae* was really important, because it was communal play, we had so many circles going and we had to train everyone to be a lead. That was really fun. I don't think we've been able to duplicate that. It was a very moving kind of experience. It was very well coordinated. We had some communal games, different performances and of course, Dohee's dance at the end when everyone was doing *kanggangsullae* together, and in that circle Dohee [Lee] dances, I was in tears, I think a lot of people were in tears at that point. (Helen Kim interview, August 7, 2005)

Despite earlier resistance, Helen Kim notes that the Korean press reviewed the event positively (figure 7.3 ◉). As a result, the larger community eventually became sympathetic with what we were trying to accomplish and came to see us "more as a peer or in a different light" (Helen Kim interview, August 7, 2005; Ko Hyunjin 2001). This episode exposes a subtle reconfiguration of the dynamics between subgroups within a Korean American community. It was also an effort to encourage audience members to be less passive and become more actively engaged in responding to an emerging crisis, the aftereffects of which would continue to be politicized for years to come.

Due to the broad outreach to the mainstream press for this event, the audience was more diverse than usual. As a result, affective moments of unexpected alliance also occurred—one of which is evident in this moving email that was sent to KYCC from an audience member:

My husband and I wish to extend a heartfelt thank you for the extraordinary "Gathering of Wishes Under the Full Moon." In this time, it is extremely difficult to find words to express all my feelings—perhaps instead I will simply share this story: My father, a dear man, but rather conservative and militaristic, came to visit from Boston for just two days. He was the last person I would have expected to travel at this time. I was—and am—deep in mourning and fear about the current events and doing what little I know to do: writing letters to congress, gathering with friends, donating, praying, mobilizing... So, while hosting my father I knew I must find some way to continue my involvement. But how? There was a gathering at Dolores Park, but I knew he would not go. On my way to the airport, I heard two minutes of broadcast from KPFA and someone mentioned the *p'ungmul* drum ceremony that would be taking place in Golden Gate Park, and I thought Dad might go to that! So, on Saturday morning we made our way to the city and spent the day in the park.

For me and my husband, we loved every moment. We were amazed how connected we felt to all aspects of the ceremonies and rituals especially to the profound intentions of the gathering and the deep connectedness with the earth. I am so thankful. But, perhaps the most amazing thing about the whole afternoon was watching my father. Beforehand he seemed bent on retaliation and "justice." But there he sat, for five hours, enraptured with the statements, the ceremonies, the hopes of those who had gathered. I watched my father, who has—forgive him—also been known to be "reserved" if not outright prejudiced towards Asian-Americans, join us as we lined up to bow at the tree of life. I watched as his hand shot up to be the one who lit the incense. I watched him dance in spirals... I watched him delight in the traditional rituals. I watched him nibble rice cakes. I watched him run to the car during intermission to get a sweater. I watched him smile when I asked if he was ready to go; no, he wanted to stay on for the afternoon, this our only day together. I felt him trying to open his heart. I listened as he began to dialogue instead of fight with me about my positions on violence and retaliation and my commitment to peaceful resolutions. This brought tears of hope and finally, after days, I felt I could breathe, at least for a moment, more freely, more hopefully. (Personal email communication)

The embodied participatory activities that became more of a focus of the event after 9/11 served to intensify affective responses and alliances among core and outside members. Interestingly, the participatory activities of the event appeared to make it possible for the father to process both physical and emotional responses to 9/11 before necessarily being able to process complex reactions and thoughts on the topic through language-based thoughts and conversation. According to Thomas Turino, this has to do with the "semiotic potential of signs" where he theorizes that musical engagement tends to heighten and prolong energetic (somatic reactions like tapping one's foot or dancing) and emotional interpretants (responses like euphoria), while postponing "rational," "conscious," or language-based interpretants (Turino 1999, 233–34). In this case, bodily participation in this event made it possible for the father to be more affectively receptive to a more peaceful and immigrant-centered response to 9/11, even if he might have been more initially resistant to this through word-based thought and conversation. The intensity and positive nature of his affective response was then reinforced by facilitating a more open dialogue between the father and daughter after the event. While KYCC did not forge a permanent association with Marx Meadow in Golden Gate Park, the ability to hold a uniquely Korean American ceremony and vigil in a well-known location in the Bay Area was critical to KYCC in asserting its right to be heard and seen in such a public space (video 7.1 🔊).[19]

Meanwhile for *p'ungmul* groups in New York City, the situation was vastly different due to their proximity to Ground Zero and the far-reaching destruction of the World Trade Center. It was not until many months later that MinKwon's Pinari organized a ritual and vigil at Battery Park on February 16, 2002, to pray for peace and remember the victims of 9/11. They were joined by others in the region, including collegiate groups from NYU and Stony Brook University and even community groups like Philadelphia's Mae-Ari, for a total of about sixty participants (Gwak 2008). According to interviews and Korean newspaper accounts, they performed *p'ungmul* in a circle and held a vigil and ritual by reciting a *chemun* prayer in front of a shrine set up with sacrificial food (figure 7.4 ⊙). When I asked Ju Bum Cha why they decided to hold the event at Battery Park, he said that they chose it because of its proximity to the former World Trade Center, but also because they were drawn by its view of the Statue of Liberty, a universal symbol of freedom. Through memorial speeches, they paid special attention to immigrant victims of 9/11 and spoke out against the rising tide of anti-immigrant sentiment, treatment, and policies. Afterward, they moved on to 32nd Street in Koreatown to conduct their regular Lunar New Year *chishinpalpki* and distribute the various shrine foods to participants there. Circling back to historical practices of *p'ungmul* in the United States, it is evident that the regular and repeated patterning of *chishinpalpki* continued to be important in creating a Korean American sense of place, solidarity, and performative sociality.

THE SONIC AND TACTICAL DEVELOPMENT OF *P'UNGMUL* IN A NEW MILLENNIAL ERA OF PROTEST

The two decades since 9/11 were especially turbulent, giving rise to numerous large-scale protests in the United States and around the world. Then-President Bush's ensuing "global war on terror" and the invasions of Iraq and Afghanistan spurred a series of anti-war peace protests and demonstrations that many US-based *p'ungmul* groups took part in. For example, KYCC was involved in the anti-war march in San Francisco that drew 50,000 people on January 18, 2003, and MinKwon's Pinari and other groups took part in a massive "Say No to Bush's Agenda" rally in New York in 2004. Concurrently, the intensified antiterrorist sentiments led to an increased attention to controlling borders and immigrants, which resulted in both sympathetic immigration bills such as the DREAM Act of 2001 (H.R. 1582), as well as harsher anti-immigration bills such as the Border Protection, Antiterrorism, and Illegal Immigration Control Act of 2005 (H.R. 4437). Although neither became law at the time of their introduction, these actions precipitated intense participation in immigrant rights demonstrations for Korean American organizations such as MinKwon in New York and KIWA in Los Angeles. Ju Bum Cha of MinKwon recounted that Pinari was involved in supporting the 2001 DREAM Act campaign and actively opposing H.R. 4437. Opposition to H.R. 4437 and immigration reform was an especially galvanizing issue for Latinx communities, culminating in the large-scale protests of 2006. These immigration reform marches began in Chicago on March 10, 2006 and gained steam over the next two months. An additional nationwide protest occurred on May 1, 2006 and came to be known as the "Great American Boycott" or "A Day Without an Immigrant." Pinari was involved in the one that was organized by the We Are America Alliance that took place in New York City, which was said to have attracted over 200,000 people.

Activist *p'ungmul* groups across the country became more accustomed to participating in large-scale protests, often encountering diverse groups in unexpected ways. In this process, these groups developed a range of techniques of contributing to and resonating with diverse US-based protest cultures. Some groups, like Pinari, chose to clearly delineate their place in a march formation. According to Ju Bum Cha, "*P'ungmul* is always in the front, that is our tradition. It really sets off a spark with people. It makes people excited!" Sometimes, groups would take advantage of spontaneous intercultural moments. Ju Bum

Cha even recounted how being next to a Mexican percussion group spurred an impromptu jam session (Ju Bum Cha interview, August 3, 2015).

Another development in the latter half of the 2000s was the formation of a small wave of activist *p'ungmul* groups, many of which were explicitly feminist and queer in orientation. These include Ieumsae, operating under the umbrella of the Korean American activist organization HOBAK (Hella Organized Bay Area Koreans) in the San Francisco Bay Area, SUBAK in Southern California, and the Poongmul Movement Builders in New York. Whereas earlier groups like KYCC sometimes had internal conflicts about whether their focus should be artistic, educational, community service–oriented, or more activist in nature, these groups view activism as central. As stated in their mission statement, Ieumsae's vision is simultaneously intersectional and transnational, stating that "As Korean immigrants, feminists, queer folks, trans folks, mixed race folks, and adoptees, we take our drumming into the streets and alongside our comrades—bringing energy, rhythm, and solidarity to people resisting police violence, war and imperialism in the US and abroad." They have also developed quite a record of participation in a diverse range of political events, from Pride parades to immigrant, women, and Indigenous rights rallies to Korean peace, reunification, and "comfort women" reparation events. This may be due to the prioritization they place on collective, non-hierarchical processes in which they "share leadership, knowledge, and decision-making with all members not dependent on age or ability." In my interview with one of their members, anyone is welcome to "propose a project, you just need two people to co-sign it." They then appoint a "chef" or "point person to round up everybody, talk about logistics, and make sure the conversation happens and that everyone is prepared properly . . . So that is all done by the chef, so you are not only vouching for it, but you are also going to chef for it." While they "uphold the legacy of resistance of *p'ungmul* drummers" in South Korea, the way that they apply *p'ungmul* and *madang*-related ideas such as community or *kondongch'e* goes a few steps further than many of the earlier Korean and Korean American cultural organizations, many of which were still based on more hierarchical structures and decision-making.[20]

Focusing on the realm of sound for a moment, there are several elements that may help to explain *p'ungmul*'s appeal in protest situations. For one, it is loud, but beyond its sheer volume, it also features a rich timbral texture that results from its unique combination of higher and lower drums and gongs that fill out the frequency spectrum in a powerful way. For example, in an article documenting the use of *p'ungmul* in Washington DC's Women's March in January of 2017, journalist Allison Kinney consulted a member of the electronic music duo Matmos, Drew Daniel, with whom she was marching. He remarked, "I loved their stately pace and big resonant gong, it made things a little ominous, like a Javanese court gamelan crossed with industrial percussion legends Crash Worship—it also made a great metronomic grid on which to place chants. They ruled!" (Kinney 2017). As each percussion instrument occupies a different sector of the frequency spectrum, there is sufficient space in between for chants to be layered into the texture. Given that songs, chants, and shouts called *ch'uimsae* are already integral to *p'ungmul*, inserting protest chants comes somewhat naturally for most *p'ungmul* players.

The Ieumsae member interviewed emphasized a different aspect of the sound itself that I had not considered:

> It's really effective in terms of drawing attention. It could be a sound action . . . meaning that sound is the action itself, like creating disruption. Some people may chain themselves to the doors to disrupt business for a day . . . we don't have to do that. We can just show up and stop everything because everyone is going to turn and look at us. Or we can use it strategically to signal, okay, this is where we are going to go now in a big protest. Or we can shift the whole energy in a street riot, where it's escalating, and the police are shooting tear gas. We can create a different kinda space where it's more calm and on our own terms and maybe even celebratory. (Ieumsae interview)

In other words, sound actions are sounds that have performative power and are tactically deployed in various contexts, at times in ways that have the potential to re-set the dynamics of an event in more self-determined ways for marginal groups. Drawing on the work of Jacques Rancière, this could be interpreted as an act of dissensus defined as a "redistribution of the sensible" (Rancière 2013, 45). Here, Ieumsae's tactic of rebellion against the "order" that is enforced by the police is deployed by re-figuring, embodying, and sounding space in a different way in order to be heard on their own terms. Ieumsae also uses this technique to purposely break from the normative conventions of a US-based protest by performing rhythms/movements that are not easily subsumed into the protest soundscape—like the Pilbong *p'ungnyu-kut* rhythmic series—in order to assert difference. Also influenced by Rancière, André Lepecki productively theorizes these types of embodied actions as "choreopolitics" and describes them as insisting on a "redistribution and reinvention of bodies, affects, and senses through which one may learn how to move politically, how to invent, activate, seek, or experiment with a movement whose only sense (meaning and direction) is the experimental exercise of freedom" (Lepecki 2013, 20).[21]

The mobile and embodied aspect of *p'ungmul* makes it especially well suited to these types of tactical actions. Interestingly, Ieumsae is very aware of their sonic, spatial, and tactical power and they deploy it in intentional and intersectional ways.

> There's awkwardness where people really want us to be in the front and we have to say no, we are going to go to the back, we want some other position in the formation. Usually for something that is that big, we will have a direct line of communication with the comms team of the day for an action so that we can say, we would rather be spaced out from other chanters because it sounds really crappy when everyone is competing and it also doesn't make sense to have a lot of chanting happening in the front of a two-mile march while in the back there is nothing going on . . . If we are drumming and all of a sudden, a bunch of grandmas from CPA (which is the Chinese Progressive Alliance), they've decided to drum that day and be spontaneous, and they are drumming on five-gallon plastic buckets, we are not going to outshine them. And same with AYPAL, they will do something similar, they are a youth group. Like we are not going to compete with them. There will be some sort of—whether it's spoken or not—exchange of giving each other space. (Ieumsae interview)

From my experience participating and playing lead gong or the *sangsoe* role in anti–Iraq War demonstrations post-9/11 in the Bay Area and more recently in the Women's March in Lexington, KY, I try to be mindful of when to play and occupy more sonic space and when to be more open and responsive to the chanting and sonic presence of others. For me, it is less important to keep playing representative Korean traditional rhythms and more important to listen to the constantly shifting soundscape to better respond to, accompany, and amplify what is going on around me (figure 7.5 ⊙). When *p'ungmul* performers do play traditional rhythms, they tend to choose simpler rhythms that fit with a 4/4 beat such as *obangjin/chinobangjin* and *hwimori*. I like to improvise on these Korean rhythms to better match the rhythmic structure of a chant. When chants arise that clearly come more from the realm of popular culture such as Kendrick Lamar's "Alright" (2015), I have often taken more license in improvising patterns with chanters in the moment, playing more with the groove of these songs. Not everyone favors the improvisatory approach. Ieumsae, for example, likes

Sounding Space in the Korean American Community **227**

TABLE 7.3 Ieumsae Collaborative Rhythm for Protest Chants

1			2			3			4		
Kung		Tak		Tak		Kung		Tak		Kung	
ONE				We		Are		The		Peo-	ple
Kung		Tak		Tak		Kung				Kung	
TWO				A		Lit-	tle	Bit		Loud-	er
Kung		Tak		Tak		Kung		Tak		Kung	
THREE				We		Want				Just-	ice
Kung	Ta	Ta	Kung	Ta	Ta	Kung	Ta	Ta	Kung		
FOR			THE-			PEO-			PLE		

NOTE: The rhythms are indicated on *changgo* drum vocables with sample protest chant lyrics underneath each line. 4/4 meter. Composed by Ieumsae with the Filipino group Mass Bass.

to work with more intentional collaboration with other groups like the Filipino hip-hop/reggae/soul group Mass Bass, even composing a new beat to pair with protest chants (table 7.3).

These spontaneous or intentional collaborations can open up new modes, occasions, and spaces for embodying activism beyond the normative protest demonstration. For example, one such event in which Ieumsae participated was put together by the "#SoulOfOakland" on October 11, 2015, in the Lake Merritt area. Here, Ieumsae played in a rally and community drum call to protest the excessive policing of music-making and other cultural activities by people of color in the park. The #SoulOfOakland movement was another dissensual effort to assert the visibility and audibility of coalition-building in a society that would render them both separate, silent, and invisible. Although marginalized people in Oakland still struggle with gentrification, this movement was able to effect political change by successfully pressuring city officials to take down the signs in the Lake Merritt area that prohibited a "musical instrument without a permit" (Levin 2015).

More recently in early October 2019, I was able to see another event that featured Ieumsae in an intentional and artistic "re-figuring" of public space in favor of the marginalized. Entitled "Mu Fall ritual," it was organized and put together by performance artist Dohee Lee and envisioned as a Korean Jeju shamanist-style village ceremony meant to bring together and share the stories of various communities in East Oakland. These communities included second- and third-generation Asian American artists from the group Corazon, Bhutanese refugee youth, Ieumsae, and a Latinx labor activist group called Labor y Dignidad. The event took place at Peralta Hacienda Historical Park in East Oakland, which is named after the Spanish colonial Peralta family, who were known to have enslaved Indigenous people (the Ohlones) to work on their land. While the Peralta estate readily acknowledges this painful history, it was still striking to hear the native descendant, Corrina Gould, give an Ohlone Land Blessing, at the beginning of this ritual, essentially welcoming this re-imagining of the park as a space of Korean shamanist ritual.

> I want to thank Dohee and all of the other performers who are creating this ceremony on our land . . . It's important for me to know that there are folks that are coming into our territory and having ceremonies, because they have made this their home as well. We always say that we want to be good hosts on our land. But in order to be good hosts on our land, we have to have good guests. And good guests welcome us into their ceremonies and into their places in order to participate as well.

Although this elaborate and creative sounding of power, space, and sociality was ultimately temporary, fluid, and partial, various intercultural relationships were forged and affirmed.

CONCLUDING THOUGHTS

As demonstrated in this chapter, *p'ungmul* practitioners in the US have been playing in political settings for at least four decades. In so doing, they have repeatedly claimed sonic, social, and physical space for themselves and the larger Korean American community. While the sonic effects on public space are never permanent, the sounds of the Korean drums and gongs can leave residual memories or "sedimented histories" as Marié Abe argues, that can be accessed by more and more people over time (Abe 2018, 29). My research also suggests that Korean American drummers have played in more intentional, sono-tactical, creative, and intersectional ways. Far from a teleological progression, however, this has happened in fits and starts, often in response to major moments of crisis such as the Los Angeles Civil Unrest or 9/11, as well as in response to several waves of more decentralized movements pertaining to immigration reform, women's rights, or Black Lives Matter. In particular, the sono-tactical or choreopolitical capabilities of *p'ungmul* have been especially helpful for groups like Ieumsae in counter-police demonstrations where the racialized criminalization of protest is especially intense.

In these ways, Korean American drumming-based groups go beyond just temporarily defining, contesting, or claiming space in ways that bear larger implications in terms of understanding the dynamics of protest in a diverse nation still negotiating complex histories of difference along multiple fault lines. First, while the consistent favoring of an older expressive Korean performing tradition such as *p'ungmul* can be critiqued as a form of ethnocentric Korean nationalism or even self-exoticization, I argue that it is coming more from a progressive need to express one's Korean identity in solidarity with other marginalized groups, while also connecting with a longer legacy of social protest in South Korea. This impulse has led to increased intergroup awareness and activity among Korean American progressive groups, even if this is largely invisible to others. For example, groups like KIWA (Koreatown Immigrant Workers Alliance) and MinKwon have both employed *p'ungmul* to advocate for diverse immigrant workers' rights (especially Latinx and other Asian workers).

Second, the protest practices of Korean American drummers shed necessary light on the tactical, on-the-ground dynamics of intergroup protest in the United States. Noriko Manabe, in her monumental 2015 book on protest music in Japan after Fukushima, writes that "a key goal of social movements is to inspire participation" and that "[p]erformances in demonstrations tend to become more participatory over time, particularly when movements are mobilizing more and more participants" (2015, 28). While this may be the case in post-Fukushima Japan, I have found that Korean American drumming groups like Ieumsae employ tactics that are not necessarily about becoming more participatory or collaborative all the time. Instead, they aim to be sensitive to various dynamics up and down the chain of power. In one moment, this may mean laying back and giving sonic and physical space to another Asian drumming group; in the next, they may decide to resist and separate themselves from the conventions of large-scale US-based protest culture. In this way, Korean drummers have become more intentional in responding to the social dynamics of a given space/time, preferring to embody space on their own terms. Given that large-scale protests, such as the 2017 Women's March, have been questioned for replicating unequal power dynamics of race, class, and sexuality (Moss and Maddrell 2017), it is critical to look at the grassroots level to bear witness to the highly intentional efforts to forge coalitions with other marginalized communities or resist in various ways.

Third, in seeking to carve out space on their own terms, Korean activist drummers such as KYCC have also organized their own rallies and political performance events. Building upon concepts of ritual *p'ungmul*, as well as *madang*-related ideas that stem from *madang* theater's turn from drama (*madanggŭk*) to ritual (*madang-kut*) in South Korea, these events have often included strong elements of ritual participation. I also argue that the melding of ritual and politics has clear links to the mobile practice of ritual *chishinpalpki*. Namhee Lee theorized that the shift from drama to ritual within the Korean *madang* theater movement aimed for the "breakdown of the division between actor and spectator, between self and other" where the goal was the "transformative participation" of the "audience from detached individuals into members of a collective that could share the vision of a new political and cultural community" (Lee 2007, 11). This very much resonates with the work of KYCC post-9/11 and continues with Dohee Lee and her collaborations with Ieumsae and others. While the effects on material space and place are usually temporary, the transformation of actual individuals and their relationships to others have the potential to be longer lasting. Given that the US is a much more heterogeneous society than South Korea, this is challenging work and can be misunderstood as "cultish" or even off-putting for some who are not comfortable with its shamanist ritual underpinning. But even so, they have made previously unimaginable strides in creating transformative ritual spaces, often through creative collaboration.

Lastly, the power of ritual can also play a role in the healing process for those who have endured trauma. In the words of an Ieumsae member:

> The process of learning *p'ungmul* has been really healing for people . . . like, [a couple of] years ago, we really wanted to address the murder of trans people of color. And people really wanted to have a ceremony and have drumming be a big part of it. (Ieumsae interview)

Circling back to an earlier theory put forward by Bateson and Turino, I posit that one way in which healing may occur is through *p'ungmul*'s aesthetic patterning, which can then lead to integrative wholeness and stronger embodied connections to place and to each other. Even if mostly symbolic in nature, this can be especially meaningful during a time when claims to public space are increasingly tenuous.

CONCLUSION

One summer when I was visiting Southern California to see my family, my mother drove us out into the high desert in Lucerne Valley to visit some Korean American farms that sell fresh *taech'u*, or jujube fruit.[1] While I always looked forward to snacking on the perfectly crisp, sweet, and earthy flavor of fresh *taech'u*, I admit I was very curious about where they came from, since they are not widely available fresh elsewhere in the US. As we drove into the dirt gravel driveway of the farm, no one seemed to be at home, but in the distance, we could hear a high, metallic clanging in the grove of *taech'u* trees. "Could that be the sound of a *kkwaenggwari*?" I thought incredulously. But instead of leading a group of percussionists, the *kkwaenggwari* player was playing all by himself as he strolled through the dusty rows of fruit trees. When he finally emerged to greet us, I asked him why he was playing *kkwaenggwari*, and he just shrugged with a mysterious smile. Was he doing it to scare off insects or other pests? Perhaps it was his daily ritual to bless his harvest? Or maybe this was just his way of communing with nature, and if so, how was he adapting his playing to the high desert environment? This experience has stayed with me as I wonder about how many people are out there creating their own site-specific or site-oriented expressive ecologies through Korean modes of sounding and moving, in both big ways and small.

While chapter 7 has explored how Korean American groups have maintained site-oriented expressive ecologies during *chishinpalpki* Lunar New Year events in "Koreatowns" across the United States, I have not come across any US-based groups who have cultivated local expressive ecologies at the level of the Imshil Pilbong Nongak Preservation Association examined in part 1. With this said, I have since learned about a small handful of farmers of Korean heritage who are thinking about ways to integrate Korean cultural and agricultural practices on their farms. One such person is Kristyn Leach, who practices sustainable agriculture at Namu Farm in California. As an adoptee from South Korea, one of Leach's motivations is to "preserve the stories of Korean heirloom crops" (Ahn 2020). She has also invited Korean American community *p'ungmul* members to Namu Farm—many of whom are from the group Ieumsae from chapter 7—to come and help celebrate the Korean *Ch'usŏk* harvest holiday (Ahn 2020). The diverse guests participate by sowing seeds in a field before dancing to *p'ungmul* and helping to "return energy back into the earth" (Gordon 2013). In addition, Kristyn Leach has worked with community organizers to start a volunteer food justice program inspired by the Korean *nonghwal* movement detailed in chapter 1. In Namu Farm's version, they strive to engage participants in *nonghwal*'s history and spirit of community and resistance to explore how this connects to their mission to share "their knowledge of sustainable production practices and food justice to community members" (Ahn 2020).

Although I have never attended *nonghwal* or *Ch'usŏk* at Namu Farm, I am inspired by how they integrate concerns about the sustainability of diverse forms of agriculture, local communities, and culture. While Kristyn Leach's work has received attention in articles, podcasts, and even a documentary film entitled *Final Straw: Food, Earth, Happiness*, I hope that more research and documentation will be conducted to see how they are adapting Korean *p'ungmul* practices to a more food justice–oriented and intersectional vision. As much as I would advocate for their continued success and believe in their potential to motivate a movement of similar sustainable and integrative activities, I also recognize that Namu Farm (and other similar places) are constantly working at the precipice of precarity. Even without climate-related problems such as water scarcity, extreme heat, fire, and environmental degradation, other issues such as the COVID-19 global pandemic, neoliberal agribusiness practices, and the unequal distribution of resources and development have been disruptive and challenging to sustainability.

In the realm of performing arts in South Korea, similar issues are threatening to local, site-specific expressive ecologies as well, even though many of these groups possess more control over their own sites than Korean Americans do in the US. For example, the COVID-19 global pandemic and other outbreaks, such as Foot-and-Mouth disease in cattle, disrupted activities at the Pilbong village and transmission center (Yang Chongyun, personal communication). Furthermore, the number of active households in Pilbong village has dwindled so much that few remain who are able to host the Lunar New Year ritual during the *madan-*

gbalbi ceremony. The IPNPA's recent recognition by UNESCO as an Intangible Cultural Heritage of Humanity in 2014 has helped as a stopgap to preserve Pilbong as a *"p'ungmul* village" and enabled them to build a traditional-style home to host a "staged" *madangbalbi*, although these and other measures have had a negative impact on the perceived authenticity of the event.

Despite these significant disruptions and unsettling truths, I am certain that the refined skills, sensory awareness, and knowledge involved in sustaining expressive ecologies by sounding, moving, and interacting with others in the *hyŏnjang* (in the actual time and place) will be critical in helping to reconnect with others in a post-COVID, climate-challenged world. Although this book covers a very small number of Korean and Korean American expressive ecologies, I think it is safe to say that many groups have already adapted their practices to become more site-oriented as opposed to anchored to one physical site, if they have not already adapted to both. Given the somewhat unstable nature of humanity's relationship to the land and other living things in a world of uneven development, migration, and climate change, more groups will have to share space, especially in South Korean urban areas and throughout the Korean diaspora. In South Korea, there are many *madangs* or other shared outdoor spaces that have been intentionally designed to present various *yŏnhŭi*, or outdoor-oriented Korean performing arts groups (chapter 6). In addition, even when Korean expressive culture is performed in other public locations, such as the temple, park, or plaza, it is generally seen as more congruent with Korean daily life and culture, despite its loud volume. However, this is not usually the case in the diaspora, and the sharing of public space is often more contentious, even in urban "Koreatowns" in the United States, for example. Because of this, during some critical situations such as the Los Angeles 1992 Civil Unrest, some Korean Americans have leaned into the counterpublic tendencies of *p'ungmul* (stemming from South Korea's democratization movement) to help bolster more oppositional forms of civic participation (chapter 7). Another issue with sharing space is that various Korean diasporic groups have very little lasting control over such spaces and must hold other institutions accountable for their equitable use and care.

As I come full circle and try to articulate the larger implications of this work, I think back on the initial question that spurred this research: "Are you a *madang* (village courtyard) type or a *mudae* (stage) type?" Only now, I dwell less on my personal answer to this question and more on other issues such as: What does it take to be a successful *madang* type? What skills are involved and how do they apply to building and sustaining expressive ecologies? When I think about all the extraordinary *madang* types I have encountered, all have high levels of fortitude, endurance, commitment, and usually skill (although high levels of skill and training are not always necessary). Beyond this, what sets them apart is that they all possess tremendous sensory and social awareness (e.g., spatial, temporal, social, aural, kinesthetic, visual, emotional), coupled with the ability to quickly respond to the moment in a manner that is sympathetic, generous, uplifting, humorous, or otherwise fitting to the moment, depending on what is needed. Looking back, I think of the time when Pilbong performers entertained a skeptical crowd as they improvised their way through the village spring ritual (*saem-kut*) when the water was clearly undrinkable. I also remember when one female Norikkot member was able to charm a diverse Seoul audience by successfully retrieving and spinning a disc thrown from a potential non-Korean "suitor." I think of the many times I was moved by masked dance performers who connected with marginalized members of society (such as migrant workers, seniors, and people with disabilities) through their performances of the *Mundungi* (leper from Goseong Ogwangdae) or *Imae* (foolish servant from Hahoe Pyŏlshin-kut T'alnori) characters. Lastly, I remain astonished by the tactical nerve of Korean American groups like Ieumsae who bravely perform sound actions to help de-escalate a protest or project calm during a chaotic street riot.

While the question of the political implications of this line of inquiry was explored in chapter 7 in the Korean American context, more work could be done in this area. With this said, my findings suggest that the skills learned in the *madang* can be effectively applied in protests or demonstrations. In particular, the ability to attend to the dynamics of a given site and situation while performing is helpful in interacting with a range of other groups within a mass protest, whether it is to collaborate with other groups to create unique ways to accompany protest chants, to make space for others, or even to protect themselves or others through sound actions. Furthermore, these skills can be helpful in defining or shaping one's space within a protest setting or other planned event. The ability to determine one's own representation in space can be especially meaningful where access to public space is limited, contested, and/or threatened by gentrification. At the same time, this can also be perceived as "claiming space" over others and should be done in the spirit of sharing and sensitivity to other groups. As theatre scholar Kathleen Irwin writes, it is important to remember that site-specific performance is "extrapolated from the specificities of the site itself and, importantly, the communities that claim ownership of it" (Irwin 2007, 10–11). In the American diasporic context, there is always the danger that the skills used to claim or define space can be used by one group to replicate settler colonial ideologies.

Much more work can be done to ascertain whether any of these related activities have impacted the political audibility or visibility of Korean expressive folk culture. My limited research in the Korean American diaspora suggests that site-oriented activist *p'ungmul* has become a visible feature of US-based mass protests. However, at the same time, the community-based, participatory orientation of many *madang*-oriented groups has limited its mainstream legibility within a performing arts landscape that is dominated by the *mudae* or stage. Perhaps one of the main legacies of creating site-oriented events in diasporic political contexts is their ability to unsettle and stimulate new and lingering questions and debates. In Kathleen Irwin's words: "The material traces [of a site] evoke worlds that are intangible and unlocatable: worlds of memory, pleasure, sensation, imagination, affect, and insight" (Irwin 2007, 37).

In terms of the implications of this work on the future of Korean performing arts or other forms of cultural heritage, I hope this research provides some insight on what it takes to cultivate and continually sustain site-specific, site-oriented, or *madang*-oriented expressive ecologies. As interest in Korean popular culture continues to rise globally, locally grounded practices will likely continue to exist in tension with these trends. While interest in regional culture flourished in the earlier *tapsa* and *nonghwal* movements, it has only continued to gain interest in more recent waves, especially as the younger South Korean generations become more disillusioned with the compulsory centrality of Seoul.

As explored in part 1 of this book, it is important to recognize all that goes into sustaining site-specific expressive ecologies located in Pilbong and elsewhere. For example, the purveyors of healthy expressive ecologies not only have to think about the robust transmission of expressive content, but also the condition of the surrounding land and natural features (such as the *tangsan namu* or tutelary spirit tree), the material buildings and all relevant cultural sites, the various material practices of adorning the sites, and all the various rituals, foodways, costumes, and props. In addition, they need to think about how to help sustain local livelihoods and the surrounding community. Each of these elements can be seen as critical to the whole, and any changes to one or more of them can have a serious impact. While nothing is permanent, site-specific expressive ecologies possess a rich array of tangible and intangible elements that are associated with both the site and with the associated group or genre, but they can also be more complicated to sustain.

As explored in part 2 of this book, site-oriented expressive ecologies are formed when an artist/performer/group forms a less exclusive relationship with a site (park, business, neighborhood, performance venue, farm, etc.). While various elements may come into play in orienting expressive content to a particular site, they are more ephemeral. Even so, if repeated in a regular fashion, these expressive ecologies and sites can gain sedimented and multilayered meanings in the memories of those who experience them regularly. Whether one is working in site-specific or site-oriented situations, I believe that more *madang*-types are needed to help groups adapt to complex situations and environments, as they are well positioned to figure out multidimensional ways of engaging contemporary audiences. Whether a site is shared or under more exclusive artistic control by one community, I hope this book demonstrates the value of stepping in the *madang* and feeling more connected to each other through music and dance.

In terms of disciplinary implications, this book intersects with several theoretical approaches that are concerned with the intersection of sound, music, movement, space, place, and the environment. These include ecomusicology (Guy 2009, Allen 2011, Titon 2013), acoustemology (Feld 1996), sound ecology (Titon 2020), soundscape and sound studies, resonance (Abe 2018), and music sustainability (Schippers 2016). While my work remains very much in dialogue with these areas, I put forth the concept of expressive ecology as a term that is more inclusive of other elements such as movement, dance, ritual, and dialogue. These extramusical elements are significant because they can be critical to contributing to the stylized "sound *and* motion" of a participatory *madang* event (Turino 2008, 28). Another thread throughout this book is the emphasis on social relationality in space as conceived by Doreen Massey (1994) and Henri Lefebvre (1991), which also echoes through Marié Abe's "resonance" concept (2018). This emphasis on the social also intersects with the epistemological concerns of Steven Feld's theorization of acoustemology, where sounding as a way of knowing can be seen to inform how we interact with others (copresence) and with the surrounding environment. Jeff Todd Titon, writing within his "sound ecology" framework, also refers to this as "copresence" (Titon 2020, 7) or "relational epistemology" (2013, 15) but is ultimately concerned with pursuing "a sound basis for a healthy economy and to a sound and just community for all beings" (2020, 3). While epistemological concerns have not been at the forefront of this study, I do believe that the skills gained in cultivating expressive ecologies can inform a more multi-sensory, embodied knowledge that can be wielded in powerful ways.

While part 1 of this book delves deeply into one site-specific expressive ecology, part 2 explores a range of different ways in which these ideas can be applied in site-oriented or *madang*-oriented ways. In actual practice, however, I contend that site-specific and site-oriented expressive ecologies operate as more of a fluid and potentially overlapping continuum. Neither operates in a vacuum and many performers and participants travel frequently from one to the other. While some of the above theoretical areas tend to focus their explanatory power on "natural," "rural," or less industrialized environments, I have tried to configure my analysis to suit diverse settings. With that said, this framework is admittedly anthropocentric, and the perspective of animals and other forms of biological life have been limited in this study although it could be expanded if applied elsewhere.

By drawing on Turino's reading of Bateson, I hypothesized in the introduction that participants may be motivated to engage in expressive ecologies in order to help integrate "different parts of the self and thus facilitate wholeness," which is "crucial to experiencing deep connections with others and with the environment" (Turino 2008, 3–4). Korean folk expressive practitioners speak about the desire for "wholeness" in terms of "becoming one" (*hanaga doeda*) in the *madang*, a sentiment that can be traced to a deeply felt post-colonial desire to contend with the rupture of Korea's occupation by Japan and subsequent division. At the end of the day, we all deserve to pursue a sense of integrated wholeness, whether we live in the streets of Seoul, a township on the southern coast of Korea, or a farm in California's high desert. At the same time, as I think about who has the power to define or access site-specific or site-oriented expressive ecologies, it is important to remember Homi Bhabha's succinct words: "The globe shrinks for those who own it; for the displaced or the dispossessed, the migrant or refugee, no distance is more awesome than the few feet across borders or frontiers" (Bhabha 1992, 88). In this way, I remain mindful of placing too much emphasis on any one mode of engaging with or defining site. Whether physical or virtual, rural or urban, raucously embodied or silently contemplative, I hope we can all find ways to become whole by participating in expressive ecologies and connecting to others in the spaces in which we live and interact.

NOTES

INTRODUCTION *Stepping in the Madang*

1. *P'ungmul* or *nongak* (literally "farmer's music") (Important Intangible Cultural Property No. 11) is a widespread percussion band genre in rural Korea. The South Korean government designated the following regional groups to represent the genre: Jinju *Samcheonpo nongak* No. 11-1 (Gyeongsang province) in 1966; Pyeongtaek *nongak* No. 11-2 (Gyeonggi province), Iri *nongak* No. 11-3 (Western Jeolla province), and Gangneung *nongak* No. 11-4 (Gangwon province) in 1985; Imshil Pilbong *nongak* (Eastern Jeolla province) No. 11-5 in 1988; Gurye *Jansu nongak* (Eastern Jeolla province) No. 11-6 in 2010; and Gimcheon Geumneung Bitnae *nongak* (Northern Gyeongsang province) No. 11-7 and Namwon *nongak* (Eastern Jeolla province) No. 11-8 in 2019. While practitioners often use the term *p'ungmul*, *nongak* is the state-sanctioned term. I prefer to use the term *p'ungmul* because it enables a more holistic understanding that goes beyond its musical elements. See Hesselink for further discussion (2006, 15).

2. Interestingly, the notion of "site" has long been alternatively considered within ethnomusicology as part of the larger social, spatial, and cultural context, and later, aspects of site and locality have been addressed in music and place studies initiated by Martin Stokes and others (Stokes 1994).

3. In his analysis of jazz performances, Jackson emphasizes the crucial role of audience members who are also "expected to bring something" to these various areas (2000, 66). Interestingly, audience participation is one of the central tenets of *madang* discourse.

4. Many of these *madang*-related discourses have also been discussed by Park Shingil in her dissertation on *p'ungmul* and *samul nori* (2000, 158–76).

5. The patterns of nature mentioned here are commonly discussed by *p'ungmul* practitioners and are useful in pedagogy. The fractal-like application of these patterns has been noted most famously by Kim Inu (1987) and has been analyzed more systematically by scholars such as Yi Chongjin (1996), Sŏn Usŭng (2000), and Cho Ch'unyong (2001). Kim Samt'ae is notable for his study on the importance of breath and the heartbeat in *ture p'ungmul* (2001).

6. Although my first experience learning and playing music outside of the Western art or popular music realms was in Korean *p'ungmul* and other folk expressive traditions, I have also spent a considerable amount of time participating and learning how to play Javanese and Balinese gamelan, Bosnian vocal music, Appalachian old-time banjo, shape-note singing, and Zimbabwean mbira dzavadzimu music. Each tradition has challenged me to stretch my musicality, voice, and ways of listening, connecting, and coordinating with others in unique ways.

ONE Pathways to Pilbong

1. Two other discursive practices that are extremely influential here are the Intangible Cultural Property Preservation system put forth by the South Korean government and revivalist practices that were spurred by the cultural arm of the democratization or *minjung* movement. In particular, *madang* theater (*madanggŭk*) and its more ritual-influenced format, *madang-kut*, were especially influential in generating *madang*-related discourse and practice. See Namhee Lee (2007) for more discussion.

2. Originally this group was named as a representative of Honam Jwado *nongak*. Here, "Honam" is a provincial term for Jeolla province. "Jwado" refers to the "left side" or eastern side of the province. The "right" and "left" orientation is from the perspective of a traveler heading south from the capital, or what is now Seoul. When other groups were added to the list of Intangible Cultural Properties for *nongak* from this region, the Honam Jwado designation was dropped. For clarity, "Imshil" refers to the county and "Pilbong" is the village. *Nongak* is the government-sanctioned term for rural percussion band music and dance while *pojonhoe* means "preservation society." Pilbong practitioners used to prefer alternative and more comprehensive terms such as *p'ungmul* or *p'ungmul-kut* (*p'ungmul* ritual), but I have noticed a trend back to using *nongak*, especially after it was recognized by UNESCO in 2014 under the term *nongak*. Interestingly, Yang Chinsŏng (the current leader of the Pilbong troupe) sometimes does away with the word *p'ungmul* altogether and refers to it simply as Pilbong-*kut*, the attached suffix of *kut* meaning "ritual."

3. For additional detail on roles, costuming, and other details, see Yang Chinsŏng (2000, 107–12) and Nathan Hesselink (2006, 66–83).

4. During my fieldwork year, women occupied somewhat diverse roles within the ensemble. However, they tend to play *chapsaek* character roles, the *changgo* (hourglass drum), or the *sogo* (handheld drum) roles.

5. The title of this chapter is a paraphrase of this citation from Ch'ae Hŭiwan's discussion of the *madang* (1992, 64).

6. It is important to note that my definition of site-specific performance as it is discussed in this chapter is specific to performances with an established continuous history and does not include contemporary site-specific performance art or other creative

engagements with space. In chapters 6 and 7, I will attend to some of the ways in which Korean professional artists and Korean Americans are drawing on traditional forms and genres and applying them in new site-specific works.

7. The most popular performance traditions that students go to *chŏnsu* to learn are *p'ungmul* and *kamyŏn'gŭk* (mask dance drama, also called *t'alch'um*), both of which have many regional styles to choose from. Other popular folk performing arts include the vocal traditions of *minyo* (folksong), *p'ansori* (narrative singing), and shamanist ritual performing arts. In *p'ansori*, instead of going to a center, students often go to practice together in a mountain, often staying at a Buddhist temple, in a practice called *sangongbu* (literally "mountain study"). I first heard about the intense nature of Korean transmission practices from my fellow members at the Korean Youth Cultural Center, based in Oakland, California. Intrigued, I went for the first time in the summer of 1999 and spent a week at the Pilbong *p'ungmul* center in Namwon, a week at the Goseong Ogwangdae mask dance center, several days on Jindo Island learning *kanggangsullae* (women's group play with movement and song) and several more days learning *buk* dance at the Miryang Paekjungnori center.

8. For an interesting discussion on the various views about interpreting the meaning of the Chinese character ideograph *mu* (巫) and how this relates to Park's definition of the *mu* religion, and on the *mu* religion more generally, see Peter Park (2014, 88–100).

9. Although it is difficult to substantiate whether students came seeking political refuge (if at all), it is clear that *p'ungmul* and other forms of Korean expressive folk culture were strongly conceived as a "repository of *minjung* (people's) *consciousness* and practice" and, as such, was considered oppositional culture (Abelmann 1996, 26).

10. According to an interview with Yang Chinsŏng, this building was used primarily for the purposes of the performing group (October 5, 2003). However, there was a period when it seems to have been used for instruction by other teachers during the same time the Namwon *chŏnsugwan* was running (Yi Chongjin 1996, 16).

11. The notion of "body techniques" was first theorized by Marcel Mauss in his seminal essay, "Techniques of the Body," as "the ways in which from society to society men know how to use their bodies" (1973 [1935], 70). In this way, Arthur Frank's formulation is quite in line with Mauss's view of the body as a medium and tool of culture and society.

TWO *"Becoming One" through Site-Specific Intermodal Transmission*

1. The reason for the long hiatus is mostly because the previous leader, Yang Sunyong, had to leave Pilbong in the mid-1980s, as detailed in the previous chapter, due to the politicization of *p'ungmul* in villages.

2. My phrasing of "way of being" draws loosely from Raymond Williams's concept of "structures of feeling" (1973, 297; 1977, 128–35). On the one hand, the *madang* can be

associated with structured experiences of class (in this case, the "farmer" or "commoner" class) within a given historical moment, as suggested in the "structures of feeling" concept. However, I have chosen to rephrase to foreground the processes of embodiment that are distinctive to "being" in the *madang*.

3. The democratization movement of the 1970s and '80s is referred to as the *minjung* or "people's" movement in modern South Korean history. It also included a cultural branch that was referred to as the *minjung munhwa undong* (people's cultural movement) of which *p'ungmul* played a significant role.

4. My use of the word "groove" will be discussed in further depth later in the chapter, but I draw from Charles Keil's and Steve Feld's definitions of the term in their book *Music Grooves* (1994).

5. Unless geopolitical circumstances prevent practitioners from doing so (as is the case for regional practices believed to have originated in present-day North Korea), these centers are usually built in or near the locale where a given genre is believed to have developed. *Gugak* [*kugak*] literally means "national music" and refers to Korean forms of vocal and instrumental music that demonstrate continuity with Korea's pre-colonial past.

6. For more information on how discourses of the cultural arm of the democratization movement (*minjung munhwa undong*) impacted expressive folk culture practice, see Hesselink (1999, 1–5; 2006, 91–92) and Katherine Lee (2012, 179–205).

7. While most of the individuals who visit the Pilbong transmission center are South Korean citizens, small numbers of foreign students have visited and developed relationships with the teachers. In addition, there are groups of diasporic Koreans who have attended, mostly from Japan and the United States.

8. For more information on state cultural policy and the Intangible Cultural Asset system, see Yang (1994), Howard (2006), and Saeji (2012).

9. A few exceptions to this in the English literature include the work of Nathan Hesselink (2006) and CedarBough Saeji (2012, 2013). In *P'ungmul: South Korean Drumming and Dance*, Hesselink devotes a chapter to comparing the transmission experiences of representative teachers from the "left-side" (*Jwado*) and "right-side" (*udo*) styles of *p'ungmul*. While Hesselink discusses transmission centers in some detail in pages 143–47, it is not the major focal point of his chapter. In addition, Hesselink's research on Pilbong's transmission center differs from mine primarily because it was conducted earlier during very different circumstances. Saeji's 2013 chapter most directly examines and elucidates the culture nurtured at these centers but does not spend as much time analyzing specific transmission techniques. For those interested in the fuller picture of South Korean Cultural Property Preservation Law and its impact on folk culture transmission, Saeji's 2012 dissertation is essential reading. Despite the diversity of disciplinary approaches to the study of *p'ungmul* in the Korean literature, there is still not that much research on transmission centers. One notable exception is Chin Chaehong's thesis (2010)

on the Pilbong transmission center in which he focuses on the *sangsoe* leader selection process.

10. For the sake of simplicity, I give preference to the word *madang*. The related term, *p'an*, is used somewhat interchangeably with the *madang*, although *p'an* usually indicates a larger space with public and entertainment-oriented connotations.

11. According to Gade, most "approaches in the history of religions are grounded in the conviction that religion is a site for the transformation of self and social order." Gade also acknowledges that "ethnomusicologists make similar claims for musical systems" (2002, 330).

12. Csordas believes that studies of embodiment should involve a mode of inquiry he has termed "cultural phenomenology," which involves "synthesizing the immediacy of embodied experience with the multiplicity of cultural meaning" (1999, 143).

13. The philosophy of *kongdongch'e* or community participation in Korean discourse does not necessarily translate as equal participation and governance. Within *p'ungmul*, *kongdongch'e* does promote increased communal awareness and blurs the boundaries between performers and audience members, but it does not necessarily do away with leadership structures that may already exist within the group. For example, *p'ungmul* ensembles always have a leader (the lead small gong player) who wields a great deal of power and responsibility across multiple realms (artistic, social, organizational). In addition, these leaders tend to be men, except when the group is either very progressive in terms of gender politics or an all-female ensemble.

14. For more information on activities that emphasize liminality and play at *chŏnsu*, see Saeji (2013).

15. These two programs were not a regular fixture of *chŏnsu*. In the summer season, they did not have the environmental program. Also, when I talked to people who had attended as recently as January of 2005, the fieldtrip, or *tapsa*, was not part of the program. When comparing 2002 and 2005 programs with more recent program schedules, the most consistently scheduled activities seem to be the *p'ungmul* classes, the *p'ungmul* lecture or "*iyagi p'an-kut*" (re-formatted as a performance), the evening practices and *twip'uri* gatherings, and the culminating *sangsoe* contest and performance. Other consistently included classes are *sogo* dance and other expressive folk culture forms.

16. *Kut* is usually defined as a shamanist ceremony or ritual. In *p'ungmul*, however, referring to a *p'ungmul* event as a *kut* acknowledges its shamanist roots but can also be used more generally to refer to a festive *p'ungmul* performance, especially because a shaman specialist does not need to be present to conduct a *p'ungmul-kut*.

17. A rhythmic series within the Pilbong *p'ungmul* style.

18. A rhythmic pattern within the Pilbong *p'ungmul* style.

19. A rhythmic series during which the players spiral in the cardinal directions.

20. A characteristic rhythmic series within the Pilbong *p'ungmul* style.

21. For personal reasons, I have chosen to withhold the identity of the teacher referred to in this document under the generic pseudonym of Mr. Kim.

22. The use of *ipchangdan* in the transmission of both *p'ungmul* and other Korean expressive traditions is extremely common. In the context of *p'ungmul*, Hesselink devotes some time discussing the use of *ipchangdan* in his book (2006, 100–110), and highlights the related importance of oral verse in his discussion of Kim Inu's seminal text *P'ungmul-kut and Communal Spirit* (1987). However, neither Hesselink nor Inu highlight their intermodal qualities.

23. It is outside the scope of this chapter to discuss the more multidimensional dancer/musician interactions in Pilbong *p'ungmul*, but for other examples of research in this area, see Chernoff (1979), Gerstin (1998), and Gerischer (2006, 115–16).

24. For example, anything approximating a delay of approximately 0.2 constituted a higher margin of discrepancy, while 0.1 or lower was considered less significant.

25. Yang Chinhwan, Yang Chinsŏng's brother and lead *changgo* player, explained that their rustic *tto-bak tto-bak* style has something to do with the rough and jagged geography of the Pilbong region (Yang Chinhwan interview, October 8, 2002).

26. It is important to mention that a small satellite transmission center was set up in Seoul during this period in 1996. Since then, others have opened in other nearby cities such as Bucheon. As the Pilbong style expands in popularity and acceptance, so the picture of Pilbong transmission becomes more fractured and multilocal. These satellite centers operate differently and serve more as community centers with regular classes. Interestingly, I found that active college students from the Seoul area prefer going to the intensive week-long *chŏnsu* experience rather than attending the Seoul center on a regular basis, supporting the idea that it is the cultural experience that is cultivated at a week-long *chŏnsu* that continues to be a significant draw for these students.

THREE *Cultivating the Village, Preparing for Ritual*

1. Within the context of *p'ungmul*, the village is crucial because it is considered to be the locational base for two of its oldest strains: ritual *p'ungmul* and *ture p'ungmul* (cooperative farming labor *p'ungmul*). Though *ture p'ungmul* has not been continuously practiced in the industrial era, ritual *p'ungmul* is still performed.

2. Among the representative groups that have been designated as Important Intangible Cultural Properties for *p'ungmul* (No. 11), the Gangneung style from Gangwon province is a notable exception that also prides itself on preserving *maŭl-kut*. When talking to other *p'ungmul* practitioners and scholars about this claim, it seems that there are several lesser-known villages that practice village *kut* but have not received national recognition. In addition, given the turbulent history of Korea in the twentieth century, it is doubtful that any village was able to practice their rituals continuously with no interruptions.

3. In Korean, the romanization of the saying is *Kuse kamyŏn, Ttŏkina mŏkŏyaji*.

4. Interestingly, when I viewed the actual broadcast of the show, they ended up using "staged" footage of *mae-kut*, in which all the performers were wearing pristine white *minbok* from a previously shot documentary.

5. These excerpts were downloaded from the Pilbong *p'ungmul* website (www.pilbong.co.kr) in December of 2002 prior to the 2003 Lunar New Year festival and were available in both English and Korean.

6. Because the overall tone of Deshpande's article is a critique of Hindu communalism as a potentially dangerous and divisive force in a heterogeneous state such as India, it is important to note that Deshpande's sense of the "ideological" has to do with a privileging of the beliefs of a particular group or class. However, it is somewhat unclear whether he is aligned with a strict Marxist sense of ideology as "contributing to a system of illusory beliefs or false consciousness" (as summarized in Raymond Williams 1977, 55). To be clear, what I take from Deshpande's formulation of heterotopias does not correspond with this more negative sense of "ideology." However, I do think it is useful to see the Pilbong village ritual as an event that has the potential to powerfully link "social subjects" with a given "political-moral" or cultural identity.

7. For more information on the heritage development of Bukchon, Hahoe, and Yangdong areas, see Radzuan, Song, and Ahmad (2015).

FOUR "Abundant Kut, Abundant Life": The Place of Ritual P'ungmul

1. As simplistic as this sounds, this phrase has been used by the IPNPA for more than a decade and should be read within the context of not only the long history of the suppression of shamanism in Korea but also its revival in South Korean cultural nationalist discourse.

2. The percussionists wear sleeveless blue vests or black short-sleeved vests (small gong players) with blue and yellow sashes that drape over each shoulder and are tied in the back alongside a third red sash that goes around the waist. Most of the players wear *kokkal moja*, or paper flower hats. However, the *soe* (small gong) players and *ch'aesang sogo* (handheld drum) players wear different types of twirling ribbon hats. Each *chapsaek*, or "character player," has their own distinctive costume and props while the *t'aep'yŏngso* (conical double-reed) player dons a pale blue robe over their *minbok* (table 1.1). For more detail see Yang (2000, 97–114) or Hesselink (2006, 66–84).

3. For notation of Imshil Pilbong Nongak rhythms, see www.pilbong.co.kr/music.php.

4. This is the same "Mr. Kim" that I am using a pseudonym for and who was featured in chapter 2.

5. This may be why folk practitioners cite the felling of *Tangsan* trees as such an effective method of cultural oppression and violence. This practice occurred in many Korean

villages during the Japanese colonial era as well as during the New Village movement (*Saemaŭl Undong*) in the 1970s.

6. More specifically, this characteristic quality of the *madang* has been articulated as *hyŏnjangjŏkin undongsŏng* (philosophy of the moment) by Im Chint'aek (1990, 85) and similarly by Pak Hŭngchu as *ili bŏlŏjinŭn jangmyŏn* (a scene where something is happening, developing) (Pak unpublished typescript, 1). Another scholar, Ch'ae Hŭiwan, describes this concept as *salmŭi hyŏnjangŭrosŏ saenghwal munhwa konggan* (in the actual every day, cultural space of life) (1992, 64). In a related fashion, the importance of temporal openness of the *madang* within a theatrical context is stressed by scholar Lee Young-mee [Yi Yŏng-mi] (1997, 50).

7. There may be more than one possibility for the meaning of *hwadong*. In *p'ungmul*, *hwadong* is the name of a common *chapsaek* character, although in this case, it is clear that the leader is addressing everyone, not just the *hwadong* character. In another sense, *Hwadong* (화동 和同) also means "unison" or "harmony," in which case this could be a call to bring everyone together in harmony or unison.

8. This is analogous to how the sliding of a wedding ring onto one's partner's finger while saying "with this ring, I thee wed" works together to performatively enact the union between two people.

9. *Chinguk* is a term for an intense, undiluted type of liquid, usually in the form of a strong soy sauce or a high-alcohol beverage.

10. *Pŏlkŏk* is an onomatopoetic word that signifies the act of "gulping" or "guzzling" water or some other kind of beverage.

11. For further explanation on *naego-talgo-maetgo-p'ulgo*, see Nathan Hesselink's excellent edited translation of Kim Inu's article "'P'ungmulgut' and Communal Spirit" (Hesselink 1999, 12).

12. In Korean the *mun-kut tŏkdam* proceeds as follows: *Chwin, chwin munyŏso, mun anyŏlmyŏn, kallayo!* (쥔, 쥔, 문여소, 문안열면 갈라요!)

13. From my experience observing similar rituals, *mun-kut* can be a source of drama. If performed truly in the moment, it is possible that the troupe might be rejected or rebuffed. On one occasion described briefly in the introduction, the Seoul division of the Pilbong drumming group had been nervously anticipating how they would be received at one of the elder's homes during a Lunar New Year ritual performance in Yangchon village. Previously, this elder had gone into a rage because his home had not been visited first. When he realized the troupe was not slighting him, but was in fact waiting to honor his home last, he calmed down and welcomed us into his home.

14. Historically, women participated in *p'ungmul* in an organized fashion in two historic contexts. The first was in the latter half of the Chosŏn dynasty (1700–1910), when women played *p'ungmul* percussion instruments as part of female song-and-dance troupes called *sadangp'ae* (also called *yŏsadang*). Given that these groups performed other song

and dance forms as well, scholars believe that their *p'ungmul* playing may not have been as distinctive or skilled as that of the all-male groups called *namsadangp'ae* (Hesselink 2012, 27). The second came after the Japanese colonial period, during a spurt of activity between the 1950s to 1970s when women played in all-female groups called *yŏsŏng nongaktan*. The first of these was based in Namwon and was called the *Ch'unhyang Yŏsŏng Nongaktan* (Kwŏn Ŭnyŏng [Kwon Eun Young] 2008). In the new millennium, the most prominent women's group is Norikkot, which is a comprehensive, creative performance team that I discuss in chapter 6 (see also video 6.1 🔊).

15. In "five-element" theory, elements are often grouped together so that "east" is connected to the color "blue" and so forth. For more in-depth discussion of cosmological patterning in Korean traditional music, see Nathan Hesselink and Jonathan Christian Petty (2004).

16. For notation of Imshil Pilbong *Nongak ap-kut* and *twi-kut* rhythms, see www.pilbong.co.kr/music.php.

17. For more detail on the reasons Yang Sunyong left Pilbong, see the "Phase 1 (1970–1983): Beginning in Pilbong Village" section of chapter 1.

18. Experiencing the full Lunar New Year ritual in Pilbong (and all the preparations that went into it), first in 2002 and later in 2016, remains one of the more indelible and influential experiences that I have sought to apply to my daily life, perhaps most directly in my work with the Korean Youth Cultural Center from 2002 to 2005, some of which I write about in chapter 7.

19. According to CedarBough Saeji, there are four main types of audiences for Korean traditional performing arts: participant or expert audiences, paying audiences, cultural experience audiences, and accidental audiences (2016, 15). In her article, she cites the IPNPA as an excellent example of a group that has cultivated expert participants, and this seems to hold true in 2016.

20. It should be noted that the concept of *samjae* (three elements of the heavens, earth, and humans) can also be considered part of a continuum of Asian cosmological philosophies that are advocated by Confucian, Taoist, and Buddhist thinkers. Nathan Hesselink and others trace the concept of *samjae* taking hold in Korea to the Chosŏn dynasty (1392–1910) when Korean elites embraced the concept, which he believes then spread to folk beliefs (Hesselink 2007, 145).

FIVE *The Madang on the Move*

1. For more research on *namsadang* troupes, see Shim Usŏng 1994; Hesselink 2012, 17–37; and Park Shingil 2000, 60–63.

2. For example, the main building usually houses the kitchen and living quarters, with separate buildings for the outhouse, granary, woodshed, and guest rooms.

3. The modeling of the Hyŏmnyulsa (later Wŏngaksa) on the Colosseum in Rome with the intention of being comparable to London's Royal Albert Hall or Vienna's Royal Theater comes from a firsthand account by Ch'oe Namsŏn (1972 [1947], 222) and is cited both by Andrew Killick (1998, 56) and Marshal Pihl (1994, 47).

4. These "traditional" elements go a long way to mark the space as distinctively "Korean," especially in contrast to the surrounding city sprawl. Even after the era of *norimadangs* had peaked, this cultural indexing of space continued in other incarnations. For more analysis of performances in the Seoul Nori Madang, see chapter 5, entitled "Madang Migrations: Performing Pilbong *P'ungmul-kut* on the Road" from the author's dissertation (Kwon 2005, 282–301).

5. In Korean, the title of the event was *Tonghak Nongmin Hyŏngmyŏng Paeksan Ponggi 108Chunyŏn Kinyŏm Taehoe*.

6. *Tonghak* means "Eastern Learning" and refers to the broader peasant-based reform movement that emerged in the 1860s and ended up being unsuccessful by 1895 due to the influx of Chinese and Japanese military forces. Even so, the *Tonghak* rebels made significant strides in 1894 under the leadership of Chŏn Pongjun, forcing the government to agree to fair taxation, the dismissal of corrupt officials, and a halt to rice exports to Japan. *Tonghak* rebels rose up all over the South; at one point, they even occupied the city of Jeonju (Cumings 1997, 115–19).

7. The title "Mung Bean General" (*Noktu changgun*) is said to have stemmed from Chŏn Pongjun's diminutive height when he was younger. In addition, the *noktu*, or mung bean, has become generally associated with the *Tonghak* movement. Interestingly, both Chŏn Pongjun (1855–1895) and Yi Sunshin (1545–1598), a famous naval commander who I focus on later in this chapter, have been memorialized as nationalist heroes fighting against Japanese imperialist forces.

8. Within the Imshil Pilbong *nongak* tradition, there is actually a precedent for portraying dramatic stories within the longer ritual form called *Todukchaeb'i-kut*. Since the late 2000s, the IPNPA has gone further to use *p'ungmul* to create new works that tell their own personal stories of prominent members, such as the story of Yang Sunyong, the previous leader of the group.

9. These groups are not actually comprised of members from North Korea. Rather, they consist of South Koreans who have some link to those regions and have been able to continue the development of these styles in South Korea.

10. Incidentally, the incorporation of "folk" crafts and the writing of wishes to burn in the bonfire has also been incorporated in the IPNPA's self-produced events.

11. In previous years, they have also performed at Goseong's "Natural Monument No. 41." This is a craggy stretch of Goseong coastline that features interesting stone walkways, and more importantly, the fossilized footprints of baby dinosaurs.

12. These invasions are also known as the Imjin Wars (1592–1598). The first invasion

began in 1592 and paused with a truce in 1596. Then, a related invasion occurred in 1597 and ended with a military stalemate and the withdrawal of Japanese forces in 1598.

13. Although most *madang*-type events usually center on one group, there are some relevant historical precedents for multiple groups sharing the same field. These would include the busy market days of the past where a mind-boggling array of things may be taking place at once: entertainment, hawking, butchering, wrestling, etc.

14. They even provided live emceeing in both Korean and English.

SIX *Creative Korean Performing Arts in National Urban Spaces*

1. This quote from Jambinai's Facebook website has since been changed, but I documented this wording when I accessed their page on May 1, 2017 (https://www.facebook.com/jambinaiofficial/about/). It is also interesting to note that culture writer, Yun Chunggang, introduced the term "post-kugak" for groups like Jambinai (Yun 2016).

2. Because this text may be difficult to find on their current website, I provide the original in Korean: "앞으로도 연희집단 The 광대는 고정되고 규정된 형태의 전통이 아닌, 현시대의 흐름과 함께 살아 숨 쉬는 전통의 맥을 이어가기 위해실험정신을 바탕으로 끊임없이 새로운 작업에 도전함으로써 전통예술분야의 젊은 선두주자가 되고자 합니다." Yŏnhŭi Chipdan The Kwangdae, "Yŏnhŭi Chipdan The Kwangdae," accessed December 15, 2015, http://blog.naver.com/the_gwangdae.

3. Yŏnhŭi Chipdan The Kwangdae, "Hwang-gŭm Kŏji," June 1, 2015, YouTube video, 2:14, https://www.youtube.com/watch?v=O9Aa2Zogzfo&t=11s.

4. See National Gugak Center, "국립국악원 별별연희: 놀이꾼들 도담도담 [2015.09.12] 03. 착작연희 (Creative Performance)," September 15, 2015, YouTube video, 25:23, https://www.youtube.com/watch?v=dTr_2OKm3ao.

5. To view these performances of Norikkundŭl Todam Todam, see their website (https://cafe.naver.com/dodamdodam12/131) and click on *Yŏnhŭi Kŏrikŭk* (연희거리극). I discuss them in chronological order, which are the fifth, fourth, and first videos listed.

6. I draw from Kiri Miller's discussion of game terminology, in particular her definition of "rhythm games" in her book *Playable Bodies: Dance Games and Intimate Media* (2017, 7).

7. Interestingly, the "Rose of Sharon Has Bloomed" game became famous around the world in fall of 2021 when it was included as the first survival game on the popular Netflix K-drama called *Squid Game*.

SEVEN *The Politics of Sounding Space in the Korean American Community*

1. Later, several prominent performers such as dancer Halla Pai Huhm in 1949, the well-known *kayagum* player Sŏng Kŭmyŏn (1923–1986), and *shinawi* musician Chi Yŏnghŭi (1909–1979) moved to Hawai'i in 1974 and opened studios that included Korean percussion

as part of their activities (Sutton 1987, 106–9). There were several other prominent figures like this who were active prior to the 1980s in the United States that I cannot cover here, but for more information, see Kim Soo-Jin 2011, 131–35.

2. Halfway between first (*il-se*) and second generation (*i-se*), 1.5 or *il-chom-o-se* designates those who were born in Korea, immigrating sometime in their childhood or teen years.

3. It is important to note that all of these Korean expressive forms were prominent in the influential *minjung munhwa* (literally, the "culture of the common people") movement that swept South Korean college campuses and activist political and labor organizations in the 1970s and '80s.

4. Due to the limitations of this chapter, I cannot cover the diversity of collegiate, community, and professional groups that developed during the 1990s and beyond. For more of the general history of US *p'ungmul* groups, see Donna Kwon (2001), S. Sonya Gwak (2008), and Soo-Jin Kim (2011).

5. Aside from the earlier evidence that Korean immigrants in Hawai'i played Korean percussion instruments in the early twentieth century, I have only heard of one instance of this with the Ieumsae group going to Namu Farm in California to celebrate the *Ch'usŏk* holiday. I address this topic in more depth in the conclusion.

6. See "Chishinpalpki," *The Korean Encyclopedia of Korean Culture*, accessed June 30, 2021, http://encykorea.aks.ac.kr/Contents/Item/E0054281.

7. This practice was especially popular in Seoul, and by the late 1990s, the Seoul Regional *P'ungmul* Council was formed (*Seoul chiyŏk p'ungmul hyŏpŭihoe*), and one of their activities was to coordinate *chishinpalpki* activities across the city. Based on research by Park Shingil, it appears that one of the earlier groups that conducted *chishinpalpki* continuously in Seoul is T'ŏullim, who focused their activity in the Pulkwang Market beginning in 1985 (Park Shingil 2000, 129–30).

8. According to Soo-Jin Kim, the Nongak Troupe of the Eastern United States did perform during Lunar New Year parades for Chinese and Korean Americans in Flushing, New York (2011, 134).

9. The most common rhythms that almost all *p'ungmul* groups would be familiar with are *ilch'ae*, *ich'ae* or *hwimori*, *samch'ae* or *jajinmori*, and the slower *kutkŏri*. The Korean Youth Cultural Center sometimes also included the march-oriented rhythms *obangjin* and *chinobangjin*. Beginning in the late 1990s, many groups became better acquainted with the P'ilbong *p'ungmul* rhythms and began to include their rhythms as well.

10. I base much of this normative description of *chishinpalpki* on my own auto-ethnographic experiences with KYCC, but much of this is very similar to Kim Soo-Jin's ethnographic research with groups in Los Angeles (2011).

11. Kyung Jin Lee, "Koreatown's 'Ghostbusters' Usher in Good Luck for the Year of

the Goat," *The World*, March 2, 2015, https://www.pri.org/stories/2015-03-02/koreatowns-ghostbusters-usher-good-luck-year-goat.

12. Lee, "Koreatown's 'Ghostbusters' Usher in Good Luck for the Year of the Goat."

13. KAFFNYDigital, "Sa I Gu (Official Full Version)," March 19, 2012, YouTube video, 41:30, https://www.youtube.com/watch?v=G_UyYj-pR8U&t=1884s. Original film directed by Dai Sil Kim-Gibson and Christine Choy (Center for Asian American Media, 1993).

14. It is also important to note that Koreatown has long had a higher concentration of businesses owned by Korean Americans than Korean American residents. Because of this, many Korean Americans came to the Koreatown Peace March from various suburbs in Southern California (Chang and Krikorian 1992).

15. The composition of the drummers are not mentioned in the *Sa-I-Gu* film (1993), the articles by Timothy Tangherlini (1999, 2001) and Elaine Kim (1993), or the news report by *Los Angeles Times* journalists Irene Chang and Greg Krikorian (1992).

16. Many groups that formed during the 1980s and early 1990s often learned and performed many genres, not just *p'ungmul*. Although many groups emphasized *p'ungmul* over the more virtuosic *samul nori* style, in actuality, many groups performed both styles. For more on these dynamics, see Soo-Jin Kim (2011) and Park Shingil (2000).

17. KYCC members were inspired by similar activities performed in *p'ungmul* and mask dance contexts, where the wishes are usually written down on strips of paper and inserted into a straw structure and then later burned in a bonfire. Due to restrictions on fire at Golden Gate Park, this was not possible and therefore the banner concept was created.

18. Ann Kwon, "Performing Korea," filmed by Michael Hurt, July 30, 2023, YouTube video, 29:08, https://www.youtube.com/watch?v=hj-MPviWYDg&t=2760s.

19. To find out more on this KYCC performance, see *Performing Korea* by Michael Hurt. Also available on the companion website (video 7.1 🔊).

20. This material is based on an interview that took place on May 6, 2019, with a representative member of Ieumsae who wishes to remain anonymous. Further citations will be cited as "Ieumsae interview."

21. In drawing on the work of Jacques Rancière and André Lepecki, I am heavily indebted to a colloquy of articles on the 2017 Women's March that was published in the Winter 2019 *Music and Politics* issue, which was adapted from a roundtable panel presented at the 2017 Society for Ethnomusicology annual conference. Although most of the authors engage productively with Rancière and Lepecki, for more discussion on dissensus, see Maria Sonevystsky's "Listening for Dissensus" and on choreopolitics, see Shayna Silverstein's "On Sirens and Lamp Posts: Sound, Space, and Affective Politics," in *Music and Politics* 13, no. 1 (Winter 2019).

Conclusion

1. According to Anita Brown, there are "approximately fifty farmers with existing or developing jujube farms" in the Lucerne Valley in Southern California and by 2013, "there were enough Korean farmers in the region to form a Cooperative" called the Hi-Desert Jujube Coop (2022).

BIBLIOGRAPHY

Abe, Marié. 2018. *Resonances of Chindon-Ya: Sounding Space and Sociality in Contemporary Japan*. Middletown, CT: Wesleyan University Press.

Abelmann, Nancy. 1996. *Echoes of the Past, Epics of Dissent: A South Korean Social Movement*. Berkeley: University of California Press.

Abelmann, Nancy, and John Lie. 1995. *Blue Dreams: Korean Americans and the Los Angeles Riots*. Cambridge, MA: Harvard University Press.

Ahn, Ashley. 2023. "South Korea Has the World's Lowest Fertility Rate, a Struggle with Lessons for Us All." *National Public Radio*, March 19, 2023. https://www.npr.org/2023/03/19/1163341684/south-korea-fertility-rate.

Ahn, Vianney. 2020. "Kristyn Leach of Namu Farm." *Agricultural Sustainability Institute*, December 2, 2020. https://asi.ucdavis.edu/programs/sf/resources/sustainable-ag-heroes/Kristyn-Leach.

Allen, Aaron. 2011. "Prospects and Problems for Ecomusicology in Confronting a Crisis of Culture." *Journal of the American Musicological Society* 64 (2): 414–24.

———. 2013. "Ecomusicology." In *The Grove Dictionary of American Music*, 2nd edition, edited by Charles Hiroshi Garrett. New York: Oxford University Press.

Appadurai, Arjun, Frank J. Korom, and Margaret A. Mills, eds. 1991. *Gender, Genre, and Power in South Asian Expressive Traditions*. Philadelphia: University of Pennsylvania Press.

Attali, Jacques. 1985. *Noise: The Political Economy of Music*. Minneapolis: University of Minnesota Press.

Austin, J. L. 1961. "Performative Utterances." In *Philosophical Papers*. Oxford: Clarendon Press.

Bateson, Gregory. 2000. *Steps to an Ecology of Mind: Collected Essays in Anthropology, Psychiatry, Evolution, and Epistemology*. Chicago: University of Chicago Press.

Becker, Judith, and Alton Becker. 1981. "A Musical Icon: Power and Meaning in Javanese Gamelan Music." In *The Sign in Music and Literature*, edited by Wendy Steiner, 203–15. Austin: University of Texas Press.

Bhabha, Homi. 1992. "Double Visions: 'Circa 1492.'" *Artforum* 30 (5): 85–89.

Bourdieu, Pierre. 1977. *Outline of a Theory of Practice*. Translated by Richard Nice. New York: Cambridge University Press.

Brinner, Benjamin. 1995. *Knowing Music, Making Music: Javanese Gamelan and the Theory of Musical Competence and Interaction*. Chicago: University of Chicago Press.

Brown, Anita. 2022. "#Fridaysonthefarm: Tending the Healing Harvest in the High Desert." Natural Resources Conservation Service, June 23, 2022. https://www.nrcs.usda.gov.

Bruner, Edward M. 2005. *Culture on Tour: Ethnographies of Travel*. Chicago: University of Chicago Press.

Bryant, Levi R. 2014. *Onto-cartography: An Ontology of Machines and Media*. Edinburgh: Edinburgh University Press.

Butler, Judith. 1993. *Bodies That Matter*. New York: Routledge.

Ch'ae Hŭiwan. 1992. *T'alch'um* [Mask Dance]. Seoul: Daewonsa.

Chang, Irene, and Greg Krikorian. 1992. "A City in Crisis: 30,000 Show Support in Koreatown March." *Los Angeles Times*, May 3, 1992. https://www.latimes.com/archives/la-xpm-1992-05-03-mn-1945-story.html.

Chernoff, John Miller. 1979. *African Rhythm and African Sensibility: Aesthetics and Social Action in African Idioms*. Chicago: University of Chicago Press.

Chin Chaehong. 2010. "Imshil pilbong nongak'ŭi chŏnsŭng kwajŏngae nat'anan pyŏnhwawa chisok: Sangsoe ppopkirŭl chungsimŭro" [Change and Continuity in the Transmission Process of Imshil Pilbong Nongak: A Study Centering on the Sangsoe Leader Selection Process]. Master's thesis, Seoul National University.

Cho, Sumi K. 1993. "Korean Americans vs. African Americans: Conflict and Construction." In *Reading Rodney King/Reading Urban Uprising*, edited by Robert Gooding-Williams, 196–211. New York: Routledge.

Cho Ch'unyŏng. 2001. "*Maŭl p'ungmulgusae issŏsŏŭi il-gwa daŭi munjae*" [Issues of Work and Other Aspects in Village *P'ungmul-kut*]. Bachelor's thesis, Inha University.

Ch'oe Namsŏn. 1972 [1947]. *Chosŏn sangshik mundap sokp'yon* [General Knowledge Questions and Answers]. Seoul: Samsŏng munhwa chaedan (Seoul: Tongmyŏngsa, original publishers).

Choi, Yoonjah. 2014. "Gendered Practices and Conceptions in Korean Drumming: On the Negotiation of 'Femininity' and 'Masculinity' by Korean Female Drummers." PhD diss., City University of New York.

Chŏng Pyŏngho. 1992. *Han'gukui minsok ch'um* [Korean Folk Dance]. Seoul: Samsŏng ch'ulp'ansa.

Chu Kanghyŏn. 1992. *Kusŭi Sahoesa* [A Social History of *Kut*]. Seoul: Ungjinch'ulp'an.

Clayton, Martin, Rebecca Sager, and Udo Will. 2004. "In Time with the Music: The Concept of Entrainment and Its Significance for Ethnomusicology." *ESEM CounterPoint* (1): 1–82.

Csordas, Thomas J. 1990. "Embodiment as a Paradigm for Anthropology." *Ethos* 18 (1): 5–47.

———. 1993. "Somatic Modes of Attention." *Cultural Anthropology* 8 (2): 135–56.

———. 1999. "Embodiment and Cultural Phenomenology." In *Perspectives on Embodiment: The Intersections of Nature and Culture*, edited by Gail Weiss and Honi Fern Haber, 143–62. New York: Routledge.

Cumings, Bruce. 1997. *Korea's Place in the Sun: A Modern History*. New York: W. W. Norton and Company.

Deshpande, Satish. 1998. "Hegemonic Spatial Strategies: The Nation-Space and Hindu Communalism in Twentieth-Century India." *Public Culture* (10): 249–83.

Dicks, Bella. 2002. *Heritage, Place and Community*. Cardiff: University of Wales Press.

Downing, Sonja. 2019. *Gamelan Girls: Gender, Childhood, and Politics in Balinese Music Ensembles*. Champagne: University of Illinois Press.

Eum Sungwon [Ŭm Sungwŏn]. 2015. "Number of Foreign Residents in S. Korea Triples over Ten Years." *Hankyoreh*, July 6, 2015. http://english.hani.co.kr/arti/english_edition/e_international/699034.html.

Fatone, Gina. 2010. "'You'll Break Your Heart Trying to Play It like You Sing It': Intermodal Imagery and the Transmission of Scottish Classical Bagpiping." *Ethnomusicology* 54 (3): 395–424.

Feld, Steven. 1994. "Aesthetics as Iconicity of Style (uptown title); or, (downtown title) 'Life-up-over Sounding': Getting into the Kaluli Groove." In *Music Grooves*, edited by Charles Keil and Steven Feld, 109–50. Chicago: University of Chicago Press.

———. 1996. "Waterfalls of Song: An Acoustemology of Place Resounding in Bosavi, Papua New Guinea." In *Senses of Place*, edited by Steven Feld and Keith H. Basso, 91–136. Sante Fe: School of American Research Advanced Seminar Series.

———. 2015. "Acoustemology." In *Keywords in Sound*, edited by David Novak and Matt Sakakeeny, 12–21. Durham, NC: Duke University Press.

———. 2017. "On Post-ethnomusicology Alternatives: Acoustemology." In *Perspectives on a 21st Century Comparative Musicology: Ethnomusicology or Transcultural Musicology*, edited by Francesco Giannattasio and Giovanni Giuriati, 82–99. Udine: Nota.

Fiol, Stefan. 2017. *Recasting Folk in the Himalayas: Indian Music, Media, and Social Mobility*. Champagne: University of Illinois Press.

Frank, Arthur. 1991. "For a Sociology of a Body: An Analytical Review." In *The Body: Social Process and Cultural Theory*, edited by Mike Featherstone, Mike Hepworth, and Bryan S. Turner, 36–102. London: Sage Publications.

Fraser, Nancy. 1990. "Rethinking the Public Sphere: A Contribution to the Critique of Actually Existing Democracy." *Social Text* 25 (26): 56–80.

Foucault, Michel. 1986. "Of Other Spaces." Translated by Jay Miskowiec. *diacritics* 16 (1): 22–27.

Gade, Anna M. 2002. "Taste, Talent, and the Problem of Internalization: A Qur'anic Study in Religious Musicality from Southeast Asia." *History of Religions* 4 (4): 328–68.

Gaunt, Kyra D. 2006. *The Games Black Girls Play: Learning the Ropes from Double-Dutch to Hip-Hop.* New York: New York University Press.

Gerischer, Christiane. 2006. "O Suinge Baiano: Rhythmic Feeling and Microrhythmic Phenomena in Brazilian Percussion." *Ethnomusicology* 50 (1): 99–119.

Gerstin, Julian. 1998. "Interaction and Improvisation between Dancers and Drummers in Martinican Bèlè." *Black Music Research Journal* 18 (1/2): 121–65.

Gordon, Melissa. 2013. "Snack Break: Rockin' Out to the Harvest Moon at Namu Farm Chuseok." Umami Mart, October 17, 2013. https://umamimart.com/blogs/main/snack-break-rockin-out-to-the-harvest-moon-at-namu-farm-chuseok.

Graham, Brian. 2002. "Heritage as Knowledge: Capital or Culture?" *Urban Studies* 39 (5–6): 1003–17.

Guy, Nancy. 2009. "Flowing Down Taiwan's Tamsui River: Towards an Ecomusicology of the Environmental Imagination." *Ethnomusicology* 53 (2): 218–48.

Gwak, S. Sonya. 2008. *Be(com)ing Korean in the United States: Identity Formation Through Cultural Practices.* Amherst, NY: Cambria Press.

Gyeongnam Migrant Community Service Center. n.d. "Sogae [Introduction]." Accessed July 10, 2022. http://www.mworker.or.kr/intro_04.

Hahn, Tomie. 1996. "Teaching through Touch: An Aspect of the Kinesthetic Transmission Process of Nihon Buyo." In *The Body in Dance: Modes of Inquiry, Paradigms for Viewing Artistic Work and Scientific Inquiry*, 77–85. Proceedings of the Congress on Research in Dance.

———. 2006. "'It's the RUSH': Sites of the Sensually Extreme." *TDR: The Drama Review* 50 (2): 87–96.

———. 2007. *Sensational Knowledge: Embodying Culture through Japanese Dance.* Middletown, CT: Wesleyan University Press.

Han Geon-Soo [Han Kŏnsu]. 2007. "Multicultural Korea: Celebration or Challenge of Multiethnic Shift in Contemporary Korea?" *Korea Journal* 47 (4): 32–63.

Hesselink, Nathan. 1999. "Kim Inu's '*Pungmulgut* and Communal Spirit': Edited and Translated with an Introduction and Commentary." *Asian Music* 31 (1): 1–34.

———. 2006. *P'ungmul: South Korean Drumming and Dance.* Chicago: University of Chicago Press.

———. 2007. "Samul nori, *Wŏn-Pang-Kak*, and Cosmological Didacticism." *Yearbook for Traditional Music* (39): 140–61.

———. 2011. "Rhythm and Folk Drumming (*P'ungmul*) as the Musical Embodiment of Communal Consciousness in South Korean Village Society." In *Analytical and Cross-Cultural Studies in World Music*, edited by Michael Tenzer and John Roeder, 263–87. New York: Oxford University Press.

———. 2012. *SamulNori: Contemporary Korean Drumming and the Rebirth of Itinerant Performing Culture.* Chicago: University of Chicago Press.

Hesselink, Nathan, and Jonathan Christian Petty. 2004. "Landscape and Soundscape: Geomantic Spatial Mapping in Korean Traditional Music." *Journal of Musicological Research* (23): 265–88.

Hŏ Kyu. 1988. "*Norimadang, Madangnoriŭi* palsang" [*Norimadang*, the Expression of *Madangnori*]. In *Norimunhwawa ch'ukche* [Play Culture and Festival], edited by Yi Sang-il, 69–81. Seoul: Sŏnggyungwan University Press.

Hollywood, Amy. 2002. "Performativity, Citationality, Ritualization." *History of Religions* 42 (1): 93–115.

Hood, Mantle. 1960. "The Challenge of Bi-musicality." *Ethnomusicology* 4 (2): 55–59.

hooks, bell. 1984. *Feminist Theory from Margin to Center.* Boston: South End Press.

Howard, Keith. 1989. *Bands, Songs, and Shamanistic Rituals: Folk Music in Korean Society.* Seoul: Royal Asiatic Society, Korea Branch/Korean National Commission for UNESCO, Seoul Computer Press.

———. 2006. *Preserving Korean Music: Intangible Cultural Properties as Icons of Identity (Perspectives on Korean Music Volume 1).* Burlington, VT: Ashgate.

Hwang Sunju. 2003. "Pilbong *chŏngwŏl taeborŭm-kut* [Pilbong Lunar New Year Full Moon Ritual]." Accessed December 20, 2002. https://www.pilbong.co.kr.

Im Chint'aek. 1990. *Minjung yŏnhŭiŭi ch'angjo* [The Creation of *Minjung* Folk Entertainment]. Seoul: Ch'angjakkwa *Pip'yŏngsa*.

Imshil P'ilbong *Nongak Pojŏnhoe* [Imshil P'ilbong Nongak Preservation Association]. 2001. P'ilbong P'ungmul *Ch'ukche* [P'ilbong P'ungmul Festival] pamphlet.

———. 2016. P'ilbong *Chŏngwŏl Taeborŭm-kut* [P'ilbong Lunar New Year Full Moon Ritual] pamphlet.

Ivy, Marilyn. 1995. *Discourses of the Vanishing: Modernity, Phantasm, Japan.* Chicago: University of Chicago Press.

Jackson, Travis A. 2000. "Jazz Performance as Ritual: The Blues Aesthetic and African Diaspora." In *The African Diaspora: A Musical Perspective*, edited by Ingrid Monson, 23–82. New York: Garland Publishing.

Jang, Mikyung. 2013. "Analytical Psychological Meaning of Masks in the Hahoe Pyŏlshin Gut Tal (Mask) Play Dance in Korea." *Journal of Symbols and Sandplay Therapy* 4 (1): 16–20.

Jeong Hyeongho [Chŏng Hyŏngho]. 2015. "Korean Yeonhui History." In *Yeonhui* [Yŏnhŭi] [Korean Performing Arts], 53–100. Seoul: National Gugak Center.

Jin, Dalyong. 2016. *New Korean Wave: Transnational Cultural Power in the Age of Social Media.* Champagne: University of Illinois Press.

Kaye, Nick. 2000. *Site-Specific Art: Performance, Place, and Documentation.* London: Routledge.

Keil, Charles. 1994a. "Motion and Feeling Through Music." In *Music Grooves*, by Charles Keil and Steven Feld, 53–76. Chicago: Chicago University Press.

———. 1994b. "Participatory Discrepancies and the Power of Music." In *Music Grooves*, by Charles Keil and Steven Feld, 96–108. Chicago: Chicago University Press.

Killick, Andrew. 1998. "*Ch'angguk*: Re-making *P'ansori* as 'Korean Traditional Opera.'" *Korean Culture* (Summer/Fall): 4–13.

Kim, Elaine H. 1993. "Home Is Where the Han Is: A Korean American Perspective on the Los Angeles Upheavals." *Social Justice* 20 (1/2): 1–21.

Kim, Sandra So Hee Chi. 2017. "Korean 'Han' and the Postcolonial Afterlives of 'The Beauty of Sorrow.'" *Korean Studies* (41): 253–79.

Kim, Soo-Jin. 2011. "Diasporic *P'ungmul* in the United States: A Journey Between Korea and the United States." PhD diss., The Ohio State University.

Kim Iktu. 1995. "*P'ungmulkusŭi Kongyŏn Wolli-wa Yŏnhaengjŏk Sŏngkyŏk*" [P'ungmul-kut's Principles and Performance Character]. *Hanguk Minsokhak: Minsok Hakhwe* (27): 97–132.

Kim Iktu, No Boksun, Im Myŏngjin, Chŏn Chŏnggu, and Choi Sang-hwa. 1994. *Honam Chwado P'ungmul-kut* [Jeolla Province "Right Side" P'ungmul-kut]. Chŏnju: Chŏnbuk taehakkyo Jeolla munhwa yŏnguso.

Kim Inu. 1987. "*Pungmulgut-kwa Kongdongch'ejŏk Shinmyong*" [P'ungmul and Communal Spirit]. In *Minjok-gwa Kut*, 102–44. Seoul: Hangminsa.

Kim-Gibson, Dae Sil, and Christine Choy, dir. 1993. *Sa-I-Gu*. San Francisco: Center for Asian American Media. https://www.youtube.com/watch?v=G_UyYj-pR8U&t=1884s.

Kim Samt'ae. 2001a. "*P'ungmul-kutkwa shimjang undong pigyo yŏngu: Shwinŭn gŏtsul jungshimŭro*" [P'ungmul-kut and Heartbeat Movement: Centering on Breathing]. In *2001 Pilbong P'ungmul-kut Ch'ukche Seminar*, 1–89. Pilbong: Pilbong Pojŏnhoe.

———. 2001b. *P'ungmul-kutp'anŭi sul-kwa shinmyŏng* [Alcohol and Shinmyŏng in the P'ungmul-kut P'an]. In *2001 Pilbong P'ungmulgut Ch'ukche Seminar*, 140–48. Pilbong: Pilbong Pojŏnhoe.

Kinney, Alison. 2017. "The Beating Heart of the Women's March." *Noisey: Music by Vice*, January 27, 2017. https://www.vice.com/en/article/aejvzk/the-beating-heart-of-the-womens-march.

Kirshenblatt-Gimblett, Barbara. 1995. "Theorizing Heritage." *Ethnomusicology* 39 (3): 367–80.

Ko, Hyunjin. 2001. "Holding an Event to Pray for Peace." *The Korea Times* (San Francisco Bay Area edition), September 24, 2001.

Komodo, Haruko, and Mihoko Nogawa. 2002. "Theory and Notation in Japan." In *East Asia: China, Japan, and Korea*, edited by Robert Provine, Yosihiko Tokumara, and J. Lawrence Witzleben, 565–84. New York: Routledge.

Kwon, Donna Lee. 2001. "The Roots and Routes of *P'ungmul* in the United States." *Umakgwa Munhwa* [Music and Culture (Korean Society for World Music)] (5): 39–65.

———. 2005. "Music, Movement and Space: A Study of the Madang and P'an in Korean Expressive Folk Culture." PhD diss., University of California, Berkeley.

———. 2015. "'Becoming One': Embodying Korean P'ungmul Percussion Band Music and Dance through Site-Specific Intermodal Transmission." *Ethnomusicology* 59 (1): 31–60.

Kwon, Miwon. 2002. *One Place after Another: Site-Specific Art and Locational Identity*. Cambridge, MA: MIT Press.

Kwŏn Tuhyŏn. 1992. "*P'ungmulŭi kinŭnggwa yŏnhaeng'yangshik yŏn'gu*" [The Function and Performance Style of P'ungmul]. Master's thesis, Andong University.

Kwŏn Ŭnyŏng. 2008. "*Yŏsŏngnongaktanŭl t'onghae pon kŭndae yŏnyenongagŭi yangsang*" [The Status of Modern *Nongak* Performance as Seen Through Female *Nongak* Troupes]. *Silch'ŏnminsokhak yŏn'gu* [The Society of Practice and Folklore] (11): 197–228.

Larmer, Brook. 2018. "South Korea's Most Dangerous Enemy." *New York Times*, February 20, 2018. https://www.nytimes.com/2018/02/20/magazine/south-koreas-most-dangerous-enemy-demographics.html.

Lau, Frederick. 2008. *Music in China: Experiencing Music, Expressing Culture*. New York: Oxford University Press.

Lee, Katherine. 2012. "The Drumming of Dissent during South Korea's Democratization Movement." *Ethnomusicology* 56 (2): 179–205.

———. 2018. *Dynamic Korea and Rhythmic Form*. Middletown, CT: Wesleyan University Press.

Lee, Kyungjin. 2015. "Koreatown's 'Ghostbusters' Usher in Good Luck for the Year of the Goat." *The World*, March 2, 2015. https://www.pri.org/stories/2015-03-02/koreatowns-ghostbusters-usher-good-luck-year-goat.

Lee, Namhee. 2001. "Making Minjung Subjectivity: Crisis of Subjectivity and Rewriting History, 1960–1988." PhD diss., University of Chicago.

———. 2003. "Between Indeterminacy and Radical Critique: *Madang-gŭk*, Ritual and Protest." *Positions* 11 (3): 555–84.

———. 2007. *The Making of Minjung: Democracy and the Politics of Representation in South Korea*. Ithaca, NY: Cornell University Press.

Lee Yong-shik [Yi Yongshik]. 2004. *Shaman Ritual Music in Korea*. Seoul: Jimoondang.

Lee Young-mee [Yi Yŏng-mi]. 1997. "Korean Traditional Theatre and *Madangguk* Theatre." *Korea Journal* 37, (3): 40–62.

Lepecki, André. 2013. "Choreopolice and Choreopolitics." *The Drama Review* 57 (4): 13–27.

Lefebvre, Henri. 2004. *Rhythmanalysis: Space, Time and Everyday Life*. London: Bloomsbury Academic.

Levin, Laura, and Marlis Schweitzer. 2011. "Editorial Performing Publics." *Performance Research* 16 (2): 1–6.

Levin, Sam. 2015. "Oakland to Take Down Lake Merritt Signs Prohibiting Musical Instruments, Activists Plan Protests." *East Bay Express*, October 8, 2015. https://eastbayexpress.com/oakland-to-take-down-lake-merritt-signs-prohibiting-musical-instruments-activists-plan-protests-2-1/.

Maliangkay, Roald. 2017. *Broken Voices: Postcolonial Entanglements and the Preservation of Korea's Central Folksong Traditions (Music and Performing Arts of Asia and the Pacific)*. Honolulu: University of Hawai'i Press.

Malraux, André. 1967. *The Museum Without Walls*. Translated by Start Gilbert and Francis Price. Garden City, NY: Doubleday.

Manabe, Noriko. 2015. *The Revolution Will Not Be Televised: Protest Music after Fukushima*. New York: Oxford University Press.

Massey, Doreen. 1994. *Space, Place, and Gender*. Minneapolis: University of Minnesota Press.

Mauss, Marcel. 1973 [1935]. "Techniques of the Body." Translated by B. Brewster. *Economy and Society* 2 (1): 70–87.

Miller, Kiri. 2017. *Playable Bodies: Dance Games and Intimate Media*. New York: Oxford University Press.

Mills, Simon. 2007. *Healing Rhythms: The World of South Korea's East Coast Hereditary Shamans*. Burlington, VT: Ashgate.

Min Pyong Gap. 1990. "Korean Immigrants in Los Angeles." *ISSR Working Papers in the Social Sciences* (1989–90), no. 2, 1–34.

Moss, Pamela, and Avril Maddrell. 2017. "Emergent and Divergent Spaces in the Women's March: The Challenges of Intersectionality and Inclusion." *Gender, Place and Culture* 24 (5): 613–20.

No Dongŭn. 1995. *Han'guk Kŭndae* Ŭmaksa 1 [Modern Korean Music History Vol. 1]. Seoul: Hangilsa.

Monson, Ingrid. 2007. *Freedom Sounds: Civil Rights Call Out to Jazz and Africa*. New York: Oxford University Press.

Onishi, Norimitsu. 2007. "Marriage Brokers in Vietnam Cater to S. Korean Bachelors." *New York Times*, February 21, 2007. https://www.nytimes.com/2007/02/21/world/asia/21iht-brides.4670360.html.

Oppenheim, Robert. 2008. *Kyŏngju Things: Assembling Place*. Ann Arbor: University of Michigan Press.

———. 2010. "Crafting the Consumability of Place: *Tapsa* and *Paenang Yŏhaeng* as Travel Goods." In *Consuming Korean Tradition in Early and Late Modernity: Commodification, Tourism, and Performance*, edited by Laurell Kendall, 106–26. Honolulu: University of Hawai'i Press.

Pak Ch'ansuk. 2013. "*Onŭ wŏnjo'kwi'nongminŭi 30nyŏn ch'onsali pogosŏ*" [30 Year Report on the Origins of the Back-to-Earth Farmer Movement]. Hwanghaemunhwa, Fall.

Pak Chinhŭi. 2001. "*Nonghwal.*" Hwabo: Sŏngkyunkwan daehakkyo dongariyŏnhamhwe yŏrŭm nongchonbongsa'hwaldong [Sŏngkyunkwan University Annual Summer Nonghwal Pictorial].

Pak Hŭngchu. n.d. *P'an-kut-iran Muŏssinga?* [What is *P'an-kut*?]. Unpublished typescript.

Park, Kyeyoung. 2019. *LA Rising: Korean Relations with Blacks and Latinos After Civil Unrest*. Lanham, MD: Lexington Books.

Park, Mi-Kyung. 1985. "Music and Shamanism in Korea: A Study of Selected *Ssikkum-gut* Rituals for the Dead." PhD diss., University of California, Los Angeles.

———. 2003. "Korean Shaman Rituals Revisited; The Case of Chindo *Ssikkimgut* (Cleansing Rituals)." *Ethnomusicology* 47 (3): 355–75.

Park, Peter Joon. 2014. "*P'ungmul Kut* (Percussion Music Rituals): Integrating Korean Traditions with Modern Identities." PhD diss., University of Washington.

Park, Shingil. 2000. "Negotiating Identities in a Performance Genre: The Case of *P'ungmul* and *Samulnori* in Contemporary Seoul." PhD diss., University of Pittsburgh.

Pearson, Mike. 2010. *Site-Specific Performance*. New York: Palgrave Macmillan.

Peckham, Robert Shannan, ed. 2003. *Rethinking Heritage, Cultures and Politics in Europe*. London: I. B. Tauris.

Phillips, Justin. 2021. "An Oakland Lake Became a Symbol of Black Resilience. Then the Neighbors Complained." *San Francisco Chronicle*, May 23, 2021. https://www.sfchronicle.com/local/justinphillips/article/An-Oakland-lake-became-a-symbol-of-Black-16194668.php.

Pihl, Marshall R. 1994. *The Korean Singer of Tales*. Cambridge, MA: Harvard University Press.

Prögler, J. A. 1995. "Searching for Swing: Participatory Discrepancies in the Jazz Rhythm Section." *Ethnomusicology* 39 (1): 21–54.

Quinn, Naomi. 1991. "The Cultural Basis of Metaphor." In *Beyond Metaphor: The Theory of Tropes in Anthropology*, edited by James W. Fernandez, 56–93. Stanford, CA: Stanford University Press.

Radzuan, Indera Syahrul Mat, Song Inho, and Yahaya Ahmad. 2015. "A Rethink of the Incentives Programme in the Conservation of South Korea's Historic Villages." *Journal of Cultural Heritage Management and Sustainable Development* 5 (2): 176–20.

Rancière, Jacques. 2013. *The Politics of Aesthetics*. Translated by Gabriel Rockhill. New York: Bloomsbury Academic.

Saeji, CedarBough. 2012. "Transmission and Performance: Memory, Heritage and Authenticity in Korean Mask Dance Dramas." PhD diss., University of California, Los Angeles.

———. 2013. "Drumming, Dancing and Drinking *Makkŏlli*: Liminal Time Travel through

Intensive Camps Teaching Traditional Performing Arts." *Journal of Korean Studies* 18 (1): 61–88.

Schippers, Huib, and Catherine Grant, eds. 2016. *Sustainable Futures for Music Cultures: An Ecological Perspective*. New York: Oxford University Press.

Seo, Maria. 2002. *Hanyang Kut: Korean Shaman Ritual Music from Seoul*. New York: Routledge.

Shelemay, Kay Kaufman. 2022. *Sing and Sing On: Sentinel Musicians and the Making of the Ethiopian American Diaspora*. Chicago: University of Chicago Press.

Shim Usŏng. 1994. *Namsadangp'ae yŏngu* [A Study of Namsadang Troupes]. Seoul: Tosŏ ch'ulp'an tongmunsŏn.

Small, Christopher. 1998. *Musicking: The Meanings of Performing Listening*. Middletown, CT: Wesleyan University Press.

Smith, Laurajane. 2006. *Uses of Heritage*. London: Routledge.

Smith, Laurajane, and Natsuko Akagawa. 2009. "Introduction." In *Intangible Heritage*, edited by Laurajane Smith and Natsuko Akagawa, 1–10. London: Routledge.

Son, Su-rak. 2001. "Opinion." *The Korea Times* (San Francisco Bay Area edition), September 18, 2001.

Son, T'aedo. 2021. "*Ch'angjak yŏnhŭiŭi hyŏnhwangkwa chŏnmang* [Current Status and Prospects of Creative Yŏnhŭi]." *Han'guk chŏnt'ong kongyŏn yesulhak* [Journal of Korean Traditional Performing Arts] (6): 97–141.

Song, Soonam [Song Sunam]. 1990. "*Shinmyŏng* in Korean Group Dance Performance." *Korea Journal* 30 (9): 32–35.

Song Bangsong [Song Pangsong]. 2000. *Korean Music: Historical and Other Aspects*. Seoul: Jimoondang Publishing Company.

Stokes, Martin, ed. 1994. *Ethnicity, Identity and Music: The Musical Construction of Place*. Oxford: Berg Press.

Sumarsam. 1995. *Gamelan: Cultural Interaction and Musical Development in Central Java*. Chicago: University of Chicago Press.

Sutton, R. Anderson. 1987. "Korean Music in Hawaii." *Asian Music* 19 (1): 99–120.

———. 1991. *Traditions of Gamelan Music in Java: Musical Pluralism and Regional Identity*. Cambridge: Cambridge University Press.

Tam, Brett. 1992. "Thousands Unite in Koreatown to Rally for Peace, Racial Equality." *Daily Bruin*, May 1992. University of California, Los Angeles.

Tangherlini, Timothy R. 1999. "Remapping Koreatown: Folklore, Narrative and the Los Angeles Riots." *Western Folklore* 58 (2): 149–73.

———. 2001. "*Chisin Palpki, P'ungmul*, Christian Surfers and 'Slamming a Ride': Folklore and the Negotiation of Korean American Identity in Los Angeles." *Acta Koreana* (4): 95–114.

Titon, Jeff Todd. 2013. "The Nature of Ecomusicology." *Música e Cultura: revista da ABET* 8 (1): 8–18.

———. 2020. *Toward a Sound Ecology: New and Selected Essays*. Bloomington: Indiana University Press.

Turino, Thomas. 1999. "Signs of Imagination, Identity, and Experience: A Peircian Semiotic Theory for Music." *Ethnomusicology* 43 (2): 221–55.

———. 2008. *Music as Social Life: The Politics of Participation*. Chicago: University of Chicago Press.

Turner, Victor. 1974. *Dramas, Fields and Metaphors: Symbolic Action in Human Society*. Ithaca, NY: Cornell University Press.

Un Yŏngja. 2017. "Sri Lanka Participates in Migrant Arirang Multi-cultural Festival 2017." *Embassy of Sri Lanka*. Accessed July 10, 2022. http://www.slembassykorea.com/eng/bbs/board.php?bo_table=s1_4&wr_id=36&page=2.

Urry, John. 1996. "How Societies Remember the Past." In *Theorizing Museums: Representing Identity and Diversity in a Changing World*, edited by Sharon Macdonald and Gordon Fyfe. Cambridge: Blackwell.

Vickers, Adrian. 1989. *Bali: A Paradise Created*. Singapore: Periplus Editions.

Warner, Michael. 2002. "Public and Counterpublics." *Public Culture* 14 (1): 49–90.

Wilkie, Fiona. 2002. "Mapping the Terrain: A Survey of Site-Specific Performance in Britain." *New Theatre Quarterly* 18 (2): 140–60.

Williams, Raymond. 1973. *The Country and the City*. New York: Oxford University Press.

———. 1977. *Marxism and Literature*. New York: Oxford University Press.

Witzleben, J. Lawrence. 1995. *Silk and Bamboo Music in Shanghai: The Jiangnan Sizhu Instrumental Ensemble Tradition*. Kent, OH: Kent State University Press.

Wong, Deborah. 2001. *Sounding the Center: History and Aesthetics in Thai Buddhist Performance*. Chicago: University of Chicago Press.

———. 2008. "Moving: From Performance to Performative Ethnography and Back Again." In *Shadows in the Field: New Perspectives for Fieldwork in Ethnomusicology*, 2nd edition, edited by Gregory F. Barz and Timothy J. Cooley, 76–89. New York: Oxford University Press.

Yang Chinsŏng. 2000. *Honam Chwado Imshil Pilbong-kut* [Cholla Province "Left Side" Style: *Pungmul-kut* of Pilbong Village]. Jeonju: Shina Chulpansa.

———. 2008. "*Pilbong nongak-ŭi kongyŏnhakchŏk yŏn'gu*" [A Study of Pilbong Nongak as a Performing Art]. PhD diss., Jeonbuk University.

Yang Jongsung [Yang Chong-sung]. 1994. "Folklore and Cultural Politics in Korea: Intangible Cultural Properties and Living National Treasures." PhD diss., Indiana University.

Yeo, Hyunjin [Yŏ Hyŏnjin]. 2018. "Voicing the Unheard: Gendered Practices, Discourses, and Struggles of *Gugak* Musicians in South Korea." PhD diss., University of Maryland, College Park.

Yi Chongjin. 1996. "*P'ungmulkusŭi karak kuchowa yŏkdongsŏng: pilbong p'ungmulkusŭl chungshimŭro*" [The Dynamics and Rhythmic Structure of *P'ungmul-kut*: A Study of Pilbong P'ungmul-kut]. Master's thesis, Andong University.

Yi Hyejin. 1998. "*Madangnori ch'umŭi yesuljŏk tŭksŏng yŏngu*" [Research on the Distinctive Characteristics of *Madangnori* Dance]. Master's thesis, Kŏnkuk University.

Yŏnhŭi Chipdan The Kwangdae. n.d. "*The Kwangdae sogae* [The Kwangdae Introduction]." Accessed December 15, 2015. https://www.youtube.com/watch?v=O9Aa2Zogzf0&t=11s.

Yu, Hongjun. 1993. *Na ŭi Munhwa Yusan Tapsagi* 1 [The Chronicle of My Field Investigation of Cultural Remains]. Seoul: Ch'angjak kwa Pip'yŏngsa.

Yun Chunggang. "Jambinaiwa posŭtŭ kugak [Jambinai Post-kugak]." *Kyŏngin Ilbo*, June 13, 2015. http://www.kyeongin.com/main/view.php?device=pc&key=20160612010003622.

INDEX-GLOSSARY

Page entries in **bold** refer to figures.

Abe, Marié, 16, 150, 173, 198, 237
Abelmann, Nancy, 37, 39, 156–57
acoustemology, 8, 237
activism, 61; and Korean American communities, 198–204, 224–25, 229–30, 233, 235–36, 250n3; and *nonghwal*, 15, 23–24, 35–40, 44, 250n3; and *tapsa*, 33–34
aesthetics, 61, 73, 77, 81, 98, 124, 129, 187; of *p'ungmul* rhythms, 76, 83, 85–86
affect, 16, 150, 173, 220, 223, 226, 236
agency, 39–40, 59–60
agriculture, 12, 24, 30, 45, 87, 91, 144, 176, 220, 232–33; and *chŏnsu*, 37–38
Akagawa, Natsuko, 142
alcohol: and ceremony, 94, 121, 123–24, 137; *makkŏlli* (milky rice beer), 4, 50–54, 104, 112, 139, 167, 205–6
Allen, Aaron, 7
amplification, 29, 167
An Daech'ŏn 안대천, 180
Andong International *T'alch'um* Festival, 154
Anseong 안성, 3
ap-kut 앞굿 (front ritual, first half of a performance), 132, 139, 247n16
Appadurai, Arjun, 2
apprentices, 95–96, 103
architecture, 15, 30, 34, 55; Korean-style, 65–66, 102, 159, 184, 247n2; and theaters, 151–52, 154
artifacts, 33–34, 55, 163, 169

Attali, Jacques, 98, 152
audiences, 18, 33, 237, 239n3, 247n19; and *ch'angjak yŏnhŭi*, 179, 181–94; and GOPA, 162–63, 165–69, 171–72; interactions with, 3–6, 12, 80, 87; and *madangbalbi*, 124, 128, 130–31, 133–35, 139; and Pilbong Lunar New Year, 108–13, 136–37, 235; and theaters, 152, 154
Austin, J. L., 119
authenticity, 48, 61, 105, 234
authority, 33, 48, 70–71, 124–26

Baeksan 백산 (White Mountain), 155–61
balance, 12–13, 145
bamboo poles, 96, 135, 163, **164**
Bateson, Gregory, 9, 231, 238; *An Ecology of Mind*, 8
Battery Park, New York, 223
Becker, Judith and Alton Becker, 11
becoming one, 11–12, 14, 57, 67, 69, 79, 161–62, 168–69, 238
Berkeley, CA, 204
Bhabha, Homi, 238
Black American communities, 207, 210, 212–13
Black Lives Matter, 229
bonfires. See *Taljip t'aeugi*
Bongsan T'alch'um 봉산탈춤 (mask dance drama from the Bongsan region of Hwanghae province), 186, 191

Boramae Park, Seoul, 183
Border Protection, Antiterrorism, and Illegal Immigration Control Act (2005), 224
Bourdieu, Pierre, 61
breath, 82–83, 85–87, 112
Brinner, Benjamin, *Knowing Music, Making Music*, 62
Brown, Anita, 252n1
Bruner, Edward, *Culture on Tour*, 109
Buddhism, 192, 247n20
Bukchon Hanok district, 107
Bush, George W., 224
businesses, 143, 202–8, 210–12, 217, 251n14
Butler, Judith, 119

catharsis, 11–12, 42, 49, 108, 167, 192–93; and *p'ungmul*, 37, 77–78. See also *shinmyŏng*
Ch'ae Hŭiwan 채희완, 14, 30, 240n5, 246n6
ch'aesang sogo 채상 소고 (handheld drummer with twirling streamer hat), 27–28, 126, 134, 245n2
chajinmori 자진모리 (fast 12/8 rhythm), 172, 182, 188
Ch'angbu 창부 (male entertainer character), 29, 116–18
changdan 장단 (rhythmic cycle), 134, 195, 201
changgo 장고 (hourglass drum; also called *changgu*), 4–5, 12, 27–28, 44, 46, 68, 71, 79, 113, 118, 126, 134–35, 160–61, 192, 194, 217
ch'anggŭk 창극 (musical theater genre derived from *p'ansori*), 153
ch'angjak yŏnhŭi 창작 연희 (creative traditional performing arts), 17, 174–75, 178–80, 195; The Greatest Masque, 185–89; Norikkot, 183–85; Norikkundŭl Todam Todam, 189–94; Yŏnhŭi Chipdan The Kwangdae, 180–83
chaos, 5, 11–12, 49–50, 71, 78, 98, 114, 121, 126–28, 134, 192. See also *nanjang*
chapsaek 잡색 (character player in *p'ungmul*), 3, 27, 78, 112–19, 126–27, 133, 138–39, 160, 205, 245n2, 246n7; as archetypal, 12, 27, 124
chapsaek nori 잡색놀이 (character play), 124

chemun (prayer), 223
ch'ibae (performers), 27, 70
Chicago, Il, 199, 201, 209, 224
chicken fighting, 193–94
Chin Chaehong, 242n9
Chinese Progressive Alliance (CPA), 227
ching 징 (large gong), 12, 27–28, 113, 127, 160, 161, 192, 206, 209
chinobangjin (fast rhythm), 211, 227, 250n9
chishinpalpki 지신밟기 ("earth spirit treading," refers to ritual that is performed during Lunar New Year), 203–9, 223, 231–32, 250n10
Cho Ch'unyŏng 조춘영, 92–93, 96, 98, 239n5
Ch'oe Ho-in 최호인, 50, 85–87, 94, 135
Ch'ŏllyung-kut 철륭굿 (storage jar ceremony), 121–22
chŏng 정 (love/affection), 67, 128
Chŏng Pyŏngho 정병호, 131
Chŏngwŏl Taeborŭm-kut 정월 대보름굿 (Lunar New Year Full Moon Ritual), 90–91, 98, 108, 113. See also Lunar New Year
Chŏn Kwangnyŏl 전광렬, 161
Chŏn Pongjun 전봉준, 156, 158–59, 248nn6–7
chŏnsu 전수 (transmission), 15, 34–35, 37–40, 52, 55, 58, 63, 202, 242n9, 243n15. See also Pilbong transmission center
chŏnsugwan / *chŏnsuhoegwan* 전구관 / 전수회관 (transmission building or center), 15, 30, 35, 47–53, 58, 60, 163
chŏnsu students, 13, 38–54, 96, 140, 163, 165, 171, 241n7, 244n26; and recent Pilbong *chŏnsu*, 58, 60–63, 65, 67, 69–72, 78–80, 85–87
choreographies, 12–13, 27, 90, 131–33, 144, 160, 191, 197, 202, 215
choreopolitics, 226, 229
chorijung 조리중 (monk character), 29
chowang-kut 조왕굿 (kitchen ceremony to appease the house god), 121, 122, 123, 127
Choy, Christine, 209
Cho Yun-Mi 조윤미, 112
Christianity, 45, 204, 218
ch'uimsae 추임새 (stylistic shouts of

encouragement), 33, 115–19, 182, 184, 190, 205, 226
chuin 주인 (owner), 120, 207. *See also* ownership
ch'ukche 축제 (festival), 162
ch'ukche p'an 축제 판 (festival space), 162
Chung-Ang University, 179
Ch'usŏk 추석 (Korean harvest moon holiday), 170, 214, 216–20, 233, 250n5
citizenship, 32–34
class, social, 121–22, 124, 172, 183, 245n6
Clayton, Martin, 81–82
cognitive musicology, 62–63
collaboration, 94, 177, 204–5, 228–31, 235
colonialism, 32–33, 100, 105, 152, 189, 236; Japanese, 152, 163, 189, 220, 246n5, 246n14, 248n6, 248n12
Colosseum, 151, 248n3
communal labor, 3, 140, 149; and *chŏnsu*, 37, 45, 54, 70–72, 78, 93
communal ways of being, 57, 59, 63–64, 79, 87–88, 241n2, 245n6
communitas, 13, 52
community, 13, 61, 73, 121, 160, 237; and *chŏnsu*, 64, 69–72, 87, 95; connections to, 3, 7, 11, 198; and Korean Americans, 202–13, 215, 231, 233, 235; and *madang*, 128, 130, 135, 139, 161; and Pilbong Lunar New Year, 105, 114, 142–43; and *p'ungmul*, 9, 93. *See also kondongch'e*
community organizations, 3, 5, 32, 39, 65, 203, 213. *See also names of community organizations*
competitions, 34, 68, 74–77, 179, 243n15
conflict, 5, 60, 71, 77, 114–16, 120, 124, 128, 210, 225
consumerism, 152, 176–77, 181
cooking, 10, 15, 39, 45–48, 78, 94, 102, 104
copresence, 237
Corazon, 228
cosmologies, 11, 13, 43, 132, 142, 247n15, 247n20
counterpublics, 33, 207
court genres, 60, 153

COVID-19, 180, 233–34
Creative Ch'angjak Yŏnhŭi Competition, 179
Csordas, Thomas, 1, 8, 59, 64, 85–86, 243n12
cultural heritage: and Pilbong, 14–15, 89, 100, 109, 142; preservation of, 2–3, 6–7, 16, 24, 105, 107, 143, 149, 184; and sites, 7, 236; and *tapsa*, 23, 31–35
Cultural Property Protection Law (1962), 60
cultural tourism, 15, 32–35, 54, 58, 60, 67, 106, 109, 142–43; and GOPA, 162–63, 169
culture industries, 175, 177

Daejeon University, 54
dancing, 33, 237, 241n7, 243n15; and *ch'angjak yŏnhŭi*, 182, 186–88, 191, 193, 195; choreographies, 12–13, 27, 90, 144, 160, 191, 197, 202, 215; and GOPA, 161, 163, 166–67, 171–73; and intermodal pedagogy, 80–81; and Korean American communities, 214–15, 219–23, 233, 235, 237; and *madangbalbi*, 125, 139–40; and *p'an-kut*, 131–35; and *sangsoe* competition, 74–76
Danghangpo harbor 당항포, 16
Danghangpo Tourist Site, 163, **164**, 169–70
Daniel, Drew, 226
decolonization, 35, 43, 59
democratization. *See minjung undong*
Deshpande, Satish, 106, 127, 245n6
diasporic communities, 12, 18, 52, 234–35, 242n7, 249n1. *See also* migration
diversity, 65, 139, 169–71, 176, 213, 219, 225
DREAM Act (2001), 224

ecomusicology, 7
economic issues, 13, 41, 176, 181, 183, 236–37
EGO, 216, 220
elders, 4–5, 39, 53, 114, 135, 137, 186–89, 246n613
embodiment, 1–3, 8, 17–18, 61–63, 173, 241n11, 243n12; and *ch'angjak yŏnhŭi*, 175, 191, 193–96; and community, 5, 16, 33–34, 130, 157, 161, 168–69, 222–23; and *madang*, 12, 96, 134–35, 242n2; and Pilbong *chŏnsu*, 59–60, 79–87; and Pilbong Lunar New Year, 110,

Index-Glossary **267**

114, 117, 119, 141; and sensory experiences, 34, 51–53, 106, 144, 226–27, 235–37; and site specificity, 6–7, 15, 141; and *tapsa*, 72–74
emotions, 4, 9, 12, 49–52, 115, 218, 222–23, 235
employment, 176–77, 183
emptiness, 80, 92–93, 96, 98
endogenous rhythms, 82
entertainment-oriented formats, 78, 90, **97**, 98, 130–31, 141, 151–53, 159–60, 206, 221, 243n10
entrainment, 81–83, 86–87, 141, 145
environment, 3, 7–9, 14–16, 55, 68, 72–74, 149–50, 233; and expressive ecologies, 35, 90, 142–43, 238
epistemology, 8, 237
Equality Summer Camp for Migrant Workers, 169–73
ethnography, 15–19, 37, 51, 93, 109
Eunyul T'alch'um 은율탈춤 (mask dance drama from the Eunyul region of Hwanghae province), 162–63, 165–67
Event in Korea (TV show), 98
everyday life, 2, 30, 46, 66, 108, 181, 191, 234, 247n18; and ritual, 42, 77, 108, 121, 135, 140, 144, 247n18
Ewha University, 36, 64, 67
experiential knowledge, 5–6, 8–13, 46, 49, 59, 93, 103, 150, 168, 193
expressive ecologies, site-oriented, 7, 17, 149–50, 238; and GOPA, 155–73; and Korean American communities, 198, 203, 214, 232; national urban spaces, 174–75; and Tonghak, 155–61
expressive ecologies, site-specific, 8, 15, 57–59, 85–87, 234–37, 240n6; definitions of, 3–8, 90; and Pilbong transmission center, 41, 54, 79; and Pilbong village, 14–17, 19, 23, 89, 100, 105–10, 120, 141–44; and South Korean geography, 24–25; and *tapsa*, 32–35, 72. See also *chŏnsu*; Pilbong transmission center

farmers, 42, 45, 143, 156, 232–34, 242n11, 252n1; and *nonghwal*, 15, 23–24, 35–40, 55; and *p'ungmul*, 47–48, 83, 86, 111–12

Fatone, Gina, 62
Feld, Steven, 8, 11, 79, 237, 242n4
festival culture, 55, 154–55, 162, 179
fieldwork, 17–18, 37, 161; in Namwon, 50–51; in Pilbong, 3–5, 25, 53, 69, 94–95, 108
Fiol, Stefan, 2
flag ritual. See *Ki-kut*
Flushing, New York, 199, 201, 205, 250n8
folk revival movement, 42, 61
folk sayings, 92, 111
folksong. See *minyo*
food, 10, 15, 39, 45–50, 78, 92, 94, 102, 104; and Korean American communities, 198, 206, 232–33; and ritual, 110, 113, 121, 123, 129–30, 139, 223
Foucault, Michel, 105–6, 127
frames, **10**, 10–13, 60
Frank, Arthur, 51, 241n11
Fraser, Nancy, 207
fusion *gugak*, 177–78

Gade, Anna M., 64, 243n11
games, 13, 34, 50, 54, 134, 152–53, 189–90, 193–94, 221. See also *nori*
Gangjin 강진, 25, 41, 111
Gangnyeong T'alch'um 강령탈춤 (mask dance drama from the Gangnyeong region of Hwanghae province), 186
Gaunt, Kyra, 8
gender, 16, 24, 30, 36, 70, 171, 177, 243n13; and *ch'angjak yŏnhŭi*, 184, 193; and *chapsaek*, 124–27; and labor, 94–95, 104
Geoje Island 거제도, 201
Gerischer, Christiane, 85
gift-giving, 39, 50, 70
global financial crisis (2008), 176
globalization, 2, 14, 169, 192
Golden Gate Park, San Francisco, 216, 222, 252n7
Goseong Ogwangdae 고성오광대 (mask dance drama from Goseong in South Gyeongsang province), 155–69
Goseong Ogwangdae Pojonhoe 고성 오광대

보존회 (Goseong Ogwangdae Preservation Association or GOPA), 16, 58, 92, 162, 165–66, 169–73, 180, 186, 214, 219–20, 235, 241n7
Gould, Corrina, 229
gravel-paved *madang*, 95, 102, 130, 153, 163
The Greatest Masque, 17, 179, 185–89
groove, 60, 63, 76, 79–80, 85–87, 145, 195, 242n4
GTA *of* 연희 (*GTA [Grand Theft Auto] of Folk Arts*, a show by Norikkundŭl Todam Todam), 189
gugak [kugak] 국악 (national Korean music), 242n5
Guy, Nancy, 7
Gwangju 광주, 30, 199
Gyeongju 경주, 34, 107
Gyeongnam Migrant Community Service Center (GMCSC), 170–71
Gyeongsang province, 162, 182, 188

Habermas, Jurgen, 207
Hahn, Tomie, 1, 8, 51, 62; *Sensational Knowledge*, 58
Hahoe 하회, 107, 245n7
Hahoe Pyŏlshin-kut T'alnori 하회 별신굿 탈놀이 (mask dance drama of Hahoe village), 107, 182, 186, 235
hallyu 한류 (Korean wave), 177
halmi 할미 (grandmother), 27, 29, 112, 127, 187
halmŏni tangsan namu 할머니 당산 나무 (grandmother tutelary spirit tree), 4, 100
Hamgyeong province Cultural Property No. 1, 162
han 한 (aesthetic concept that refers to pent-up sorrow), 187, 212, 220
Han, Geon-Soo [Han, Kŏnsu], 169
hanbok (Korean traditional dress), 4, 112, 177
Han Chaehun 한재훈, 25–26, 71–74, 94
Handong school, Geoje Island, 169
Han'guk Ilbo 한국 일보 (*The Korea Times*), 217
Hanin Ch'ŏngnyŏn Munhwawŏn 한인 청년 문화원 (Korean Youth Cultural Center [KYCC]), 18, 58, 199, 203–4, 206, 213–24, 231, 241n7, 247n18, 250nn9–10, 251n17
Haninhwe 한인회 ("Korean organization," used to refer to Korean American business-oriented organizations), 217
Hanmadang 한마당 ("one madang," refers to the Korean Youth Cultural Center's *p'ungmul* group), 199, **200**, 201, 204
hanok 한옥 (traditional Korean-style architecture), 65–66, 184
Han Ool Lim 한울림 ("one reverberation," UCLA *p'ungmul* group), 211
HanUri 한우리 ("one us," San Jose *p'ungmul* group), 220
haraboji tangsan namu 할아버지 당산 나무 (grandfather tutelary spirit tree), 4, 100, **101**
Harvard University, 201
Hawai'i, 198, 250n5
healing, 17, 198, 219, 231
Hella Organized Bay Area Koreans (HOBAK), 225
Hell *Chosŏn*, 176–77, 194
Hesselink, Nathan, 79, 242n9, 244n22
heterotopias, 105–6, 127, 245n6
Hobokdong 호복동, 41, 44–47
Hŏ Ch'angyŏl 허창열, 180–82, 185–87
hohŭp 호흡 (breathing), 82–83, 85–87
Hollywood, Amy, 119
Honam region, 24, 240n2
Hongik University, 191
Hood, Mantle, 18
hooks, bell, 207
Human Cultural Asset holders, 44, 48
hwadong 화동 (village character), 29, 138, 246n7
Hwang Chonguk 황종욱, 58, 162, 165, 171
Hwanghae province, 162
Hwang Sunju 황순주, 127
Hwangtojae Battleground and Memorial Hall, 158–59
Hwangŭm Kŏji 황금 거지 (*Golden Beggar*, show by Yŏnhŭi Chipdan The Kwangdae), 181, 183

Index-Glossary **269**

hwimori 휘모리 (a common fast rhythm, also the name of the Stanford *p'ungmul* group), 118, 125, 182, 227, 250n9

Hyŏmnyulsa (theater), 151, 248n3

hyŏnjang 현장 (site), 11, 13–14, 34, 72–73, 78; and ritual, 110, 113–16, 119, 135, 141, 156, 160

hyŏnjangjŏkin undongsŏng 현장적인 운동성 (philosophy of being attuned to the moment/scene), 14, 246n6

Hyosŏng Senior Cultural Center, 186, 188

ich'ae 이채 (fast rhythm), 83, 211, 250n9

iconicity of style, 11, 14

identities, 59, 109, 169, 208, 212; author's, 18, 52; of Pilbong *p'ungmul*, 90, 245n6; regional, 24, 60; South Korean, 24–25, 106–7

Ieumsae [*Iŭmsae*] 이음새 (an activist *p'ungmul* group in the San Francisco Bay Area named after the term for "connective rhythm"), 226–31, 235, 250n5

ilch'ae 일채 (a fast rhythm), 192, 206, 250n9

Ilkwa Nori 일과 놀이 ("work and play," Chicago *p'ungmul* group), 199

Imae 이매 (foolish servant character in the mask dance drama of Hahoe village), 181–82, 187–88, 235

Im Chint'aek 임진택, 14, 115, 246n6

IMF Crisis (1997), 176, 183

immigrants, 197, 203, 218, 223–25, 230, 238, 250n5

Important Intangible Cultural Properties, 34, 58, 62, 65, 91, 153, 155, 177–78, 240nn1–2, 244n2; No. 7, 161; No. 11-5, 14, 24–25, 42, 44, 47, 89, 100; No. 61, 162

improvisation, 141; dramatic, 13, 115–19, 124, 138, 140, 172, 182, 235; and misfiring, 119–20, 123; musical, 12, 28, 118, 133–34, 192–93, 227

Imshil Pilbong Nongak Pojonhoe 임실 필봉 농악 보존회 (Imshil Pilbong Nongak Preservation Association or IPNPA), 58, 168, 232; description of, 3–4, 14–15, 23–27, 30–31, **31**, 63, 240n2, 245n1; and GOPA, 162, 165–66; groove of, 60, 63, 76, 79–80, 85–87, 145; and Korean American communities, 205, 212–29, 232, 234–36; leadership of, 35, 53, 65, 72–78, 90, 100, 105, 175; members of, 129–30, 138–42; and Pilbong expressive ecology, 89–91, 96, 99–100, 104–10, 144–45; rhythms of, 83, **84**, 247n19; and social relations, 64–65, 67–71; and *Tonghak* Peasant Uprising Commemoration, 155–61; troupe, 72, 121, 126, 131, 135, 140, 166. *See also* Pilbong; Pilbong transmission center

Incheon, 186, 188

indoor performance, 5, 30, 34, 89, 154, 197–98, 215–16

insagut (rhythm), 206

intangible cultural heritage, 31–32, 34, 44, 60, 236. *See also* Important Intangible Cultural Properties

Intangible Cultural Heritage of Humanity, 14, 100, 234

Intangible Human Cultural Asset Holders, 42

intermodal techniques, 62, 79–87, 193

internalization, 59, 63, 79, 83

intersectionality, 198, 225, 227, 229, 233

intersubjectivity, 64, 85

ipchangdan 잎장단 ("mouth rhythm," refers to drum vocables), 80, 85–86, 244n22

Irwin, Kathleen, 235–36

itinerant performers, 30–31, 38, 149–52

Ivy, Marilyn, 2

Jackson, Travis, 10, 239n3

Jamaesori [Chamaesori] 자매소리 ("sister sound," a women's *p'ungmul* group in the San Francisco Bay Area), 204, 216

Jambinai [Chambinai] 잠비나이, 178

Jang Woo Nam, 203, 208, 211, 213

Japanese colonialism, 152, 163, 189, 220, 246n5, 246n14, 248n6, 248n12

Japantown, 206, 213

Javanese gamelan, 226, 240n6

Jeolla province, 24–25, 41, 128, 157, 162, 240n2

Jeonju, 25, 30, 92–93, 111, 248n6

"Jindo Arirang" 진도 아리랑 (Arirang folksong from Jindo Island), 124, 206

Jindo Island, 220, 241n7
Johnson, Mark, 9
Ju Bum Cha, 203–4, 223–24

kaeinnori 개인놀이 ("individual play," refers to individual or group solos in a *p'ungmul* performance), 134
kaenjigaeng 갠지갱 (a medium fast rhythm in P'ilbong nongak), 74, 76–77
Kajin Yŏngsan 가진 영산 (a complex rhythmic series in P'ilbong nongak, normally played in the second half), 133
kakshi 각시 (young woman or bride), 27, 29, 112, 125–27, 134, 166
"Kakshi Bang'ae" 각시 방에 ("In the Bride's Room," newly composed folksong), 130
kamyŏn'gŭk 가면극 (mask dance drama), 11–12, 40, 178, 241n7. See also Hahoe Pyŏlshin-kut T'alnori; *t'alch'um*
kanggangsullae (women's group play), 65, 214–15, 219–21
kangyak 강약 ("strong weak," refers to a dynamic aesthetic), 83, 85. See also yin and yang
Kaye, Nick, 6
Keil, Charles, 79, 242n4
kibon ch'um 기본 춤 ("basic dance," represents characteristic moves in mask dance dramas), 163, 165
Ki-kut 기굿 (flag ritual), 27, 103, 110, 112–13, 136
kil-kut 길굿 ("road ceremony," refers to a rhythmic series in P'ilbong *nongak*), 205, 219
Kim, Elaine, 209, 212
Kim, Helen, 216, 218, 220–21
Kim, Soo-Jin, 199, 250n8
Kim Anju 김안주, 156, 158
Kim Chihun 김지훈, 189
Kim Dae-Jung [Kim Taejung] 김대중, 175
Kim-Gibson, Dai Sil, 209
Kim Inu 김인우, 1, 76, 121, 239n5, 244n22
Kim Jungwoon 김정운, 183, 185
Kim Myŏngkon 김명곤, 44

Kim Pongjun 김봉준, 44, 199
Kim Samt'ae 김삼태, 52–53, 82
Kim So Ra 김소라, 183
King, Rodney, 209, 212
King Kojong, 151
Kinney, Allison, 226
Kirshenblatt-Gimblett, Barbara, 142
kisu 기수 (flagholders), 27, 29
kkoktugakshi norŭm 꼭두각시 놀음 (puppet play), 178
kkwaenggwari 꽹과리 (small gong), 28, 46, 71, 161, 192, 209, 232
kokkal moja 고깔 모자 (flower hats), 5, 96, 111, 144, 205, 245n2
kokkal sogo 고깔 소고 (flower handheld drum players), 27–28
kondongch'e 공동체 (community), 11, 12, 40, 54, 59, 64, 114, 243n13; and *chŏnsu*, 70–71, 93; and GOPA, 163, 165; and ritual, 119–20. See also community
Korea National University of the Arts, 179, 192
Korean Community Center of the East Bay (KCCEB), 213, 215
Korean Demilitarized Zone (DMZ), 24
Korean Immigrant Workers Alliance (KIWA), 230
Korean Resource Center, 211
Korean subjectivities, 59, 87, 106–7, 127–28, 156; intersubjectivity, 64, 85
Korean War, 38, 152
Korean Youth Cultural Center. See *Hanin Ch'ŏngnyŏn Munhwawŏn*
Koreatown Immigrant Workers Alliance (KIWA), 203, 224
Koreatown Peace March (1992), 209–13
Koreatowns, 202–13, 215, 223, 232, 234, 251n14
Kosa / kosa-kut 고사 / 고사굿 (ritual in which food is offered to spirits), 219
Kotkan-kut 곳간굿 (storage shed ceremony, also called *nojŏk-kut*), 121
K-pop, 176–78, 195
Kugyŏngkkun 구경꾼 (spectator), 3, 129
kŭmjul 금줄 (prohibitive rope), 96, 102, 111, 142

Index-Glossary **271**

kut 굿 (ritual), 42–43, 57, 62, 149, 165, 191, 236, 240n1, 243n16; and *ch'angjak yŏnhŭi*, 178, 180; and Korean American communities, 203, 205, 214–16, 218, 223, 227, 229–32; and *madang*, 1–2, 10–12, 64, 70; and *madangbalbi*, 98, 104, 110, 113, 119–29, 134–41, 145, 207, 234; and Namwon *chŏnsu*, 49–50; in Pilbong, 14–16, 57, 71–73, 76–79, 87–92, 91, 96–98, 105, 110; *p'ujin-kut*, *p'ujinsalm* (abundant kut, abundant life), 108, 135, 140; *p'ungmul*, 3–5, 29, 42–43, 54–55, 90; and *tapsa*, 30, 32–33. *See also* Lunar New Year

Kutkŏri 굿거리 (medium slow rhythm in 12/8, also name of a Harvard-based *p'ungmul* group), 125, 201, 211, 250n9

kutnaenŭn karak 굿내는 가락 ("ritual producing rhythm," or warm-up rhythm), 112

kutp'an 굿판 (participatory ritual space-time), 71

kwangdae 광대 (folk entertainer), 180

Kwon, Ann, 217

Kwon, Miwon, 6

Lake Merritt, Oakland, 216, 228
Lakoff, George, 9
Lamar, Kendrick, 227
Latinx communities, 207, 213, 224, 229–30
Leach, Kristyn, 233
leadership, 61, 69–70, 72–78, 102, 115–19, 243n13
Lee, Dohee, 220, 231
Lee, Edward Song, 209–10
Lee, Katharine, 153, 201–2
Lee, Namhee, 33, 156, 207, 231
Lee Myung-bak [Yi Myŏngbak] 이명박, 175
Lee Soobeen [Yi Subin] 이수빈, 201–2
Lefebvre, Henri, 191–92, 237
Lepecki, André, 226, 251n21
Levin, Laura, 208
lighting, 35, 131, 140, 166–67
liminality, 52

lion characters, 167, 182, 190
Los Angeles, CA, 199, 202, 207, 209, 224; Civil Unrest in, 198, 203, 208–12, 229, 234
Lunar New Year, 1, 3–5, 31–32, 53, 126, 152, 205; and Korean American communities, 214, 223, 232; in Pilbong, 15–16, 57, 72, 78, 88–91, 105–10, 128, 132, 143–45, 203, 234, 246n13; in Pilbong (2002), 92–98, 110–35, 247n18; in Pilbong (2016), 98–104, 135–40

Madang 마당 (village courtyard, multidimensional cultural trope), 234–35, 239n4, 240n1, 246n6; and architecture, 150–52, 154; and *ch'angjak yŏnhŭi*, 178, 181–82, 184, 186–88, 190, 193–94; discourses of, 5–18, 40–41, 49–54, 57, 72, 92–93, 98, 109; and GOPA, 161–68, 170, 172–74; and Korean American communities, 198, 203, 207, 215, 225, 230; and *madangbalbi*, 120–24, 127–28, 144; Namwon, 47, 50–52; and *p'an-kut*, 133–34, 138–41; and pedagogy, **10**, 63–64; and performance, 81, 102–3, **103**, 113, 149; Pilbong, 53, **56**, 66–67, 70, 80, 85, 100, 112, 119; Pilbong, preparation of, 94–96, 102–3, 110; and *sangsoe*, 74, 76; village, 1–3, 23, 30, 33–35, 46; and way of being, 57, 59, 63–64, 79, 87, 241n2. *See also* *hyŏnjang*; *kondongch'e*; *nanjang*; *shinmyŏng*; yin and yang

madangbalbi 마당밟이 ("stepping on the madang"), 98, 104, 110, 113, 120–35, 137–39, 203, 207, 234

madanggŭk 마당극 (madang-theater), 154, 179, 201, 207, 231, 240n1

madanghwa 마당화 (madang-ization), 154

madang-kut 마당굿 (madang ceremony), 121–24, 128, 231, 240n1

madang-oriented expressive ecologies. *See* expressive ecologies, site-oriented

Mae-Ari 매아리 (Philadelphia *p'ungmul* group), 223

Mae-kut 매굿 (a village ritual held on New Year's Eve of the lunar calendar where a *p'ungmul* band goes to each house), 98, 245n4

makkŏlli 막걸리 (opaque rice-based alcoholic drink), 4, 50, 52, 104, 112, 139, 167, 205–6

Malraux, André, 34

malttugi 말뚝이 (horse groomsman mask dance drama character), 167

Manabe, Noriko, 230

marches, 16, 159, 205, 209–12, 224–27, 230, 250n9, 251n14, 251n21

marginalization, 17, 40, 171, 197–98, 207, 212, 228, 231, 235

marriage migrants, 170, 176

Marx Meadow, San Francisco, 216, 223

mask dance drama, 33, 44, 58, 62, 65, 92, 107, 151, 201; and *ch'angjak yŏnhŭi*, 178, 181–82, 186–94; Goseong Ogwangdae, 16, 58, 92, 154–73, 214, 219–20; tropes of, 125–27

mask-making, 65

Mass Bass, 228

Massey, Doreen, 14, 237

master teachers, 39, 214, 216

mat 맛 (taste), 58, 80

material culture, 31–34, 150–54, 236

maŭl hoegwan 마을 회관 (village center building), 4–5, 41, 94, 99

maŭl-kut 마을굿 (village ritual), 89–91, 105, 214, 244n2

maŭm 마음 (heart mind soul), 91, 98

Mauss, Marcel, 86, 241n11

May 18 Democratic Uprising (1980), 199

Mead, Margaret, 9

media coverage, 169–70, 210–12, 217, 221, 223, 226, 233, 245n4; in Pilbong, 98, 124, 128, 136–37

melodies, 12, 28–29, 80, 161

memory, cultural, 16, 72, 88, 119, 157, 159–61, 229, 236–37

metaphor, 9–11, 57

methodology of book, 14–19

Midongbu nongakdan / Pyŏnghwa t'ongil nongakdan 미동부 농악단 / 평화 통일 농악단 (Nongak Troupe of the Eastern US/Peace and Unification Nongak Troupe), 199

Migrant Arirang Multi-Cultural Festival, 171

migrant workers, 169–73, 176. *See also* diasporic communities

migration, 26, 99, 143, 170, 238

mijigi 미지기 (two line formation in Pilbong *nongak*), 133

Miller, Kiri, 249n6

minbok 민복 (peasant traditional wear generally made of white cotton), 111, 159, 211

Ministry of Culture, Sports, and Tourism, 60–61, 169, 179

minjung kayo 민중 가요 (protest songs), 201

Minjung Munhwa Yŏnguso 민중 문화 연구소 (Minjung Cultural Research Center), 199, 211

minjung undong 민중 운동 (people's movement or democratization movement), 112, 127, 154, 156–57, 169, 175, 212; and Korean Americans, 199, 202, 208; and *p'ungmul*, 2, 32–33, 36–38, 43–44, 59–61, 241n9, 242n3, 242n6

MinKwon Center for Community Action (Minkwon), 201, 203–4, 214, 223–24, 230

minsok 민속 (folk, folklore), 2

minsok-ak 민속악 (folk music), 3. *See also* regional folk expressive cultures; transnational folk expressive cultures

minsok-ch'um 민속춤 (folk dance), 3. *See also* dancing

minyo 민요 (folk song), 65, 68, 158, 166–68, 171, 184, 241n7; and Korean American communities, 205–6, 214; during ritual, 124, 127–28, 130, 138; studies of, 43, 57, 62, 145

"Miryang Arirang" 밀양 아리랑 (Arirang folksong from Miryang region), 130

miryang haengjinkok 밀양 행진곡 (a march-like rhythm), 211

Miyal 미얄 (an older female wife and grandmother character in mask dance dramas, also a shaman), 186–87

mobilization, 157, 159–61, 168
modernization, 16, 33, 120, 152, 237; and *ch'angjak yŏnhŭi*, 174–75, 181, 184, 190, 192–93; and Korean subjectivities, 59, 64, 105, 156
Mokchung 목중 (apostate monk character), 186
Monson, Ingrid, 61
Mosswood Park, Oakland, 216
mothers, 102, 104, 128, 138, 185, 232
mountains, 24–26, **66**, 156, 158–59, 220, 241n7
mourning, 52, 168, 212, 217–19, 222
Mr. Kim, 79–84, 112, 125–26, 244n21, 245n4
mu 무 (Korean religion), 43, 241n8. See also *kut*
mudae 무대 (stage), 1, 152, 234, 236
multiculturalism, 169–71, 176, 213
multi-sensory knowledge, 34, 62, 144, 237
Mundungi 문둥이 (leper character in Goseong mask dance drama), 167, 171–72, 186–87, 235
Mundung Pukch'um 문둥 북춤 ("Leper Drum Dance," from Goseong Ogwangdae mask dance), 171, 186–87
Munhwajae pohopŏp 문화재 보호법 Cultural Property Protection Law (1962), 60
mun-kut 문굿 (gate ceremony), 121–22, 138, 246n13

nabal 나발 (valveless bugle), 27, 29, 111, 136, 160
naego-talgo-maetgo-p'ulgo 내고-달고-맺고-풀고 ("produce-heat up-tighten-release"), 76–77, 121, 129, 246n11
Naminsa Madang 남인사 마당 (*madang* in Insadong area of Seoul), 181, 184
namsadang 남사당 (itinerant troupe of male performers), 149, 153
Namsan Hanok Village park, 184, 195
Namu Farm, 233, 250n5
Namwon 남원, 41, 247n14
Namwon *chŏnsugwan* 남원 전수관 (Pilbong nongak transmission center at Namwon), 47–54, 73, 241n7, 241n10

nanjang 난장 (chaos), 5, 11–13, 49–50, 70, 78; and ritual, 114–15, 126, 128, 130, 134
National Farmers Coalition, 38
National Folk Arts Competition, 153
National Gugak Center, 60–61, 154, 189
nationalism, 7, 24, 33, 60, 106, 143, 169, 174, 212, 242n5; and commemoration, 16, 157, 248n7
National Korean American Service and Education Consortium (NAKASEC), 199, 201, 203
National Korean Theater, 154
nature, 34, 98, 144, 238; patterns of, 11, 13, 239n5
neoliberalism, 7, 37, 64, 176, 193, 233
New Village movement, 153, 246n5
new works, 130, 181–84, 186, 189–90, 214–15, 248n8
New York, NY, 17, 199, 202, 204, 207, 209, 214, 223–25
New York University, 204
9/11, 17–19, 198, 213–23, 229
noise, 98, 192, 197, 216
Nojŏk-kut 노적굿 (storage shed ceremony, also called *kotkan-kut*), 121–22
nongak 농악 ("farmer's music," rural percussion band music and dance). See *p'ungmul*
nongch'on bongsa hwaldong 농촌 봉사 활동 (farming village service activity), 36
nongch'on hwaldong 농촌 활동 farming village activism, 35–36
nong-gi 농기 (village farming flag used in *p'ungmul*), 27
nonghwal 농활 (farming village activism, common abbreviation for *nongch'on hwaldong*), 15, 23–24, 35–40, 43, 55, 233
norae-kut 노래굿 (song ceremony performed in P'ilbong *nongak*), 134
norae undong 노래 운동 ("song movement," political movement songs), 214
nori 놀이 (play), 12–13, 23, 70, 87, 98, 114, 119–21, 136, 165, 189; and *ch'angjak yŏnhŭi*, 185, 193–94; and *chŏnsu*, 50, 54, 61, 71, 78; and Korean American communities, 207; and *madangalbi*, 129–30, 134, 138–39
Norikkot 노리꽃 (a women's creative

traditional performing arts team), 17, 183–85, 235
Norikkot P'ida 노리꽃 피다 (*Blooming Norikkot*, a show by Norikkot), 183–84
norikkun 노리꾼 (entertainers to excel at cultivating play), 189
Norikkundŭl Todam Todam 놀이꾼들 도담도담 (a creative traditional performing arts team), 17, 189–94
norimadang 놀이마당 ("play madang," village courtyard), 154
norip'an 놀이판 ("play p'an," village common or field), 183
North Korea, 24
NYURI (New York University *p'ungmul* group), 204

Oakland, CA, 18, 58, 199, 204, 213–16, 228–29, 241n7
obang 오방 (five directions), 144
obangjin 오방진 (a medium tempo march-like rhythm), 205, 211, 227
ogŭm 오금 (stylized bending of the knees), 82–83, 85–87
ohaeng 오행 (five directions: east, west, north, south, center), 144, 247n15
Ohlone people, 229
Oh Mi-ae 오미애, 45–47
ŏkkaech'um 어깨춤 (shoulder dance), 81, 86
older generation performers, 30, 34, 39, 49–50
ontology, 161
openness, 11, 92–93, 130, 165, 181, 207, 246n6
Oppenheim, Robert, 31–34
outdoor performance, 5, 11, 27, 30, 34, 48, 50, 89, 102, **103**; and Korean American communities, 215–16, 234; and site-oriented expressive ecologies, 149, 151–54, 163, **164**, 171, 178, 189–90, 198
outsiders, 90, 110, 114, 120, 123, 128
ownership, 120, 124, 128–29

Pabo 바보 (idiot character), 190
p'aejang 패장 (group leader), 69–70

Paekche kingdom, 156
Pak Ch'ansuk 박찬숙, 36
Pak Hŭngchu 박홍주, 57, 115, 246n6
Pak Hyŏngnae 박형래, 48, 135
Pak Insŏn 박인선, 186
Pak Insu 박인수, 189–90
P'an 판 (village common or field, multidimensional cultural trope), **10**, 63–67, 76, 130–33, 150, 152–53, 160, 165, 221, 242n10
p'anhwa 판화 (print), 199
p'an-kut 판굿 (entertainment-oriented p'ungmul performance), 90, 95–96, 100, 111, 130–35, 139–41, 158–59, 193, 221
pan-p'ungnyu 반풍류 (a commonly played medium fast 12/8 rhythmic cycle from the *p'ungnyu-kut* rhythmic series), 80, 83
p'ansori 판소리 (a vocal storytelling genre that incorporates narration, singing, and dramatic gesture), 150–51, 153, 183, 185, 241n7
paraem-kut 바램굿 (wish ceremony), 214, 219–20
Park, Kyeyoung, *LA Rising*, 210
Park, Peter, 43
Park Chung Hee [Pak Chŏnghŭi] 박정희, 33, 36
Park Chung Hee regime, 153
Park Geun-hye [Pak Kŭnhye] 박근혜, 175
participatory performance, 3–9, 12–13, 33, 87, 154, 237, 239n3; and *ch'angjak yŏnhŭi*, 181–95; and GOPA, 165–69, 171–72; and Pilbong, 57–59, 80, 110–15, 119, 140–42; and Pilbong *madangbalbi*, 124, 127, 131–33
patronage, 120, 149
patterns: as maps, 8–9, 13–15, 131–32, 150, 231; in ritual, 121–22
Peace and Unification Nongak Troupe, 199
pedagogy, 15, 45–46, 48, 58–60, 62, 72, 79–87
Peralta Hacienda Historical Park, Oakland, 229
performance theory, 6–7, 208
performative misfiring, 119, 123
performative utterances, 119
phenomenology, 5–6, 8, 79, 242n12

Index-Glossary **275**

Pibi kwajang 비비 과장 ("Play of Pibi the Beast"), 167

Pilbong 필봉, 3–4, 14–15, 54, 59, 63, 68; description of, 25–27, 244n25; development of, **99**, 135–36; expressive ecology of, 66–67, 79, 89–91, 94, 96, 100, 107, 120, 141–44; residents of, 114, 129, 135, 141, 143; *tapsa* to, 60, 72–74

Pilbong *p'ungmul*. *See* Imshil Pilbong Nongak Pojonhoe

Pilbong transmission center, 15, 24–25, 135, 233, 241n7, 242n7; current, 61, 63–71, 106, 141; growth of, 30–31, **31**; and pedagogy, 79–87; phases of, 41–54; and *sangsoe*, 72–78. *See also* Imshil Pilbong Nongak Pojonhoe

Pinari 비나리 (New York *p'ungmul* group at MinKwon), 199, **200**, 203, 214, 224

place, 113, 174, 239n2; connections to, 3, 7–9, 41, 58, 89, 119, 149–50; as constructed, 14, 55; and GOPA, 161–63, 170; and Korean American community, 197, 213, 231; and Pilbong groove, 63, 87; and site-specific pedagogy, 15, 60, 141

Pojonhoe 보존회 (preservation association), 240. *See also* Goseong Ogwangdae Pojonhoe; Imshil Pilbong Nongak Pojonhoe

political ecology, 8

politics, 19, 24, 33, 41, 59, 88, 175–77; and folk genres, 2–3, 36–40, 169; and Korean American activism, 225–30, 235; and LA Civil Unrest, 198, 203, 208–12; and 9/11, 213–24; and *p'ungmul*, 36–40, 44, 197–98, 203, 245n6; and reunification, 214, 217, 225; and *Tonghak* uprising, 155–61

pŏna 버나 (a type of entertainment developed by itinerant troupes that involves spinning discs and other objects with a stick), 178, 184–85

post-colonialism, 33, 88, 156

poverty, 13, 181, 183

Psy, "Gangnam Style," 177

public space, 150–51, 196–98, 203, 215, 223, 231, 234

public sphere, 207–8

p'ujin-kut, p'ujin-salm 푸진굿, 푸진삶 ("abundant kut [ritual], abundant life"), 108, 135, 140

puk 북 (barrel drum), 12, 27–28, 113, 160–61, 183, 191–92, 209, 217

pukch'um 북춤 (barrel drum dance), 184

p'ungmul / p'ungmul-kut 풍물 / 풍물굿 (percussion band music and dance), 52–53, 79, 95, 115, 153, 161, 244n1; and *ch'angjak yŏnhŭi*, 178, 190, 192–93; descriptions of, 11–12, 27–29, 239n1; government support for, 175; and Korean American communities, 202–6, 211–31, 233–34, 236; and protest, 36–40, 44, 197–202; regional styles of, 62, 90; and *Tonghak* uprising, 157–59. *See also* Imshil Pilbong Nongak Pojonhoe

p'ungnyu-kut 풍류굿 (a rhythmic series in P'ilbong *nongak*), 156, 205, 226

Quinn, Naomi, 9

racism, 210, 216, 230

Rancière, Jacques, 226, 251n21

regional folk expressive cultures, 3, 14–16, 24–25, 87, 150, 155, 162–63, 168–70, 173

repetition, 119–20

resonance, philosophy of, 16, 149–50, 173, 198, 237

responsorial performance, 115–19, 133–34

reunification, 156, 169, 214, 217, 225

Rhee, Liz Chong Eun, 199

rhythmanalysis, 191–92, 194

rhythms, 46, 50, 78, 144, 174; and *ch'angjak yŏnhŭi*, 182, 188, 190–96; at GOPA, 166, 168, 172; and Korean American groups, 205, 209, 211, 219–20, 226–28, 250n9; and *madangbalbi*, 122–23, 125, 128, 138; and *p'an-kut*, 132–35; Pilbong, 15, 79–87, 112–13, 243nn17–20, 245n3, 247n16; and protest, 201–2; and *sangsoe*, 74–77; of *tŏkdam*, 115, 118; and *Tonghak* commemoration, 156, 159–60

Rice, Timothy, 62

ritual. See *kut*; *mu*
Roh Moo-yun [No Muhyŏn] 노무현, 175

Sabal T'ongmun 사발통문 ("Round Robin" document used in the Tonghak Movement), 160
sacred spaces, 54, 95, 96, **97**, 100, 106, 113, 136. See also shrines
Saeji, CedarBough, 52, 242n9, 247n19
Saemaŭl undong 새마을 운동 (New Village movement), 153, 246n5
Saem-kut 샘굿 (spring ceremony), 114–19, 121–24, 137, 140–41, 235
Sager, Rebecca, 81–82
Sa-I-Gu 사이구 (literally "4-2-9," the date of the Los Angeles Civil Unrest on April 29, 1992), 209, 213, 251n15
samch'ae 삼채 (an extremely common 12/8 medium to fast rhythmic cycle), 205, 209, 211, 250n9
samjae 삼재 [三才] (three elements of heaven, earth, and humans, also called *ch'ŏn chi in* or 천지인 [天地人]), 145, 247n20
sampo sedae 삼포세대 ("three giving-up generation," referring to courtship, marriage, and having kids), 185
SamulNori 사물놀이 (founding group or quartet that created a new genre also called *samul nori*), 197
samul nori 사물 놀이 (genre of Korean drumming), 90, 153, 190–91, 194, 214, 251n16
San Francisco, CA, 17, 204, 206, 224; Golden Gate Park, 216, 222, 252n17
San Francisco Bay Area, 18, 199, 203–4, 218–19, 225
sangmo 상모 (the twirling of streamers or feathers attached to special hats), 160
sangsoe 상쇠 (lead small gong), 27–28, 68, 70–78, 102, 115–20, 220, 243n10; and GOPA, 165; and Lunar New Year, 137; and *madangbalbi*, 122–28, 134–35, 138, 140
sangsoe ppopki 상쇠 뽑기 ("picking the sangsoe" competition), 68, 74, **75**

sanjŏng madang 산정 마당 (mountaintop madang), 95, **97**, 130–31
"Sarangga" 사랑가 ("Love Song"), 130, 206
Saturday Night Live Korea, 189
schizophonia, 2
Schweitzer, Marlis, 208
Sehan University, 179
sensory experiences, 34, 51–53, 62, 106, 144, 226–27, 235–37
Seo, Maria, 43
Seoul 서울, 3, 99, 107, 154, 203, 236, 244n26, 246n13, 250n7; and *ch'angjak yŏnhŭi*, 17, 174, 181, 183; Fringe Festival, 191–92; Namsan Hanok Village park, 184; and transportation, 25, 30, 54
Seoul International Park, LA, 211
Seoul Nori Madang, 154–55, **155**, 248n4
sexuality, 185, 230
Shakespeare, William, *Othello*, 186
shamanism. See *kut*; *mu*
Shelemay, Kay Kaufman, 17
shinmyŏng 신명 (spiritual catharsis), 10–12, 42, 172; and *ch'angjak yŏnhŭi*, 187–88, 193; and *chŏnsu*, 49–52, 71, 78; and *kut*, 108, 130. See also catharsis
shrines, 4, 92, 94, 104, 141–42, 158, 204–6, 223
site-oriented expressive ecologies. See expressive ecologies, site-oriented
Small, Christopher, 152
Smith, Laurajane, 142
social drama, 116–19
social media, 177–78, 249n1
social relations, 4–5, 14, 17, 52, 59, 176, 235; and *chŏnsu*, 35, 37, 41, 60–64, 67–68; discourses of, 9–11, **19**, 74; and GOPA, 161, 165, 168; and Korean American communities, 202–8, 210; and *madangbalbi*, 121–22, 130, 132; and Pilbong *chŏnsu*, 69–72, 78–79, 81, 87; and Pilbong Lunar New Year, 105, 116; and resonance, 16, 149–50
soe 쇠 (small gong), 12, 27–29, 44, 76–79, 113, 116, 118, 125, 133–34, 137, 160

Index-Glossary **277**

sogo 소고 (small handheld drum), 12, 74, 76, 112–13, 125, 160, 243n15

sŏlchanggo 설장구 (first *changgo* player; solo *changgo* dance; *changgo* performers' group dance, also called *sŏlchanggu*), 68

solidarity, 17, 38, 162, 198, 212, 220, 223, 225, 230

solos, 29, 68, 125–27, 134, 166, 186

somatic attention, 85–86

Sŏngju-kut 성주굿 (tutelary or family spirit ceremony), 121

"*Sŏngjupuri*" 성주풀이 (tutelary or family spirit appeasement song), 124, 138, 206

Song Soonam [Song Sunam] 송수남, 12

Son Su-Rak 손수락, 217

Son T'aedo 손태도, 178

Sŏn Yŏng'uk 선영욱, 181, 183

Sori 소리 (early UC Berkeley *p'ungmul* group), 199

#SoulOfOakland, 228

South Korean government, 153, 179; and cultural heritage, 7, 14, 47, 60–61, 100, 108, 144, 175, 239n1; and Important Intangible Cultural Properties, 34, 62, 65, 91, 153, 155, 178, 240nn1–2; and repression, 36, 38, 40, 44

South Korean identities, 24–25, 106–7

Space Theater, 153

spatial discourses, 9–13, **19**, 34, 74, 78, 87, 163, 241n6; and *ch'angjak yŏnhŭi*, 184, 186, 190, 196; and Korean American communities, 197, 213, 227, 230, 235–36; and Pilbong village, 23, 54, 105–6; and *Tonghak* commemoration, 157, 160–61

spectrogram analysis, 83, **84**

spirits, 43, 96, 208, 220; and *p'ungmul*, 1, 4, 51–52, 67, 76, 123, 141, 144–45

springs, village, 4, 63, 92, 114–15, 118–19, 123, 140–41, 144, 235; and ritual, 96, **97**, 100–102, 137

Statue of Liberty, New York, 223

stepping, spirit of, 51–52, 81, 98, 106, 123, 138, 237

stone prayer cairns, 100, 111, 142

subakch'igi 수박치기 (patty-cake games), 134–35, 193

sul-kut 술굿 (alcohol ceremony), 121–24

Sungkyunkwan University, 37

sustainability, 35, 38, 40, 143, 233, 236–37

synchronization, 52, 79, 81, 112–13, 140 144, 172, 192–95, 211

Taeborŭm p'an-kut 대보름 판굿 (full moon *p'an-kut*), 111

Taeborŭm Paraem-kut 대보름 바램굿 (Gathering of Wishes Under the Full Moon), 214, 219–20

Taedong-kut 대동굿 (group ritual play or dance), 190–92

taedongnori 대동놀이 (group play), 13, 33, 193–94

taep'osu 대포수 (hunter character), 27, 29, 116–18, 120, 124–26, 134

t'aep'yŏngso 태평소 (conical double reed), 3, 12, 27–29, 47, 125, 161

t'alch'um 탈춤 (mask dance), 36–37, 186, 191

Taljip t'aeugi 달집 태우기 (bonfire), 37, 78, 96, 162–63, 167, 171–72, 248n10, 251n17; in Pilbong, 100–105, 111, 130–31, 135, 140–44

T'al Kosa 탈고사 (opening mask ceremony with altar and ritual offerings), 163, 165

Tangherlini, Timothy, 208, 212

tangsan 당산 (tutelary spirit), 94, 113–14

Tangsanje 당산제 (a rite to give offerings to the village tutelary spirit), 112–13, 136–37, 141–42

tangsan-kut 당산굿 (tutelary spirit ceremony), 113

tangsan madang 당산 마당 (tutelary spirit tree madang), 95, 245n5

tangsan namu 당산 나무 (tutelary spirit tree), 27, 63, 99–100, 104, 112, 136, 144, 153, 236

tapsa 답사 (fieldtrip), 15, 23, 31–35, 54, 58, 143, 243n15; to Pilbong, 60, 72–74, 95

tchaktŭrŭm (hocketing rhythm featuring the *soe*), 118

teachers, 39–45, 48–50, 70–71, 79–87, 90, 94, 135

tempo, 1, 13, 80, 86, 130, 132, 145, 174; changing, 77, 206–7; medium, 83, 125, 191–92, 205

278 *Index-Glossary*

temporality, 14, 74, 78, 87, 157, 198; and *ch'angjak yŏnhŭi*, 184, 190; discourses of, 9–11, **19**, 246n6; and GOPA, 163, 165–66, 170; and *tapsa*, 34, 60

theaters, 151–54

Titon, Jeff Todd, 7, 237

tŏkdam 덕담 (oral verse; stylized speech or chants), 115–19, 122–23, 127, 144, 205, 207

Tondollari 돈돌라리 (a series of folk activities from Bukcheong, South Hamgyeong Province that incorporate games, songs, and dances performed during the holidays), 162–63, 165–67

Tongch'ŏng madang 동청 마당 (village common madang), 110, 112

Tongdaemun History and Culture Park, Seoul, 183

Tonghak 동학 ("Eastern Learning," indigenous religious and social movement): Peasant Uprising Baeksan Revolt 108th Year Commemoration, 16, 155–62, 168–69, 248n6

Tonŭn Nom Ttwinŭn Nom Nanŭn Nom 도는놈 뛰는놈 나는놈 (*Spinning Guy Running Guy Flying Guy / I'm a Guy*, show by Yŏnhŭi Chipdan The Kwangdae), 181

totem pole carving, 162–63

tourism, 176–77, 181–82

Toyotomi Hideyoshi, 163

transformative practices, 10–13, 43, 59, 63–64, 87, 128, 168, 185, 215, 231, 243n11

transmission practices, 2–3, 15, 35, 62–63, 149, 241n7; and Pilbong, 14–15, 23–24, 42–43, 66–67, 79–87, 107, 110. See also *chŏnsu*; Pilbong transmission center

transnational folk expressive cultures, 3, 14, 16

transportation, 24–25, 54, 92

ttŏk 떡 (chewy rice-cake), 92

ture 두레 (communal labor; communal work group), 11–12, 47, 70, 86, 144, 244n1

Turino, Thomas, 5, 8–9, 195, 222, 231, 238

Turner, Victor, 13, 52, 96, 116–19

twaeji-chapki 돼지 잡기 (pig-catching), 94

twi-kut 뒤굿 (after ritual, second half of a performance), 132–33, 139, 219–20, 247n16

twip'uri 뒤풀이 (after-party), 67–68, 132, 140, **155**, 166, 168, 221, 243n15

ŭm-yang ohaeng 음양오행 (yin-yang five direction philosophy), 113, 121, 131–32

UNESCO, 14, 32, 100, 142, 234

University of California, Berkeley, 199, 216, 220

University of California, Los Angeles, 211

university students, 35–40, 61, 139, 202; and transmission centers, 42, 44–45, 49–54, 65, 106

urban space: and *ch'angjak yŏnhŭi*, 174–75, 181–83, 192–95; expressive ecologies of, 17, 248n4; and Korean American communities, 203–13

Uri Munhwa Kondongch'e 우리 문화 공동체 ("Our Culture Community," Los Angeles group), 203, 211, 213

utopias, 105–7, 127

venues, 149–54, 163, **164**, 197. See also indoor performance; outdoor performance

Vickers, Adrian, 9

video games, 189, 193, 249nn6–7

village life, 15, 38, 83, 150; and authenticity, 31, 90, 100, 104–7, 138, 244n1; and *chŏnsu*, 42, 45–54, 58–59; and Koreatowns, 209; and *maŭl-kut*, 89–94; and modernization, 120, 143–44, 152–53, 170; in Pilbong, 23, 67, 72–74, 99

volunteerism, 61, 140, 163

Warner, Michael, 207

War on Terror, 18–19

We Are America Alliance, 224

Wilkie, Fiona, 6–7

Will, Udo, 81–82

Williams, Raymond, 241n11

wishes, 135–37, 162, 214–15, 218–21, 248n10, 251n17, 251n20; in Pilbong, 111, 114, 128

women, 18, 115, 171, 229, 243n13; comfort

Index-Glossary **279**

women, 184; and Jamaesori, 216; and *kanggangsullae*, 65; mothers, 102, 104, 128, 138, 185, 232; and Norikkot, 17, 183, 185, 235; in traditional arts, 126, 138, 177, 240n4, 246n14; as wives, 9, 46, 73–74, 134, 168

Women's Marches, 226–27, 230, 251n21

Wŏngaksa 원각사 (historic theater), 151

wŏnhyŏng 원형 (standard form; primary form), 87

Wonkwang Digital University, 179

yangban 양반 (aristocrat character), 29, 166

Yang Chinhwan 양진환, 30, 48, 94, 130, 244n25

Yang Chinsŏng 양진성, 23, 28, 48, 104–5, 128, 135–38, 202, 218; on *chŏnsu*, 65, 67, 69–70, 74, 78–79, 241n10; and IPNPA, 30, 35, 90, 94, 100, 102, 109, 165, 175; on *kut*, 2, 42–45, 108, 111, 115, 122, 126, 129–31, 136, 240n2

Yangchon 양촌, 3–6, 246n13

Yang Sunyong 양순용, 41, 42–48, 72–74, 105, 108, 127, 135, 153, 202, 241n1

Yeongnam 영남, 24, 203

Yeongnam nongak samul nori 영남 농악 사물놀이 (a canonic *samul nori* repertoire from the Yeongnam region), 219

Yi Chongjin 이종진, 92, 239n5

Yi Chuwŏn 이주원, 186, 189

Yi Hyejin 이혜진, 151

yin and yang, 83, 113, 121, 131–32. See also *kangyak*

Yi Sŏkkyu 이석규, 201

Yi Sunshin 이순신, 16, 163, 169, 248n7

yŏlyŏitnŭn piyŏissŭm 열여있는 비어있음 (a state of open emptiness), 92

yong-gi 용기 [龍旗] (dragon flag), 27

yŏng-gi 영기 [令旗] (signal flag), 92

yŏnhŭi 연희 (a term for folk arts including *pungmul*, mask dance drama, *namsadang*, and shamanic performances that are generally performed in *madang* or *p'an* spaces), 178–79, 184, 189, 191, 234

Yŏnhŭi Chipdan The Kwangdae 연희 집단 The 광대 (creative traditional performing arts team), 17, 179–84, 186–87

Yŏnhŭi Madang 연희 마당 (*madang* for Korean performing arts at the National Gugak Center), 154, 190

younger generation performers, 17, 30, 85, 170, 199; and *ch'angjak yŏnhŭi*, 177–78, 180; and *chŏnsu*, 43, 48, 53, 57, 103

Young Koreans United (YKU), 199

Yu Hongjun 유홍준, 31–34

Yun Hanbong 유한봉, 199

Yushin Constitution era, 36, 43

MUSIC / CULTURE

A series from Wesleyan University Press
Edited by Deborah Wong, Sherrie Tucker, and Jeremy Wallach

The Music/Culture series has consistently reshaped and redirected music scholarship. Founded in 1993 by George Lipsitz, Susan McClary, and Robert Walser, the series features outstanding critical work on music. Unconstrained by disciplinary divides, the series addresses music and power through a range of times, places, and approaches. Music/Culture strives to integrate a variety of approaches to the study of music, linking analysis of musical significance to larger issues of power—what is permitted and forbidden, who is included and excluded, who speaks and who gets silenced. From ethnographic classics to cutting-edge studies, Music/Culture zeroes in on how musicians articulate social needs, conflicts, coalitions, and hope. Books in the series investigate the cultural work of music in urgent and sometimes experimental ways, from the radical fringe to the quotidian. Music/Culture asks deep and broad questions about music through the framework of the most restless and rigorous critical theory.

MUSIC/CULTURE FALL 2024

Benjamin Barson
*Brassroots Democracy: Maroon
Ecologies and the Jazz Commons*

Donna Lee Kwon
*Stepping in the Madang:
Sustaining Expressive Ecologies
of Korean Drumming and Dance*

Sumarsam
*The In-Between in Javanese
Performing Arts: History and Myth,
Interculturalism and Interreligiosity*

A COMPLETE LIST OF SERIES TITLES CAN BE FOUND AT
https://www.weslpress.org/search-results/?series=music-culture

ABOUT THE AUTHOR

Donna Lee Kwon is associate professor of ethnomusicology at the University of Kentucky and the author of *Music in Korea: Experiencing Music, Expressing Culture* (2011).